DOING ETHICS IN MEDIA

Doing Ethics in Media: Theories and Practical Applications is an accessible, comprehensive introduction to media ethics. Its theoretical framework and grounded discussions engage students to think clearly and systematically about dilemmas in the rapidly changing media environment.

The 13-chapter text is organized around six decision-making questions—the "5Ws and H" of media ethics. The questions encourage students to articulate the issues; apply codes, policies or laws; consider the needs of stakeholders; sift and sort through conflicting values; integrate philosophic principles; and pose a "test of publicity." Specifically, the questions ask:

- What's your problem?
- Why not follow the rules?
- Who wins, who loses?
- What's it worth?
- Who's whispering in your ear?
- How's your decision going to look?

As they progress through the text, students are encouraged to resolve dozens of practical applications and increasingly complex case studies relating to journalism, new media, advertising, public relations, and entertainment.

Other distinctive features include:

- Comprehensive materials on classic moral theory and current issues such as truth telling and deception, values, persuasion and propaganda, privacy, diversity, and loyalty.
- A user-friendly approach that challenges students to think for themselves rather than imposing answers on them.
- Consistent connections between theories and the decision-making challenges posed in the practical applications and case studies.
- A companion website (www.routledge.com/textbooks/Black) with online resources for students, including additional readings and chapter overviews, as well as instructor materials with a test bank, instructor's manual, sample syllabi and more.
- A second website with continuously updated examples, case studies, and student writing—www.doingmediaethics.com.

Doing Ethics in Media is aimed at undergraduates and graduate students studying media ethics in mass media, journalism, and media studies. It also serves students in rhetoric, popular culture, communication studies, and interdisciplinary social sciences.

"*Doing Ethics in Media* has the needed antidotes for contemporary media students on a global level. There are so many moral dilemmas that media practitioners and media consumers have to grapple with—is it really enough these days to be a reporter and present solely the facts? Should you present multiple angles? What about the complicated ethical decisions one has to make as a PR professional—how do you remain loyal to the companies you work for but also remain accountable to the public at large? These are just some of the questions we deal with in Media Ethics courses. And I am pleased that Doing Ethics in Media helps students and instructors successfully work through these challenges."

—*Zaneta Trajkoska, Macedonian Institute for Media*

"*Doing Ethics in Media* is a book that lives up to its name. It enables readers to wrestle with the significant philosophical foundations through a lens of reality. It lives up to the definition of ethics as being values in action, ensuring readers get hands-on experience with dilemmas that face those in the mass communication professions."

—*Lois A. Boynton, University of North Carolina at Chapel Hill*

"Black and Roberts have put together in one book excellent content and hands-on analysis techniques that one finds scattered through the best existing texts in the field."

—*Deni Elliott, University of South Florida*

Doing Ethics in Media

Theories and Practical Applications

Jay Black
Chris Roberts

 Routledge
Taylor & Francis Group

NEW YORK AND LONDON

Acquisitions Editor: Linda Bathgate
Senior Development Editor: Nicole Solano
Editorial Assistant: Katherine Ghezzi
Production Editor: Sioned Jones
Project Manager: Rosie White
Text Design: Susan R. Leaper

Copyeditor: Jeff Nosbaum
Proofreader: Lynda Watson
Indexer: Jo Wilkinson
Cover Design: Gareth Toye
Companion Website Designer: Natalya Dyer

Published 2011
by Routledge
270 Madison Ave, New York, NY 10016

Simultaneously published in the UK
by Routledge
2 Park Square, Milton Park, Abingdon, Oxon OX14 4RN

Routledge is an imprint of the Taylor & Francis Group, an informa business

© 2011 Taylor & Francis

Typeset in Palatino and ITC Stone Sans by
Florence Production Ltd, Stoodleigh, Devon
Printed and bound in the United States of America on acid-free paper by
Edwards Brothers, Inc.

Library of Congress Cataloging in Publication Data
Black, Jay.
  Doing ethics in media : theories and practical applications / Jay Black, Chris Roberts.
  p. cm.
  1. Journalistic ethics—United States—Handbooks, manuals, etc. 2. Journalistic ethics—United States—Case studies—Handbooks, manuals, etc. 3. Mass media—Moral and ethical aspects—United States—Handbooks, manuals, etc. 4. Mass media—Moral and ethical aspects--Case studies--Handbooks, manuals, etc. I. Roberts, Chris, 1965– II. Title.
  PN4888.E8B535 2011
  174'.907--dc22   2011001661

ISBN13: 978–0–415–88150–0 (hbk)
ISBN13: 978–0–415–88154–8 (pbk)
ISBN13: 978–0–203–82951–6 (ebk)

To Leslie, Laura, and Stephanie, who do ethics in the real world.

—Jay Black

To Melissa and James, who might one day want to read the pages that follow. Or they might say what Pee Wee told Dottie at the end of his Big Adventure: "I don't have to see it . . . I lived it."

—Chris Roberts

Contents

Case Studies

Journalism

New Media

Public Relations

Advertising

Entertainment

ABOUT THE AUTHORS

Jay Black is Poynter Jamison Chair in Media Ethics, Emeritus, at the University of South Florida, St. Petersburg. He is founding co-editor of the *Journal of Mass Media Ethics* and has authored or edited ten volumes, including books on media ethics and five editions of an introductory mass media textbook. He was named co-winner of the first Freedom Forum Journalism Teacher of the Year Award in 1997. His Ph.D. in Journalism was earned at the University of Missouri; other degrees were from Miami (Ohio) University and Ohio University. He has worked as a reporter and copy-editor and in public relations, and he has held tenured positions at the University of South Florida, the University of Alabama, Utah State University, and Bowling Green State University. He has published or presented more than 500 papers and seminars, primarily in media ethics.

Chris Roberts is an Assistant Professor at the University of Alabama, where he earned his Bachelor's and Master's degrees (and was Black's assistant with the *Journal of Mass Media Ethics* in the late 1980s). He started his media career before he could drive, working for newspapers and radio stations in his hometown before becoming a full-time reporter and editor for newspapers in Birmingham, AL, and Columbia, SC. He earned his doctorate and started his academic career at the University of South Carolina, before returning to the University of Alabama in 2008.

Acknowledgments

Countless mentors, and the occasional tormentor, need to be acknowledged.

Jay Black was turned onto media ethics in the 1970s by fellow grad student Ralph Barney and mentor John Merrill at the University of Missouri. In the early 1980s he fell under the spell of Cliff Christians, Lou Hodges, Deni Elliott, and Ed Lambeth at a week-long workshop on teaching the subject. With their encouragement, and nudging from numerous colleagues at the Association for Education in Journalism (now the AEJMC), he and Dr. Barney launched the *Journal of Mass Media Ethics* (*JMME*) in 1984. Untold thousands of pages of manuscripts and a quarter century later, despite the assistance of an incredibly dedicated editorial board, he was happy to turn that chapter of his life over to friend and colleague Lee Wilkins, who has improved the journal. (A special shoutout to Linda Bathgate, *JMME*'s faithful editor at LEA, now with Routledge/Taylor & Francis.) In the interim, he was inspired by team-teacher Frank Deaver at the University of Alabama, Bob Steele and his colleagues at the Poynter Institute, hundreds of colleagues in the Society for Professional Journalists, and dozens of really bright participants in the "Colloquium 2000" series on media ethics research. As he enters retirement, he is newly inspired by the zeal and quality of work coming from the emerging generation of media ethicists, some of whom have been his students. Chris Roberts is atop the list, joined by Susan Keith, Patrick Plaisance, Rick Kenney, Lee Anne Peck, Wendy Wyatt, Sandra Borden, Aaron Quinn, and Kevin Stoker.

Chris Roberts has been grateful to Jay Black for more than two decades—first as a graduate student and research assistant, for years as a *JMME* board member, now as a yokefellow on this project, and always as a friend. That friendship shaped Chris's decisions while doing media as ethically as possible for decades as a journalist, as did the influence of scores of upright journalists and advertising/public relations practitioners. Deserving of special mention at *The Birmingham News* are Greg Garrison and the late Randy Henderson. At *The State* newspaper in Columbia, SC, editors Mark Lett, Steve Brook, Scott Johnson, and Sara Svedberg made it possible for Chris to pursue a Ph.D. at the University of South Carolina while working at the paper. While a doctoral student (and, later, as a faculty member), dissertation committee members Augie Grant, Ran Wei, Pat McNeely, and Richard Wertz were among many who provided guidance. Now, back home in Alabama as a middle-aged junior faculty member, he is thankful for the colleagues who encouraged him during this project and the students he hopes he can influence in the manner that Jay influenced him.

The authors want to thank those who reviewed and nurtured the book manuscript and helped it change from a bunch of interesting but somewhat disconnected ideas to a comprehensive and original approach to the subject matter. We especially acknowledge the efforts of Lois Boynton of the University of North Carolina, Chapel Hill. Others (who were willing to be identified) deserving thanks are Deni Elliott of the University of South Florida, St. Petersburg, Pat Gehrke of the University of South Carolina, Walt Jaehnig of Southern Illinois University, Susan Keith of Rutgers, Paul Lester of California State University, Fullerton, Ian Richard of the University of South Australia, Zaneta Trajkoska of the Macedonian Institute for Media, and Herman Wasserman of the University of Sheffield. Their efforts, and the scholarly efforts of several others who preferred to remain anonymous, are deeply appreciated . . . even the occasional caustic criticisms.

What began as Jay's brainchild became a collaborative effort. He developed the "5Ws and H" questions that frame this textbook, and he wrote the drafts for all but Chapter 13, which Chris wrote between multiple trips to Utah between semesters. Chris wrote all but one case study, conceptualized the book's "5Ws and H" framework, built the graphics, shepherded it through the production process, and is primarily responsible for the online material.

The shortcomings of the book now in your hands, we're supposed to say, are there despite the good efforts of the reviewers.

Introduction
Welcome to the Media Ethics Environment

THIS BOOK is based on several premises:

1. Media ethics is not an oxymoron.
2. "Doing ethics in media" should be based on moral philosophy and theory, not mere moralizing.
3. Students and instructors share the challenge of meeting substantive course objectives.

People who work in traditional and emerging forms of journalism, public relations (PR), advertising, and entertainment media play significant roles in contemporary life. A society that expects its citizens to be informed and its consumers to be discriminating must be served by moral media. The overwhelming majority of media practitioners take their ethics seriously. They may not always get it right, however, in part because commercial and other pressures often complicate their decision making. And they know their decisions will not always be popular. When faced with a choice between doing the right thing and being popular—which are often at odds with one another—ethical media practitioners opt for the high road. They "do ethics."

Learning to do ethics in media is not simple. Students preparing for careers in media, and people who see themselves only as media consumers, benefit equally from a systematic understanding of the complex subject matter. Instructors and students should work together to create and maintain an environment in which the subject matter receives intellectual and pragmatic life.

On one hand, media ethics investigates academic and abstract concepts that for millennia have intrigued philosophers, historians, sociologists, psychologists, economists, political scientists, and other thoughtful observers and policy makers.

On another hand, students of media ethics are immersed in controversial current events while learning decision-making processes that may have to be applied daily—often on deadline. They recognize that media practitioners may make the decisions on their own, or with a group of peers; while working at the bottom of the corporate food chain, or while serving as supervisors or executives. Those decisions may have little impact, or they may affect vast numbers of stakeholders. Regardless, media practitioners will be "doing ethics" while being pushed and pulled by a variety of moral and pragmatic concerns.

Many who study this subject matter are driven to become the very best professional practitioners they can be. For them, one hallmark of becoming a professional is the ability to make connections between classical theory and current practice. (Later in this book we'll discuss the pros and cons of being "professionals," and why media practitioners don't always qualify. However, on occasion we will use the word "professional" to describe the ideal moral practices of those who work in media jobs.) Meanwhile, for those with no expectation of working in media, the capacity to apply theory to current issues should help them be more sophisticated consumers and critics of media fare.

MORAL PHILOSOPHY AND MORALIZING

Ethics is a branch of moral philosophy, or philosophical thinking about morality, moral problems, and moral judgments. The study of ethics challenges us to apply the wisdom of the ages carefully and systematically. When we thoughtfully use these theories of moral philosophy to resolve real-world moral dilemmas, we are engaging in applied, practical ethics. Consistency in moral decision making is a goal—consistency over time, from case to case, from rule to rule, from person to person. The insights we bring to the enterprise have broad, general application to other dilemmas on other days. They help us learn to think for ourselves, make the tough calls—to become autonomous decision makers or moral agents, even in a workplace environment that all too often devalues independent decision making. When we get it right, we are "doing ethics," and in the long run there is a positive payoff.

Unfortunately, much of what passes for "doing ethics" is based on precious little systematic moral philosophy. Instead, it consists of narrowly pragmatic decisions based on expedience, gut reactions, dogmatic opinions, imposition of a manager's or culture's values, and arbitrary and often inconsistent invocation of rule books or codes of ethics. In these cases, the variables that go into making a decision one day are not necessarily used to make other decisions the next day. And, while it might get us through one dilemma, this approach does little to help us become careful, thoughtful professionals. It is *ad hoc* moralizing, rather than moral philosophy, and it mitigates against moral autonomy. This pattern of moralizing confuses media consumers, who wonder how and why media practitioners make their decisions. It contributes very little to civic life.

Read (a slightly edited version of) what one of our graduating seniors wrote at the end of a semester's study of media ethics. He had worked for the campus newspaper and was a sports stringer for a metropolitan paper. He had long wanted to be a sportswriter, so his mind focused on that field even though the course dealt with media in the broadest sense. Nevertheless, his study of ethics deeply affected how he continued to pursue his career:

> I have learned more about "doing" journalism in this course than through all my other classes combined. In other classes, I learned how to write a lead, conduct interviews, edit, and enough media law to stay out of trouble. In this course, I have begun to recognize moral issues facing journalists today, developed my ability to analyze those issues from different points of view and have changed my outlook on the profession as a whole.
>
> Before I started this class, I envisioned myself in a journalistic world of black and white. I found myself reading stories and thinking, "I just wouldn't do that story" or vice versa. I believed I could avoid doing harm by avoiding stories that could cause harm. I realize now that journalists live in a perpetual gray area where the potential to do harm is a constant concern. Where there is truth and accuracy in reporting, there is the potential to create difficult situations for those being reported on.
>
> Before this class, I could not (or would not) recognize the moral issues represented by the case studies discussed in class or assigned in the readings. When the class began, I felt completely lost in many such discussions because I had no ammunition to attack the issues. It was easier for me to say, "I just wouldn't do that story."
>
> Reading about the philosophers and working through the models provided me with that ammunition. I started to feel like I could participate in class discussions and bring something insightful to the conversations. Working through some of the issues in my journal, while becoming more comfortable with the models, I realized that my attitude toward journalism was changing. Through close analysis, my sense of journalistic moral obligations was developed for the first time.
>
> If I had to sum up the course, I would say that I better understand the daily dilemmas facing journalists. I better understand the obligations journalists have to their readers, their subjects and themselves. I can better recognize moral issues in many news pieces; in print and on broadcasts. I have a better sense of my moral obligations as a journalist. I feel I am much better prepared to deal with ethical dilemmas when they arise in my future profession.

Most media ethicists believe that the development of individual moral agency—moral autonomy—is necessary for the media to fully assume their important roles in society. Media fare that reflects the collective judgment of autonomous moral agents is far preferable to media content determined by unquestioned adherence to tradition and myth; or determined by ethics rules drafted by management and dogmatically imposed on staffers; or based on government-imposed rules for individual practitioners. The constant struggles between or among these forces for autonomy and conformity make the study of media ethics one of the most interesting and challenging courses in the pre-professional curricula.

OBJECTIVES OF THE COURSE

In her Harvard doctoral dissertation, Deni Elliott (now the Poynter Jamison chair in Media Ethics at the University of South Florida, St. Petersburg) critiqued various pre-professional ethics course objectives, before stating her list of what to include in a course that stresses moral autonomy and avoids indoctrination. She concluded that:

> Within the context of basic shared values of the profession, the main goals in the teaching of professional ethics would be to help the student better understand the moral requirements of the profession and help the student develop and test his/her own system of professional moral belief. At a minimum, I suggest that pre-professional students should (1.) become aware of their own systems of professional moral belief, both in terms of approved actions, attitudes, and justifications for that approval, (2.) recognize that there are alternative systems of belief both among peers and from traditional ethical theory, (3.) be challenged to test one's own system of professional ethics by grappling with cases and be willing to adopt new processes and standards based on critical exploration into one's own system, and (4.) understand that the obligations of the profession delineate moral boundaries to professional action by individuals, attempt to isolate those moral boundaries into a class of essential shared values, and become skilled in utilizing those obligations and moral boundaries as criteria for judging the adequacy of professional moral decisions.
>
> (Elliott, 1984, pp. 154–155)

This textbook incorporates Elliott's objectives and insights from the Hastings Center Institute of Society, Ethics, and Life Sciences,* a major ethics think tank that has helped many academics frame their ethics courses. The Hasting Center (1980) suggests that five instructional goals appropriate for any ethics course are to help students in:

1.   recognizing moral issues
2.   developing analytical skills
3.   tolerating—and resisting—disagreement and ambiguity
4.   stimulating the moral imagination
5.   eliciting a sense of moral obligation and personal responsibility.

We will consider each objective as it applies to students and instructors of media ethics. The first three objectives are especially adaptable to media education; the other two are difficult to achieve.

---

* The following argument was developed in two previous publications (Black, 1992, 2004) and strongly influenced by Clifford Christians, particularly in his book with Catherine Covert (Christians & Covert, 1980).

Recognizing Moral Issues

This objective is entirely consistent with a pre-professional curriculum. It is vital to be able to define problematic areas, recognizing that although something may be legal this does not necessarily make it ethical. It is equally vital to understand the duties of communicators and their impact on society, and other variables in the nexus of professional practice in a business whose social significance has provided it with a number of freedoms and responsibilities. With all this in mind, we do well to devote a good deal of attention to raising—and attempting to answer—the deceptively simple question: "What's your problem?"

The Socratic method works particularly well here, according to Christians and Covert (1980). The classroom is a safe environment in which to provide each other with ethically acceptable reactions to mass media problems and sharpen our ability to discover the ethical dimensions of practices and policies. This skill, as with most skills, is built upon insight and knowledge. When done well, in an open classroom, these discussions naturally move from "moralizing" toward "moral philosophy."

Students with practical experience—such as internships or working on student publications or other productions—may have less difficulty recognizing issues in media ethics than students whose primary exposure to media practices has been as members of media audiences or as students in classrooms. However, all students can benefit from an ethics course that asks them to become more precise in their definitions of concepts and principles, to articulate the moral dimensions of case studies, and to delay final judgment until they have systematically thought through the problems at hand.

Developing Analytical Skills

This pragmatic objective is also quite compatible with media education. The subject matter of ethics is often in dispute, and the dynamic tension arising from an open marketplace of philosophical positions becomes very stimulating. It is sometimes a stretch to connect hypothetical and real issues raised in this course with the classical and contemporary theories we will discuss throughout the book. However, when the connections are made and the case studies can be analyzed in accordance with the new vocabularies that such theories provide, a significant improvement in the intellectual endeavor is likely to be shown. Likewise, analytical skills come with learning and applying various decision-making models or justification processes.

By the time students take the media ethics course, they probably already have learned practical skills such as news gathering and reporting, visual communication, online and desktop publishing, developing public relations and advertising campaigns, photography, and the like. However, it may well be that such skills were learned more through instruction and rote than through individual exploration. The ethics course should take a different path. In developing analytical skills, students should learn to demonstrate intellectual coherence and consistency. Because media professions demand powerful skills for interpreting complex events, analytical abilities should be sought to varying degrees in all media courses. And, as we heard from our graduating senior quoted on page 3, the ethics course should hone these abilities.

Rigorous argumentation with attention to evidence, not rampant moralizing, is the key to building analytical skills. Students should be motivated to state why a particular problem has ethical dimensions, and to formulate a hypothesis. Possible solutions to the problem should be explored during a brainstorming session, but a halt to brainstorming should then be called and students should be asked to pay careful attention to detail—to causes and consequences, to people affected by ethical or non-ethical decisions, to institutional norms and values. The solutions should then be tested against traditional philosophic principles.

One tried-and-true way to develop analytical skills is to use a template or justification model. A good model frames our decision making by asking us to respond systematically to a specific set of questions. If the questions and answers are based on moral philosophy and reflect a high grip on reality, we are "doing ethics" as it should be done in the professional arena. This is why this textbook is framed around six fundamental, easily remembered, but philosophically sound questions. The questions, akin to the "5Ws and H" taught in almost every introductory mass communications or news-writing or reporting course, are:

- What's your problem?
- Why not follow the rules?
- Who wins, who loses?
- What's it worth?
- Who's whispering in your ear?
- How's your decision going to look?

We have already introduced the first question, and we will say much about all six questions throughout the text.

Tolerating—and Resisting—Disagreement and Ambiguity

The media ethics classroom has a natural proclivity toward open discourse. It is only normal for such discussion to entail a great deal of disagreement and ambiguity. Many of the questions and case studies seemingly have no clear answers at first, and articulating opinions is likely to take up much class time. However, not all opinions have equal intellectual or ethical weight. To put the disagreements in their proper pedagogical perspective, the probing has to go far beneath the surface, asking the "why" about the "what." Instead of relying upon convention and the "of course" syndrome (reflected in assertions that something "just is because it just is"), layers of that anti-intellectual moralistic onion should be peeled away.

Insights into epistemology—the study of how we know what we think we know—might help clarify the formation of our opinions and beliefs. A natural and healthy evolution may occur: opinions and beliefs that were imposed by authority and tenaciously adhered to suddenly seem inadequate; in their stead we begin to tolerate disagreement and ambiguity. We ultimately develop an individual commitment and sense of personal responsibility, taking ownership of our opinions and beliefs and having acute awareness of the consequences of our actions.

It is natural to be uncomfortable with the recognition that there may be no single "right" answers to many of the questions raised in this class. Why, we ask, if philosophers have been working for two millennia on these issues, aren't there more absolutes? Frustrated with the inherent disagreements among various schools of philosophic thought, and concerned that there seem to be no clear and universal moral absolutes governing media ethics, we might tend to revert to relativism, arguing that all opinions have equal value. When the tendency to rampant relativism happens, we do well to widen the arena of investigation, to help one another work through various moral points of view to discern for ourselves a justifiable system of ethical decision making. If everyone in the class (including the instructor) is willing to grapple honestly with areas of disagreement, all should be receptive to the analytical skills-building exercises as their individual and collective moral imaginations are stimulated. Members of the class may take steps toward developing a sense of moral obligation and personal responsibility.

It would be nice to say that the call for tolerance of disagreement needs little further comment. We try in our schools and colleges of journalism and media studies to avoid mindlessly promoting ideological ethics and undisputed conventions; we assume that all of us will naturally appreciate the need for some discussion, disagreement, and tolerance. However, in times of "politically correct speech," with institutional intolerance for extreme utterances, we may be unnecessarily restricted in exploring the natural boundaries of our ideologies and value-based words, ideas, and behaviors. An intellectually honest media ethics course is a natural venue for such an exploration.

Stimulating the Moral Imagination

Unlike the first three objectives outlined above, this fourth goal of media ethics instruction is not fully compatible with typical mass communication practice and instruction. Stimulation of the moral imagination demands that the course work involve more than practical skills or even abstract intellectual exercises. It also means that our feelings and imagination must be prodded. According to Christians and Covert (1980), moral imagination will not be stimulated until live human beings and their welfare become central to the classroom enterprise. And that is difficult, given the "realities" of traditional and online journalism, advertising, public relations, and entertainment media as they are taught and practiced today.

Traditional mass communicators tend to lack one central characteristic shared by other professionals. Whereas other professionals have individual clients with articulated needs and expectations, mass communicators tend to deal with customers—undifferentiated members of the public. As a result, it is hard for mass communicators to sense empathy for individuals they report about, persuade, entertain, and report to—their sources and audiences. They may pay lip service to the needs of T.C. Pits ("The Celebrated Person In The Street"), but mass communicators in daily practice are more likely to focus on appealing to a vast, anonymous, heterogeneous, undifferentiated mass audience. These realities of traditional mainstream media may explain why many young people have turned elsewhere for entertainment, information, and persuasion. Internet-driven media sources provide a sense—real or imagined—of interconnectedness, recognizing sources and subjects as "real people" co-existing in "real time." Little wonder traditional media practitioners, who have always held to a top-down model of experts-serving-masses, are struggling with the changing media environment. As far as media ethics is concerned, the ramifications of this shift could be enormous.

Meanwhile, it is hard to be idealistic and empathic in today's increasingly depersonalized mass media institutions, where neophyte practitioners see themselves as interchangeable cogs in a corporate machine. Many students worry about finding a media job that pays a living wage, let alone one that offers occupational if not moral autonomy. To them, the professional trait of "servant" or "steward" may not come naturally. Our study of media ethics should reinforce the fact that the public has a right to the best information, entertainment, and persuasion we can provide them, and that producing these "products" in accordance with moral principles often entails suffering or happiness on the part of "real" people.

By definition, serving media audiences means practitioners must help them make sense out of the myriad conflicting messages that clutter communication channels. Doing so means the communicator must take a long, hard look at the world, to try to understand the forces that make it work, and to choose a position from which to communicate. Raising such questions in the media ethics class invariably means we should begin questioning such standard operating principles ("craft values") as objectivity, or such bromides as "go with what you've got," "if the competition's going to do it, so should we," or "if it's legal, it's ethical." After all, the classroom is a far safer place than the establishment media to be an iconoclast!

Stimulating the moral imagination means asking why deadlines and technological or economic constraints can produce behaviors that would be less tolerable if such pressures were absent or lessened. In the quiet after the deadline has been met, introspection and second guessing may give rise to questions of impact and empathy. If an ethics course stimulates the moral imagination, such questions will become internalized, and media practitioners might consider their permutations before the next deadline.

A typical concern expressed by students in this class is that it is all well and good to sit around and discuss these issues at our leisure over the course of a semester, but that in "the real world" there is scarcely time to tend to the task at hand, let alone play abstract intellectual games. A logical response is that if the process is undertaken in the classroom often and well enough, the synopses will be in place for more rapid and sophisticated decision making under pressure, so that each new dilemma is not written upon a blank tablet. (As a surgeon might argue, she cannot wait for the badly injured patient to show up on the operating table before learning how to do medical ethics. Just as ethical "front-loading" is a worthy goal in medical school, so it should be in schools of mass communication.)

Before we leave this topic, consider another problem with stimulating the moral imagination of media students and practitioners. We tend to think it is the public's responsibility, not the communicators', to impose meaning onto and deal with consequences of news, persuasion, and entertainment. Journalists, for instance, may think that their major responsibility is to meet the deadline, to be published. If that is so, they spend little time considering the consequences of what they write. They provide the "facts"; once they are published, it is assumed that an abundance of ideas competing in the marketplace will make all come out right—as suggested by utilitarians and libertarians such as John Stuart Mill, Thomas Jefferson, and John Milton. If individuals' rights are considered, they are often thought of in terms of legal rights, such as privacy, intrusion, libel, fair trial, etc., rather than moral rights, such as dignity, well being, peace of mind, etc. Likewise, advertisers and public relations practitioners motivated by the sometimes contradictory goals of informing and persuading may quickly turn from one campaign to the next, without considering the impact of the first. Often persuaders claim it is not their responsibility to control the effects of their messages—they just present them for public consideration, hoping their messages will get through and bring the desired results. Given this attitude, and the pressures of the moment, advertisers and PR practitioners may be acting irresponsibly—without even knowing it.

Eliciting a Sense of Moral Obligation and Personal Responsibility

The fifth and final objective, as with the fourth, is difficult to attain in a media ethics class but well worth attempting. At several points throughout the semester, we would do well to face such questions as "Why should I be moral?" "What are my ethical duties and obligations as an individual, as a student, and as a professional mass communicator?" "Given my freedoms, what are my responsibilities?" The abstract questions cut to the quick of the enterprise. They ask us to take ethics seriously and to recognize that there is more to ethics than recognizing ethical problems, having analytical abilities, staying open minded, and being morally stimulated. At the same time, this fifth objective may be the most problematic, because it opens the Pandora's box in which reside all the concerns about education *vis-à-vis* indoctrination, learning-about-ethics *vis-à-vis* being-expected-to-be-ethical.

As Christians and Covert wrote decades ago, in order to elicit moral obligation, it is necessary that ethics instruction appeal to the will, expect some sort of action, and engage decision making. For all practical purposes, it is presupposed that individuals are free to make moral choices and be held responsible for them. However, this freedom to make moral choices may be limited in mass media because practitioners usually operate within profit-centered institutions, carry out their chores under conditions of controlled pandemonium, and remain somewhat removed from the people affected by their actions—factors that tend to isolate ethical decisions from other routine decisions. If, as more than one philosopher has said, the ultimate ethical decision may be whether to accept the universe or to protest against it, many media practitioners—particularly those working within mainstream media institutions—are not routinely in the position to make ultimate ethical decisions. Bloggers, freelancers, and other entrepreneurial media practitioners may actually be in a better position to make "the ultimate ethical decision"—meaning that the bar for moral obligation and personal responsibility may actually be set higher for these people than for mainstream media practitioners. The irony will not be lost upon us as we consider the dozens of case studies throughout this textbook.

Honing a sense of moral obligation and personal responsibility goes hand in hand with leading an examined life—surely a worthy goal for any university experience. Moral psychologists tell us that acting out of a sense of commitment and principled behavior occurs only at higher stages of moral development. This stage of development comes once we learn to internalize, reflect upon, and operate out of moral principles. Our conscience has become refined after we have progressed through stages of egoism, relativism, and culturally defined goals and rules. The process of internalization tends to occur as we move from an illusory kind of inner direction to a more rational and realistic one. We can achieve an examined life and a degree of moral autonomy, become moral agents on our own, and even reach a point at which we can criticize the rules and values of our society. (We commit Chapter 4 to this topic.)

If we think we will progress through these stages and emerge as "moral heroes and sheroes" by the end of this semester, we may be setting our sights unrealistically high. Research indicates that the overwhelming majority of us operate at conventional stages of morality, motivated largely by tradition and temporal pressures. But we should hope for more than that.

CONCLUSIONS

This introduction—indeed, this entire book—argues that media practitioners should overcome a propensity to view life as a series of disconnected episodes rather than as a continuing stream of experience. We are concerned when media workers react rapidly to situations on the basis of unexamined internalized standards of news/advertising/ public relations/entertainment judgment, focus on action rather than consequences, expect immediate gratification, and reach conclusions quickly. We believe it is prob-lematic for media practitioners to remain aloof from events, to suspend judgment, to act as disinterested observers rather than participants. Likewise, it is disconcerting to see too many *ad hoc* responses to morally challenging incidents, and a paucity of appeals to principle or theory as a framework for decision making.

Thus, our study of media ethics must encourage us to consider long-term consequences as well as immediate action, the tolerance of ambiguity and unresolved dilemmas, the slow and deliberate coming to judgment, the invocation of principle, and a sense of moral obligation.

All of these qualities are devalued when people have an episodic view of the world. Consider what happens if we accept without question a premise of traditional objectivity, which says that news stories should be balanced and should present "multiple sides of the question." When seeking this artificial balance, journalists may have become professionally detached from distinguishing good and evil in what they observe. Likewise, advertising and public relations and entertainment media workers who accept without question the myths and standard operating procedures of their crafts have shortchanged themselves and their audiences intellectually and morally. The end result of such unquestioned acceptance of their crafts is that practitioners become excluded from the ultimate ethical decision: to accept the universe or to protest against it.

Certainly the goal of professional education is to provide immediately usable skills and attitudes valuable on the job. But it has a companion purpose—realizable in an ethics course—to preserve and protect those more humane considerations sometimes trampled in the professions' rush to deadline, the controlled pandemonium of the broadcast control room, the account executives' harried schedules and conflicted loyalties. The prospective media practitioner should be conditioned to the more philosophic long-term view to balance the pressures toward the narrow and the episodic approach that will characterize the "professional" milieu.

EPILOGUE: ETHICAL THEORY AND PRACTICAL APPLICATIONS

Theory

While we work to expand our ethical horizons, we do so with a constant eye toward ethical theory. As Kurt Lewin and others have said (it's unclear who originated the expression), "There's nothing quite so practical as a good theory."

Theory does not flow full-blown from the pens of casual observers. Rather, it is an end result of long, careful analysis of many variables. Theories are not universal laws explaining in complete and unquestionable detail all the causes and effects of phenomena being studied. Rather, theories are systematically related generalizations, calling for further analysis of phenomena and variables. In the case of media scholarship, theory emerges from social scientists and humanities scholars who have coupled the tools used in such fields as psychology, sociology, anthropology, history, economics, and philosophy.

Ethical theory is of this nature. When couched in a valid theoretical framework, our study of the media ethics environment should tend to counterbalance all the pressures to just get on with the job, finish it quickly, and hang the consequences.

We are working in a theoretical realm when we grapple with a never-ending series of questions about the nature of our work and its impact on the political, social, and individual environment.

Development of such a theoretical foundation also gives us cause to question the integrity of the corporations that employ us. As professional media workers sandwiched into a corporate structure whose executives are primarily concerned with profit, our creative energies—be they in producing news, persuasion, or entertainment—can easily become just another product to be stamped out as the market demands. Hanging out our own shingle, and saying "to heck with the corporate rat race," makes us no less susceptible to these moral challenges.

All of us bear some responsibility for ethical decision making at the organizational as well as the personal level. Our course in media ethics must give us some guidance in bringing ethical insights to bear on conflicts between personal and organizational commitments. The responsibility to the public sphere must be borne by both individual and organization.

Practical Applications

The compound title of the book you are reading reflects the authors' conviction that making ethical judgments is a process ("doing ethics") that meshes theory with practice. In media ethics, useful theories should be closely connected to a world in which multiple stakeholders constantly make decisions that have an impact on other stakeholders and shape the larger environment.

This book is divided into six sections and thirteen chapters. Each section carries the title of one of the six "5Ws and H" questions we introduced a few pages back: (1) What's your problem? (2) Why not follow the rules? (3) Who wins, who loses? (4) What's it worth? (5) Who's whispering in your ear? and (6) How's your decision going to look? In less colloquial terms, we are assessing moral problems, codes and rules, stakeholder theory, competing values, moral philosophers, and accountability. (For what it's worth: The "5Ws and H" approach has met with a good deal of success in seminars and professional workshops with executives and middle managers, as well as with young people just beginning their careers.)

A brief introductory essay follows each of the six questions, describing the chapters that will flesh out the questions. Each question stands alone as a line of inquiry into media ethics, but the questioning process and the answers that emerge are cumulative. In our experience as media practitioners and instructors we have found the six-step justification process to have good value, as it encourages us to stay on track, consider numerous alternatives, and reach justifiable conclusions.

Most chapters conclude with several practical applications and five case studies. The cases are for:

- journalists

- new media practitioners, such as bloggers or people who run websites

- public relations practitioners

- advertising practitioners

- people in entertainment media, such as television and film.

Each set of case studies is designed to help you consider the chapter's focus as you work through situations you may one day face in your career, or situations you'd do well to understand in your quest to be a more informed media consumer. While many of these case studies ultimately require you to make a binary "yes-or-no" decision, the goal is to think about your thinking as you work your way through each situation. As others have said, there may not always be a right or a wrong answer, but there are relatively good or bad processes to get there.

The cases in this text are increasingly complex, asking you to incorporate your growing body of knowledge about ethical decision making. You may find it tempting to focus on the cases most closely connected to your immediate career interests. However, it is useful to work through related cases that are based on the same scenario but focus on different communication specialties. Thinking about other media careers is useful for at least two reasons: (1) because many mass communicators shift specialties throughout their careers, and you may someday find yourself in an entirely different environment from the one you are anticipating, and (2) because thinking about other communication specialties can both stimulate your moral imagination and increase your media literacy as citizen-consumers and media critics.

Most of the case studies, strictly speaking, are hypothetical. (Many are based in Freedonia, the name of a fictional country in the Marx Brothers' 1933 movie *Duck Soup*. Some names in the case studies are based upon characters or people associated with this madcap movie now in the National Film Registry.) But many of the cases are *romans-à-clef*, in which actual people and events are fictionalized—in part, to save some of the stakeholders from probable embarrassment. These "based-on-reality" situations let the authors introduce more nuances—more ethical gray areas—into cases that may already have been resolved. We'd like to discourage you from doing *post hoc* analyses, with 20–20 hindsight, on well-known cases; we'd prefer that you look at general cases with fresh eyes.

Just because a case is hypothetical is no reason to lighten your intellectual grip, since many of the cases actually occurred in real life and are as thorny as situations you might face in the real world. How you work through those situations now may well affect how you deal with complicated ethical issues once you are on the job.

One more observation about the casework: Most of the scenarios are typical of dilemmas faced by neophytes in the early stages of their media careers. We see little value in asking you to think like a network CEO before you've finished an internship or your first year on the job. This does not mean the cases are simplistic. Far from it. But they're not bogged down with all the extraneous variables that impact decision making in the corporate towers. However, if you learn to work smoothly through the level of cases in this book, you'll find yourself front-loaded and well prepared to tackle much tougher dilemmas as your careers develop.

Where to Find More

The changing nature of mass media and the desire to offer more than mere text are reasons why *Doing Ethics in Media: Theories and Practical Applications* is more than a book. The authors have also provided:

- An area on the publisher's website, www.routledge.com/textbooks/black, with more media ethics material for students and instructors. Among other things, students will find printed and audio summaries for each chapter, a glossary, study helps, and links to ethics codes and other useful sites. Instructors will find ancillary material to assist in their preparation for the course, too.
- A new site—www.doingmediaethics.com—we hope will become a landing point for up-do-date discussions of media ethics for students, instructors, and the general public. We'll post there frequently with discussion points for class, new case studies, new ideas, and ways for you to (civilly) argue with one another.

The www.doingmediaethics.com site also will provide you an easy way to contact the authors. We are eager to hear feedback about what works, what doesn't, how to improve the site, and what needs to be added to (and subtracted from) new editions of the textbook.

■ ■ ■

CHAPTER VOCABULARY

Note: Definitions are available at this book's companion website.

- *ad hoc* moralizing
- autonomous moral agent
- epistemology
- libertarian

- moral imagination
- moral philosophy
- Socratic method
- utilitarianism

What's Your Problem?

Moral dilemmas may be defined as situations in which we find it necessary to choose between two (or more) equally compelling, but incompatible, alternatives. One scholar calls these "right-versus-right" situations (Kidder, 1995, pp. 113–114). In such cases we are expected to resolve conflicts between core moral values—truth versus loyalty, self versus community, justice versus mercy, etc. Making choices between or among unsatisfactory alternatives is difficult work.

> Spell out, in some detail, what makes this situation a moral dilemma. Leave yourself with a clearly stated question to be answered.

The work of moral decision making—a process we call "doing ethics"—cannot begin until we thoroughly understand our problem. Is this a routine, craft-based problem, or a moral dilemma? Who are the stakeholders, and how might they be affected by choices being proposed? What rights or values or obligations seem to be in conflict? How can we make clear, rational, and publicly defensible choices? Etc.

To help us understand moral dilemmas, Chapter 1 offers a primer on ethics and morality. It outlines several categories of ethics and shows how we "fix" our beliefs or reach conclusions, including reliance upon the "authority" of law, codes of ethics, and individual and professional judgments. The primary goal of the chapter is to help us articulate and solve problems by employing principled decision making rather than shooting from the hip.

The more practical experience we have, the easier it is to recognize the nuances of our problems and to keep on task. The task becomes more manageable when we have the necessary tools: the vocabulary of ethics and a commitment to do the right thing for the right reasons. (Crass self-interest is not one of "the right reasons.")

1. <u>**What's your problem?**</u>

2. **Why not follow the rules?**

3. **Who wins, who loses?**

4. **What's it worth?**

5. **Who's whispering in your ear?**

6. **How's your decision going to look?**

CHAPTER 1

Ethics and Moral Reasoning

INTRODUCTION

THE FIRST step in making good decisions is to recognize the problems at hand. Some problems are routine, craft based, or professional— what we might call "non-moral" issues. Others are complex matters of morality and ethics—the subject matter of this textbook. Both categories of problems become easier to resolve with practice. Experience teaches mainstream and new media journalists how to do a better job gathering information and converting it into powerful news stories; it teaches advertisers how to craft messages effectively to promote ideas, goods, and services; it teaches public relations practitioners how to assist clients and the public in meeting common ground; it teaches people in the entertainment media how to attract audiences with a wide array of media and messages. And experience teaches audiences of this media cornucopia how to master the important skills demanded of citizen-consumers.

Making good decisions in matters of morality is also a skill that improves with practice. That skill—a process we call "doing ethics"—begins by carefully articulating the problem, and then systematically resolving it.

If ethical decision making were simply a matter of choosing between right or wrong, good or bad, this would be a very short book. However, such choices are not always black or white; they're much more likely to be arrayed in a rainbow of gray. We cannot resolve these moral dilemmas simply by invoking institutional traditions or routinely obeying someone else's rules or codes of ethics.

To help us identify and resolve problems in the media ethics environment, this chapter:

- sets the stage with a pair of case studies
- offers a primer on ethics and morality
- defines several categories of ethics
- shows how people "fix" their beliefs—from visceral responses to principled decision making
- suggests pros and cons of reliance upon the "authority" of law, codes of ethics, and individual judgments
- describes the place of ethics in different types of personal and professional relationships
- provides several practical applications for further study.

CASE STUDIES

The following hypothetical case studies reveal the complexity of media ethics and the challenge of "getting it right." The first case explores a perplexing challenge in modern media: conflicts of interest for online publications. The second is based on a composite of events and choices faced by a public relations practitioner. For each case, you (and your classmates) are first asked to identify the central problems, and then to define the moral dilemmas. You will find a number of problems nestled within each case. Not all the problems are moral or ethical ones. Some are personal, pragmatic, or craft-based "non-moral" concerns that impinge upon essential moral dilemmas. The goal at this early juncture is not to completely work through all the subtleties of both cases, but to discover the basic nature of the problems. Once you've carefully defined the problems, the job of resolving them becomes much easier.

CASE 1-1 **Keep the Money—and Your Self-Respect?**

In your spare time you have built a successful website, www.freedonialive.com, dedicated to all things in your native land. It is a collection of your thoughts on the day, whether on politics, the news of the day, or even the movies you have seen, the restaurants you visit, and the products you use. Your smart writing and wry sense of humor have made it a credible destination for thousands of readers each day, and even the Freedonia mainstream media link to your work.

But now it's time to show yourself the money. Your site generates a little revenue—you have a few local sponsors, an online "tip jar," and Google's "AdSense" program, which pays you for clicks on ad links placed by Google—but the Web doesn't cover your household bills. After a few years, your site remains a labor of love that you hope will one day become a career.

So you are intrigued when a Freedonia-based firm, MarketingMarx, comes to you with an offer. The firm represents many local potential advertisers, and it promises a steady income if you provide at least three favorable references per week to the products and services of its clients. Moreover, the company will pay for the products and services you use.

It is enough money that, with a little penny pinching, you could fully focus on the site to make it even better (and attract more readers and advertisers, and therefore become even more lucrative) over time.

You accept MarketingMarx's offer to see how it goes. Your first assignment is to eat at a restaurant in town and write about the duck soup, the restaurant's newest dish.

MarketingMarx has given you no guidelines beyond "favorable reference" requests, but it is clear its goal is to use your site's credibility for its "word-of-mouth" campaigns. Your first concern is about transparency, because the Freedonia Trade

continued

CASE 1-1 *continued*

Commission requires bloggers to tell readers that posts may be sponsored by advertisers. The Word of Mouth Marketing Association's (WMMA) code of ethics frowns upon "shilling," which it defines as paying someone to promote a product "without disclosing that they are working for the company." However, the WMMA code does not say how this can be avoided, and you are not a member, anyway.

So before you eat that bowl of duck soup, you must make some decisions.

What's the Basic Problem Here?

Is this an everyday routine situation with an everyday routine solution—or are you facing a moral dilemma? If it's a moral dilemma, describe what variables you should consider as you try to reach a defensible solution. Have economic realities and options for financial independence put you into a win–win, a win–lose, or a no-win situation? Are any of your loyalties in conflict? Is the problem resolved by following a set of rules or code of ethics? What's to be gained or lost by not telling anyone about the financial ties to MarketingMarx, or by fully disclosing the ties? Can you follow the letter of the law yet still not meet the spirit of the law, such as if you disclosed the deal with MarketingMarx in a separate "about me" page that does not link to the duck soup review and would be less likely to be read than the review itself? (Simply put, can you follow the law yet still hide the MarketingMarx deal so readers who aren't careful might not know you have a deal?) What are the short- and long-term consequences of your choices?

CASE 1-2 **A Dilemma About Loyalty and Promise Keeping***

You are the public affairs (public relations) officer in Freedonia for the city's largest employer, the National Paper Corporation (NPC). Your middle-management position gives you access to the company's immediate and long-range plans. You are at the meeting where top managers decide that economic conditions have made it necessary to permanently close NPC's Freedonia plant and cut 3,000 jobs. Factors

continued

* This hypothetical case is based on first-hand experiences with a gypsum mine and paper mill in Ohio and a steel mill in Utah, and second-hand experiences relayed by numerous participants in a series of middle-management ethics workshops over the past several years. The boyhood company town of one of the authors, in Ohio, was hauled away on flatbed trucks after the mine petered out and the wallboard, paint, and paper divisions closed. Versions of this case, with commentaries by four philosophers and public relations practitioners, appeared in the inaugural issue of the *Journal of Mass Media Ethics* and in five editions of the textbook *Media Ethics: Issues and Cases*. This case raises timeless dilemmas about truth telling, promise keeping, and loyalty that cut across professional and personal domains.

CASE 1-2 *continued*

include a glut of inexpensive, imported paper products, which is diminishing the market for NPC's products, plus the government's insistence that the Freedonia plant's sixty-year-old production processes pose environmental hazards that will cost too much to remedy.

Freedonia is in a sensitive economic position. There are few job possibilities for Freedonia's unemployed, who probably would have to sell their houses and move.

The region was primarily agricultural before World War II, with only a moderate amount of manufacturing. After the war, the NPC plant's growth changed the economic balance. The children of farmers developed skills in fields related to the plant, and numerous family farms were consolidated into several larger farms, offering far fewer employment possibilities. The plant has paid decent wages, and most of its workers own their own homes in or around Freedonia.

You are a single parent of two high school children. You own your own home and have been saving money to send your children to college. Your sister, Elizabeth, is a real estate agent. Elizabeth is very excited about having five "hot" prospects for house sales in town; the deals should go through in about three weeks. Elizabeth's husband, Frank, has worked at NPC for fifteen years and now has a high-paying job as a shift foreman. Elizabeth and Frank have been very close to you, especially since your spouse died a decade ago in an industrial accident at the NPC plant.

At the meeting where the company decides to close the plant, arguments are made that a great deal of harm would come to the company—damage to its reputation, an inability to fill a final set of orders for one last major contract, and the response of the stock market to the corporation—if word leaked about the impending closure. Everyone at the meeting is asked to promise not to say anything to anyone about the closure, nor to do anything that would set off rumors or a panic.

NPC managers told you they would make every effort to find a similar job for you at another division of the parent corporation, in an out-of-state location. Your boss reminds you of how well the company treated you after your spouse died: You had quickly jumped from secretary to executive secretary to public relations assistant to public relations officer.

What's the Basic Problem Here?

Has management placed you in an untenable position, or is this a routine PR dilemma that requires a routine PR solution? At what point, in what way, and to whom could/should you speak out? What should you tell the Freedonia newspaper's business reporter, who is certain to be calling within twenty-four hours? Are you

continued

CASE 1-2 *continued*

being asked to deceive others? Are you a powerless "decision taker" or an empowered "decision maker"? The case study doesn't say whether you are male or female; would your gender make any difference in how you address the problem? To whom should you remain most loyal? Why? Do your professional loyalties trump your personal loyalties? Why, or why not?

Thinking About the Cases

Listen closely to your own arguments and to those of others as you and your classmates talk about the blogging case study and the professional and personal situation involving the closing paper mill. In each case, ask and answer:

- What's the central problem? To what extent is this a moral dilemma, and to what extent a "non-moral" one? (Describing something as a "non-moral" dilemma recognizes that many routine decisions are based on practical, pragmatic, or craft-based considerations rather than moral or ethical ones.)
- What variables are people focusing on? Are they the same variables that concern you?
- What are your initial perspectives, your first set of conclusions? How quickly did you reach any conclusions? On what were they based? (Don't be surprised if your first response is a "gut level" or visceral response, deeply rooted in your own experiences or values.)
- How do you react when you hear others reach very different conclusions? Does it cause you to defend your initial conclusions strongly, or to become more open to alternatives?
- Are you comfortable having to say, "I don't know"?
- In both cases, we used "you" as the person facing the ethical situation. Might your decisions be different if the events were happening to someone else?

Elsewhere in this book we discuss such topics as professional and moral values, loyalty, privacy, truth telling, credibility, accountability, moral development, and various schools of philosophy. We'll refer to these initial case studies throughout the book and in the book's online component. At this point, however, just jot down the key ideas or arguments that you and your colleagues expressed while defining and attempting to resolve the problems. Later, when you have studied the variables in more detail, you might want to revisit—and rethink—your and your colleagues' initial perspectives. Weeks from now you might change your mind about *what* you would do if you had the opportunity to turn a profit on your website and what it would mean to the merchants and consumers of freedonialive.com, and *what* you should have done as a PR practitioner (and parent, sister, and member of the larger community). On the other hand, you might have the exact same set of conclusions, but our bet (and hope) is that you use a different set of criteria to reach them!

At this point we should define our key terms. Identifying the moral or ethical problem is the essential first step in doing ethics, but the entire journey demands a detailed map of the territory.

DEFINING ETHICS AND MORALITY

Students asked to define ethics and morality usually say these subjects deal with human values and conscience; creating and using standards agreed upon by a particular group of people; choices between good and bad, or between two troublesome options; decisions about whether to go against the norm or even break a law for a greater good; and clashes among competing core principles. These are astute observations about complex ideas.

Philosophers and other scholars have struggled for millennia to define ethics and morality, and to distinguish between the two. They know the term "ethics" comes from the Greek "ethos," meaning character, or what a good person is or does to have a good character. In general, ethics deals with decision making; it deals with good and bad, right and wrong. In the original Greek, "ethos" meant "dwelling" or "stall." That suggests the stability and security a person needs to act at all. The term at first referred to animals, not to humans. Thus the germinal idea in the word "ethos" is the stability and security provided by a "stall" or "dwelling" for animals. The verb root of ethics, in Greek, was "iotha," which means to "be accustomed to." There is a relationship between stability and custom. For humans, our customs serve the same purposes as stalls do for animals: They provide security and stability. Ethics, according to Diogenes, is concerned with the foundations of human behavior.

"Morality" is often used interchangeably with ethics, although philosophers maintain the words emerge from different traditions and have subtle distinctions. Some see ethics as the foundations of human behavior, and morality as the actual practice or behavior on these foundations. Morality is of Latin origin, not Greek; it referred to the way or manner people behaved—their "customary" behavior. Given this distinction, "morality" describes behavior based on custom; "ethics" describes behavior according to moral philosophy, reason, or reflection upon the foundations and principles of behavior. (One shorthand way to remember the difference is to think of ethics as behavior that occurs above the neck, and morality as behavior that occurs below the neck!)

As a practical matter, in media ethics—as in many practical arenas—there is a substantial overlap between concerns over ethics and morality. This book does not obsess about the distinctions. Both terms are concerned with the cement of human society that provides the stability and security we need to flourish. When applied to the media environment, practitioners might ask and try to answer basic questions about how they fit into society:

"What are we, as believers in the precepts of public relations or advertising or journalism or media entertainment, to do? What are our obligations? To whom are we accountable? What are the consequences of doing a good job, or a poor one?" The answers are complex; the route to those answers is rarely as simple as we might imagine.

Writers have crafted an array of definitions of ethics and morality, and some are more helpful than others. Consider these:

1. The philosophical investigation of the principles governing human actions in terms of their goodness, badness, rightness, and wrongness. (D.M. Borchert & D. Stewart, 1979)
2. Ethics is obedience to the unenforceable. (Moulton, cited in R. Kidder, 1924/1995)
3. It is normal to think about ethical issues not only in terms of right behavior, but also in terms of appropriate feelings, attitudinal responses, and ways of being. We urge the person to *be* a certain way, not just to *do* something. This raises questions of virtue and character. (K. Lebacqz, 1985)
4. Ethics is a branch of philosophy; it is moral philosophy or philosophical thinking about morality, moral problems, and moral judgments . . . Moral philosophy arises when, like Socrates, we pass beyond the stage in which we are directed by traditional rules and even beyond the stage in which these rules are so internalized that we can be said to be inner-directed, to the stage in which we think for ourselves in critical and general terms . . . and achieve a kind of autonomy as moral agents. (W.K. Frankena, 1973)

These diverse insights suggest that ethics and morality are philosophical and practical enterprises dealing with "owes" and "oughts." Unlike law, which concerns itself with obligatory behavior ("What's the bottom line, below which we should not fall lest we be punished?"), ethics concerns itself with unenforceable behavior ("Given freedom to choose, what should we do?") and maximum standards that require near perfection to achieve. (If law is "thou shalt not kill," then maximum standards would be to show love continuously "with all your heart, mind, and soul.")

When "doing ethics," we consider the nature of competing values, virtues, and responsibilities. The questions we grapple with include:

*   "Which values take precedence?"
*   "What would my moral heroes and sheroes do?"
*   "To whom do we owe something?"
*   "Why ought we behave in a particular way?"
*   "What are the consequences of our behaviors?"

These definitions help us focus on the ethical and moral issues we face and help us define problems as something other than routine, pragmatic, garden variety dilemmas. To keep us on track in our exploration, we also need to describe several categories of ethics.

SOME CATEGORIES OF ETHICS

We are now ready to look more closely at the nature of philosophical ethics and moral philosophy. Our brief foray will define and deal with descriptive, normative, and meta-ethics, and with the notion of applied, practical ethics.

Consider first what philosophical ethics is *not*. Philosophical ethics is *not* the same as *descriptive ethics*. Descriptive ethics involves chronicling what sorts of beliefs certain individuals hold about morality or describing a society's set of moral customs.

Sociologists are engaging in descriptive ethics, for example, when they report that more than half of people who belong to the Republican Party believe that the use of marijuana is immoral; sociologists are simply describing the results of an empirical study revealing that certain individuals hold a particular moral belief. Anthropologists who report the sexual mores of Freedonia also are engaged in descriptive ethics. They do not report *moral* facts, but report facts about the beliefs of Freedonians regarding sexual conduct. Journalists interested in financial meltdowns, Ponzi schemes, and crises of leadership may write stories that include quotes and sources' opinions about right and wrong; these journalists are likewise engaged in descriptive ethics. But journalists who write opinion columns or editorials or blogs on the same topics, drawing their own conclusions about right and wrong based on moral principles, may venture into the domain of philosophical ethics.

Philosophical ethics is not *non-theoretic ethics*. Non-theoretic ethics involves discussing one's views on moral problems without appealing to any general moral principles. Usually, this involves passionately airing one's mere opinions or "feelings" about the moral status of, for example, abortion, capital punishment, drugs, pornography, or sex. Non-theoretic ethical talk runs rampant in bars, dormitories, political rallies, and cocktail parties. It also shows up during heated debates over case studies and sometimes in answers to essay questions.

Philosophical ethics includes the study of *normative ethical theory*. Normative ethical theorists strive to formulate the broad, general moral theories that can explain exactly why certain actions are right and others wrong. Those theories can be used to untangle and resolve complex moral problems. Therefore, as you unravel our case studies about a blogger's temptation to take the money and run, and a public relations practitioner's concerns about loyalty and truth telling, you would be doing normative ethics if your decision making relied upon systematic moral theories.

Not only must the normative ethical theorists articulate their general moral theory, but they also must *defend* it by offering positive arguments for their own theory, by defending their theory against criticisms, or by criticizing alternative normative theories. Defending such a thesis lies at the heart of what it means to "do" philosophy, just as it is essential when "doing ethics."

Another part of philosophical ethics is *meta-ethics*. Although meta-ethicists address a variety of philosophical puzzles, one problem they address is how to define our moral terminology (e.g., something "is obligatory" or "is immoral"). The distinction between normative ethical theory and meta-ethics is not hard and fast; drawing the distinction does not serve our present purposes. However, we cannot resolve our first two cases without some basic understandings of the nature of "truth," "deception," and "loyalty." The terms should not be used too loosely, especially at the initial stage when we are defining our problem.

So that all of this thinking and discussion reaches some practical ends, we employ one more notion from philosophical ethics: *applied ethics.* Applied ethics involves connecting a particular normative theory to a particular moral problem. This suggests that thoughtful responses to ethical dilemmas—when systematically following philosophical principles about right or wrong acts, about positive or negative consequences—are based on applied normative ethics.

With the exception of the few meta-ethical issues, this book is primarily a work in normative ethical theory and applied ethics. This will involve explicating in detail a classic normative ethical theory, followed by an application of that theory to particular moral problems faced by media practitioners.

FROM VISCERAL REACTIONS TO PRINCIPLED DECISION MAKING

Ethics ultimately demands decision making. The first step is to know a dilemma when we see one: What moral and non-moral issues are we grappling with, and what essential question(s) do we intend to answer? That crucial first step is not taken in isolation, but is inextricably connected to the other steps we must take if we intend to reach a defensible conclusion and take appropriate action. How we define our problem is the stage-setting question. Beyond that essential step—as much of this book maintains—the process of making good decisions should be clear and rational.

Media practitioners make decisions daily; some are minor and bear little consequence. Other decisions are more important and may involve greater consideration. Occasionally, decisions may be of such magnitude that many stakeholders are greatly affected by them.

How do we make decisions? Without an analytical study of the process, most of us make decisions instinctively, even carelessly. Indeed, when we first confront an ethical dilemma, our natural inclination is to react viscerally—from the gut, if you would. "This just doesn't feel right," we might say. Or, on the other hand, "I feel comfortable with this." Of course, hardcore philosophers will say they are not particularly interested in what we "feel," but only what we "think." They might even accuse us of deferring too often to our reptilian brain rather than our cerebral cortex. In reality, however, we're only acting in a normal, human way when we rely on our "feelings" as the initial response to a dilemma.

However, can you imagine what the world would be like if we all relied solely upon our gut reactions? Looking back at the case studies at the outset of this chapter, what would happen if all the journalists, advertisers, PR practitioners—rookies to top managers—based all their conclusions upon nothing other than their "feelings"? How narrowly would they have defined the problems in the first place? How likely is it that they would have considered the needs and interests of all the other stakeholders? What compromises would they have unwittingly made, and with what short-term and long-term consequences?

How We Fix Beliefs

Charles Peirce (1839–1914), an American pragmatist, philosopher, mathematician, and physicist, explored these questions when he outlined his notion of "epistemology"—how we know what we think we know; how we "fix our beliefs." His conclusion was that individuals and societies rely upon four basic and hierarchical ways of knowing:

- tenacity
- authority
- intuition
- science.

The most primitive or fundamental way of fixing our beliefs is tenacity, or merely believing in something out of blind prejudice or through unquestioned adherence to tradition. We may have learned some "eternal verities" at our parents' knees, at our places of worship, in our villages and communities, from our teachers and coaches, and from our professional colleagues. Once we latch onto these simple all-encompassing explanations, we use them automatically to define and resolve continuing problems and as shortcuts to handling new problems. Holding tenaciously and dogmatically to our beliefs is easier than grappling with troubling nuances. It should come as no surprise to hear that dogmatic and visceral people make decisions more quickly—and, seemingly, with more certainty—than people who spend more time weighing all the subtleties. In the mass communication environment, as in many places of business, the method of tenacity is found in the words and actions of traditionalists who say, "We've always done things this way around here." The consequences of dogmatically and tenaciously fixing beliefs are often alarming.

The next step in Peirce's schema is to accept ideas passed on to us by various authority figures—secular or religious, personal or institutional, etc. The extent to which we tentatively or wholeheartedly accept opinions from authority figures says a lot about how open or closed minded we are. Careful, rational filtering of opinions from authorities is a sign of mental and moral maturity; blind obedience and willful deference are not. For example, if media neophytes find themselves automatically deferring to the "tribal elders"—their editors, account executives, directors, or to knowledgeable veterans who have accumulated years of practical experience—the young practitioners are not likely to develop decision-making skills on their own. In some environments, tribal elders make it perfectly clear that their experience and opinions are not to be challenged; authority serves as a form of social control. In other cases, an open environment encourages exploration and even tolerates some mistakes along the way.

Numerous examples of reliance upon authority are found in everyday media practices: Journalists are expected to interview and cite reliable sources for their stories; advertisers are expected to back up any "factual" claims with hard evidence; public relations people are expected to conduct solid research before making claims about "public opinion"; documentarians are expected to film and record actual events, and so forth.

Not all authorities are human. Other forms of authority are embedded in institutional practices—the practice of objectivity in journalism, puffery in advertising, and selective editing in entertainment are examples of tradition-based authority. In these examples "authority" is an asset that can help media achieve excellence. However, merely following authority will not always lead to excellent journalism, advertising, public relations, documentaries, or entertainment work. Media practitioners need other ways of fixing beliefs to go beyond tradition or undue reliance on authority. Put another way, authority is a necessary but not sufficient means of establishing truth.

Beyond authority-based beliefs are those Peirce said we generate by our own intuition, or best judgments. We take in a wide variety of opinions and observations, running them through our individual filters—filters created by our particular lot in life, our professional backgrounds, our demographic (age, sex, education, income, place of residence, etc.) and psychographic (our values and motivations) variables, our attentiveness or indifference, our self-interest, etc. For example, in an open environment we all are welcome to articulate our unique and diverse opinions, and put our conclusions into action. Professionals rely upon finely honed intuitions to make good decisions.

All well and good—we've transcended tenacity and authority and have come to rely on good intuition. But, Peirce and pragmatists ask, what happens when the well-meaning intuitions of one person are not in accord with the well-meaning intentions of others? What happens when "good people" see the world differently, because their filters are dissimilar? How then do we reach meaningful consensus?

Peirce's answer was to use the scientific method. He did not necessarily mean we should run all our decisions through laboratory instruments or systematically produce and test hypotheses about everything. But he suggested that the ideas behind the scientific method have much to offer us in everyday life. Science does not reach decisions until evidence is gathered; it asks us to try to be objective in assessing ideas and experiences rather than jumping to conclusions; it says our opinions and conclusions should stand up to public scrutiny. In essence, we are describing *principled decision making*.

> To satisfy our doubts, therefore, it is necessary that a method should be found by which our beliefs may be determined by nothing human, but by some external permanency—by something upon which our thinking has no effect.
>
> —C.S. Peirce, 1877

We should note that it is completely normal to jump back and forth among these four means of fixing beliefs. On many issues it makes little if any difference what framework we employ. On others, particularly those with significant potential impact on others or on public policy, we do well to move toward the more sophisticated and principled stages of decision making.

How can Peirce help us resolve our first two case studies? He might say that:

1. it is natural to have a gut reaction to the situations, but . . .
2. we should test those reactions by asking what authorities/rules/policies should be considered
3. what other stakeholders and rational observers might intuitively decide about the dilemmas
4. and what we would decide if we were to make careful, systematic, and transparent choices.

THE LEGAL-ETHICAL WALL

When answering the question, "What's your problem?" we should decide how much of our problem lies within the moral or ethical domain, and how much lies within the legal or authority-based domain. Until we sort that out, we won't do a very good job of reaching defensible conclusions.

Earlier we quoted William Frankena's definition of ethics. When describing the ethical maturation of Socrates, he said ethical considerations arise when we pass beyond the stage of only considering rules and legalistic arguments about why we should behave certain ways. Ethical considerations and moral philosophy emerge when we begin to think for ourselves in critical and general terms, and achieve a kind of autonomy as moral agents.

This is not to say that what is legal and what is ethical are always in agreement. In fact, we may categorize the characteristics "legal–illegal" and "ethical–unethical" in four groups to see where our ethical dilemmas may exist.

Let us construct a "wall," with desirable decisions on one side and undesirable decisions on the other side. (This assumes, of course, that ethical and legal decisions are desirable; that unethical and illegal decisions are undesirable.) Then we will represent decisions in four categories, and evaluate each category.

Many decisions are easy to make positively, because they are both legal and ethical. Similarly, many decisions are easy to make negatively, because they are both illegal and unethical.

We have more difficulty in other cases, such as when a decision can be defended as legal, but in our conscience we deem it unethical. We sometimes hear people justify a questionable decision by saying, ". . . but it's not illegal." That response is an ethical

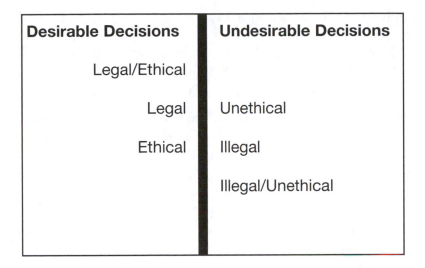

FIGURE 1.1 | Legal vs. Ethical

"cop-out" because it subjugates conscience to authority. It is an exercise in "buck-passing," in refusing to take an ethical stance considered to be correct.

In the third instance we have even more difficulty, when a decision is clearly illegal but we deem the decision to be ethical and the law to be wrong. In such a situation, we may have to defy the law—the modern term is "civil disobedience"—to stand up for our ethics. Great moral heroes of all societies and eras have dared to stand against convention and put personal principle above societal conventions. Examples include Jesus Christ, Buddha, Gandhi, Dr. Martin Luther King, Rosa Parks, and Mother Teresa.

But people who defy the law in the name of ethical principle must then be willing to offer themselves as test cases when challenging the law. This may mean arrest and imprisonment for civil disobedience, and lengthy trials and appeals in the testing of a law's ethical validity. For media practitioners, it could mean losing a job and being ostracized.

A number of journalists have refused to testify in court when asked to reveal names of their confidential sources—in essence violating legal mandates but upholding personal and professional principles. Some public relations practitioners have been those confidential sources, breaking laws and commitments to their organizations by providing information they think serves a greater good. Whether these and other activists are ultimately viewed as ethical—judged to be "moral heroes or sheroes"—may depend on society's ultimate decision regarding the rightness or wrongness of their positions and their (at least temporarily) illegal actions.

Our moral and ethical development can be put to the ultimate test when law and ethics collide, and our principles may cause us to sacrifice friendships, employment, even freedom.

But consider more precisely the distinctions between law and ethics. To behave legally, within legal limits, is not necessarily to behave ethically. Note the big difference between the ethical question of "What behaviors do I choose to engage in?" and the legal question of "What behaviors are we unwilling to tolerate in this society?"

Law tells us how badly we may have behaved. Ethics tells us how we may behave well.

Law is the court of last resort; it reflects society's inability to resolve issues involving civil and other rights. Socrates maintained that good people thinking well should have resolved these through application of moral philosophy.

Ethical thinking is contextual and introspective, concerned with reordering and/or redefining social virtues. Moral philosophy seeks truth, justice, and consistent advice in an open, dialectical, analytical, and cathartic manner.

Legal thinking is linear, with a logical progression to some ultimate conclusion. It is rule oriented. Law does not seek virtue but a preponderance of evidence. The adversarial legal system can lead to justice, but it does not necessarily lead to truth.

Ethical decision making is also linear, albeit without being as rule oriented as law. Taking advice from pragmatist Charles Peirce and moral philosophers, we can systematically use evidence and logic to reach justifiable conclusions. We approximate the scientific method by carefully utilizing a "justification model." In the next chapter we will explore several such models, including the "5Ws and H" checklist that frames this book. If we apply these models properly, we will find ourselves using Charles Peirce's higher levels of epistemology—refining our intuitions and "scientifically" considering the variables that can lead to justifiable resolutions.

As we claimed earlier, the first step in making defensible decisions is to articulate the problem. To what extent does our definition of the problem focus our attention on external authorities, such as the law or various rules and regulations imposed on us, or on self-chosen authorities or autonomous "moral agency"? Not to complicate the picture, but these authorities often meld.

AUTHORITY: ETHICS IN LAW

Lawful authorities have already made many of our decisions for us. But doesn't this violate the definition about "individual" decision making? Yes, of course, but this is only one of many apparent contradictions we shall see in this study. All societies, from the most primitive to the most advanced, have reached certain decisions by consensus. As the society develops, many of these right-or-wrong decisions become law. We may find it useful, then, to assert that law is a moral consensus, defined and made enforceable. On the other hand, it may be just as useful to say that law is a means of protecting ourselves against the potentially immoral behavior of others.

In any case, societies have developed bodies of laws, a large percentage of them defining the minimum behavior deemed to be ethical. We are asked to respect the rights of others.

We are told to respect private property. We learn that it is wrong to kill or deprive others of their property. These and many other definitions of society are laws that define our collective ethic.

In the case of mass communication in developed societies, we find a limited number of formal controls over press freedom and free expression. For example, we may not damage the good name or reputation of people, nor should we invade their privacy. We are limited in our use of copyrighted material. We should not advertise or promote harmful goods or services, and we should be truthful in promoting the quality and health implications of goods and services. But beyond these minimal definitions, most "free world" societies impose few legal prohibitions or mandates on mass communication.

AUTHORITY: ETHICS IN CODES

Mass communication codes of ethics are controversial, to say the least. It has been said that if I am ethical, I do not need a code to define my actions; and if I am unethical, my actions will not be affected by a code anyhow. Nevertheless, recent years have witnessed a proliferation of codes for news and entertainment media, advertising, and public relations. The codes range from nationally circulated codes by organizations of professional communicators, to locally adopted codes of individual media and agencies.

A code of ethics may be defined as a statement of beliefs, principles, and acceptable behavior of people in a common vocation. The statement, or code, is normally published, often displayed, and commonly referenced as a definition of peer-group practices.

A significant characteristic of a code of ethics is that it is unenforceable in court. It is not defined by a legislative body or subject to litigation in a judicial body. Some peer groups include a procedure for internal punishment of violators, as in the denying of a doctor or lawyer the right to practice in a hospital or a court. But there is no enforcement mechanism in the ethics codes of many peer groups, most communicator groups included. Violators of codes are often ignored, or at the worst may be criticized, by their peers in an assembly.

Because codes of ethics are becoming increasingly common and increasingly controversial among communicators, we dedicate much of Chapter 2 to the subject of media codes.

AUTONOMY: ETHICS IN INDIVIDUAL JUDGMENTS

No set of laws, no detailed codes, can possibly anticipate and identify all the ethical decisions that professional communicators must make. We cannot escape the necessity to think for ourselves, which brings us full circle to the definition of ethics as "individual decision making about right and wrong." And, should we decide not to decide, that in itself is a decision that may create significant consequences.

It is not enough for anyone, especially a professional communicator, to make ethical decisions carelessly. Decisions should be rational. Decisions should be fair. Decisions should be defensible. Decisions should be externally consistent. Decisions should be internally consistent. For all these reasons, and more, decisions should be arrived at carefully.

All of this is to say that the professional communicator should be a responsible, ethical person.

ETHICS AND RELATIONSHIPS

Finally, we do well to ask: How is society best served when there are few or no legal restraints on mass communication? What are the real and assumed contracts when communicators sell their persuasion, their information, their entertainment, their culture? On whom does society rely for competent communication?

Human beings are inescapably and simultaneously individual and social. We are free agents living together. Our actions affect each other, and we are radically dependent upon each other. The fact that we affect each other deeply, for good and for ill, requires that we must act responsibly toward each other if society is to endure. The greater our power to affect others, the heavier our ethical duty.

Morally mature individuals take on specific responsibilities with respect to others. Those responsibilities are considered at every stage when doing ethics, including the initial act of defining our problem. From the outset, we must recognize that our dilemma is not isolated from other beings. "What's your problem?" asks, in essence, that we consider our options in terms of their impact on others.

As we consider how our decisions affect others, it is useful to consider several kinds of relationships we have with others: *assigned*, *contracted*, and *assumed*. Philosopher Lou Hodges said:

- *Assigned relationships* require us to act responsibly out of threat of power or simply because we lack power to act otherwise. Such relationships are most obvious in authoritarian states, but are also seen in the military, in some employer–employee relationships, and elsewhere where there is a significant power imbalance, where someone simply assigns responsibility to another. In many instances as a mass communicator, you are an employee or create messages under "work-made-for-hire" contracts that mean you are subservient to a boss—or that you may be the boss. When you are the boss or decision maker, subordinates take their ethical cues from you and must act upon your ethical decisions. When you are the worker bee or decision taker, you must carry out the wishes of your boss. Sometimes you must decide whether your moral compass will not allow you to carry out an order you perceive to be unethical. The media world is filled with stories of the actions of unethical bosses, unethical workers who fail to carry out the ethical decisions of their bosses, and workers who quit rather than compromise their ethical beliefs. There are significantly fewer stories of assigned relationships that work smoothly, because that is the non-newsworthy norm in the workplace.

- *Contracted relationships* describes interaction between parties who have agreed to share more-or-less equally in power and authority. The agreements range from written contracts to informal understandings of obligations. For example, we act responsibly out of having voluntarily accepted some duty to others and because we have a general duty to keep promises. As a journalist, we sometimes make "deals" with sources, such as refusing to reveal a source's name in order to protect a whistleblower. We would face a dilemma if a court ordered us to reveal the name. As advocates in advertising or public relations, we may sign agreements not to reveal proprietary information—and struggle if it might be in our (or the public's) best interest to break that promise.

- *Assumed relationships* are self-imposed—both individual and personal. They come into play when we voluntarily identify ways in which we might—but are not required to—benefit another person or group and then voluntarily accept responsibility for doing so as an expression of character or virtue. Ultimately, these commitments tend to be stronger and more enduring than assigned or contracted responsibilities. We act responsibly in these relationships because we feel we owe it to ourselves to be persons of principle and character, and because we feel we have an obligation to act ethically with respect to others in society. An example might be the many codes of ethics drafted by groups such as the Society of Professional Journalists or the Public Relations Society of America. We have no legal or moral obligation to join those groups in order to practice in those fields, but we may feel a higher moral calling to try to follow those codes' precepts once we become members.

Note the similarities between the three types of relationships and our discussion of law, codes, and ethics. Ethics plays a role in each of these three kinds of relationships. Assigned relationships have much in common with legal relationships, in that there is little wiggle room for independent decision making. Contracted relationships are similar to those prescribed by professional codes: they may be entered into voluntarily, but decisions and behaviors are often predetermined. Assumed relationships encourage the greatest degree of moral autonomy, as they encourage each of us to use ethical theory to sift and sort through our conflicting institutional and community obligations and duties and to make defensible decisions and take appropriate actions.

SUMMARY AND CONCLUSIONS

Let's return to the two case studies presented at the start of the chapter and attempt to apply the chapter's key concepts. Our goal is not to fully resolve the cases. Our initial challenge is to define the problems, because we must define well before we can choose well. By carefully defining the problems, listing the practical and moral considerations, we can avoid lumbering around aimlessly as we "do ethics." Without a clearly articulated problem, all sorts of extraneous variables will contaminate our effort to systematically resolve the case at hand.

Once we outline the pragmatic and ethical issues, we can see the problems of the blogger and the PR practitioner through the lenses of tenacity, authority, intuition, and science. How problematic are the blogging and PR crafts' reliance upon tradition or arbitrary authority? What do the practitioners' intuitions tell them, and what is to be done when their intuitions clash with the intuitions of other stakeholders? Is there any way the problems can be systematically—even scientifically—approached? Or are the problems so fuzzy that they are doomed to be hashed and rehashed and unsatisfactorily resolved because we find ourselves mumbling, "It all depends . . ."?

The problems can be outlined along the domains of authority (legal and codified) and individual, autonomous judgment and the nature of the relationships among the stakeholders. What laws and codes affect the problems? To what extent are the central characters in the cases decision makers or decision takers? What binds the stakeholders together, and what freedoms do each have to be autonomous moral agents?

So many questions, so few answers.

Satisfactory answers may be found for these and the dozens of other case studies we present in this book—if we continue to systematically ask and attempt to answer the other guiding questions for doing ethics. In the next two chapters we take up the second of our six questions: "Why not follow the rules?"

■ ■ ■

CHAPTER VOCABULARY

Note: Definitions are available at this book's companion website.

- analytical
- applied ethics
- assigned relationships
- assumed relationships
- cathartic
- contracted relationships
- descriptive ethics

- dialectical
- epistemology
- ethics
- meta-ethics
- morality
- non-theoretic ethics
- normative ethical theory

PRACTICAL APPLICATIONS

1. Think of a time in your life when you made a mistake in defining the problem you were facing. What were the results? How could you have done a better job in defining the problem?

2. Name some movies and situation comedies whose storylines are predicated on people not having the same understanding of a problem.

3. Who are your moral heroes and sheroes? What unpopular and difficult decisions did they make?

4. Describe some situations in which each of Charles Peirce's four "methods of knowing" or "fixing beliefs" have been evident. What were the strengths and weaknesses of each method?

5. What experience have you had with assigned, contracted, and assumed relationships? Which experiences were most satisfactory, and which were problematic?

■ ■ ■

THE SECOND QUESTION

Why Not Follow the Rules?

The first section of the book asked us to describe our "problem" or moral dilemma, and to leave ourselves with a clearly stated question to be answered. Now it's time to answer the question as clearly and systematically as we can.

If our problem is one that others have faced before, some moral, legal, or routine institutional precedents may already be in place. A code of ethics or institutional policy statement may offer resolutions to our specific problem, or to one reasonably similar to ours. A professional community may have incorporated resolutions into its conscious or unconscious culture. If the problem is serious enough to pit institutional or professional interests against public interests, it might have been addressed by a body of law or a governmental policy. In such instances it would be folly to ignore history and to plow ahead as though our problem were unique.

The second section of our textbook asks us to stop momentarily in our decision making and consider some of the pertinent "rules" of media ethics—formal and informal policies, codes of ethics, justification models, and historical, legal, and cultural forces. Collectively, they show that the decision-making process should not occur in a vacuum, but should be informed by precedents and an awareness of the interplay between media and other institutions. We cannot decide whether to follow the rules unless we understand where they came from and what difference they make when invoked or violated.

Two chapters are dedicated to this quest. Chapter 2 explores the pros and cons of ethics codes and other formal guidelines drafted by large professional organizations and specific media institutions. In keeping with our sense that codes are incapable of

> **Are there some precedents, guidelines, codes, or laws you should keep in mind? If so, are there reasons your dilemma can't be resolved by them?**

resolving the myriad and nuanced problems arising in media work, the chapter then looks to more generic models for decision making. Several justification models or decision trees are presented, including the "5Ws and H" checklist that frames this textbook.

The second part of our inquiry into "following the rules" involves understanding the evolution of media traditions and cultures—the formal and informal "rules" that have shaped the world's rich tapestry of mass communications. This means we are venturing onto political, economic, philosophical, technological, and cultural turf. No single textbook chapter can provide a full treatment of these traditions. A rich literature has emerged from the pens and keyboards of thousands of scholars over a great many years, so the best we can offer in Chapter 3 are some idiosyncratic highlights. Even if you have encountered some of this material in other mass communications courses, you should find it helpful to put these matters in the broader context of the media ethics environment.

What are we to conclude from these two chapters?

There are plenty of good reasons to follow the rules. But when a perplexing right-versus-right choice has to be made, it may not be enough to "trot out the rulebook." We have our work cut out for ourselves when facing a moral dilemma that demands a choice between compelling but unsatisfactory alternatives. The rest of this book should help us do the heavy lifting.

1. **What's your problem?**

2. <u>**Why not follow the rules?**</u>

3. **Who wins, who loses?**

4. **What's it worth?**

5. **Who's whispering in your ear?**

6. **How's your decision going to look?**

CHAPTER 2

Codes of Ethics and Justification Models

INTRODUCTION

IN THE previous chapter we pondered the first question, "What's your problem?" Now it's time to build upon that practical framework by focusing on the second question: "Why not follow the rules?"

There's nothing inherently wrong with rules. Legislators, regulators, and code writers will maintain that their rules are historically grounded codifications of decisions agreed upon by all reasonable stakeholders. With that in mind, it would be folly to skip over the laws, codes, and policies affecting any enterprise—let alone mass communications—that affects society. So why not follow the rules?

Even at this early juncture in our media ethics journey, it should be evident that doing ethics entails much more than merely following rules created by someone else. Sometimes, doing ethics means transcending our own rules, and even our own codes of ethics! While this sounds contradictory, overly complicated, and bordering on moral anarchy, it makes a certain amount of sense. Philosophers and other well-meaning decision makers may quibble about some things, but they generally agree that whatever decisions we make should be based on clear and defensible thinking rather than arbitrarily following a bunch of rules or authority-based rationales.

Remember the point made earlier, that media practitioners too often wait until deadline before thinking through ethical quandaries? What is suggested here is that we front load our decisions. We should decide in advance which rules, policies, codes, or procedures to follow in general, and which are inapplicable to the dilemmas *du jour*. Doing ethics this way means we should have already discerned, in

In a continuing effort to promote autonomous moral decision making, this chapter:

- considers the pros and cons of ethics codes
- notes the recent flurry of code writing, and some basic differences among media codes
- discusses the strengths of codes as voices of consensus and conformity, but also notes some areas of concern, especially over issues of enforcement and accountability
- proposes alternative ways of doing ethics; a variety of "justification models" for defensible decision making will be examined, concluding with a fuller discussion of the six-question model that frames the textbook you are now reading.

general, which philosophic principles, values, loyalties, etc., we are comfortable relying upon, and which ones we tend to reject. Having the *general* framework in place makes it significantly easier to make *specific* calls when deadlines loom. And simply knowing the rules can help us determine when, if ever, we should break those rules in order to meet a higher ethical calling.

This chapter occasionally refers to the two cases introduced in Chapter 1—one in which you must decide whether to change your principles to add profit to your website; the other in which you must decide what (if any) information to release about a planned plant closing. In addition, five new case studies from the fields of news reporting, advertising, entertainment, and public relations let you apply new insights about codes, rule following, and justification models.

CODES OF ETHICS

One prerequisite of being a professional is to have a code of ethics. Mass communications is just one of many fields struggling with notions of professionalism and seeing a flurry of "codism" triggered by changing issues, changing technology, and changing public opinion.

Codes of ethics are supposed to act as the conscience of the professional, of the organization, of the enterprise. Think of codes as part of the middle ground between law on one hand, and internalized societal values (or personal values) on the other. Codes can be the place where formal social and economic sanctions or a social group (a profession, an industry, a firm, a company) seek to ensure conformity by defining acceptable standards of behavior and penalizing deviance.

Purposes for Codes

Associations and professional groups have several reasons to write and revise their codes of ethics. One good reason is for public relations: A good code contains a set of ideals that justify and rationalize a profession's activities to a larger society, including governments—especially during times of diminished credibility and intensified public scrutiny.

Codes also provide an educational function. A good code promotes ethical thought and behavior within a profession. This is especially important for newcomers, who may not know the complexity of the craft's moral landmines. But it also helps veterans faced with pressures from peers, higher-ups, and outsiders to violate a profession's values and norms.

Codes that take their educational function seriously seek to highlight and anticipate ethical dilemmas, so it is not necessary to reinvent a decision-making process with each new dilemma. Codes inspire us about our unique roles and responsibilities. They make each of us custodians of our profession's values and behaviors, and they beckon us to emulate the best of our profession. They promote front-end, proactive decision making that occurs before our decisions "go public." Unless a code serves these purposes, it may be little more than an impotent façade hanging on the office walls. Poorly constructed codes falsely imply that the profession has agreed upon a uniform set of ethical practices, or they suggest that all the important questions have been settled once and for all. As we will see, these matters have not been settled—neither within the rank-and-file memberships of the various media professions nor in the minds of the various publics. Drafting, reconsidering, and revising codes should encourage further conversation within the field and better dialogue with the public and other stakeholders.

And then, after a couple of years, it is probably useful to tear up the code and start over—if only because the process of drafting a code of ethics is intellectually invigorating and pragmatically cathartic!

The bottom line: If we want to be taken seriously as ethical communicators, we need codes that mean something to practitioners and the general public. If we want to be ethical, we need to articulate our ideals, remind ourselves and others of our unique contributions to the world's civic health, and then act accordingly. If we want to continue to claim freedoms to communicate and advocate, then we should accept concomitant responsibilities. To some extent, codes of ethics can help on all counts.

Two Types of Codes

People who are serious about ethics are concerned with self-imposed behaviors and with moral obligations to keep commitments and honor relationships with colleagues, clients, sources, and intended audiences. Two significantly distinct types of codes address those tasks; neither does the whole job, but one comes closer than the other. The first we will call codes of minimal standards; the second, codes of ideal expectations or "aspirational" codes.

Codes of minimal expectations spell out, in sometimes excruciating detail, the hard and fast rules of the game. They typically go on for pages—some advertising, business, and journalism codes are a hundred-plus pages. Noteworthy examples are the 64-page code of ethics of Enron and the 52-page *New York Times* code. They list every imaginable form of behavior their authors find reprehensible. They are filled with legalistic "thou shalt not's," a litany of sins that morally immature individuals might be tempted to commit.

For instance, the Texas-based Enron Corporation's 64-page code of ethics spelled out, in minimalistic and legal terms, all of the expectations for its employees—including the rule that all ideas that an employee has about Enron's business belong to Enron. A section titled "How to Use this Booklet" told employees to sign a Certificate of Compliance, "as a statement of your personal agreement to comply with the policies stated herein" (2000, p. 3). The code's foreword, by CEO Kenneth Lay, said, "We want to be proud of Enron and to know that it enjoys a reputation for fairness and honesty and that it is respected." Enron, which for six years was named America's most innovative company, collapsed in 2001 because of accounting fraud. It remains widely regarded as one of America's least fair, honest, and respected corporations.

On the other hand, one of the world's most authoritative newspapers, the *New York Times*, also resorted to numerous minimalistic provisos in its lengthy code. Drafted following a scandal over Jayson Blair, a reporter who had fabricated numerous stories, the *Times'* "Code of Conduct for the News and Editorial Departments" told how to deal with 155 problem areas. One of the eight subsections under "Speaking Engagements," for example, says staffers:

> . . . should be especially sensitive to the appearance of partiality when they address groups that might figure in coverage they provide, edit, package or supervise, especially if the setting might suggest a close relationship to the sponsoring group. Before accepting such an invitation, a staff member must consult with the associate managing editor for news administration or the deputy editorial page editor. Generally, a reporter recently returned from the Middle East might comfortably address a suburban synagogue or mosque but should not appear before a group that lobbies for Israel or the Arab states.
>
> (*New York Times*, 2003, p. 14)

A later topic, "Voting, Campaigns and Public Issues," say journalists "have no place on the playing field of politics. Staff members are entitled to vote, but they must do nothing that might raise questions about their professional neutrality or that of *The Times*" (p. 19). Among other things, staffers cannot wear campaign buttons or put campaign signs on their lawns.

If we violate a code's minimal standards, we are blameworthy, and we deserve to be disciplined. But just because we uphold those minimal standards does not mean we are morally praiseworthy, because they are bottom lines below which we should not fall. For instance, we should not expect to be rewarded for not plagiarizing or not abusing a client, but codes feel free to offer penalties for people who drop below the line.

The fixed rules found in minimal standards codes might serve to focus discussions on moral issues. However, they may short-circuit the process of "doing ethics" if we expect such codes to resolve all our concerns. The argument against these legalistic codes is not new: Aristotle pointed out in Book 5 of *Nichomachean Ethics* that minimum codes cannot solve the majority of ethical dilemmas, and no one could write a usable code that would do so.

Is there an alternative, a more philosophically defensible type of code? Yes, in codes that are basically statements of ideal expectations, or perceived ideals. Such aspirational codes include lofty and sometimes abstract statements of expectations. Followers of such codes strive to reach the ideal standards set forth. Practitioners are not punished for not achieving those ideals, any more than show dogs or horses or painters or sculptors or journalists are punished for not winning "best-of-show" competitions, for not being awarded Pulitzer prizes, for not achieving perfection.

Box **2.1** | SOME STATEMENTS OF MINIMAL EXPECTATIONS IN MEDIA CODES OF ETHICS

From the Radio-Television Digital News Association Code of Ethics and Professional Conduct:

Professional electronic journalists should not:

- Report anything known to be false.
- Manipulate images or sounds in any way that is misleading.
- Plagiarize.
- Present images or sounds that are reenacted without informing the public.

From the National Press Photographers Association Code of Ethics:

Photojournalists and those who manage visual news productions are accountable for upholding the following standards in their daily work:

2. Resist being manipulated by staged photo opportunities . . .
5. While photographing subjects do not intentionally contribute to, alter, or seek to alter or influence events . . .
7. Do not pay sources or subjects or reward them materially for information or participation.
8. Do not accept gifts, favors, or compensation from those who might seek to influence coverage.
9. Do not intentionally sabotage the efforts of other journalists.

From the International Public Relations Association Code:

In the conduct of public affairs, practitioners shall:

5. Falsehood. Not intentionally disseminate false or misleading information, and shall exercise proper care to avoid doing so unintentionally and correct any such act promptly;
6. Deception. Not obtain information from public authorities by deceptive or dishonest means . . .
9. Profit. Not sell for profit to third parties copies of documents obtained from public authorities.

From the American Association of Advertising Agencies Standards of Practice:

. . . Specifically, we will not knowingly produce advertising that contains:

- False or misleading statements or exaggerations, visual or verbal.
- Testimonials which do not represent the real opinion of the individual(s) involved.
- Price claims that are misleading . . .
- Statements, suggestions or pictures offensive to public decency or minority segments of the population . . .

Note: Full text of these and other codes are available through the book's companion website.

An aspirational code can broadly define the good communicator, the virtuous communicator, the committed communicator, the noble communicator. It accepts—yet transcends—the minimal code, acknowledging its failings while attempting to provide exemplars and guidance for the resolution of hard cases. The Code of Hammurabi is an example; its nearly 300 legal provisions address in positive terminology the principle that the strong shall not injure the weak. The preambles and general framework of several recently revised media codes also provide good examples of aspirational statements: the Society of Professional Journalists, the Public Relations Society of America, the Radio-Television Digital News Association, Public Radio News Directors Inc., the National Press Photographers Association, and the Society for News Design.

The highly significant differences between these two types of codes say a great deal about human nature.

Codes of minimal standards seem to reflect a world of neuroses if not outright paranoia. The fundamental assumption of minimal standards codes implies that, at worst, people for whom the codes were drafted are morally primitive or at least inherently flawed; that they lack independent judgment and need authority figures to lead them through the decision-making process; that they respond best to threats and fear of punishment; that their natural inclination is to abuse others and misuse their power. A more generous assessment is merely to say that such codes are written for the professionally uninformed (a.k.a., the ethically challenged), who would be better served by a good textbook or course in their profession's history and principles than by a legalistic litany.

On the other hand, codes of ideal expectations reflect a different universe. Their lofty and abstract standards indicate a faith in one's fellow beings, a recognition that inherently decent people are trying to do better, and a sense that gentle reminders of our lofty goals are more effective means of achieving an ethical society than are base-level, punishment-oriented rules and guidelines. Finally, codes of ideal expectations acknowledge our imperfections and generally offer positive "thou shalt" suggestions that will make the world a better place.

You may have noticed that some of the same institutional or organizational codes appear in Boxes 2.1 and 2.2, as examples of both minimal and aspirational standards. In a couple cases, the lofty ideal standards appear in the preliminary or framing section of the code, and the minimal standards appear as a list of specific applications or checklists later in the code. In some codes, however, the language jumps back and forth with a somewhat disconcerting array of standards. In the grand scheme of things this may not be crucial, but in terms of getting buy-ins from practitioners, such codes tend to be confusing and difficult to implement.

Minimal expectations codes tend to be created by management and imposed on newcomers, while ideal standards codes are developed by people who expect to follow them. It would be ironic for an organization's rank-and-file employees to draft a code that implies a general lack of faith in themselves.

Box 2.2 | SOME STATEMENTS OF IDEAL EXPECTATIONS IN MEDIA CODES OF ETHICS

From the Society of Professional Journalists Code of Ethics:

- Seek Truth and Report it. Journalists should be honest, fair and courageous in gathering, reporting and interpreting information.
- Minimize Harm. Ethical journalists treat sources, subjects and colleagues as human beings deserving of respect.
- Act Independently. Journalists should be free of obligation to any interest other than the public's right to know.
- Be Accountable. Journalists are accountable to their readers, listeners, viewers and each other.

From the Radio-Television Digital News Association Code of Ethics and Professional Conduct:

Professional electronic journalists should operate as trustees of the public, seek the truth, report it fairly and with integrity and independence, and stand accountable for their actions.

From the Al Jazeera Code of Ethics:

6. Recognize diversity in human societies with all their races, cultures and beliefs and their values and intrinsic individualities in order to present unbiased and faithful reflection of them.

From the National Press Photographers Association Code of Ethics:

Photojournalists operate as trustees of the public. Our primary role is to report visually on the significant events and on the varied viewpoints in our common world. Our primary goal is the faithful and comprehensive depiction of the subject at hand. As photojournalists, we have the responsibility to document society and to preserve its history through images.

From the Society for News Design Code of Ethical Standards:

Courage. Journalists need moral and, at times, physical courage to fulfill their responsibility to serve the public. It takes courage to stand behind values such as accuracy, honesty, fairness and inclusiveness. Such courage is necessary to achieve personal integrity and build credibility.

From the Public Relations Society of America Member Code of Ethics:

The value of member reputations depends upon the ethical conduct of everyone affiliated with the Public Relations Society of America. Each of us sets an example for each other—as well as other professionals— by our pursuit of excellence with powerful standards of performance, professionalism, and ethical conduct.

From the American Association of Advertising Agencies (AAAA) Standards of Practice:

[S]ound and ethical practice is good business. Confidence and respect are indispensable to success in a business embracing the many intangibles of agency service and involving relationships so dependent upon good faith.

Note: Full text of these and other codes are available through the book's companion website.

Carefully constructed codes of ethics should clearly distinguish between minimal standards and perceived ideals (Elliott, 1985–1986). They also should articulate *group norms*—largely unstated expectations of how all people within the group should or do perform. Because it is "normal," adhering to group norms is not particularly praise-worthy—or even noticeable. And we should beware the dangers of group-think, of blind conformity. A code is valuable if it articulates group norms so that new and veteran practitioners discuss these norms and do not just take them for granted.

The strength of an ethics code lies not only in its words, but in its legitimacy and power in the eyes of those for whom it is written. People will obey because they willingly subject themselves to ethical standards above and beyond their own personal belief, or because the code has specific provisions for enforcement they feel will be invoked should they violate it.

Code Enforcement and Accountability

Longstanding debates over how to enforce codes of ethics reflect a serious flaw in understanding the nature of *accountability*, which is the topic of Chapter 13. To say that agents are accountable for their behavior means they can be called to judgment in respect to their obligations. That is, one can legitimately raise questions or even raise accusations if necessary, and expect reasonable answers. An account is a reckoning properly requested and given, a statement explaining conduct to legitimately designated parties. Professions may be said to be accountable to government, to fellow professionals, and to the public (Christians, 1985–1986). It can be argued that mass communicators owe accountability to:

- *Government*, which makes us liable to punishment when we violate legitimate laws.
- *Fellow professionals*, which means that our peers can publicly disapprove of our morally questionable activities; punishment takes the form of public or private censure, criticism, outrage. We intuitively recognize this form of accountability when distinguishing the moral from the legal, when realizing that although we are not breaking any laws, we have a moral obligation not to violate a commitment or dishonor a relationship. In mass communication, professional accountability is difficult because ethical codes tend to be unenforceable. Lawyers and doctors who break ethical codes can be drummed out of their professions, but journalists, advertising experts, public relations practitioners, and entertainment personnel can continue to work in communication jobs that have no barriers to entry. We'll have more to say about this in our Chapter 3 discussion of professionalism.
- *The public*, which implies a more general notion of answerability in that huge social arena constructed largely of custom and convenience. The public can seek answers and explanations from professionals whose behavior appears unacceptable. Professionals can be accused of neglect or irresponsibility and punished by scorn or indignation, and the public can refuse to buy their products, services, or ideas.

Box **2.3** | CODE ABUSE? ONE JOURNALIST'S TRIP TO COURT

Ethics codes—especially ones filled with ideal expectations—can be double-edged swords in dealing with the public. Unless the public understands that the code's aspirational expectations are not minimal standards, people who live by the code may be unfairly judged by people who do not understand just how high the bar has been set.

Take the case of Cindi Scoppe, an editorial writer in 2000 at *The State* newspaper in Columbia, SC. In writing against plans for a state lottery, she used information from another newspaper (a story that had been reprinted in her newspaper) that incorrectly claimed the governor's former chief of staff worked for a lottery company. When the error was called to her attention, *The State* promptly corrected the mistake.

Still, former chief of staff Kevin Geddings sued Scoppe in a state court, claiming his reputation was damaged and that Scoppe should sign an agreement that she should research her work more carefully and follow the code of ethics of the Society of Professional Journalists (SPJ). (He did not sue the newspaper that made the original error.)

As it turns out, Scoppe wasn't a member of the SPJ. But when she learned of the mistake, she followed the SPJ code's edict to "[a]dmit mistakes and correct them promptly."

The case was withdrawn quietly a year later, but not before Geddings used the code to make points with the public against a newspaper editorially opposed to his administration's lottery plan. Stories about the lawsuit moved on the Associated Press wire, giving Geddings the publicity he wanted and perhaps further confusing people about the purposes of codes of ethics.

Scoppe says the experience taught her that "people don't have to have a legitimate claim in order to sue you." The incident also is a reminder that while codes of ethics may not work against you in a court of law, they can be used against you in the court of public opinion.

A team effort is necessary to make codes of ethics work, media ethicist Clifford Christians says (1985–1986). Accountability implies moral sanction, and we cannot maintain a community with explicit functions without attaching specific rebukes for failing to meet obligations. Fellow practitioners/peers need to be the ones calling each other to account. People cannot be called to account for violating their communal obligations unless there are norms by which they can assign obligations and decide innocence or guilt. No accounting occurs without a visible process whereby agreed-upon principles function as arbiters of obligation.

For people who question whether codes of ethics are worth anything if they have no enforcement provisions, remember that minimal standards codes usually contain some means of enforcement. The codes often clearly include the nuts and bolts of behaviors that even a "knuckle-dragging, mouth-breathing moral troglodyte" (a term coined by one of our students) should follow. However, this is not the nature of ideal expectations codes.

In other words, it is easier and more appropriate to punish the morally primitive than to punish people who fail to live up to our ideal expectations.

Applying Codes to Two Case Studies

It may be helpful to see how codes of ethics might apply to the two case studies in Chapter 1—the website and the public relations practitioner. Bloggers have only recently begun to draft codes; PR people have had ethics codes for decades.

What did you decide were the essential problems facing the blogger and PR person? For the sake of argument, perhaps you agreed that the blogger was trying to resolve a financial conflict of interest, while the PR person was trying to balance competing loyalties and having to decide whether—and to whom—to be a truthful communicator.

Why not follow the rules laid down by fellow practitioners in media codes of ethics? The blogger might turn to a proposed code of blogging ethics (Kuhn, 2007), which says to "Strive for Factual Truth" ("Never intentionally deceive others" and "Be accountable for what you post") and to "Be as Transparent as Possible" ("Reveal your personal affiliations and conflicts of interest"). These succinct, positively stated principles would caution the blogger to be a transparent truth teller. But is that enough? Remember, the blogger has been slogging in the Freedonian trenches for years and finally has a chance for financial independence and time to improve the blog dramatically and serve the community. Do the "rules" explicitly forbid taking the offer from MarketingMarx, or is more hard thinking called for? (In the United States, Federal Trade Commission rules demand transparency in such cases, but—as we saw in the case itself—there are ways around those rules, meaning that it remains an ethics dilemma.)

In the PR case, consider the Public Relations Society of America (PRSA) code. Its list of values includes both honesty and loyalty: "We adhere to the highest standards of accuracy and truth in advancing the interests of those we represent and in communicating with the public," and "We are faithful to those we represent, while honoring our obligation to serve the public interest." Several pages describe core principles and guidelines for achieving them—but do not tell PR practitioners whether to accept management's request for silence when there are compelling reasons not to remain silent. We might even conclude that the PRSA code offers contradictory advice in this case.

To sum up: The codes offer helpful but inconclusive insights. There is more work to be done, if the blogger and PR person hope to "do ethics."

Some Conclusions About Codes

Creating a code of ethics for one's professional group is a worthwhile and challenging project. Rank-and-file employees gain a greater appreciation of the organization's roles and goals when they participate in the code-building exercise. However, employees have a tendency either to follow meekly or resent code provisions imposed on them by management. Code building, when done well, can be an exercise in moral philosophy. Code imposition, when arbitrary, is an exercise in moralizing.

JUSTIFICATION MODELS

While codes may be useful, they are often inadequate in our quest for sound and defensible ethical decisions. Moral philosophy and normative ethics involves going beyond rules and codes, and utilizing *justification models*—ethics formulas or decision-making matrices that we follow to their logical conclusions. We can choose from a number of justification models. Some are more linear than others, but all push us to apply systematic (even "scientific") thinking when we do ethics. This section describes several models that have worked well in the past, and it leads up to a model created for this book.

The Rotary Four-Way Test

Rotary International, a global service organization of more than a million business and professional people, asks its members to adhere to a "Four-Way Test" affecting things they think, say, or do:

- First, Is it the TRUTH?
- Second, Is it FAIR to all concerned?
- Third, Will it build GOOD WILL and BETTER FRIENDSHIPS?
- Fourth, Will it be BENEFICIAL to all concerned?

Rotarians are asked to consider a business or professional dilemma and then "walk it through" this four-way test. They might find how difficult—if not impossible—it is to satisfy all four steps simultaneously. For instance, will telling the truth necessarily build good will and better friendships? Can truth and good will be fair and beneficial to all concerned? Notwithstanding the semantic and logical glitches, this challenging test has remained immensely popular in Rotary International since its adoption by the group in 1942.

There are other such models, some more appropriate to one field of communication than to others.

Bok's Test of Veracity

For a generic justification model to apply whenever we are tempted to lie or deceive others (a dilemma faced by advertisers, public relations practitioners, journalists, entertainers, and all of us ordinary people on a daily basis), we might consider using the three-stage justification model suggested by Sissela Bok, in her excellent book *Lying: Moral Choice in Public and Private Life* (1978). Bok says we can decide whether to deceive once we ask and answer the following:

1. Are there alternative actions that will resolve the difficulty without lying?
2. What are moral reasons to excuse the lie, and what reasons can be raised as counter-arguments?
3. As a test of the first two steps, what might a public of reasonable persons say about such lies?

Bok's test demands a satisfactory answer at each step along the way. If there are alternatives to lying, we should use them. If not, let's move to the second step. If our moral reasons to excuse the lie are more justifiable than those forbidding it, we can move to step three. Otherwise, we shouldn't lie. Even if we do go all the way to the third step, lying is not a good option if our decision is not transparent and cannot pass the "test of publicity."

The TARES Test

A model gaining popularity in the fields of public relations and advertising ethics is known as the TARES Test. To be an ethical persuader, ask and answer questions about the appropriateness of the following:

T Truthfulness of the claims made by the persuader.
A Authenticity of the persuader—integrity, virtue, sincerity, loyalty, independence.
R Respect for the "persuadee's" dignity/rights/interests/autonomy.
E Equity of the persuasive appeal—fairness/justice/parity of the persuasion "playing field."
S Social responsibility for the wider public interest or public good rather than self-interest.

(Baker & Martinson, 2001)

The TARES test demands fairly sophisticated moral thinking on the part of persuaders. It is as philosophically complex as the decision-making model found at the end of the PRSA's code of ethics. To do good ethics in PR, the PRSA code says practitioners should:

1. Define the specific ethical issues and/or conflict.
2. Identify internal and external factors (e.g., legal, political, social, economic) that may influence the decision.

3.   Identify key values.
4.   Identify the parties who will be affected by the decision and define the public relations professional's obligation to each.
5.   Select ethical principles to guide the decision-making process.
6.   Make a decision and justify.

These six steps are not the PRSA code *per se*. That code is many pages long, and it offers a good deal of advice on such matters as the free flow of information, the nature of competition, the disclosure of information, safeguarding confidences, dealing with conflicts of interest, and various ways to enhance the profession . . . all followed by a pledge to be taken by PRSA members. The six steps above come at the very end of the code, and have been reprinted on business-card stock to help PRSA members "do ethics" on the spot.

Society of Professional Journalists Model

Other professional societies seek to provide guidance in decision making, some within codes of ethics, some in internal publications. The Society of Professional Journalists, for example, framed its 1996 code around four guiding principles, each of which is followed by examples and specific advice:

1.   Seek Truth and Report It.
2.   Minimize Harm.
3.   Act Independently.
4.   Be Accountable.

A handbook produced by the SPJ, *Doing Ethics in Journalism* (Black et al., 1999), expands upon the code. A four-part diagram shows that the four principles work in tandem as a justification model that shows how to do journalism ethics. The goal is to maximize each principle. For instance, journalists can seek and report important truths while minimizing harm to sources and subjects. See Figure 2.1. Meanwhile, they can simultaneously remain independent from those who would inappropriately manipulate the news while remaining accountable to stakeholders.

The SPJ handbook also offers a ten-point checklist, modified from a procedure first developed at the Poynter Institute for Media Studies. It asserts that to make good ethical decisions a journalist should ask—and then carefully answer—good questions. Although the ten questions were designed for newspaper and broadcast journalists, they can provide an equally appropriate checklist for communicators in public relations, advertising, and any other communication vocation. Decision makers should ask:

1.   What do I know? What do I need to know?
2.   What is my journalistic (i.e., my "professional communication") purpose?
3.   What are my ethical concerns?

4. What organizational policies and professional guidelines should I consider?
5. How can I include other people, with different perspectives and diverse ideas, in the decision-making process?
6. Who are the stakeholders—those affected by my decision? What are their motivations? Which are legitimate?
7. What if the roles were reversed? How would I feel if I were in the shoes of one of those stakeholders?
8. What are the possible consequences of my actions? Short term? Long term?
9. What are my alternatives to maximize my truth telling responsibility and minimize harm?
10. Can I clearly and fully justify my thinking and my decision? To my colleagues? To the stakeholders? To the public?

FIGURE 2.1 | Balancing the SPJ principles

The Potter Box

One of the most frequently cited justification models is known as the Potter Box. The Potter Box (shown in Figure 2.2) is a model of moral reasoning designed by Dr. Ralph Potter of Harvard University's Center for Population Studies and popularized by Clifford Christians and his colleagues in numerous editions of their media ethics textbook. It is a series of logical steps that conscientious people can use as they work through an ethical quandary. The Potter Box provides a rational and systematic approach that leads a person to . . .

1. define the ethical situation or dilemma objectively and in detail
2. identify values that relate to the situation
3. inject moral philosophy as justification for a decision and
4. choose to whom one is ultimately loyal.

Start in Box 1 by defining the situation. Then proceed systematically through the remaining quadrants. The lines indicate that you may return to any previous box—and should at least consider doing so—to apply insights gained from the other boxes.

A significant discovery is that reasonable, open minded, and intellectually honest people who use the box may reach different ethical decisions, based on their individual input in each or all of the four quadrants. (Potter realized this while working on his doctoral dissertation on how Christians should view nuclear weapons. As he worked his way through the moral ambiguities, he found himself sorting his notes into four piles he later identified as the four boxes in the model.) The goal is not to force a choice, but to help the individual understand and ethically justify a decision.

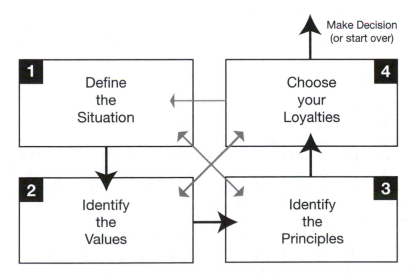

FIGURE 2.2 | The Potter Box

DOING ETHICS BY ASKING AND ANSWERING THE "5WS AND H"

Drawing from a variety of justification models, and anticipating the insights shared by philosophers in the following chapters, we now offer a comprehensive process for doing ethics. This process is useful not only in professional communications fields, but in everyday life—on deadline, and in the quiet *post mortem* period. It is the checklist first introduced in this book's Introduction, and its questions frame the six sections of the book.

By asking and answering these (deceptively) simple questions, we push ourselves to apply moral philosophy directly, systematically, and publicly. The "5Ws and H" list asks:

1. What's your problem?
2. Why not follow the rules?
3. Who wins, who loses?
4. What's it worth?
5. Who's whispering in your ear?
6. How's your decision going to look?

1. What's your problem?

Spell out, in some detail, what makes this situation a moral dilemma. Leave yourself with a clearly stated question to be answered. Look at your problem in detail and from different points of view. As the case develops, recognize that additional events and new insights may cause you to adjust your preliminary answers to one or more of the other questions. You may have to return to the problem and repeat the cycle. For example, looking once again at our Chapter 1 case studies: a blogger must decide whether to accept payment for mentioning specific products and how transparent to be, and a PR person must decide whether to remain silent when silence may harm a community. Such cases hinge on understanding the entire dilemma. If we become hung up along the way, it may be because we have not defined the situation thoroughly enough.

2. Why not follow the rules?

Are there some precedents, guidelines, codes, or laws you should keep in mind? If so, are there reasons your dilemma cannot be resolved by them? As we have explored throughout this chapter, codes of ethics and policy statements have their strengths and weaknesses. Chapter 3, on media traditions and the paradox of professionalism, offers further thoughts on informal "rules." And, as every student of media who has ever taken a course in media law knows, there is virtually no end to the applicable statutes, legislative and executive acts and policy statements, constitutional interpretations, and other formal and informal governmental actions that impinge upon media practices. Recognizing and adhering to these precedents, guidelines, codes, and laws should be considered necessary, but not sufficient, in doing ethics.

3. Who wins, who loses?

Who are the stakeholders, and what impact is your decision likely to have on each of them in the short term and in the long term? This question asks you to identify your loyalties: To whom are you ultimately loyal, and to whom at intermediate steps are you loyal? Who benefits? Who gets hurt? Do any particular people or institutions deserve special loyalties, especially those who are weaker or have faced discrimination? You may have competing loyalties to yourself, your family and friends, your boss, your company or firm, your professional colleagues, your clients/customers/audiences, and society at large. You may feel one loyalty has supremacy at one stage of the decision-making process, but other loyalties may dominate at another stage. The theories of moral development described in Chapter 4 show that self-loyalty motivates us at low or pre-conventional stages of moral development; that group conformity/collectivist thinking occurs at the middle or conventional stages, and that moral philosophy—especially autonomous use of moral principles and rules and loyalty to all humanity—occurs at the highest or post-conventional stages of moral development. Applying these insights to our case studies in blogging and PR, we can see that the more narrow our sense of loyalty, the easier it would be to do the expedient thing; the more universal our loyalties, the more difficult. Additional insights into loyalty appear in Chapter 5, which explores the complex nature of loyalty as a general construct and the need for loyalty to increasingly diverse audiences and stakeholders.

4. What's it worth?

Prioritize your values—both moral and non-moral values—and decide which one(s) you won't compromise. Values help us rationalize or defend behavior. They are standards of choice through which we individually and collectively seek meaning, satisfaction, and worth. We seek consistency in our values. Values can describe desirable conduct (such as "being helpful" or "being independent") or describe end results (such as "happiness" or living "an exciting life"). We might conclude that values define what we stand for. Applied to our Chapter 1 case studies, the blogger and PR practitioner may be motivated by the values of security, a comfortable life, being honest, and being independent. But can they resolve their problems without deciding which of these values are more important than the others?

In this text we devote one full chapter (Chapter 6) to philosophers' and social scientists' insights into values; a second chapter (Chapter 7) to the values of truth telling and the problems of deception; a third chapter (Chapter 8) to the value of privacy; and a fourth chapter (Chapter 9) to the complicated values dilemma arising in media persuasion and advocacy.

5. Who's whispering in your ear?

In general—and specifically in this case—which school of philosophy or set of moral principles provides you with a moral compass? We shouldn't moralize or give inconsistent, *ad hoc* or dogmatic advice; instead, we should use moral philosophy to discover general, consistent advice drawn from the wisdom of the ages. Chapters 10 through 12 will discuss ethical principles, as laid down by philosophers, that should illuminate the issues.

Some well-known principles include Aristotle's theory of virtues, Kant's categorical imperative, Mill's utilitarianism, Rawls's theory of justice, Ross's "Prima Facie Duties," and the feminist "ethics of care." People who seek to do the ethically right thing usually follow one or more of the principles consistently. Until we have a more complete grasp of these principles, we may not be able to apply them thoroughly to the case studies. However, our intuition may have already told us that we want to do the greatest good for the greatest aggregate of stakeholders while harming the fewest number (Mill's utilitarianism). Or we may sense that certain moral duties—such as honesty—can never be compromised (Kant's categorical imperative). If so, we would see how this general perspective fits with our case study process. For instance, if we think the blogger and PR practitioner ought to value independence and a comfortable life (question 4), we may also be inclined to think utilitarianism is the most appropriate principle (question 5). On the other hand, if we put "honesty" at the top of our values inventory, we're likely to be motivated by Kant's notion of following our duty. Unless our values and principles align with one another, we will have difficulty doing ethics.

6. How's your decision going to look?

State your conclusion, and imagine what your friends and people you respect will think about your decision making. The bottom line should emerge logically from your responses to the first five questions. You should be willing to be accountable for those choices; your justification process should be transparent, and it should withstand the test of publicity. Chapter 13 is dedicated to these topics, intermixed with the constant concern of media practitioners to establish and maintain credibility.

As with other useful justification models, this checklist is simple enough to grasp readily yet flexible enough to apply broadly. It can guide our decision making, while simultaneously stretching it. It works particularly well for mass communicators, because it focuses our attention on a specific quandary while testing broader variables in a public arena. It acknowledges the importance of rules, policies, and codes, reminding us that many of the issues we face may have been directly addressed in the past. It demands that we pay close attention to the needs of numerous stakeholders. It expects us to clarify conflicts over professional and non-professional values. It challenges us to make decisions consistent with principles of moral philosophy. And—perhaps of unique importance in a profession whose work product is on constant public display, and whose jobs involve critiquing others—it wants us to be transparent and to hold ourselves accountable.

We will rely upon the "5Ws and H" test throughout this book, and we will attempt to resolve a number of case studies with it.

SUMMARY AND CONCLUSIONS

In this chapter we asked, and started to answer, our second question: "Why not follow the rules?" We focused on codes of ethics as statements of institutional and professional rules, and found them to have merits and shortcomings. There is much to be said for the codification of media rules, but there are definite limitations when relying upon them if our goal is to do ethics carefully and systematically.

When codes and rules don't solve our problems, we do well to use a systematic justification process—one that asks us to take one careful step at a time until we reach a conclusion we believe will hold up to public scrutiny. In some ways, the justification models described in this chapter are indistinguishable from professional codes of ethics. The lines blur between the two means of making ethical choices. However, one way to separate them is to think of the justification models as calling for systematic application of normative ethics, whereas the detailed professional codes of ethics are more likely to be sets of specific guidelines regarding daily occupational practices. Thus, one can apply the Rotary four-way test, Bok's three-step test of truth telling, the TARES test, the Potter Box, or the "5Ws and H" checklist in any number of situations, be they personal, social, or occupational; the media codes have more limited objectives and applications.

As you may have surmised when considering justification models, the questions that frame them are not "no brainers." They demand a certain amount of moral philosophy. At a minimum, they challenge us to think carefully about what we do, what we owe one another, and what happens when we make choices. They are part of what is meant by being an ethical communicator. They are "brainers."

When using justification models, we may find that reasonable, open-minded, and intellectually honest people can reach different ethical decisions, based on their individual input in each or all of the steps along the way. The goal of these models is not to force a choice, but to help the individual understand and ethically justify a decision. If we find ourselves in a quandary after having gone through the entire justification model, we may have to go through the process a second or third time, seeing where there has been inconsistency in some of our choices.

It is safe to conclude that the study of ethics is the study and commitment of the conscience, of individual and collective moral autonomy, of the responsible use of freedom. Achieving these objectives demands hard work. The numerous codes of ethics in the media environment provide guidance but were never intended to do our thinking for us. There are no short cuts if we are to do ethics properly. However, understanding and applying justification models may make the effort seem somewhat more fruitful and less frustrating.

To add context to the problem raised by asking "Why not follow the rules?" the next chapter discusses a number of traditions and cultural variables in mass communications, including the informal "rules" emerging from the quest for professionalism.

CHAPTER VOCABULARY

Note: Definitions are available at this book's companion website.

- categorical imperative
- ethics of care
- justification models
- persons-as-ends

- prima facie duties
- the Potter Box
- the TARES test
- theory of justice

PRACTICAL APPLICATIONS

1. Write your own code of ethics. Think of an enterprise in your life—or your life in general—and create a code of ethics that can serve you or the organization you have in mind. Before and as you write, consider:

    A. Whether an aspirational code or a code of minimum standards is more appropriate. If you mix them, how can you make sure that one is not mistaken for the other?

    B. Whether you would include an enforcement clause that details penalties for breaking minimum standards.

    C. Whether, after stating the important values and stakeholders, you will try to rank them in order of importance.

    D. Whether you would seek to impose this code on others.

    E. What ethics code (found in the online resources for this book) makes the most sense for your situation.

2. How useful are the justification models surveyed in this chapter? For instance, if you were tempted to tell a lie or otherwise deceive someone, would Sissela Bok's three questions be helpful to you? What about the Rotary four-way test?

3. Revisit the two cases that introduced Chapter 1—the blogger and the PR person. Although it is still early in our exploration of media ethics, can you expand upon your preliminary analysis of the case by "plugging into" the "5Ws and H" checklist? We will return to these cases in later chapters, but you might find it helpful to see where you feel confident, and where you feel uncertain, about how to "do ethics" in these cases.

■ ■ ■

CASE 2.1 **Journalism: The Club and Code**

You are a young reporter for *The Freedonia Times*, a 15,000-daily-circulation newspaper in your hometown. You are now a third-generation member of the local chapter of the Rotary Club, an international fraternal and service organization. The local chapter's members include many movers and shakers in your small town, including your publisher. You joined only because your dad insisted, and you do not consider yourself an especially active member.

You also are a member of the Society of Professional Journalists, a large national organization whose code of ethics has four guiding principles:

1. Seek truth and report it.

2. Minimize harm.

3. Act independently.

4. Be accountable.

After a Rotary Club meeting a week ago, you overheard a quiet conversation between two members and learned that a club member misspent money that was to have been used on college scholarships for needy students. You discover that a minister took the money. When you talk to the minister—telling him you are acting as a reporter—he says he used the money to cover a temporary financial shortfall in his church's daycare. He says he expects to repay it within two weeks, that you (and the people you overheard) are the only people who know, that the students will receive their scholarships, that the daycare would have closed without the short loan, and that his reputation will be ruined if you continue asking questions—much less wrote a story. The minister even reminds you that a pillar of the Rotary Club is that members ask themselves whether what they are thinking, saying, or doing would be beneficial to all concerned.

Questions
- **What's your problem?**
- **Why not follow the rules?**
- What else do you need to know?

Thinking it Through
1. How helpful is the SPJ code of ethics in this example? How could it be more helpful?
2. In this case study, what specific parts of the SPJ code of ethics appear to be in conflict?
3. Can a journalist really be "free of associations and activities that may compromise integrity or damage credibility," as the SPJ code requests?
4. Is the SPJ code in conflict with the Rotary Club's code, which says that thoughts, words, and actions should be "beneficial for all concerned"?

5. How might your actions be different if you were not a member of the club? Or if your dad were not a member? Or if your publisher were not a member?

6. What else do you need to know before you take action?

7. Do you continue to ask questions?

8. If so, do you write a story? Why or why not? How do you defend your actions?

For more information, see the SPJ code of ethics, linked from this book's website.

■ ■ ■

CASE 2.2 **New Media: Make a Link—or Not?**

You run www.freedonialive.com, a website that focuses on local politics and other news in your home. As with any good weblog, your site is filled with links that take readers to other sites for more information. You take seriously the "Bloggers' Code of Ethics" stated at www.cyberjournalist.net, which says bloggers should do their best to identify and link to sources. "The public is entitled to as much information as possible on sources' reliability," the code says.

Since you like to post breaking news, you are intrigued late on a Friday when a competing blogger posts a note saying Sen. Margaret Dumont of Freedonia is about to become engaged. This is surprising, because it was never reported that she was dating.

The senator, aged 45, is a widow. Her husband died of a heart attack last year while serving his first term in office, and she was given her late husband's seat as a humanitarian gesture that let her stay in the capitol with her children and complete his term. She is not a candidate in next month's election, and she has served the term very quietly and kept her two children out of the spotlight.

The blogger's bare-bones post does not name a single source of the information, makes no mention of any effort to contact the senator or her staff, and does not even name the potential new spouse. You have followed the blogger's work for several years. While you have never met this person—you don't even know if it's a man or a woman—you have seen some of the blogger's posts that were uncannily accurate, and others that were 180-degrees wrong. Simply put, you cannot make an educated guess about the truth of the post.

The "Bloggers' Code of Ethics" says it's OK to link to other websites, but this case gives you pause. The code also says that if bloggers post "questionable information, make it clear it's in doubt." And while the code also notes that public officials have fewer rights to control information about themselves, it also says that a blogger should be compassionate toward "those who may be affected adversely by Weblog content." Your thoughts briefly turn to her young children.

The code also says that bloggers should remember that "gathering and reporting information may cause harm or discomfort," but also that a blogger should use "good taste" and "avoid pandering to lurid curiosity," and that it should require an "overriding public need" to justify invading someone's privacy.

➤ **You need to decide whether to link to the blog post or not, because when you've made that decision you can finish work for the day.**

Questions
- **What's your problem?**
- **Why not follow the rules?**
- What else do you need to know?

Thinking it Through

1. How helpful is the "Bloggers' Code of Ethics" in helping you make a decision?

2. Do you feel an obligation to try to contact the senator's office before posting the link? Should you try to do any additional reporting before putting the link online?

3. Do you feel an obligation to try to contact the blogger for more information before posting the link?

4. If you post the link, what do you write to explain your justification to readers?

5. If you do not post the link, do you say anything to readers about your decision?

6. To what extent is it news that Sen. Dumont might be getting married?

7. To what extent, if any, do privacy rights related to Sen. Dumont's children enter your thinking?

8. Do you post the link or not? How do you defend your decision?

9. If you post the link to the information and it's wrong, what obligation (if any) do you have to explain or apologize to readers? To Sen. Dumont?

10. If you were working for the web operation of a newspaper or television station, would your decision-making process be different? If so, what does that say about the ethics of online posting?

For more information see Cyberjournalists.net's "Bloggers' Code of Ethics," linked from this book's website. It was adopted in April 2003, just as the word "blog" started to become a household word, and is adapted from the Society of Professional Journalists' code of ethics.

■ ■ ■

CASE 2.3 **Public Relations: The Truth of "Left to Pursue Other Interests"**

As the junior staffer in the two-person public relations office of First Freedonia Financial Inc., your job includes writing press releases and taking calls from working media. Two months ago the board of directors hired a new chairman, William Worthington, intending him to turn around the company's falling fortunes. You wrote the press release announcing his hire and coordinated media coverage as he made the rounds of local media. Worthington seems to trust you.

After six weeks at his new post, Worthington's first major decision is to clean house among the company's highest-level employees. He fires the company's chief financial officer, who was in his mid-forties. The company's chief lawyer, in his late fifties, takes early retirement instead of being fired. Both of the departing executives are well known in the community. Worthington replaces them with two new executives from outside Freedonia.

Your boss tells you to write a press release that focuses on the two new executives with quotes about the new management's plans.

Your first question to your boss: "What do we say about the two executives who are out? The first question I'll get from the newspaper reporter is, 'What happened to the other guys?'"

Your boss's answer is that if you have to mention it at all, just write in the last paragraph that they are leaving the company "to pursue other interests." He says, "You read that all the time when executives leave companies. But I'll leave it up to you whether you mention them at all."

Your boss is right, of course. A quick search of www.prnewswire.com, one of the sites that hosts press releases, shows dozens of examples in which companies say that former executives are "leaving to pursue other interests" or "other business opportunities" or "other career opportunities."

The phrase sounds nice, but—strictly speaking—it is not true that they left to "pursue other interests," since one was fired and the other was essentially pushed out the door. On the other hand, it might seem mean-spirited to write the truth in the press release.

You are a member of the Public Relations Society of America, so you take a look at its code of ethics. It says members should be "honest and accurate in all communications" and "avoid deceptive practices." On the other hand, the code also says that practitioners should "protect the privacy rights of clients, organizations, and individuals by safeguarding confidential information." It could be argued that the executives' dismissal should be a private thing and not highlighted in a press release.

Deadline is approaching, because the boss wants the press release issued before the stock market closes, in hopes that the news will give the company's share price a quick bump.

Questions
- **What's your problem?**
- **Why not follow the rules?**
- What else do you need to know?

Thinking it Through
1. How useful is the Public Relations Society of America's code of ethics to guide you in making a decision?
2. Why not just follow the PRSA code?
3. What will you do?
    A. Will you write what the boss says?
    B. Will you suggest to your boss that the "pursue other interests" line isn't truthful?
    C. Will you find a better way to say it and suggest that wording to your boss?
    D. Will you decide not to mention anything about the departing executives?
4. If you choose to find another way to disclose the information about the two departing executives, will you draw a distinction between the one who was fired and the one who was allowed to retire instead of being fired?
5. What will you say to the reporter who asks you to clarify what leaving to "pursue other interests" really means?
6. What will you say to one of those two executives if they ask you why their names had to be in the press release, and why the "pursue other interests" line had to be included in the release?

For more information, the PRSA Member Code of Ethics and the International Public Relations Association (IPRA) Code of Brussels for the conduct of public affairs worldwide are available at the book's website.

■ ■ ■

CASE 2.4 **Advertising: Does This Ad "Suck"?**

You are starting your second year at an advertising firm and have a new client: Cramrick's Clothing, a retail chain known for low prices and older customers. The chain plans to start stocking more merchandise aimed at the 18-to-35 age range, and it needs your help in an ad campaign aimed at them.

In a brainstorming session, your agency comes up with a radio and TV campaign geared toward younger buyers. The campaign's slogan: "High prices suck. Cramrick's doesn't."

You've used the term "sucks" to describe something you don't like since you were a middle-schooler. But you know the term might offend older people; your parents still look at you askance when you say it in front of them. It also would be the first time in your community that the term has been used in a mainstream advertising campaign.

You are a member of the American Advertising Federation, the 40,000-member organization that calls itself the "unifying voice for advertising." Its code of ethics and principles include a section on taste and decency that says ads "shall be free of statements, illustrations or implications which are offensive to good taste or public decency."

➤ **You wonder whether that part of the code relates to the proposed slogan. You've got to recommend to your boss—and to the client—whether to use the slogan. What do you do?**

Questions
- **What's your problem?**
- **Why not follow the rules?**
- What else do you need to know?

Thinking it Through
1. How helpful is the American Advertising Federation's statement of ethics and principles in making your decision?
2. How much responsibility do you feel in maintaining standards of decency and good taste stated by the American Advertising Federation's statement of ethics and principles?
3. How much conversation might you have about whether different age groups might react differently to the slogan? What about different types of shows in which the ad might be broadcast? What about the network's reaction?
4. Children will hear the slogan, too. Does that factor into your decision?

For more information, the American Advertising Federation statement of ethics and principles is linked from this book's website.

■ ■ ■

CASE 2.5 **Entertainment: So What's Gratuitous Violence?**

You are writing the pilot episode of *Canadian Cop Chronicles*, to be broadcast on Canadian television nationwide. The nonfiction show uses dramatic recreations to tell the stories of actual events and people.

You are writing about a 19-year-old man who was suspected of four random homicides. Police shot and killed the man while trying to arrest him five years ago. In researching his story, you learn that he had tortured neighborhood dogs when he was a child. You read* that there may be a connection between animal cruelty and serial killers. Your producers agree that it's an intriguing topic that may be relevant to the story. It also would spark discussion by viewers and by news media, which will create a buzz about the show in free media and likely boost ratings.

The topic of animal cruelty is tough, because it may well be that some viewers would be more upset about the depiction of a puppy's death than by a person's death. But you believe the topic, which is rarely talked about in society, would be powerful.

The question: How far do you go in depicting violence against animals? You believe that it is not enough simply to use dialogue explaining that the killer also abuses animals; you know that not everyone pays attention to the dialogue in a show. You know the power of TV visuals, and the depiction of a man kicking a dog would be much more powerful than talking about it.

Since this is Canadian television, you are aware that its prime-time shows are replete with violence.** You also are aware of the Canadian Association of Broadcasters' code of ethics regarding violence on television.† Among other things, the code states that "programming containing gratuitous violence [should] not be telecast," and that a television show should include violence when it is "relevant to the development of character, or to the advancement of the theme or plot."

➤ **A draft of the episode is due in ten days, and you've got to decide what to do quickly in order to start writing.**

---

* See, for example, Wright, J. and Hensley, C. (2003). From Animal Cruelty to Serial Murder: Applying the Graduation Hypothesis. *International Journal of Offender Therapy and Comparative Criminology, 47*(1), 71–88.

** Paquette, G. (2004). Violence on Canadian television networks. *The Canadian Child and Adolescent Psychiatry Review, 13*(1), 13–15. Retrieved from www.pubmedcentral.nih.gov/articlerender.fcgi?artid=2533816.

† The Canadian Association of Broadcasters' code regarding violence in television programming is at www.cab-acr.ca/english/social/codes/violencecode.shtm.

Questions

- **What's your problem?**
- **Why not follow the rules?**
- What else do you need to know?

Thinking it Through

1. How helpful is the Canadian Association of Broadcasters' code regarding violence in TV programming?

2. If you were in charge of the Canadian Association of Broadcaster's code regarding TV violence, what (if anything) would you do to change the code?

3. The US Supreme Court in 2010 overturned a federal law* that made it a crime to make, own, or distribute some depictions of animal cruelty. Do you think such a law is necessary, or do you agree with the court's 8–1 decision in the *US v. Stevens* that it violated the First Amendment.

4. How do you solve the tension? Do you:

    A. Decide to find another approach to the story, because the animal cruelty angle could be too controversial?

    B. Use the animal cruelty angle, but use dialogue (or interview experts) to let viewers know of the animal cruelty?

    C. Use the animal cruelty angle and include a scene that depicts the killer kicking a puppy—but put the actual kicking off the screen, so the moment of impact isn't shown but viewers hear the howling and dying dog?

    D. Use the animal cruelty angle and actually show the scene in which the killer kicks a puppy? (The dog isn't real, of course, but the scene is shot so viewers think the dog is real.)

    E. Think of something else not listed here?

5. Can you make arguments that including the animal cruelty in the show could be both "gratuitous" as well as integral to the plot?

6. What moral obligation, if any, would you have if you learned a teenager watched your show and then attacked a puppy in the same manner that was depicted (if you choose to show the scene) or alluded to (if you don't actually show the scene) in your show? If your answer is "I cannot be responsible for one person's actions," then at what point do you think you should begin to feel responsible for others' actions based on what you broadcast?

■ ■ ■

---

* The statute is at www.law.cornell.edu/uscode/18/usc_sec_18_00000048----000-.html.

CHAPTER 3

Media Traditions and the Paradox of Professionalism

This chapter:

- briefly introduces media history
- notes the ethical implication of media through their evolution from elite, to mass, to specialized institutions
- speculates about what is happening as "many-to-many" communication models emerge through the Internet
- explores how media respond to rules and conditions unique to the cultures of the societies in which they operate
- reminds us that no society has complete freedom to its media to report, to persuade, and to entertain; rather, media practitioners must make judgment calls within a variety of constraints
- discusses what it means to be a "professional" communicator— and how the cultures of professionalism and accountability are factors shaping media performance
- provides practical applications and five case studies that encourage you to think about rules and cultures.

INTRODUCTION

THE PREVIOUS chapter began to explore the question, "Why not follow the rules?" In keeping with our argument that autonomous decision making is not the same as rule following, we considered a number of codes and guidelines that should be of some help when doing ethics in media. The second part of our inquiry into "following the rules" involves understanding the evolution of media traditions and cultures—the formal and informal "rules" that have shaped the world's rich tapestry of mass communications.

Whether they acknowledge it or not, media practitioners are influenced by an enormous number of historical forces— political, economic, philosophical, technological, and cultural. Mainstream media institutions are more likely to recognize that heritage than are the new media enterprises emerging like wild flowers in the late twentieth and early twenty-first century. Regardless, it is possible to point out some trends that influence media behavior. Those trends include (but are not limited to) struggles for freedom and autonomy, or acquiescence to authority; the necessity of being economically and socially responsible within the broader political and cultural arena; the quest for professional status. There are other trends, as captured by thousands of scholars who have written hundreds of books and course syllabi. However, we are limited in this text to a single chapter that considers how history and culture impact media ethics.

MEDIA EVOLUTION

Before they became big businesses in the nineteenth century, western media started as local institutions produced and consumed by economic and political elites. Media products were expensive and slow to create and expensive to buy—but they had a long shelf life. Elite print media, in particular, had serious content of a political, philosophical, literary, or economic nature. They had limited circulation. Before they could become mass media they had to overcome a number of geographic, technological, and political barriers. The isolation of cities meant media developed strong local allegiances—local ownership, local news, local audiences, local advertising. Only later did regionalism and nationalism become a factor. But even today, despite chain ownership and network television, the US government only licenses local radio/TV stations and holds them responsible for their programming. It does not license the national networks.

Elite media were underwritten by special interest groups, which meant they often had a strong political and economic bias. They also had high per-unit subscription costs, so their loyal audiences knew what they were buying. This began changing in the 1830s in the United States, as improvements in technology and tides of newcomers to America led to the development of the "penny press." Advertising paid the majority of the bills, shifting the economic model from subscribers to advertisers. High-speed printing presses led to mass production of newspapers and magazines. Their growth mirrored the mass production of other factory products, all eagerly consumed by an emerging middle class. The content of these mass-produced products—media included—appealed to the "lowest common denominator." As far as news media were concerned, this meant news that was engaging—often titillating—and generally inoffensive politically. Objectivity emerged, in part, as a marketing tool, when news media discovered that neutrality in reporting was the best way to sell to large, heterogeneous audiences.

By the twentieth century, the same evolutionary processes began with electronic media. Initially expensive to produce and distribute, radio and television quickly leapfrogged the barriers of geography and illiteracy to become mass media. As they did, they joined newspapers and mass circulation magazines in attempting to be all things to all people. The need to produce the least objectionable programming (the theory of "LOP") was a natural result of media maximizing audience appeal.

Johannes Gutenberg's fifteenth century moveable type printing press sped up the process and lowered the cost of information flow, even though book publishing was quite slow and expensive by today's standards. In one sense, the magazine sped up the book, and then the newspaper sped up the magazine. A slightly different pattern held true for electronic media: The cumbersome telegraph gave way to the wireless radio, while cinema and radio were trumped by television, and the best feature of each medium seems to have emerged into some of today's internet technology. (Samuel Morse's 1844 telegraph message between Baltimore and Washington, DC, was "What hath God wrought?" from the Old Testament, Numbers 23:23. Imagine what he might have tweeted on his new iPad.)

When media become institutionalized—that is, produced and distributed on a regular basis—they can count on a specific circulation/distribution pattern and can anticipate a certain level of income. They can plan their investment and technology. Hence, the media are big businesses. PriceWaterhouseCoopers (2010) estimates that global revenue for entertainment and media will top $1.7 trillion by 2014. That's roughly the value of the goods and services produced in Brazil, a nation of nearly 200 million people with the world's tenth-largest economy.

As with other big businesses, media organizations must adapt to change or die. The recent history of media shows that no single medium "owns" the mass audience. In a free enterprise system with new technology, audiences demand specialized media fare, and media institutions have had to adapt. People with leisure time (or "psychic leisure"), discretionary income, and special interests have become the market for new media and new advertisers. Emerging and relatively inexpensive communications technology means all of us can be both publishers and specialized consumers, so "many-to-many" social networks and other internet-based means of communicating are transforming the old "one-to-many" models of the media environment. Older media such as newspapers have specialized internally, with sections and columns and advertising supplements intended to appeal to the broader spectrum. Their struggles to adapt to new competition have met with mixed success, as their audiences—particularly the younger audiences—have shifted to more "consumable-upon-demand" media such as the Internet. The same has happened with commercial television. Instead of three networks "owning" the audience, hundreds of cable and other programming options now pander to audiences' special interests. Mass circulation, general appeal magazines have either shriveled or died.

The transitions—from elite, to popular, to specialized and "many-to-many" media—did not occur in a vacuum. In addition to geographic, technological, and economic considerations, the world's media have grown up reflecting the political and philosophic systems of the nations where they operate. No matter their nation's stage of development or the corner of the globe where they have struggled to survive, all media have faced ethical and moral dilemmas. In a sense, all media had to become socially responsible to the environments of which they are a part.

THEORIES OF THE MASS MEDIA

Mass media are no different from other institutions in taking on the form and coloration of the social, economic, and political structures and philosophies within which they operate. Media and other institutions appear to reflect two basic systems: one stresses control (authoritarian-tending) and the other stresses freedom (libertarian-tending). Authoritarian systems are disposed toward a well-structured, disciplined worldview with definite rules and an ordered society. Libertarian systems are disposed toward an open, experimental, nonrestrictive society with a minimum of rules and controls. Governments are designed on the philosophical base somewhere along the continuum of one of these two basic orientations. The reality, of course, is that neither "theory" exists in a pure form, so the following discussion considers tendencies rather than absolutes.

Leading scholars have offered tentative explanations of the different systems under which media have evolved. Among the most durable is *Four Theories of the Press*, the 1956 treatise by Frederick Siebert, Theodore Peterson, and Wilbur Schramm. The authors argue that, in general, media operate under authoritarianism and libertarianism systems, or their respective offshoots of communism and social responsibility.

Critics continue to quibble over the imprecise designations of media systems. Some point out that all media are inherently socially responsible to their social, economic, and political environment. Media ethicist John Merrill used to argue in his University of Missouri lectures that the title of the Siebert, Peterson, and Schramm book was a misnomer, as it described not four but two basic systems, as these were not really theories, and as they weren't just talking about the press. ("Sort of like the Holy Roman Empire," which, Merrill would quip, was neither holy, nor Roman, nor an empire . . .)

More recently, a group of scholars from the University of Illinois, in *Last Rights: Revisiting Four Theories of the Press* (Nerone, 1995), explored flaws in the original *Four Theories* book, including: the loose rhetorical use of "theory"; a single-minded bias: pro-classical liberalism and anti-communism (not altogether surprising given the book's Cold War publication date and its sponsorship by the National Council of Churches); the focus on the printed press rather than other mass communication forms; little mention of economics as a force that shapes the press; the watered-down and idiosyncratic use of philosophy (especially the notion that a free press was a natural right); and, in general, a bad fit between press theory and press practice.

Despite these criticisms, *Four Theories of the Press* has greatly influenced generations of media students grappling with basic questions: How and why do media operate within the political and regulatory system? Who and what permit media to exist? For what reasons: To inform? To make a profit? To entertain? To persuade? To challenge conventional wisdom? Who and what require and ensure that the media are *responsible*?

The subtle differences in media systems should not be underestimated. Many of the world's media systems differ considerably from one another; sometimes, well established systems undergo significant changes—particularly when a new political regime takes power. Acceptable journalism, entertainment, and persuasion in the American system might be considered highly irresponsible under a different system, in a different time and place, a point that necessitates an appreciation of cultural relativism. Therefore, we will borrow from *Four Theories* and augment the classic book's four theories. We also consider additional "theories" or descriptions of the media proposed by scholars who describe media operating in *revolutionary* cultures, in third-world *developmental* systems, in modern European *democratic socialist* conditions, and in the *cultural relativism* of Asian and other societies.

Authoritarianism

Authoritarianism is the oldest and most widespread type of media control. It appears in many guises, most of which hold that what the people don't know won't hurt them. Controllers of mass media content ("keepers of the established truth") release enough information to the masses so society can function, but they keep the masses from coping with material that they decide is not good, clean, and authoritative. The theory holds that over time, the masses will never become aware of what they don't know, and will be easily manipulated by propagandists or any number of authority figures.

A great many writers and thinkers have advocated one form or another of authoritarianism. In ancient Greece, Plato advocated rule by philosopher-kings, assuming that even an enlightened society should be kept in check by the wisest and strongest leaders rather than through a completely open and shared government. In the late years of the Middle Ages, the Italian political adviser Niccolo Machiavelli suggested in *The Prince* that leaders should exercise any and all options available to maintain their authority. (From Machiavelli we get the expression, "The ends justify the means.") Numerous advocates of totalitarianism, statism, religious fundamentalism, and other top-down theories of control have contributed to the literature and realities of authoritarianism.

More people in more societies have lived under authoritarian regimes than under any other form of government in history. It seems that humankind has produced far more oppressive and abusive leaders than ideal "philosopher kings." Beginning with ancient cave dwellers, through the growth of mass cultures in Mesopotamia and the Holy Roman Empire and on to today's multifaceted cultures from Asia, Africa, Latin America, and most of the civilized world, the general history of civilization demonstrates a pattern of oppression, of subjugation of the people to the control of leaders. Post-colonialism notwithstanding, governments have a natural tendency to control their societies' means of communication.

The truism that "knowledge is power" requires authorities to retain power by hoarding knowledge, or at least define it by their own terms for their subjects. Under authoritarian regimes, the media (which are often not owned or operated by government) are controlled through a variety of forms of "prior restraint," including government patents, guilds, licensing, taxation, sedition laws, and direct censorship.

After the printing press came into use during the fifteenth and sixteenth centuries, English monarchs (especially Henry VIII and Elizabeth I) devised new strategies to exert their authority. They exercised strict control over printed material through licensing, taxation, and laws of seditious libel. Licensing, a form of direct censorship, began during the reign of Henry VIII. Religious or secular authorities approved every word published. Printers who cooperated with authorities received numerous side benefits, such as lucrative printing contracts. Printers who violated the laws were punished, sometimes severely.

Parliament in 1712 passed the first Stamp Act, another effective means of controlling the press by imposing taxes on newspapers and pamphlets, on advertising, and on paper itself. This tax on knowledge forced printers to register with the government and therefore bolstered the treasury. These laws eventually migrated to the colonies that are now the United States. The refusal by the colonists to pay the 1765 Stamp Tax fomented the American Revolution.

Laws regarding sedition—criticism of the state—originated during the thirteenth century in England. Spreading rumors about the crown and nobility, whether truthful or not, became a serious offense. Until the eighteenth century, all a jury had to do was to determine whether the accused had indeed published the rumor or criticism. Because truthful criticism was more likely to stir up angry crowds than readily disproved untruthful criticism, the general principle for many years was that "the greater the truth, the greater the libel."

Our discussion of authoritarianism cannot be limited to the past. Even today, most of the people of the world live under authoritarian-tending rather than libertarian-tending governmental systems. Despite the fact that since the late 1940s the United Nations' Universal Declaration of Human Rights has demanded that its members guarantee freedom of speech, only one-sixth to one-fourth (depending on who is counting) of the world's people actually receive this and other parallel freedoms, including freedom of assembly, freedom of religion, and freedom to petition their governments. Annual analyses of worldwide trends in freedom and control demonstrate the fragility of such assurances. Indeed, after the attacks on New York and Washington, DC, on September 11, 2001, groups that monitor freedoms worldwide criticized the United States for authoritarian practices with its Patriot Act, its watering down of freedom of information laws and rules on *habeas corpus*, its treatment of prisoners of war, its increasingly intrusive security provisions, etc. The message may be universal: a society, institution, or leader under threat tends to exert more controls and restrictions than one not under threat.

Before continuing, we do well to take a recommendation from the authors of *Last Rights: Revisiting Four Theories of the Press*. Nerone and his colleagues maintained that authoritarianism is a fuzzy concept—not a complete theory—that is better understood in terms of practice than theory. They noted that all institutions—traditional or contemporary, public or private, large or small, tightly controlled or relatively free—engage in authoritarian practices whenever there is a concentration of authority or power "exercised to limit or suppress or define people's thought and expression" (Nerone, 1995, p. 38). Therefore, we will note the authoritarian or control tendencies in the following descriptions of the world's media systems.

Communism

The communist "theory" of the press is a logical extension of authoritarianism, with one important exception. Authoritarian theory recognizes the press as an entity *outside* the government; the communist press is part of the state. Communist-owned media reflect the national policy or party line, and media attempt to further the state's aim. Communism is based on the ideas of Karl Marx, among others, who believed improving

Box 3.1 | MASS MEDIA FACE ATTACKS ON FREEDOM WORLDWIDE

Freedom House (2010) says media freedom is declining in the world, and only one in six people live in nations that provide free speech to their citizens and media. The organization, a non-profit think tank based in Washington, DC, was founded in 1941 as a response to Nazi interests in the United States. Its annual report defines freedom largely based on the United Nations' Declaration of Human Rights, which states that:

Everyone has the right to freedom of opinion and expression; this right includes freedom to hold opinions without interference and to seek, receive, and impart information and ideas through any media regardless of frontiers.

The Freedom House's annual report is built on how nations stack up on 23 questions related to each nation's legal environment for press freedoms, political environment (including intimidation of journalists), and the economic environment of media.

The organization's 2009 report on 195 nations says that, after two decades of improvements, free press is on the decline worldwide. The report notes that:

- 17 percent of the world's residents live in the world's 70 free countries
- 41 percent live in 61 "partially free" countries
- 42 percent live in 64 "not free" countries.

Topping the 2009 list as the most free were 11 European nations—Iceland, Finland, Norway, Denmark, Sweden, Belgium, Luxembourg, Andorra, the Netherlands, Switzerland, and Liechtenstein—and New Zealand.

The United States tied for twenty-fourth, down from recent years because of concerns about journalists being jailed for refusing to reveal anonymous sources. Canada tied for twenty-seventh. North Korea, as usual, ranked last, below nations that include Cuba, Libya, Burma, and several former Soviet Republics.

Go to www.freedomhouse.org to see its reports on media freedom.

---

society would best serve the needs of each individual. Given this view, collectivism serves governments' ends far more effectively than individualism.

Because the communist press operates as the voice of the government, it suppresses ideas or views that oppose the state. Media serve to inform and indoctrinate society to achieve governmental social control. Under these conditions, intimidation, meddling, surveillance, and economic or political actions by government agencies work to control the media. There is not repression of the press under this system, *per se*, because the press *is* the state.

Obviously, the dissolution of the Soviet Bloc in the early 1990s challenged the traditional Soviet-totalitarian concepts of media control and purpose as originally outlined in *Four Theories of the Press* (which had been published during the heart of the Cold War). Under Mikhail Gorbachev's liberalization policies of *glasnost* ("openness") and *perestroika* ("wholesale restructuring of society"), in the late 1980s and early 1990s, established mass media could challenge the status quo. Under President Boris Yeltsin, state control of radio and television was relinquished to a great degree, yet entrepreneurs found it difficult to raise the money needed to establish broadcast stations. As of this writing, however, a variety of moves by Russia's current government seem to indicate that while communism may have waned, authoritarianism continues unabated.

In the People's Republic of China and Cuba, liberalization has been less successful than in Russia. The crackdown in Tiananmen Square in 1989 showed the world that elderly traditionalists within the communist government would not tolerate Chinese students' mass demonstrations and pleas for democracy. The subsequent manipulation of domestic and international news media (the official press joined the military in urging citizens to turn in people who had participated in the demonstrations and protests) was a clear and painful reminder that totalitarian media still operate under the premise of perpetuating and expanding the socialist system. The first of many signs of change came in 1992, when Chinese Communist Party policies changed dramatically. In depoliticizing socialism, the government promised writers, editors, and producers more freedom than they had enjoyed since the mid-1980s. In that climate, a number of new media were born. Many of them experimented with ways to reach divergent audiences, funded by the capitalist notions of advertising and circulation rather than government subsidies.

Promises of greater openness and tolerance for human rights swayed the International Olympic Committee in awarding Beijing the 2008 summer Olympics. However, the global spotlight on China, largely because of its Olympics but also because of its emergence as a world economic power, has shown the country still struggling with openness vs. control. Its historical collectivist orientation saw it exercising control over bloggers and other dissidents critical of the nation's problems with pollution, human rights, the handling of devastating natural disasters, and economic disparity—"dirty laundry" the government didn't want aired while China mobilized its massive propaganda efforts for the Olympics. The nation's "Golden Shield Project"—known better as the "Great Firewall of China"—is its efforts to block websites and online content that runs counter to its party's wishes. As of this writing, China's government has blocked mainstream sites such as CNN and NBC, and "many-to-many" sites such as as Youtube and Wikipedia. Google left China in 2010 instead of censoring searches at the behest of Chinese government, but returned after extended negotiations.

Libertarianism

The premises of authoritarianism have been seriously challenged during the past three centuries, particularly in the Western world. The Protestant Reformation, the Age of Enlightenment, the ascendancy of science as a means of "fixing our beliefs," global exploration, and the rise of the middle class are among the forces that have been giving rise to libertarianism. Starting in Western Europe in the sixteenth century, an emerging philosophy questioned the authoritarian notion of state control over its citizens. Instead, primacy was placed on individual rights, and the notion that people are fully capable of self-governance when they are well informed and free to choose from among multiple points of view. In other words, while authoritarians and collectivists insist that improvements in society at large would result in the greatest benefits for individual men and women, libertarians argue that the fulfillment of the individual is the ultimate goal, and that rational and well-informed individuals will create a good state or society.

Numerous philosophers and political theorists articulated the libertarian argument. Key among those whose ideas contributed to understanding how media function in a free society were Great Britain's John Milton, John Locke, and John Stuart Mill, and the United States' Thomas Jefferson.

In 1644, poet John Milton argued the basic tenets of libertarianism in a speech before the British Parliament. The speech, *Appeal for the Liberty of Unlicensed Printing* (later published as *Areopagitica*), called for an "open marketplace of ideas" and the "self-righting process" that would occur once the authoritarian licensing of books, pamphlets, and papers were repealed. Milton wrote:

> Let truth and falsehood grapple; whoever knew truth to be worse in a free and open encounter . . . Though all the winds of doctrine were let loose to play upon the earth, so truth be in the field, we do injuriously by licensing and prohibiting, to misdoubt her strength.

Milton called licensing the "evil child of evil parents," given that licensing was invented by the Roman Catholic Church and used to prohibit anything the Church found unpalatable. Furthermore, licensing is impractical and unworkable because it:

1. Assumes infallible and incorruptible censors; if such people could be found, licensing would be a waste of their time and wisdom.
2. Is not broad enough to control people's minds, since it only censors current news/topics. It would have to censor everything else.
3. Hinders people's search for truth, which will win in any open encounter with falsehood.

Milton's idea of press freedom was narrow and negative—"freedom from" governmental control rather than "freedom for" achieving any specific ends. While he was most critical of pre-publication censorship, he nevertheless thought government should censor blasphemy, atheism, and libel. He advocated burning books that were "mischievous." His view was also somewhat elitist and self-serving: He would have denied free expression to people who disagreed with him on fundamentals, such as Royalists and Catholics, and people of lesser intellect (read: "journalists"). Several years later, in fact, he was Oliver Cromwell's official censor (Sackville, 2009).

Despite the obvious authoritarian undercurrent, Milton's eloquent appeals for an open marketplace of ideas have echoed across the generations and centuries.

Writing in the seventeenth century, English philosopher John Locke proposed a radical new view of government, society, and the individual. Locke articulated the theory that justified revolution against tyranny and gave the British Parliament supremacy over the Crown. As described in *Four Theories:*

> The law of nature and the social compact are essential doctrines of Locke's philosophy. He argued that man under the guise of reason has surrendered his personal rights to the state in return for a guarantee that the state will recognize and maintain his natural rights. He denied the political validity of church government and argued cogently for religious toleration, excluding, of course, elements subversive to the state.
>
> (Siebert, Peterson, & Schramm, 1956, p. 43)

Locke's perspectives on popular sovereignty, legal rights, religious diversity, and free enterprise inspired the American *Declaration of Independence* and the French Revolution. He helped shape Thomas Jefferson and James Madison's notions of democracy and press freedom.

Jefferson's views on a free press were soundly libertarian. Although individual citizens may err in exercising their reason, he felt that the majority would inevitably make sound decisions as long as society consists of educated, informed citizens. The qualification is significant, because it recognizes that even the philosophy of libertarianism is meaningless if the people being promised liberties have no way to use them. The way to help people avoid making errors of judgment, wrote Jefferson to Edward Carrington in 1787:

> . . . is to give them full information of their affairs through the channel of the public papers, and to contrive that those papers should penetrate the whole mass of the people. The basis of our government being the opinion of the people, the very first object should be to keep that right; and were it left to me to decide whether we should have a government without newspapers, or newspapers without government, I should not hesitate a moment to prefer the latter.
>
> (January 16, 1787)

Many who are fond of this quotation forget its conclusion: "But I should mean that every man should receive those papers, and be capable of reading them."

Jefferson's view of the press became more cynical 20 years later, at the close of his presidency. After years of abuse from Federalist editors, Jefferson seemed to say that the reality of free speech fell far short of the libertarian ideal. He wrote to John Norvell in 1807:

> It is a melancholy truth, that a suppression of the press could not more completely deprive the nation of its benefits, than is done by its abandoned prostitution to

falsehood. Nothing can now be believed which is seen in a newspaper. Truth itself becomes suspicious by being put into that polluted vehicle ... I really look with commiseration over the great body of my fellow citizens, who, reading newspapers, live and die in the belief that they have known something of what has been passing in the world in their time.

(June 11, 1807)

Another major contributor to libertarian theory was English philosopher John Stuart Mill, who viewed liberty as the right of mature individuals to think and act as they pleased so long as they did not harm others in the process. The "father of modern libertarianism" argued for the right of every person to be heard:

If all mankind minus one were of one opinion, and only one person were of the contrary opinion, mankind would be no more justified in silencing that one person than he, if he had the power, would be justified in silencing mankind.

(Mill, 1947, p. 16)

Mill's argument for freedom of expression was based not on theories of natural rights but on utilitarianism, a concept to be discussed in Chapter 10. He said all human action should aim at creating the greatest aggregate good or "happiness" for the greatest number of persons and the least aggregate harm or "pain." This good/happy state is most likely to occur when individuals are free to think and act as they please. Individuals need freedom to optimize their potential, and society benefits as each individual reaches his or her potential.

He emphasized that government was not the only threat to individual liberty, because the majority might stifle minority thought. For its own protection, society may try to advise, instruct, and persuade individuals; it may, indeed, ostracize them. But it may not restrain them out of some paternalistic notion of society's own good.

Four major arguments underlie Mill's case for free expression:

1. If we silence an opinion, we may be silencing the truth.
2. A wrong opinion may contain a grain of truth necessary to find the whole truth.
3. Even if a commonly accepted opinion is the whole truth, people will hold it not on rational grounds but as a prejudice unless they are forced to defend it.
4. Unless commonly held opinions are contested from time to time, they lose their vitality, their effect on conduct and character.

All of the philosophers cited above—and many others, such as Thomas Paine, John Erskine, Samuel Adams, Alexis de Tocqueville, and James Madison—argued in favor of freeing individuals from outside restrictions that would impede their search for answers to political, religious, social, or other questions. On its face, their libertarianism called for "freedom from" governmental or other barriers. The appeal to negative freedom made good sense as a challenge to the authoritarian mindset. However, "freedom from" provided little guidance to journalists and other writers who were testing their wings. How far could they go in criticizing government officials or private citizens? Could they tell lies and harm reputations, without repercussion? Mill suggested that they couldn't, but others were not so sure.

On its face, the First Amendment to the US Constitution seems unequivocally libertarian:

> Congress shall make no law respecting an establishment of religion, or prohibiting the free exercise thereof; or abridging the freedom of speech, or of the press; or the right of the people to peaceably assemble, and to petition the Government for a redress of grievances.

History tells us that these words have been subject to continued and contentious interpretations. The bottom line—after more than two centuries of constitutional law, legislative fiat, administrative policy, and everyday use—is that free speech and a free press have limits.

The controls placed on free media in the United States differ from the draconian "prior restraints" from days of yore. American law eschewed licensing and most other forms of before-the-fact censorship—at least for print media and now the Internet. However, broadcasters still need a federal license to use public airwaves. Cinema has not always enjoyed full First Amendment protections. Neither has advertising. Public relations practitioners are limited by various statutes and administrative fiats regarding contracts and disclosure of information. Legal reasoning behind such restraints includes the argument that the public airwaves should be regulated in the public interest; that cinema was commercial entertainment not deserving of full First Amendment protection; that advertising and public relations were commercial ventures subject to the same controls affecting other interstate commerce. Courts have decided that governments can restrict the time, manner, and place of speech for the purposes of the greater good, whether it be universities restricting protesters in public areas or city councils limiting the placement of newspaper sales racks on sidewalks. Some of these arguments are more persuasive than others, but the fact remains that the United States places prior restraints on mass communication.

In addition, nations have created massive libraries of legal decisions and statutes describing the consequences of committing libel, invading privacy, violating copyright, publishing obscenity, revealing state secrets, and engaging in other not-quite-free-speech acts. These are not instances of prior restraint, but they invoke punishment after the fact. In other words, you may have the freedom to say what you'd like, but you will be held accountable if you cause harm. One result could be the chilling of free speech, given concerns that mass communication managers cannot predict whether exercising their free speech rights could lead to harm.

The laws and administrative policies affecting broadcasting, cinema, advertising, and public relations grew from economic, technical, and political realities. Those realities tempered the basic eighteenth and nineteenth century notion articulated by British jurist

Sir William Blackstone. His view was that while liberty of the press meant there would be no prior restraints, "improper, mischievous, or illegal" publications should be held accountable. "The dissenting, or making public, of bad sentiments, destructive of the ends of society, is the crime which society corrects," Blackstone wrote (1899, p. 1327). It is not surprising, then, that the struggle between freedom and responsibility has been at the heart of the communications media's history over the past century or so.

Siebert's conclusion about libertarianism, drafted a half century ago, still has some validity. He admitted that the theory is "vague, inconclusive, and sometimes inconsistent," but added that:

> Its greatest assets . . . are its flexibility, its adaptability to change, and above all its confidence in its ability to advance the interests and welfare of human beings by continuing to place its trust in individual self-direction.
>
> (Siebert, Peterson, & Schramm, 1956, p. 71)

Social Responsibility

The notion of social responsibility lays the foundation of most of this text's treatment of the media ethics environment.

Social responsibility, at least as it has been applied to contemporary Western media, is a natural extension of libertarianism. It emerged once it was recognized that the negative freedoms of libertarianism were overly idealistic and impractical. Calls for socially responsible and ethical media—"freedom for" and not just "freedom from"—were heard ever since the first printer in the American colonies got crosswise with authorities or offended public sensibilities. However, an articulated "theory" is recent. It emerged following challenges to theories of *laissez-faire* economics and natural rights. It also questioned whether people were as rational as libertarians maintained. Theodore Peterson said:

> Under the social responsibility theory, man is viewed not so much irrational as lethargic. He is capable of using his reason, but he is loath to do so. Consequently, he is easy prey for demagogues, advertising pitchmen, and others who would manipulate him for their selfish ends . . . Without . . . goading, man is not likely to be moved to seek truth.
>
> (Siebert, Peterson, & Schramm, 1956, p. 100)

Mass media ethics basically began in the twentieth century. During the early years of the American republic, political interests dominated the press by subsidizing many newspapers. Political control of the press diminished with the success of the penny press starting in the 1830s and the growth of advertising. Throughout the rest of the century, the press reflected the spirit of the times—freewheeling days of national expansion, the winning of the West, and social Darwinistic ideas of the survival of the fittest.

This climate lasted until the turn of the twentieth century, when investigative journalists—muckrakers—and individual journalists discovered their considerable influence and touched a public nerve with their crusade against business corruption and government collusion. For a decade, they attacked social injustice through books, magazines, and newspapers. Not surprisingly, when journalists did their muckraking of other powerful institutions in society, other critics found plenty to complain about the press.

A great deal of media self-criticism arose in the 1920s, as thoughtful journalists recognized public dissatisfaction with media excesses and called for commitments to journalism's professional status (Christians, 1977). The introduction of schools of journalism, most offering courses in journalism ethics, attempted to place journalism in an academic framework. The ethics literature of the period demonstrated a strong moral responsibility to one's professional community, with ethics being construed as right action toward one's fellows.

Codes of ethics and courses in media ethics emerging from this period displayed a concern for common values of a shared culture, even though codes probably had minimal effect on the daily performance of journalists. However, media and the public took notice when influential external groups seriously questioned the craft's basic operating premises. This was particularly true in 1947, when the Commission on the Freedom of the Press, a sort of blue-ribbon public conscience, issued its broad- ranging report. The commission had been created during World War II in 1942 with University of Chicago Chancellor Robert M. Hutchins as chairman. It was funded by *Time* magazine's Henry Luce and the *Encyclopedia Britannica*. Among its aims was to assess media organizations controlled by an oligopoly of companies that were accused of being concerned only with profits and wielding power.

The Hutchins Commission viewed freedom of the press as a moral rather than a natural right that could be lost if abused. The basis of social responsibility theory comes from the committee's two fundamental propositions:

1. *Whoever enjoys freedom has obligations to society.* Because the media enjoy a libertarian heritage, they have the concomitant responsibility to use those freedoms to serve the welfare of society as a whole.
2. *Society's welfare becomes the most overriding concern.* This statement demonstrates a shift in the theoretical foundation of press freedom from the individual to society. Individual rights to speak out are balanced by group rights to be free from invasion of privacy or libel; personal rights to free expression are described in terms of public access to the media, or the "public's right to know."

Based largely on testimony from journalists and from the literature of journalism organizations, the Hutchins Commission settled on five basic requirements, or expectations, society believes the press should fulfill. Those requirements have been the subject of a great deal of debate since the time they were outlined. Hutchins said our society needs a:

1. truthful, comprehensive and intelligent account of the day's events in a context that gives them meaning
2. forum for the exchange of comment and criticism
3. means of projecting the opinions and attitudes of the groups in the society to one another
4. method of presenting and clarifying the goals and values of the society
5. way of reaching every member of the society by the currents of information, thought, and feeling, which the press supplies.

These five charges constitute an ethics mandate for the media. They spell out a list of moral obligations, a set of policy guidelines or goals that ask media to use their resources in a positive, socially beneficent manner. Beneath and/or beyond these five "require-ments" are calls for media to reexamine their fundamental operating principles. They asked for a moral foundation to be built under an enterprise that the Hutchins Commission implied was in danger of losing its constitutionally protected place in America because its foundations and joists were becoming eaten away by the bugs of power, commercialization, and "technicism"—the over reliance on technology as a benefactor of society.

Hutchins asked mass communicators to rethink such notions as objectivity, profession-alism, and their implied contract with audiences and citizens. It is no longer enough to report the fact truthfully; it is now necessary to report the truth about the fact, the commissioners argued in their plea for an ethic of commitment.

Hutchins also asked journalists and other media practitioners to focus on responsibil-ities ("freedom for") rather than rights ("freedom from"), on stewardship rather than privilege, and on community connectedness rather than individualism or detachment.

The social responsibility theory suggests that journalism should be in the constitutionally or legally protected business of gathering and distributing truthful, accurate inform-ation as a stimulus for civic conversation; it should hold the powerful (including

> With its vast and direct influence on public opinion, journalism cannot be guided only by economic forces, profit, and special interest. It must instead be felt as a mission in a certain sense sacred, carried out in the knowledge that the powerful means of communication have been entrusted to you for the good of all.
>
> —Pope John Paul II, in his declaration of the Vatican's Holy Year Day for Journalists in 2000 (quoted in Kovach & Rosenstiel, 2007, p. 15)

journalism itself) accountable; it should give voice to the voiceless; it should attempt to minimize harm. It should foster "social response-ability"; to do so it should become ecumenical by promoting good relations among different factions of society, recognizing the public's right to know and its right to be heard. To do all of these things, to do ethical and excellent journalism, practitioners must have examined, professional lives.

The Hutchins Commission's agenda for media reform was not widely accepted at the time, because of its academic tone and because it challenged long-held beliefs of media practitioners. *Editor & Publisher*, the trade publication for the newspaper industry, derided the report as the high-falutin' work of ". . . 11 professors, a banker-merchant and a poet-librarian" (Bates, 1995).

A fair-minded assessment of media reform in the ensuing decades, however, would indicate that most of the recommendations have been addressed. Among the trends to be noted:

- an increase in media criticism in academic, professional, and public circles
- greater efforts at transparency, so the public knows the sources of information, the potential biases of journalists and sources, and the efforts undertaken to obtain information
- higher accountability, including improved ways for the public to contact media organizations and organizations that hire ombudsmen—people paid by the organization to make public and independent critiques
- new and diverse media outlets that challenge both the status quo and traditional economic models; the boom in these media outlets have been driven especially by the Internet and the rising number of broadcast channels
- experiments with journalism, including:
  - New Journalism techniques of the late 1960s and 1970s, in which journalists were committed to accuracy while using literary techniques such as "point of view" and full dialogue
  - Public Journalism, which began in the 1980s as a way for journalists to include the public and community members as participants and not just as spectators or readers (this also is known as civic or communitarian journalism)
  - Citizen Journalism, in which people are empowered as journalists and produce their own journalistic content.

Related to the call for journalism to be socially responsible is the call for media's persuaders and entertainers to act responsibly. In most nations with a libertarian or social responsibility bent, political and journalistic speech receives more freedom than artistic and persuasive speech. This suggests that governments are more likely to use laws requiring that commercial persuaders use "social responsibility" than other communicators, such as those delivering messages about news, politics, and art.

In advertising, for example, law punishes advertisers that mislead or flat-out lie to potential customers. Beyond that, many governments restrict ads for some products that are legal to buy—such as bans on cigarette advertising across Europe and the Americas—

but have deleterious health effects. Other nations ban ads aimed at children: Sweden bans ads aimed at children under 12, Greece bans toy ads between 7 a.m. and 10 p.m., and Belgium and Denmark forbid ads within five minutes of children's shows (Clarke, 2001). While broadcasters say the bans make it difficult to produce quality programming, and some researchers say the bans do not change behavior in children, the government has decided that the bans are socially responsible.

Entertainers also occasionally show some desire to be socially responsible, especially through trade groups. While the First Amendment does not require movies to be rated, the Motion Picture Association of America set up a voluntary ratings system in 1968. The system is designed for moviemakers to show their social responsibility by helping parents determine what movies might not be appropriate for children.

A cynic might argue that American mass communicators fall far short of being socially responsible, and it is easy to cite case after case of irresponsible behavior by individuals and corporate practitioners. The observer with a "glass half full" would counter that the public awareness of good or bad media behavior is in and of itself an indication that social responsibility is working well, because only in a vibrant, open society could such scrutiny and criticism flourish.

Meanwhile, a plausible argument can be made that all media systems, in all countries, tend to be socially responsible if only because in order to survive they have to conform to their national or regional political, philosophical, and economic pressures. In a sense, they reflect cultural relativism (Yin, 2008), a belief that each culture is entitled to its own standards and should be assessed on its own terms. To do otherwise would risk alienating their audiences, their advertisers, and their governments.

Revolutionary Media

In countries coping with revolutions against the existing government or foreign domination, the media appear to be in a transitional stage, divorced from normal state–media relationships (Hatchen, 1981). The stage of unrest is initially fomented by the media. Recently liberated media practitioners consider it their role to question authority, and as a result, their reporting often lacks fairness and balance. Their papers and other media tend to be strident and intemperate. Unfortunately for the cause of freedom, overt racism or other examples of closed-mindedness can be present.

Revolutionary publishing or broadcasting involves risks for media managers who alienate themselves from the government. If the revolutionaries succeed in replacing the old regime, they are likely to become the established media managers of the new order. The mood and philosophy of the victorious revolutionaries, along with other factors, can shape the new government and its media system. For instance, the Soviet communist media system emerged from Lenin's writings, whereas the American libertarian media system emerged from the revolutionary words of journalists such as Samuel Adams. The revolutionary press theory is not necessarily authoritarian or libertarian in nature, but it can create the stimulus for either. It therefore tends to be transitory in nature.

Developmental Media

A natural offshoot of the revolutionary press theory, at least in twentieth and twenty-first century third-world, anti-colonial, and post-colonial societies, can be called the *developmental theory* of the press. It reflects modern nationalist and political independence movements and draws upon socialist thought and developmental principles. Media promote social and economic development and nationalism. Developmental theory shares characteristics with revolutionary theory but differs in important ways. Both can be transitional, but a developmental press usually lasts longer than a revolutionary one, as settled nations move slowly toward modernization. Also, it is nearly impossible to predict whether developing nations will move toward the libertarian or toward the authoritarian ends of the government/press continuum; too many variables can affect and determine the emerging form of government (Picard, 1982–1983). Take, for example, the status of the 15 nations that split from the Soviet Union in 1991. The 2009 Freedom House listing of press freedoms worldwide listed Estonia, Latvia, and Lithuania as having free media systems. Georgia and Ukraine were listed as partially free, and the rest were not free. In nearly two decades of independence, the nations have splintered in their tradition of free speech.

A dominant trend among developing nations is the resentment many feel toward the Western world. Their cries against cultural imperialism or communications colonialism have resulted in calls for a New World Communications Order, or a New World Information Order. Such concerns are natural, given that most people in developing nations are poor, malnourished, and illiterate persons of color and resent the affluent, well-fed, literate, and primarily caucasian "West" (Hatchen, 1981). Given vast disparities among developing nations and Western nations, it is unlikely the developing nations will gravitate spontaneously toward a media system created by and suited to the Western world.

The ethics and professionalism of journalists in developing nations have been questioned, because many media practitioners seem morally ambivalent. On the one hand, journalists try to be accurate truth tellers and reporters, so newly enfranchised citizens can make informed decisions. On the other hand, there is a great deal of pressure to be cheerleaders and to cooperate with the government in building a viable nation-state. This creates angst on the part of conscientious journalists who want to take a longer view of the role of journalism in fostering nation building. Are they more responsible by being hard-nosed investigative journalists who advance democracy and human rights, or by being public relations flacks and propagandists for a struggling young government, which may have a different set of ideas about how to advance the quality of life?

Musa and Domatob (2007) describe the tough balancing act. They say developmental journalism's central philosophy is that:

> . . . journalists and national leaders are citizens who share the common goal of building a progressive and peaceful society. The role of the journalist is to advocate and support policies that are in the interest of the society.
>
> (p. 318)

The role conflict may lead to relativistic journalism, as media find themselves trying to be truth tellers, civic advocates, investigative watchdogs, economic boosters, and liberators.

The challenges are legion, particularly given the communal values said to characterize many cultures in developing nations: "family above self, community above individual, constructive engagement as opposed to confrontation" (Wong, 2004, p. 27). These values differ somewhat from Western priorities, and certainly would lead to a different kind of journalism: non-adversarial, non-dogmatic, flexible news coverage. And, in transitional countries experimenting with Western-style *laissez-faire* economics, where media success depends on drawing large audiences and garnering advertising support, the tendency is for media to be sensational and for media personnel's ethics to be relativistic (Yin, 2008).

Democratic Socialist Theory

In some Western societies, especially Scandinavia and elsewhere in Europe, a modified form of social responsibility theory has emerged. *Democratic socialism* combines Marxist thought and the writings of classical libertarian philosophers. It recognizes the uniqueness of a fully developed media system that has been given free reign in a *laissez-faire* marketplace but frowns upon increased monopolies and concentration of media ownership. Abuse by private owners, motivated by the economic bottom line, differs little from abuse by despots, according to adherents of democratic socialism.

Advocates of democratic socialism ask that the media exercise positive freedoms to achieve certain goals, and they advocate regulatory measures to assure accountability. For instance, the media are expected to open their editorial columns to a wide diversity of opinions and "to fuel the political and social debates necessary for the continued development of democratic governance" (Picard, 1982–1983, p. 27). If the press refuses to open itself to these diverse views, someone or something will intervene. That "someone or something" could be a citizens group, a press council, or a governmental agency. Outgrowths of this system include collective management, legal constraints, and governmentally enforced ownership by political, social, and racial minorities.

Libertarians do not take such suggestions lightly. They see little difference between the democratic socialism brand of media responsibility and the old-fashioned theory of authoritarianism. They argue that once the public and government are given control over the press, the Marxist philosophy of state ownership is inevitable.

PROFESSIONAL CULTURES

In addition to the many external controls over media, mass communicators also have significant internal or institutional controls, which motivate us to continue asking, "Why not follow the rules?" Among the strongest of these is the trend toward professionalism.

Professionals are supposed to be socially responsible, but there is a cost. To better understand whether media are, can be, or should be professions, consider the origins, nature, and ramifications of professionalism—including the power, privilege, and prestige that professionalism seems to provide (Black & Barney, 1990). This task can be undertaken from perspectives that include occupational sociology, social psychology, economics, political theory, and philosophy.

Occupational Sociologists' Definitions

Occupational sociologists are the scholars most frequently cited for insights into professionalism. They tend to agree that to qualify as a profession, an occupation is represented by the following characteristics:

- It must be based on a body of systematic theory, with esoteric but useful knowledge skills gained from education or training of exceptional duration or difficulty and culminating with certification based upon passing a "professional" examination or test.
- The professional is an independent practitioner with individual clients, not customers. Professionals have a fiduciary relationship with those clients, who compensate the professional by paying a fee or fixed charge.
- Services provided by professionals are indispensable for the public good, and such services are (ideally) offered impartially without regard to any special relationships.
- The professional is the authority in this complex relationship.
- Community sanctions of the powers and privileges of the professional must be present.
- A profession has a regulative code of ethics that serve as the conscience of its members, insuring the public against abuse of the profession's monopoly.
- Professionals subscribe to a set of enduring norms and expectations that generally are reinforced by membership in a professional culture. Professionals create a network of formal and informal groups—occupational associations of distinctive character—through which its members operate. (For these characteristics see Allison, 1986; Barber, 1963; Flexner, 1915; Greenwood, 1957; Kultgen, 1988; Singletary, 1982; Wilensky, 1964).

Autonomy is the most important criterion for professionalism. Professionals are committed to their occupation as a calling; work is a central life interest and a valuable source of self-identification (Moore, 1970; Orzack, 1959). And they exhibit an altruistic or service orientation, a desire and readiness to identify and treat the needs of their clients.

Media Professionals?

Given these criteria, it is intriguing to ask whether media practitioners are professionals. Our tentative answer is: "No, not strictly speaking."

We note that media practitioners:

- lack a body of systematic theory; while there are some generally agreed upon operating principles, there is not a holistic theory
- generally do not have real autonomy and power; most practitioners are not autonomous but work for commercial, profit-oriented media that appear to operate as though service to advertisers, stockholders, and (in the case of advertising and public relations) clients takes precedence over service to readers, viewers, and listeners (Kwitny, 1990)
- have relatively ineffective community sanctions over fellow media workers' powers and privileges
- lack enforceable codes of ethics
- use an often random nature of training and education for a wide diversity of careers in their media work; that randomness eventually minimizes a professional culture of "calling," and it may be why few practitioners join occupational associations.

Philosophers' Definitions of Professionalism

To advance the discussion beyond the criteria defined by occupational sociologists, insights from philosophers are instructive.

Karen Lebacqz, in her highly readable and provocative *Professional Ethics: Power and Paradox* (1985), asks us to move beyond the mechanistic list of qualities that occupational sociologists require of professionals: "What we expect of professionals is not simply a task to be done, but a way of doing it" (p. 72). Lebacqz stresses not just doing a competent job, but fulfilling a role with commitment and integrity.

To understand professional ethics, Lebacqz says we should consider notions of action (the profession's unique goals, its role in society, its jobs, its moral demands), character (integrity), and institutional structure. When defining and arguing about professionalism, philosophers ask: Does the institution use its power for personal gain, or to improve society? Can its practitioners be morally autonomous, or are they trapped in a web of powerlessness? Is competency/expertise applied to decision making? Lebacqz goes further, emphasizing the need of a professional institution to concentrate on justice and to curb its own power in order to liberate and to empower clients and the public.

Mike Martin argues that discussions of professionalism, particularly in the business world, require professionals to think differently. As he wrote:

> We usually think of professional ethics as shared duties and episodic dilemmas: the responsibilities incumbent on all members of specific professions, together with the dilemmas that arise when these responsibilities conflict. More recently, attention has been paid to the virtues, although usually limiting their role to promoting shared duties. I seek to widen professional ethics to include personal commitments, especially commitments to ideals not mandatory for all members of a profession.
>
> (2000, p. 8)

Power, Privilege, Prestige

Professionals are sometimes seen as engaging in a complex struggle for power, privilege, and prestige (Allison, 1986; Child & Falk, 1982). Media practitioners are not exempt from this generalization. Economists and political theorists join occupational sociologists and philosophers in offering useful insights into the nature of professionalism and the cultural controls professions impose on practitioners.

"Power advocates," or sociologists and political theorists who study the nature of power, look at the stakes that occupations have in acquiring professional status. To maintain power and prestige, professional groups often engage in self-serving practices—exclusive membership requirements and the acquisition of specialized knowledge, vocabularies, and practices that set them above their clients or customers to limit public criticism yet permit full credit for successes. In the media world, as in most professional arenas, practitioners often join professional groups, advocate specialized university and on-the-job training, and often distance themselves from their audiences (most media practitioners do not have "clients").

Media scholar James Carey (1978) expressed concern over the power of the professional, and he seriously questioned whether media practitioners ought to seek professional status. He said professionals and specialists have extended their control over our private lives by supervising and professing professional knowledge of any and all departments affecting us. Professionals erode the moral basis of society by setting themselves up as a special class, making "distinctive moral claims with judicial, financial and authoritative power" (p. 850).

Of particular interest to power advocates are professional codes of ethics and licensing practices. Both are used as public claims for high status; neither exists strictly as a vehicle to ensure ethical performance. Through codes, professions demonstrate their ability to handle transgressions "in house," away from the public view and without outside intervention. Likewise, self-licensing restricts public influence on the profession and keeps professionals from being accountable to the public. Indeed, this view of professionalization suggests that people calling themselves professionals tend to be more concerned with serving the interests of their fellow professionals than with serving clients or the general public. This characteristic puts them at odds with one of occupational sociologists' important criteria of professionalism: the focus on others. Arrogance, not humility, is a hallmark of such a professional attitude. And, as we have seen repeatedly in this text, arrogance is not a quality to be lauded in media practice.

Professionalism can work either for noble or for self-serving ends. Unfortunately, when professionals, like most humans, find themselves under siege, the all-too-common response is to circle the wagons and use their power, privilege, and prestige to serve their own interests. Media are most certainly not exempt from this all-too-human trait. The first line of defense against media criticism is often a series of self-serving actions that further the distance between media and the public.

Economic and Political Considerations

Some economists and political theorists have a line of reasoning similar to that raised by "power advocates." They maintain that true professionals do not work as employees in bureaucratic settings, but operate with a good deal of autonomy and decision-making powers. They are independent operatives, responsible for generating their own incomes and perks and are not tied to the whims and inexorable economic forces levied by bureaucracies and conglomerates.

As D. Hugh Gillis sees it, news media fail this test of professionalism because advertisers control the core of the activity of a news organization. While the need for information in society is clear, it would be unavailable, expensive, or less trustworthy if advertisers did not provide a way to pay for it. Either way, journalists indirectly owe their livelihood to a source other than a mere demand for their services and are therefore not working in a true professional environment (Gillis, 1966–1967). Arthur Kaul states the case more directly, arguing that journalists are in the contradictory position of being "proletarian professionals," economically subordinated to owners/managers in "America's news factories" (Kaul, 1986). Kaul sees the twentieth century professionalization of journalism, with its "public service" ethos, as an "adaptation maneuver to insulate newspaper owners/publishers against profit-threatening crises, class conflicts and public disenchantment with the press" (p. 48).

Whereas traditional journalism establishments—mainstream media—may preclude individual practitioners from claiming unilateral professional status, some interesting twists have occurred recently. Independent and freelance journalists have always been part of the scene, but only recently their independence has become a major national and international movement. Bloggers have become this century's cousin to the eighteenth and nineteenth century entrepreneurs who went from town to town with their aprons of type and small printing presses. Bloggers tend to work on their own, answerable only to their conscience, their sources, and their consumers. No specific training or education is required to be a blogger. A few—seeking credibility—have developed codes of ethics, but many question the value of doing so. As one blogger asked, "What do I do if I break a rule? Fire myself?" (Perlmutter & Schoen, 2007).

Because they are independent operatives, professionals such as doctors and lawyers find themselves constantly engaged in public lobbying or political agitation to ensure public support. Unlike media workers, such professionals have no constitutional guarantees to protect their rights and privileges. First Amendment protection works as a double-edged sword in the realm of professional/ethical behavior of media workers in general, and journalists more specifically. Economists and political theorists who develop this line of thinking also point out that until the public perceives an occupation as being a profession, it will not be a profession. Given the public's ambivalence (if not downright hostility) toward many media fields, journalism, advertising, public relations, and other media work probably fail this particular test of professionalism. Whether this is to the media's benefit or detriment, it is yet another form of pressure on the media ethics environment.

THE PATH TO PROFESSIONAL, ETHICAL MEDIA

The current trend toward some loosely defined "professionalization" may be merely a rhetorical stopover on the road toward outside forces imposing enforceable ethics on journalists and other mass media practitioners. Enforceable ethics may give us confidence in the accuracy, balance, and fairness of our media, but at what cost does such confidence come? Can we—or is it desirable for us to—have that confidence? What are the tradeoffs? What are the implications for media freedom?

Professional accountability seems to be one useful compromise between inflexible government or external regulation and the anarchy of no regulation at all (Christians, 1985–1986; Davis, 2010). Media personnel are accountable to government when they violate minimal standards spelled out by laws and doctrines of libel, invasion of privacy, obscenity, copyright, fairness, and the like. Media practitioners demonstrate their accountability to fellow practitioners by creating codes of ethics and putting in place such vehicles as professional conferences and workshops, press councils, movie ratings systems, ombudsmen, consultants and outside reviews, house organs, and trade publications. Indeed, much professional behavior is judged according to group norms. Peer groups, through codes of ethics and other vehicles, reinforce the professional climate, alternatively condoning and condemning practices of their fellows. In a third general type of accountability, media are answerable to the marketplace, to their readers and viewers and listeners who may find them irresponsible and "punish" them by indignation or by boycotting their product. That accountability to clients/customers is crucial, for without them there would be no need for service or call for professional productivity. (We develop this argument more fully in Chapter 13.)

How is the public to be reasonably certain that people who provide information, persuasion, and entertainment to the public adhere to reasonable standards of fairness, accuracy, truth, and so forth?

Publicity and transparency—that is, open accountability to the public—seems to be one answer to the question. That is, the same audiences pressuring government to change as a result of disclosures through the media should be pressuring—or be perceived as pressuring—media to change behaviors when audiences believe such behavior is outrageous. The basic principle, of course, is that media people are as responsive to public opinion as are others who rely on public favor for their survival, and media people seeking to take the high road and serve the general welfare are naturally sensitive to, although certainly not panderers to, public sentiment. On the other hand, as we will discuss in Chapter 4, there may be times when media practitioners work at higher levels of moral development that call them to ignore the public's whims.

SUMMARY AND CONCLUSIONS

This chapter was intended to help answer the question, "Why not follow the rules?" However, it raises additional questions as it explores media history, theories of media practices, and professionalism.

Modern media are the sum of a highly complex set of variables: technological, political, economic, geographic, cultural—and moral. Some patterns are evident as media evolve from elite, to popular, to specialized, and even to "many-to-many" institutions. No mass media arose or flourished without overcoming a plethora of constraints. Each reflects the political philosophy that dominates its nation-state or region of operations. Whether authoritarian-tending or libertarian-tending, each media system must be socially responsible or it will not survive. Doing so may seem to reflect a relativistic world. On the surface this seems to be true. On deeper reflection, however, the media discussed in this chapter try to gather and report information, share opinions, produce entertainment, and engage in persuasion that their societies need in order to function well. As the authors of *Last Rights* conclude, we all believe in some version of democracy, some notion of freedom, and some role that the media can play in achieving these (Nerone, 1995).

The current trend toward professionalizing media institutions and practices raises another set of questions about controls over media performance and impact. The accountability systems being suggested are calls for media practitioners and the public to reallocate unequally distributed powers of information, persuasion, and entertainment. The standards of professionalism to be sought are the standards of behavior articulated by morally mature peer groups and mediated by the cleansing light of publicity. They are not the minimal standards of expectation required by governmental statutes and court decisions. They are calls for moral autonomy, because they ask media workers to act on one essential element found in most classical definitions of professionalism: An obligation to humbly serve the public, and to operate in the best traditions of the caring professions. To do so means to be socially responsible, regardless of the political, social, economic, or philosophical context in which the media operate. And it means professional practitioners have come up with good answers when answering the question, "Why not follow the rules?"

■ ■ ■

CHAPTER VOCABULARY

Note: Definitions are available at this book's companion website.

- authoritarian theory of the press
- autonomy
- Commission on the Freedom of the Press
- communist theory of the press
- cultural relativism theory of the press
- democratic socialist theory of the press

- developmental theory of the press
- First Amendment
- Hutchins Commission—see "Commission on the Freedom of the Press"
- *laissez-faire*
- libertarian theory of the press
- Locke, John
- Machiavelli, Niccolo

- Mill, John Stuart
- Milton, John
- prior restraints
- revolutionary theory of the press
- sedition
- social responsibility theory of the press

PRACTICAL APPLICATIONS

1. **The 'Net Effect**: Just as the Internet was becoming a household term (even if it wasn't available in many households,) the Church of England's Archbishop of York, David Hope, argued that the Internet could destroy society. Hope said computers are creating "a society without a soul," because people have "no interaction when they stay home and glued to screens" (British Broadcasting Corp., 2000). The church in 1999 warned its congregants to consider the moral issues raised by the ability to communicate without the safeguards and considerations that are built into one-on-one communication. "This technology is something that could ultimately devour us," Hope said.

   A. Now, more than a decade later, how right (or wrong) do you think his warnings seem?

   B. In the continuum of authoritarian to libertarian, where does the Internet fall as a communication means in your nation? Where do you think it should fall?

   C. Have you ever written anything about someone on the Internet that you would not say to that person's face? How would your online life be different it you were required to read, face-to-face, what you wrote about the person who was your target?

2. **Professional or Not**: Choose a field of work and, using the occupational and philosophical definitions discussed in this chapter:

   A. determine whether that field is a profession, and explain why or why not

   B. decide what difference, if any, the presence or absence of a professional status makes to the industry and stakeholders.

■ ■ ■

CASE 3.1 **Journalism: Can You Show Readers What the Fuss is About?**

You are editor of *The Freedonia Times*, the leading newspaper in a land known for its tradition of unfettered press, speech, and religion. Those rights are not as established in Sylvania, which shares a 500-mile border with Freedonia and has tens of thousands of citizens living in your nation.

Sylvania is ruled by a monarchy. King Zeppo is fairly benevolent and has let a minor cult of personality develop. His image adorns stamps, money, road signs, and even hangs in places of worship. It is against Sylvanian law to deface the monarch's image or use it in any unapproved way—not that anyone would do that, because King Zeppo's subjects have ascribed him a near-deity status.

So it is a jolt to King Zeppo's subjects in and out of Sylvania when *Freedonia Comment* magazine publishes a dozen editorial cartoons that are fairly disrespectful of the monarch. The magazine has long been critical of the king, but this is the first time it has portrayed his image in a manner that would be illegal in his country.

The reaction is immediate. Protests in Sylvania quickly become violent, with fires set to the Freedonia embassy and several office buildings owned by Freedonia citizens. Protesters and the Sylvania government are deeply offended that a respected media organization would go out of its way to be disrespectful. They accuse the magazine, its editor, and the cartoonist of breaking Sylvania law. They also suggest that the issue involves racism and classism, claiming that many in Freedonia see themselves as superior because they have a different skin color and have a higher national standard of living.

The cartoonist and editors of *Freedonia Comment* do not back down from the issue, saying Freedonia's free speech tradition means they should not have to censor themselves in order to avoid offending a foreign king.

The Freedonia Times clearly must cover the issue, you decide, and your staffers are writing about the protests and the larger issue. Thousands of copies of each day's *Freedonia Times* go to Sylvania, and the newspaper's tradition has been to respect the king's wishes. In fact, you've never thought much about the issue of "misusing" his image before. You routinely print the king's image in photos taken by your staff, but drawn images have not been an issue because the newspaper does not have a political cartoonist.

But this may be different, because the issue is the images. In fact, the paper's main story in tomorrow's edition is about the images. The question is, should you publish the images in question?

The editor of *Freedonia Comment* has given you permission to run them, so it's not a legal issue in Freedonia.

➤ **Deadline comes in two hours. What do you do?**

Questions
- **What's your problem?**
- **Why not follow the rules?**
- What else do you need to know?

Thinking it Through

1. What's your first instinct?
    A. If you're inclined not to run the images:
        a. How will you justify your decision to readers who think you have given up your right to a free press through self-censorship?
        b. How can you explain to them that it's possible to fully inform readers without providing the images?
    B. If you're inclined to run the images:
        a. How will you justify your decision to Sylvanians who are certain to be offended?
        b. How can you explain to them that it's impossible to fully inform readers without providing the images?

2. Would you publish the images if Sylvania were not the country next door, and if Freedonia were home to just 100 or so Sylvania natives?

3. Will you run the images in question?

4. Regardless of your decision:
    A. How much concern should journalists have about offending people of other cultures and nations? What factors should a journalist consider when deciding whether to publish something that may be perceived as offensive or stereotypical for another culture?
    B. Is the rule of thumb "when in Rome, do as the Romans" a reasonable rule to follow for journalists in other nations?
    C. Have you ever been offended by a media message that was irreverent to your nationality or closely held beliefs? What did you do?
    D. How big of an issue is self-censorship in media? Name times when self-censorship would be ethical—and times when it may not be.

CASE 3.2 **New Media: When in Sylvania, Do You Do as the Sylvanians?**

Your website, www.freedonialive.com, has become a hit. Even better, it has branched into the adjacent nation of Sylvania. It's doing so well, in fact, that you've hired additional staff and opened a site specific to Sylvania, which has triple the population and seemingly limitless growth potential.

Unlike your nation's tradition of free speech, Sylvania is controlled by a royal family that tolerates less dissent and free speech than your home. It is an authoritarian government, in which private companies such as yours are allowed to own mass media outlets but face government control over content. The Sylvania rulers are benevolent but serious: while they say they have not killed or injured people they believe have crossed the line with dissenting messages, they have jailed dozens of people over the years for speech deemed contrary or disrespectful to the government. There are whispers that the Sylvania rulers were lying when they said no dissenters have been killed or injured, but you cannot be sure.

One day you are summoned to the Sylvania embassy, where you are told that members of the royal family generally like your website, and they hope that one day they can offer you more complete access to their nation and advertisers.

But there's a catch: an anonymous blogger on your site, who calls himself FinkKing, has written scathing entries about the king, including a claim that the King of Sylvania had sex with his son's wife.* The embassy staffer wants to know the real identity of FinkKing, because Sylvania law forbids making such scandalous comments about the king or any members of the royal family. If you reveal the name, you will receive greater access to Sylvania. If you do not identify the blogger, it is likely that Sylvania will use its powerful firewall software to block your websites from the kingdom.

➤ **You have two hours to decide.**

Questions
- **What's your problem?**
- **Why not follow the rules?**
- What else do you need to know?

---

* This is not as far-fetched as it seems. The first newspaper in the American colonies, *Publick Occurrences Both Forreign and Domestick,* published such a claim in its one-and-only edition in September 1690. See Williams, J. (1999). *The Significance of the Printed Word in Early America Colonists' Thoughts on the Role of the Press.* Santa Barbara, CA: Greenwood Publishing Group, p. 189.

Thinking it Through

1. Can you justify your decision by referring to the laws of Sylvania, which you personally detest but understand you must follow in order to do business there? Put another way: Is this a business decision or an ethical decision?

2. Does it make a difference if FinkKing the blogger:

   A. Is someone you do not know, and all you have is an IP address that would let Sylvania authorities find the blogger?

   B. Is someone you know?

   C. Lives in Sylvania and is much more likely to be arrested?

   D. Lives in Freedonia, where he/she might be safer but still might need to be concerned about actions taken by Sylvania agents in Freedonia?

   E. Lives in Freedonia but has family in Sylvania?

   F. Is you, writing anonymously?

3. Does it matter if the blogger's accusations are true? What if the claims about the king are lies?

4. Does it matter if the Sylvania embassy official says that no harm will come to the blogger once he/she is identified?

5. If you were somehow able to pierce the Sylvania firewall, would that make a difference in your decision?

6. If you give up the blogger's identify and keep access in Sylvania, what might happen next time the nation wants information from you about a dissident?

7. The bottom line question: Do you give up the blogger's name?

CASE 3.3 **Public Relations: Pay for Play in Another Country?**

You are a former television journalist now working for a public relations firm in your native country of Freedonia, which has long enjoyed a free and (mostly) responsible press. You constantly deal with reporters, and your years as a journalist have given you a firm understanding of how the Freedonia press revels in its independence. Many reporters won't let you buy them so much as a cup of coffee, so something as brusque as your offering to pay a reporter to include a favorable mention about one of your clients would kill your favorable image among reporters. In fact, you made sure to include a ban on "pay for play" in your public relations firm's code of standards and best practices.

Your first foray into international public relations comes when your client, an agency of Freedonia's federal government, hires you to promote a new trade agreement with Sylvania, which borders your country. Sylvania has a lower standard of living than your country—and its own way of doing business.

As part of your client's plan to promote the treaty with Sylvania, you and the director of the Freedonia Trade Agency arrange to have lunch with a prominent journalist who works for Sylvania's biggest newspaper. Her story will be crucial in conveying your client's message to Sylvania, and you need her to provide that third-party boost that is particularly important when delivering an international message.

The lunch goes well until the end of the dessert course, when the journalist says she will be pleased to write a story in which you are the topic—for a payment equivalent to $1,500. She wants it in cash, up front, before she writes. She makes no promises of what she will write, and there's no offer that you will see her copy before it is published.

You knew this might happen because you understand it to be a fairly standard practice for Sylvanian journalists to seek payment from sources. Because Sylvanian journalists generally receive low pay, Sylvanian public relations practitioners put journalists "on the payroll" from time to time.

You don't make a decision at the lunch table, but you tell her you'll be in touch soon.

> After the meeting, the Freedonia Trade Agency head is ecstatic: "A mention for $1,500? That's a bargain at triple the price," he says. "But I'm not the PR expert here. What do you think?"

Questions
- **What's your problem?**
- **Why not follow the rules?**
- What else do you need to know?

Thinking it Through

1. What are you thinking?
   A. If you're inclined to recommend payment to the journalist:
      a. How do you justify your actions, especially given your own journalistic background?
      b. Do you seek pre-publication review or other concessions from the journalist to be sure of a favorable mention? What if the journalist is offended by your request? How do you guarantee that you'll get your money's worth?
      c. Would you consider this an example of your paying a bribe to the journalist, or an example of extortion by the journalist? Is there an ethical distinction between the two?
   B. If you're inclined to recommend against payment to the journalist:
      a. How do you justify your actions to the director, who only seems to care about the result?
      b. What happens if the journalist writes about the client anyway? What if the story is negative?
2. Other questions, regardless of your decision:
   A. Is there a "middle ground" in this situation?
   B. Do you feel a moral obligation to introduce Freedonia's national standards of journalistic and public relations ethics to Sylvania?
   C. Would your decision change if Freedonia had a federal law making it illegal to make payments to Freedonia journalists?
   D. Would your decision change if Freedonia had a federal law making it illegal to bribe foreign companies? (Would this be a bribe, given that it goes to the journalist and not the newspaper for which she works?)
   E. How would you respond if Freedonia journalists discovered that its federal government was making payments to another nation's journalists?
   F. Should there be an international code of public relations ethics to deal with situations such as this? (See, for example, the IPRA code on this book's website.)
3. The bottom line question: What do you say to the director of the Freedonia Trade Agency?

■ ■ ■

CASE 3.4 **Advertising: Selling Tobacco Abroad**

FIGURE 3.1 │ The Marlboro Man (and other cigarette ads) is gone from US billboards, but he still sells tobacco in places such as Dakar, the capital of the West African nation of Senegal. (Photo: Chris Roberts)

This is a true story. The Marlboro Man was an advertising icon for more than four decades in the United States, with television commercials and print ads showing rugged men smoking cigarettes while surrounded by rugged nature. *Advertising Age* called the Marlboro Man the "most powerful—and in some quarter, most hated—brand image" of the twentieth century. Marlboro went from having 1 percent of sales at the campaign's start in 1955 to becoming the top-selling cigarette brand worldwide (adage.com, 2005).

You don't see the ads in the United States anymore. The US campaign ended as the government cracked down on tobacco advertisements, including bans on outdoor advertising (CNN, 1999). It also ended after at least two men who were in Marlboro ads died of lung cancer, but not before becoming anti-smoking advocates (snopes.com, 2007).

But the Marlboro Man isn't dead—he just moved overseas. One of this book's authors took the photo in Figure 3.1 during late 2007 in Senegal, where 15 percent of children aged 13 to 15 smoke, a fifth own an object with a tobacco logo, and 75 percent routinely see cigarette ads (World Health Organization, 2007). Senegal is one of many nations with fewer restrictions on tobacco advertising than the US—while other nations have tighter restrictions.

The tobacco industry would note that it is doing what is legal: selling legal products and only targeting people who are old enough to make the choice about smoking. Its proponents would argue that it should not be held to the most restrictive rules of another nation.

➤ **Answer these questions as you consider the ethics of international advertising of a controversial product.**

Questions
- **What's your problem?**
- **Why not follow the rules?**
- What else do you need to know?

Thinking it Through
1. What, if anything, do the *Four Theories of the Press* and other theories discussed in this chapter have to do with this discussion?
2. Does the difference between law and ethics play a role here? Why or why not?
3. Should the ads use natives instead of stylized Americans? Why or why not?
4. What other thorny legal and ethical issues do companies face in international advertising? How might these be resolved?
5. Should there be an international code of ethics for advertisers? Why or why not?

■ ■ ■

CASE 3.5 **Entertainment: A Pitch Too Good to Turn Down?**

You are a movie executive who hears ideas that your company could turn into feature films. You hear dozens of "pitches" a month, and your job is to summarize the best ideas and take them to a higher-level executive who ultimately decides what ideas go into production.

One of the best ideas you've heard in a long time came your way the other day: It's a political thriller involving the relationship between your nation of Freedonia and the neighboring country of Sylvania, which holds a longstanding grudge against Freedonia. It's based on a true story involving those two nations.

The story involves a Sylvanian special agent—code name Harpo—who is ordered to be part of a plan to assassinate Freedonia's president. If the plot works, no one would ever know that Sylvanian spies were responsible. But Harpo worked with the Freedonia president on a previous mission and concludes that killing the president is wrong. He decides that, even as it appears he is going along with the mission, he essentially must become a traitor and warn Freedonian officials. Sylvanian officials suspect Harpo may reveal their plan, so the movie is filled with multiple action sequences in which they try to kill Harpo. One attempt fails, but not before his wife is killed. Harpo finds a way to take revenge on his wife's killer and come out looking like the only good guy among the many Sylvanians portrayed in the movie.

You take the pitch to your boss, who thinks it's a good idea. She knows that one of Freedonia's most famous actors, Donny Jepp, is looking for just this type of movie. And another top box-office draw, Annifer Jeniston, can play his wife.

The big problem: Jepp and Jeniston are Freedonian, not Sylvanian. It would take a great deal of makeup to give them the different physical attributes that most people associate with Sylvanian natives, and even then the pair would not be totally convincing.

You can think of other problems, too:

- While Sylvania has fewer actors and actresses working in Freedonia, you could recommend several who could play the parts. However, none has the box-office draw of Jepp and Jeniston.
- All of the Sylvanian characters, except for Jepp and Jeniston, are portrayed as "bad guys." Tensions between the countries always exist, and you worry about how a major motion picture might affect international relations. If the project isn't careful, the Sylvanian bad guys will come across as stereotypes—a real possibility in an action movie.
- There's long been some racial prejudice by Freedonians toward Sylvanians. You wonder whether the project could contribute to the prejudice.

Your boss sees you as the "conscience" of the company. Even though she might decide against you, your boss still wants to hear what you have to say.

➤ **So what *do* you say?**

Questions

*   **What's your problem?**
*   **Why not follow the rules?**
*   What else do you need to know?

Thinking it Through

1. What's more important, telling a "truthful" story or commercial success? Can you find a balance?
2. What moral obligation do storytellers have to be inclusive of different races, genders, etc.?
3. How can entertainment media avoid portraying "others" as caricatures?
4. What other ethical issues might a movie executive face when thinking about foreign distribution of films?
5. Should filmmakers have to worry about the implications toward foreign policy in their movies?
6. Should filmmakers worry about whether their audiences will understand the depictions of people of different races?
7. How might your decision be affected if you had relatives living in Sylvania?
8. Do you recommend to your boss that the executive:
    A. Green-light the movie with the cast as is?
    B. Green-light the movie after it changes some cast members? Or change the countries?
    C. Decide against the project?

■ ■ ■

Who Wins, Who Loses?

The third of six questions that frame this book is: "Who wins, who loses?" This question doesn't presume that ethics is a zero-sum game, or that for each winner there is a loser. Rather, it merely asks us to identify the stakeholders and anticipate the impact our decision may have on each of them—including ourselves. We will take two chapters to explore this question. The first focuses on theories of moral development; the second, on loyalties and diversity.

> Who are the stakeholders, and what impact is your decision likely to have on each of them in the short term and in the long term?

Chapter 4 moves beyond moral philosophy by introducing theories of developmental psychology. It summarizes the work of a number of psychologists concerned about the stages people go through when developing morally, intellectually, professionally, and personally. The theories offer opportunities for self-exploration as well as a chance to examine the motives and behaviors of mass media practitioners. The theories help us understand the need to expand our levels of empathy, caring for and caring about others; they remind us that all stakeholders have needs and rights; they challenge us to progress in our individual and professional decision-making skills.

Wrestling with theories of moral development anticipates the very pragmatic issues discussed in Chapter 5: loyalty and diversity. These issues are closely connected; each demands that we understand and apply the virtues of respect, allegiance, and obedience. The challenges are obvious: Everyone deserves respect, but it is impossible to show equal loyalty to everyone. Media workers must be loyal to their institutions and clients, but they should never lose sight of the public interest. Underrepresented segments of an increasingly diverse society need to be heard, but great care must be taken in choosing how to give "voice" to the voiceless.

Together, these two chapters help us answer the question, "Who wins, who loses?"

1. What's your problem?

2. Why not follow the rules?

3. <u>Who wins, who loses?</u>

4. What's it worth?

5. Who's whispering in your ear?

6. How's your decision going to look?

CHAPTER 4

Moral Development and the Expansion of Empathy

INTRODUCTION

THIS CHAPTER introduces a number of perspectives on how we grow morally, intellectually, professionally, and personally. Leading theorists, coming at the subject from very different perspectives, seem to agree that most of us progress through predictable stages of thinking and decision making: from pre-conventional to conventional to post-conventional. The process is neither absolute nor immutable. A significant factor in moral growth is the expansion of our sense of empathy: As we mature, our sense of "the other" changes, and we employ increasingly sophisticated and sensitive ways to resolve moral problems.

Whether we are independent practitioners or part of a corporate enterprise, our capacity to cope with the inevitable workplace pressures is improved when we have a better understanding of "Who wins, who loses?" And we all do a better job as media consumers when we understand the moral psychology of all the stakeholders in the media ethics environment.

> This chapter:
> - considers how different responses to case studies reflect varying stages of moral development
> - summarizes theories of moral psychology and the expansion of empathy
> - introduces and critiques the work of William Perry, Lawrence Kohlberg, Carol Gilligan, Mary Belenky, James Rest, and others who have studied moral and intellectual growth
> - challenges you to apply the theories in several exercises and case studies.

TEST CASES FROM FREEDONIA

Let's return to Freedonia and the case studies that began this text: The "keep the money" case involving www.freedonialive.com (Case 1.1), in which you finally can make a steady income if you agree to make favorable references to a sponsor's clients and services, and the public relations officer for the National Paper Corp. (Case 1.2), in which you must decide whether to remain silent about your plant's imminent closing.

Please reconsider the moral dilemmas. This time, don't concentrate on *what* you should decide as the blogger and PR person. Rather, please focus on *how you argued*: What kinds of arguments did you and your classmates present to buttress whatever conclusions you ultimately reached about the cases?

Consider some potential lines of reasoning. Did you or your classmates argue that:

1. As a blogger you should not take the money from MarketingMarx unless you follow the Freedonia Trade Commission's rules (even though you think those rules violate your right to free speech), because you may be breaking the law and could get caught.

2. As the PR person, you should absolutely abide by the managers' request for silence, because they are your superiors and you are basically powerless to do otherwise. Indeed, they would fire you if they found you leaked the secret.

3. As the blogger or PR person you can safely assume that, if you are clever and careful, you will not get caught or punished regardless of your decisions.

4. The primary motivation of the blogger and PR person should be to "look after Number One," because as a blogger you have worked hard to make the blog profitable and as the PR person you have no assurance that anyone else will look after you.

5. As the PR person you should generally follow the company's wishes. After all, the company treated you well in the past, and your bosses implied that you would be rewarded for cooperating.

6. You work and live in an extremely relativistic world, where everything is uncertain, and there's no single satisfactory resolution to any of your dilemmas. It all depends.

7. As the PR person, you owe a special allegiance to your sister and brother-in-law, so you are justified in telling them and only them that the plant will be closing.

8. As the PR person, you should disclose the plant's imminent demise to anyone who would be in a position to help you if—or when—you lose your job.

9. As the PR person, you should generally do whatever it takes to be a good team player at work and not to rock the boat, even if it means sacrificing some of your own self-interests.

10. As the blogger and PR person, you should always abide by your crafts' codes of ethics and the pertinent laws.

11. As the blogger and PR person, you should live up to the expectations and fulfill the duties any professional would be expected to live up to.

12. As the blogger and PR person, you need to abide by the "social contracts" you have made with your sponsor and employer, your family, and your community. You should try mightily to reach a conclusion that will bring about the greatest aggregate of good, and a minimum of harm, over the long term.

13. Your conscience should be your guide in both cases. You made tacit promises to your sponsors and bosses, and everyone should always keep promises, regardless of the consequences.

14. Your conscience should be your guide in both cases. You cannot live in a community that is not completely honest and forthright or does not respect the notions of justice, dignity, and human rights.

15. As a good person and competent professional as a blogger or PR practitioner, you must resolve contradictions between your personal and professional roles. You must consider the need for all bloggers and PR people—indeed, all persons—to develop and abide by professional norms and individual conscience.

16. As a good person and competent professional who has resolved contradictions between your personal and professional roles, you should anticipate ways to minimize harm to all stakeholders. For instance, as a PR person you can speak up eloquently at the meeting to say the company should pursue other ways to remain open or, at the very least, to treat everyone in the community equally by immediately and fully disclosing the company's plans.

17. Your decisions should be based on genuine caring and the desire to maintain the greater community. As the blogger, you should consider whether to disclose your financial entanglements fully. As the PR person, you should consider whether to tell your family, the local newspaper, and other stakeholders that the plant will soon close.

18. Regardless of your decisions, you should show strength of conviction by openly disclosing your decision-making processes. As the blogger and PR person, you strongly believe that your clients, company, and community should be morally sensitive, make defensible moral judgments, and act out of articulated values that demonstrate motivation and commitment. The bottom line: your decisions should pass the test of publicity.

You'll notice immediately that these arguments differ widely, and at first glance each of them (except perhaps argument six) seems to provide a plausible rationale for whatever decisions you make. That is because each answer reflects a position reflected in the body of knowledge known as moral development, or moral psychology.

As we review some of this field's literature, we'll apply the theories to the two case studies and suggest where each of the 18 arguments falls along scales of moral development. At that point, you should be better able to decide which decisions are more morally justified, based on higher levels of moral development, and which are morally problematic. These insights won't necessarily tell you what conclusion to reach, but they should help you understand how to reach them. At base, they begin to address this chapter's key question: "Who wins, who loses?"

MORAL PSYCHOLOGY RESEARCH: SOME BASICS

Research in moral psychology has led to a number of theories explaining how we progress through a logical set of hierarchical stages in our moral development. Despite their many differences, the theories suggest that:

- In general, our individual moral development parallels our intellectual development. We tend to progress systematically from lower stages to higher stages of development as we mature.
- At the lowest stages we are ego-centered. We operate out of fear of punishment or to seek reward; there is little consciousness of behaving morally.
- At middle stages we try to "work and play well with others," to be a "good boy or a good girl," or to be self-sacrificing to meet others' needs. We tend to be moral relativists.
- At higher stages we think about the "social contract" we have with one another. We recognize the inherent worth of everyone (including ourselves), and we behave out of idealistic universal principles. In short, we become autonomous moral agents who seek to lead a good life and leave our campsites better than we found them.
- Moral maturity occurs when we recognize the flaws inherent in "lower-level" stages and as we watch people around us demonstrate the values of higher-stage reasoning and behavior.
- For many reasons, we can more readily "regress"—acting and thinking at a lower stage than we generally reside in—than we can jump to a higher stage.

The Expansion of Empathy

Developmental psychologists often focus on the notion of empathy—our capacity to be sensitive to the presence, interests, and needs of others.

It is natural for us to begin life as self-centered. As infants, we are wholly dependent upon others; in our narrow view of the world, our own needs are paramount. Recent research (Bloom, 2010) draws the fascinating conclusion that some children demonstrate moral awareness as early as one year of age, but by and large, their "sense of other" is limited. As we mature, we become aware of and respond to "immediate" others who are just like us and/or who can help or hurt us. Only then do we start to recognize the needs of, and to care about, a wider community. Ultimately, as we mature morally, we may have an intense sense of empathy for humanity in general—people who are like us, and people who are very different from us. Seen in these terms, empathy entails "caring for" and "caring about." The obvious implication is that heightened empathy means our circles of care grow ever wider.

In *Emotional Intelligence: Why It Can Matter More Than IQ*, Daniel Goleman says the roots of morality are to be found in empathy, and that empathy underlies many facets of moral judgment and action:

There is a natural progression of empathy from infancy onward . . . at one year of age a child feels in distress herself when she sees another fall and start to cry . . . By late childhood the most advanced level of empathy emerges, as children are able to understand distress beyond the immediate situation, and to see that someone's condition or station in life may be a source of chronic distress. At this point they can feel for the plight of an entire group, such as the poor, the oppressed, the outcast. That understanding, in adolescence, can buttress moral convictions centered on wanting to alleviate suffering, misfortune, and injustice.

(1995, p. 105)

Perplexing questions thus arise from our discussion in Chapter 3 on professionalism, and in Chapter 5's upcoming discussion on loyalty and diversity: At what stage of moral development do media professionals tend to function, and at what stage should they function? (Coleman & Wilkins, 2009). Do they naturally empathize/identify with professional peers, with company or institutional norms and values, with accrediting and prize-awarding committees? Do they "feel" for their sources and subjects, their clients, their audiences, the general populace? In Goleman's rubric, true professionals have evolved through stages of reward-seeking and punishment-avoiding self-interest, and moved to a universal stage of caring for and caring about others—friends and strangers, known and unknown.

INSIGHTS FROM MORAL PSYCHOLOGISTS

This section considers the contributions from several well-known moral psychologists who offer insights that we can apply to ourselves as individual decision makers and to the work of others, including media practitioners. In particular, we will note the work of five theorists who took different approaches to understanding the nature of moral development:

- William Perry, who describes students' intellectual and moral growth, focusing on their reliance upon authority figures and their sense of relativism and commitment.
- Lawrence Kohlberg, whose theory of moral development focuses on rights and justice.
- Carol Gilligan, whose theory of moral development focuses on care and community connectedness.
- Mary Belenky, who focuses on women's way of knowing and of expressing themselves.
- James Rest, whose theory focuses on four components: moral sensitivity, moral judgment, moral motivation and commitment, and moral character and implementation.

As we introduce the moral psychologists, we will connect their theories to the 18 lines of reasoning cited earlier as resolutions for the case studies about the blogger and the PR practitioner.

WILLIAM PERRY
Intellectual and Ethical Development in Young Adults

A good reason to start with Harvard director of counseling William Perry (1970; 1981) is because he deals specifically with the changes experienced by college students and young adults. Whether you are a college student or a media professional, Perry's insights should serve as a map for the journey at hand. In brief outline form, he said typical students and young adults undergo three major adjustments in their ways of coping with what seems to be a changing world:

1. Modifying a dualistic view of a black-and-white world.
2. Realizing that many things are relative.
3. Developing commitment.

The evolutionary process of intellectual and moral growth begins within a comfortable worldview where everything is clear-cut, a world where teachers and other authority figures know and provide the "right" answers to students. In such a world, uncertainty or a lack of absolute answers appears to be a fraud or a "head game." Later, this uncertainty about diverse ideas becomes tolerable if students think it's just a matter of time before authority figures find the absolute answers. All of this can be called a "pre-conventional" phase of dualism.

At the second, or conventional, phase, students move into a relativistic world. Some issues are matters of opinion, and all opinions seem equal. The students' job often seems merely to "shoot the bull" or give teachers what they want to hear. Eventually, it is an uncomfortable phase to be in, unless or until the students make an effort to orient themselves in an uncertain world.

The third or post-conventional phase is sometimes called Contextual Relativism, or "The Evolving of Commitment." As part of becoming oriented in an uncertain world, students start to put things into context and to use meaningful background. They recognize the need to reach reasoned decisions about their answers. They make tentative commitments—to answers and to lifestyle choices—and explore the implications of those commitments. Finally, they begin to live their commitments, walking the walk.

In outline form, Perry's three-phase, nine-position scheme looks like the following. To put the theory into context, we'll show where many of the 18 arguments about the blogger and the PR person (Cases 1.1 and 1.2) seem to "fit" the theory. Some of the following may stretch Perry's theory, but the general pattern seems to hold true.

First (Pre-conventional) Phase: The Modifying of Dualism

Position 1 (black and white) : Students perceive the world to be highly polarized: we-right-good versus other-wrong-bad. There are absolutely right answers for everything.

Authorities know these absolutes, and their job is to teach them to students. Answers are "written on tablets in the sky." Through hard work and obedience (such as learning the stylebook or passing a spelling test), students "collect" these absolutes, piece by piece. In doing so, they also gain goodness.

Arguments 1 and 2 for the case studies, in which we worry about breaking the law or obeying the boss, definitely reflect this perspective. Arguments 3 and 4, in which we worry about not getting caught and looking out for ourselves, probably reflect it. The black-and-white world is often defined by our authority figures, who seem to expect our obedience. Disobedience entails risk.

Position 2 (uncertainty as fraud or merely an exercise): Students recognize a diversity of opinion and uncertainty, and they account for the diversity as unwarranted confusion in poorly qualified Authorities, such as a bad or poorly prepared teacher. Or they might see these as mere exercises set by Authority "so we can learn to find The Answer by ourselves." This often begins in English class, where teachers disagree about the same poem. The students think teachers give them problems to solve so that they can develop independent thinking and find answers on their own. According to students in this position, math and science teachers seem to "see" more clearly, and teach more effectively, than English or philosophy teachers.

Arguments 5 and 6, in which we focus on promises of rewards and the fuzziness of the dilemma, seem to reflect a beginning of this relativistic perspective. Things are no longer black and white, but we're not sure what should replace that duality. The authority figures aren't quite as authoritative as we previously thought.

Position 3 (uncertainty is temporary): Students accept diversity and uncertainty as being legitimate but still temporary in areas where the Authority "hasn't found The Answer yet." Students suppose Authority grades them in these areas on "good expression," but students remain puzzled as to the standards being applied. The clouds begin to spread to the social sciences. It seems authority doesn't have the answers yet for lots of questions—and won't have them for a long time. It begins to get scary when the physics teacher says, "We don't have the answer to that yet."

Arguments 5 and 6 seem to apply here as well: We accept—but don't fully buy into—the relativistic perspective. We're not sure how much to rely upon our authority figures. This is a fairly uncomfortable position in which to be.

Second (Conventional) Phase: The Realizing of Relativism

Position 4 (some things are a matter of opinion, but others are certain): Students perceive legitimate uncertainty (and therefore diversity of opinion) to be excessive, and begin to think that the world is not divided between right and wrong, but into two realms: one where everyone has his or her own opinion ("It's just the way I feel.") and another where right and wrong are still certain. (Here the students may come to believe that literature or art can be interpreted from a variety of valid perspectives, but they will remain convinced that scientific principles are fixed.)

In the working world, we're entitled to our own opinion, even if that opinion is egoistic and based as much on "I feel . . . " as "I think . . . " It makes sense to pander to people who can help us, or those with whom we have special relationships. This is another way of looking at arguments 5, 6, 7, and 8, which suggest that we make decisions that are solely in our best interest.

Position 5 (all is relative): Students perceive all knowledge and values (including Authority's) as contextual and relativistic. Everything is relative but not equally valid. You have to understand how each context works. Theories are not Truth but metaphors with which to interpret data. You must think about your thinking. It dawns on students that there is a relationship between the validity of opinions and the data to support them. Wonder and despair. Crisis. Some turn back to dualism with vehemence. Some escape out of responsibility and become drifters, just doing what they must to get by. Most recover from emotional crisis and go on.

We don't know what the "correct" answer is, but some tentative answers seem to make more sense than others. However, in our discomfort, we may revert to the comfortable dogmatism of our earliest responses in arguments 1 through 3, and the fuzzy relativistic answers in arguments 4 through 8. Or, we might just throw up our hands and say, "What the heck!"

Position 6 (orientation to a relativistic, uncertain world): Students recognize that even in a place where there are several interpretations in the world, some positions may be correct for them. They realize the necessity of getting oriented in a relativistic world through some form of personal commitment (as distinct from unquestioned or un-considered commitment to a simple belief in uncertainty). They realize the decision is ultimately personal, and the agency for choice lies within. At this point, Authorities become resources or mentors for the students to tentatively rely upon.

We're still OK with the relativistic arguments 4 through 8, but with an increasing awareness that ultimately, it's up to us to decide. We're not expecting our bosses or our codes of ethics to solve our problem, but eventually it will need to be solved.

Third (Post-conventional) Phase: The Evolving of Commitment

Position 7 (commitment is begun): Students make an initial Commitment in some area. They sense the necessity of narrowing options, of giving up the "freedom" to choose and/or do absolutely anything. This causes some grief. But then they realize the expansion that can lie deep within the chosen field of commitment.

No longer comfortable with a fuzzy, relativistic response, we begin to turn to a general, theoretical framework for guidance. It may be argument 9's appeal to not rocking the boat, or argument 10's invocation of codes, laws, or statutes. These are not appeals to authority, but to something over and above our self-interest.

Position 8 (implications of commitment explored): Students experience the implications of Commitment, and they explore the subjective and stylistic issues of responsibility. It becomes necessary to decide how widely to spread themselves; how focused they should be. Students realize they have a number of simultaneous commitments, and may develop a sense of irony regarding the implications of multiple commitments.

Many of the ideas raised in arguments 11 through 18 can apply here. We recognize that we have several commitments, so we might balance those commitments by tentatively "trying on" one or more of the morally mature perspectives—adhering to self-chosen duties, or a social contract, or relying on an examined conscience.

Position 9 (commitment lived): Students experience the affirmation of identity among multiple responsibilities and realize Commitment as an ongoing, unfolding, constantly evolving activity through which they express their lifestyle. They may try to maintain continuity in life and commitments, but they recognize that change is constant.

Positions 11 through 18 are not just "tried on," but committed to. Argument 18 is particularly appropriate here, because it entails a commitment to caring or justice, and a willingness to expose that commitment to the test of publicity. If we made a legitimate commitment that helps us resolve these specific moral problems, that commitment should be generalized to other problems on other days, because it speaks to who we are.

Perry has much to teach us about the college experience *per se*, but also how young adults adjust to the world of work. For instance: As we learn our jobs, how much do we rely on our bosses or other authority figures, and how much on ourselves? How important is it to hear a diversity of perspectives from a wide variety of sources if we're really interested in finding the "truth" and sharing it with our sources, subjects, clients, or audiences? What are the implications of surrounding ourselves with like-minded colleagues instead of with people who constantly challenge our conventional thinking? Does our profession have any norms or "givens"? If so, where did they come from? What happens when they are challenged? What kinds of commitments have we made freely and of our own accord, and what are the implications of making them in our work and non-work lives?

LAWRENCE KOHLBERG
A Cognitive-Social Theory

A contemporary of Perry's at Harvard in the late 1950s, psychology professor Lawrence Kohlberg, developed a cognitive-social theory of moral development. Kohlberg argued (1969; 1981) that moral development may be identified and defined through six progressive stages of moral judgment. He concedes that most people become stagnated at an intermediate/conventional stage and few fully attain the final stage that reflects the moral sophistication of some of the world's great philosophers.

Kohlberg's six stages are grouped within three levels: pre-conventional, conventional, and post-conventional. These stages and levels show a natural evolution from focusing on and serving self interests, to the interests of others, and to the interests of abstract moral principles.

Stages 1 and 2 ("self-serving" pre-conventional stages): These are almost universally experienced by young children. Without an awareness of alternatives, children accept parental authority and make moral decisions based on avoiding punishment (stage 1) or pragmatically "making a deal" or following a rule or "being fair" when it satisfies their own self interests (stage 2).

Again looking at the blogger and PR cases, we can see that arguments 1, 2, 3, and 4 clearly reflect Kohlberg's first stage of moral development. It's all about obeying authority or finding a way not to be caught or punished. Kohlberg's second stage, "use or be used," is seen most clearly in arguments 5, 7, and 8. Here the media personnel use others to satisfy their own self-interests.

Stages 3 and 4 (the "other-serving" or "good boy/good girl" conventional stages): These extend from adolescence into adulthood. The "conventional" person begins to react more to the expectations of family, peers, and society. Acceptance according to the standards of group norms sometimes becomes an obsessive motivation for making "acceptable" moral decisions. Decisions are based on recognizing social expectations and seeking approval—following a "Golden Rule" (stage 3), or respecting and not questioning the rules of society (stage 4).

"Working and playing well with others" is best represented by argument 9, which advises the decision makers not to rock the boat.

Stages 5 and 6 (the law abiding/rights-respecting fifth stage and the justice seeking/conscience-driven sixth stage): These are considered to be "post-conventional principle-serving" stages of moral development.

At Kohlberg's fifth stage, individuals abide by a "social contract" with others, a freely entered upon contractual commitment to friends, family, trust, and work obligations—and to a wider society. The contract is utilitarian in nature, focusing impartially on rights, life, liberty, due process, etc., for the greatest number. Persons at this stage have a combination of legal and moral points of view, perspectives that often conflict and are difficult to resolve.

A number of arguments reflect Kohlberg's fifth stage, particularly arguments 10 through 12 with their appeals to codes of ethics, general professional duties, and social contracts with stakeholders. Arguments 13 through 17 also might apply, to the extent that the blogger and PR person are considering how to make general decisions based on their special professional roles. However, to the extent that arguments 13 through 17 can be seen as applying universally, regardless of any special professional roles, those arguments reflect Kohlberg's sixth and final stage.

The sixth stage, with its universal perspective, is reached only by the truly conscience-driven adult. At this level, "right" moral decisions are not made because of authority, or fear of punishment, or peer pressure, or conformity to social standards. Rather, they

---

Box **4.1** | **MARTIN LUTHER KING AND KOHLBERG Level 6**

Martin Luther King, Jr., eloquently explained the nature of post-conventional moral choices in his historic *Letter from a Birmingham Jail*. He was arrested in Birmingham in 1963 for breaking the city's draconian racial segregation laws, and from his cell he wrote that "one has a moral responsibility to break unjust laws."

After clergy wrote to tell him that the battle over civil rights should be waged in court instead of in the streets, Dr. King told his fellow clergymen about the pros and cons of civil disobedience. His argument is similar to that of Socrates, who demonstrated respect for the law of Athens (by accepting the death sentence) even while violating one component of it ("corrupting the youth" by teaching philosophy). As King wrote:

> You express a great deal of anxiety over our willingness to break laws . . . I agree with St. Augustine that "an unjust law is no law at all." . . . In no sense do I advocate evading the law . . . That would lead to anarchy. One who breaks an unjust law must do so openly . . . I submit that an individual who breaks a law that conscience tells him is unjust and who willingly accepts the penalty of imprisonment in order to arouse the conscience of the community over its injustice is in reality expressing the highest respect for the law.

> (quoted in Hornsby, 1986, pp. 40–41)

---

emerge as self-chosen ethical principles. Stage 6 people show self-actualized respect for broad general principles of justice, dignity, and human rights. In this stage, decision makers treat all people as ends in and of themselves. One is not law-bound when law violates these principles; one acts in accordance with the principles, knowing that to do so may mean having to pay the consequences.

As noted above, once we move beyond "special circumstances" of our personal or professional roles and think in universal terms about everyone's *obligation to* everyone else, *regardless of time, place, or other variables, we have moved to Kohlberg's sixth and most morally mature stage of development. In particular, argument 18 reflects this post-conventional reasoning.*

In summary, here's how Kohlberg's theory would play out in the "real world" of mass media work:

- At the pre-conventional level, do we basically do whatever the boss tells us to do, thinking that we will be penalized if we don't? Do we make special deals or promises with sources or clients, thinking that if we look out for them, they'll look out for us?
- At the conventional level, do we strive hard not to rock the boat at work, thinking that if we want to get along with our colleagues, we need to go along, or thinking

that we need to do whatever it takes to win recognition or prizes? Do we follow the rules, codes of ethics, or other professional standards merely because that's what good workers are supposed to do?

- At the post-conventional level, do we find ourselves asking whether we're doing the right thing for society in general, rather than just for ourselves, our co-workers, or folks we are in immediate contact with? Do we base our decisions on freely agreed upon moral principles, knowing the implications of adhering to a substantive moral philosophy, even if it entails breaking a conventional rule?

CAROL GILLIGAN'S ETHICS OF CARE
Augmenting Kohlberg

Critics have challenged both Kohlberg's philosophical assumptions and the methodologies of his social experimentations. Among his key critics was Harvard colleague Carol Gilligan, who noted that Kohlberg's research was exclusively with male subjects. Gilligan insisted that Kohlberg's theory does not recognize dimensions of moral development that are especially characteristic of females.

Gilligan's research showed that females do not fit the Kohlberg mold of moral stages because compassion, not justice, is a dominant ethic of women. Such a differentiation, she argued, leaves "caring women" permanently at the third or fourth stage—the conventional level—of Kohlberg's moral hierarchy. It ignores alternative criteria based on the importance of felt relationships, and emphasizes instead decision making based on justice and rules.

In a 1982 article, Gilligan maintained that:

> Beginning with Freud's theory that tied superego formation to castration anxiety, extending through Piaget's study of boys' conceptions of the rules of their games, and culminating in Kohlberg's derivation of six stages of moral development from research on adolescent males, the line of development has been shaped by the pattern of male experience and thought . . .
>
> The notion that moral development witnesses the replacement of the rule of brute force with the rule of law, bringing isolated and endangered individuals into a tempered connection with one another, then leads to the observation that women, less aggressive and thus less preoccupied with rules, are as a result less morally developed.
>
> (p. 201)

Gilligan buttressed her argument by drawing on psychological theories that have identified a strong bond between mother and daughter—a bond that imbues a primary value of protecting relationships and the caring that supports them. The same theories hold that a similar bond between father and son emphasizes rules and systems, and a disciplined orderliness that ensures greater control over their lives.

Other feminist moral psychologists have stressed the nature of "caring for" and "caring about." The first—captured in Gilligan's mother-daughter example—describes who or what we empathize with and provide direct care for. The second describes who or what we empathize with in a more abstract sense. Not surprisingly, some of the arguments insist that the truly morally developed individual—man or woman—cares *for* as well as *about* humanity in general.

Comparing the "Morality of Justice" with the "Morality of Care"

Media ethicist Deni Elliott (1991) spelled out significant differences between the theories of Kohlberg and Gilligan. Within Kohlberg's morality of justice, which uses "a language of rights that protects separation," Elliott noted that:

1. Individuals are defined as separate from one another.
2. Relationships are grounded in reciprocity.
3. Conflicting claims are resolved by invoking impartial rules or standards.
4. Morality is determined by whether each party was treated with equity.

Gilligan's "morality of care" uses a "language of responsibilities that sustains connection." Elliott noted that:

1. Individuals are defined as connected in relation to others.
2. Relationships are grounded in response to others on their terms.
3. Moral problems are considered as issues of relationship or response.
4. The morality of action is determined by whether relationships were maintained or restored.

Gilligan said people developing "the morality of care" move from care of self to care of others to a final, mature level of integrating the care of self and others. In a pattern that again shows the distinctions among pre-conventional, conventional, and post-conventional morality, Gilligan described the three positions as follows.

Position 1. Selfishness (orientation to individual survival): A person at this stage is concerned solely with herself, a self she perceives as powerless.

Returning to our blogger and PR case studies, we see that the arguments most representative of the "individual survival" and "powerlessness" position would be numbers 2 and 4. Several other justifications imply some selfishness and deference to authority, but 2 and 4 directly make the case.

Position 2. Goodness as giving to others (self-sacrifice): A person determines that "being good" entails sacrificing herself for the good of others. Since she perceives herself as good if she is being a good caretaker, she considers herself responsible for the actions of others.

Argument 9 is the clearest example of this line of thinking: doing whatever it takes to be a good team player. Another argument that appears to reflect Gilligan's second position is 5, with its implication of some sacrifice as the PR person. Several arguments suggest that as the PR person you should be willing to do whatever it takes to help your children and immediate family survive the plant's closing.

Position 3. Giving becomes a more social, global responsibility, and includes one's own welfare (nonviolence): At this level, the moral agent is no longer troubled by a perceived conflict of caring for self or caring for others. Once obligation to care for all persons is understood, it automatically includes the self. The person accepts nonviolence as the ultimate principle; being moral means minimizing harm and pain for everyone.

The final five arguments reflect this nonviolent, universal, caring perspective. Obviously, 17 states the case most directly, but several of the other arguments appear to resolve the conflicts between "care of self" and "care of others." Argument 16 is an especially telling statement about care: the competent professional can be proactive and seek to minimize harm before it occurs.

What would Gilligan's theory look like elsewhere in the media world?

- At the pre-conventional stages, do we as media practitioners and media consumers perceive ourselves as victims, powerless in a world that imposes decisions with no consideration of their impact on us? Do we treat our sources, subjects, or audiences in the same vein, assuming that they too are powerless? Do our entertainment programs and advertising and PR campaigns stereotype and objectify individuals or classes of society?
- At the conventional level, is self-sacrifice rewarded? Do we media workers take on extra assignments for little or no additional compensation, doing what we can to help our colleagues, subjects, and sources, all the while trying to balance the equally compelling demands of our own families and friends? Do we feel guilty when our efforts fall short of our self-imposed expectations? Do entertainment and persuasion media continually depict characters and stakeholders as self-sacrificing, struggling to cope with mini-dramas of 10-to-30 seconds (ads) or 30 minutes (dramas)?
- At the post-conventional level, do we focus on the broad goals of nurturing everyone, including ourselves, by sustaining a constant community of persons who deserve to be cared for and cared about? As journalists or documentarians, do we seek out and report stories that show community connectedness, stories of hope and non-violence? As persuaders, do we try to move public opinion away from its fixation on all the big and little things that are going wrong, and shift it toward solutions that have more general value?

Gilligan does not insist that morality is gender-based. In fact, she says justice and care are closely connected characteristics of morally mature people. She implies that we all should recognize and try to overcome inequality (lack of justice) and violence (lack of care), which work against both parties in an unequal relationship.

As Gilligan wrote: "While an ethic of justice proceeds from the premise of equality—that everyone should be treated the same—an ethic of care rests on the premise of nonviolence—that no one should be hurt" (1982, pp. 173–174). (Late in his career, Kohlberg incorporated some of Gilligan's argument when revising his theoretical framework; the revisions have resulted in women and men showing relatively similar scores on tests of moral development [Coleman & Wilkins, 2009, p. 43].)

MARY BELENKY
Women's Ways of Knowing

Gilligan's perspective was that women speak in "a different voice" when describing their ethical decision making. Feminist scholars have studied how "voice" emerges and changes. Their insights are helpful to students who want to self-monitor as they develop into competent, morally mature professionals. This literature also provides us with new ways of looking more deeply at the media environment, with its depictions of "who wins, who loses" in news, entertainment, and persuasion fare.

One of the most powerful discussions of this topic is by Mary Belenky and her colleagues, who wrote *Women's Ways of Knowing: The Development of Self, Voice, and Mind* (1986). Like others, they describe a hierarchical model of epistemological development. Their book outlined a moral and epistemological evolution from "silent" to "fully integrated" voices.

The book characterizes the development of self, voice, and mind by a series of five general positions, outlined in seven stages. The five positions are silence, received knowledge, subjective knowledge, procedural knowledge, and constructed knowledge.

1. Silent women, on the bottom rung of the *Women's Way of Knowing* ladder, tend to see life in terms of polarities. "Silent women have little awareness of their intellectual capabilities. They live—selfless and voiceless—at the behest of those around them. External authorities know the truth and are all-powerful" (p. 134). The silent women tended to be the youngest, least educated, and most disconnected (feeling "deaf and dumb" or "seen but not heard") in the authors' survey.

2. Received knowledge/listening to others describes women who defer to the authority of others. Authorities provide black-and-white answers to issues (similar to Perry's "dualism" stage). Women at this stage seek gratification in pleasing others, living up to external standards—sex-role stereotypes or second-rung status—while remaining selfless. There is little awareness of a centered self or a unique voice (similar to Gilligan's middle, "self-sacrifice" position).

3a. Subjective knowledge/inner voice thinkers are women who begin to see truth as subjective and personal. They begin to doubt external authority, particularly male authority. Multiple personal truths emerge, intuitively derived from "the still, small voice within." "Occasionally women distinguish between truth as *feelings* that come from within and *ideas* that come from without" (p. 69). People at this level turn from others and from the past—even sometimes rejecting science and scientists as "too objective"—and have a new sense of their powerful intuitions. They begin to assert authority and autonomy and forge new rules and boundaries for relationships, although they may have few tools for expressing themselves or persuading others to listen.

3b. Subjective knowledge/quest for self describes women's application of subjective knowledge toward a "new world," which they insist on shaping and directing on their own. They may break old relationships—including marriages and family ties—to seek new turf independently. They trust their intuitions and have a newfound energy and openness to novelty. "Inward watching and listening" are their tools for self-discovery. In their journey toward independence, however, they may not be grounded in a secure, integrated, and enduring self-concept. As a result, they may take out their frustration on others—particularly men. "Going it alone" has consequences, many of them negative. In general, however, this stage of awareness and development of voice provides a logical transition from the subjectivists' reliance on outside authority figures to the development of a truly integrated "voice," which is similar to Perry's conventional/relativism phases.

4a. Procedural knowledge/voice of reason is more complex than the received or subjectivist knower stages. Progress from the previous stage begins with skepticism about the infallibility of gut-level reasoning. Women realize that personal experience and intuitions can be deceptive. Knowledge is seen as a process honed and developed by authorities, "interested not just in *what* people think but in *how* people go about forming their opinions and feelings and ideas" (p. 97).

Knowing requires careful observation and analysis: "You must 'really look' and 'listen hard'" (p. 94). Objectivity is valued. There is an increased awareness that some truths are truer than others. The possibility of knowing things outside one's own experience allows a new respect for expertise that can become exaggerated. "Ways of looking" can become central, and a concern for *how* people go about forming their opinions, feelings, and ideas can take precedence over *what* people think. Women at this phase experience an increased sense of control: "The world becomes more manageable" (p. 96). Procedural knowers are practical, pragmatic problem solvers, with their feet firmly on the ground (p. 99).

4b. Procedural knowledge/separate and connected knowing takes two forms. Critical thinking and doubting the word of others are at the heart of "separate knowing," while empathy and care are essential for "connected knowing." In Kohlbergian terms, separate knowing emerges from autonomous experiences of the self and reciprocal, logical, tough-minded and justice-based relationships with others or with sources of knowledge. Separate knowers assume that everyone—including themselves—may be wrong; they are suspicious of ideas that "feel right" and examine ideas critically and objectively, regardless of their source (p. 104).

Although they engage in critical thinking, women at that phase tend to be uncomfortable with debate and argument (especially with authority figures) to resolve differences. In contrast with separate knowing, Belenky says that in connected knowing, empathy and sustained caring relationships are valued on their own terms. Connected knowers rely on historical and personal events to seek uniqueness, complexity, and connections. Their capacity to listen deeply to others provides many insights. They see others not in their own terms but in the others' terms (p. 113). Belenky notes that separate and connected knowing do not appear to be gender-specific, although evidence suggests that men are more likely than women to be "doubters," and women more likely than men to be "believers." As Belenky puts it, "believing" feels real to women, "perhaps because it is founded upon genuine care and because it promises to reveal the kind of truth they value—truth that is personal, particular, and grounded in firsthand experience" (p. 113). Connected knowers share small truths (a.k.a. "gossip") with one another. They refuse to judge, seeking rather to understand. They collaborate in nurturing groups and are "generous thinkers" who abide by "receptive rationality" (p. 121).

Overall, both separate and connected knowers tend to be oriented away from "the self." They accommodate either toward objective knowledge or knowledge gained from being connected with others, selflessly understanding others' ideas in terms other than their own. They do not yet have a single, unified "voice."

5. Constructed knowledge/integrating voices is the reasoning used by women at the highest stage of development. Each has developed an integrated, individual, and original voice. Belenky and her colleagues found that for the women they studied, the climb to this stage:

> began as an effort to reclaim the self by attempting to *integrate* knowledge that they felt intuitively was personally important with knowledge they had learned from others ... weaving together the strands of rational and emotive thought and ... integrating objective and subjective knowing.
>
> (p. 134)

Women in this stage, with a thorough self-examination, have successfully grappled with the pieces of themselves that seemed to be fragmented and contradictory. They deal comfortably with ambiguity, with conflicting role-based responsibilities, integrating rather than compartmentalizing "thought and feeling, home and work, self and other" (p. 137). They are open-minded, seeing truth in context, with rational rather than blind reliance upon "experts" and authority figures. They are passionate knowers, undergoing an intellectual renaissance. They "care for" and "care about" at the highest and most genuine levels of moral development. Their conversation includes "discourse and exploration, talking and listening, questions, argument, speculation, and sharing" (p. 144). They grapple with moral dilemmas by exploring them fully and openly, with sensitivity to situation and context. They believe in commitment and action. Ultimately, they listen to their own voices. And they want those voices to be heard and heeded.

As we have done with others, we can apply Belenky to the world of media work. In doing so, we would note the journey a young person—particularly a young woman—could take from being a silent victim to having a fully integrated, moral voice. We would note the comfort (reluctant, perhaps) she might feel while working in a highly structured, autocratic, moralizing workplace. We would then watch her begin to test her inner voice as she grows more independent. She might then base her judgments on the voice of reason, looking and listening hard before taking anything for granted from her colleagues, superiors, sources, clients, and others. She could integrate—or struggle with—notions of separate and connected learning. She could balance judgments based on Kohlberg's notions of justice with Gilligan's notions of care. Ultimately, she might become a fully integrated "knower," an open-minded, rational, highly competent communicator who truly cares for and cares about others.

The 18 statements about the blogger and PR person, at the outset of this chapter, show the steady progression from silent powerlessness to fully integrated, open-minded caring and justice seeking.

JAMES REST
The Four Components of Morality

University of Minnesota cognitive psychologist James Rest, his colleague Muriel Bebeau, and others spent 30 years integrating the various theories of moral development—particularly Kohlberg and Gilligan. Rest was a student of Gilligan who was concerned that she and Kohlberg were both right and wrong. He said they were right in seeking variables that determined moral decision making (he concluded that it was not one or the other, but *both* care and justice). But he said they were wrong in presuming a cause-effect relationship between moral sophistication or decision-making skills on the one hand and actual moral behavior on the other. Rest was particularly concerned that many people who scored at the highest stages of Kohlberg's moral development taxonomy, people with advanced moral reasoning skills, still behaved in extremely immoral ways. The disconnect between reasoning and behaving needed a good deal more investigation, Rest thought.

Rest and his colleagues—cognitive psychologists who no longer claim the clear distinction between cognitive (thinking) and affective (emotional) realms—created the Defining Issues Test (DIT) to measure moral development. The DIT was not gender biased, and it assessed differences across a wide range of professional groups. Their research focuses on moral sensitivity, moral judgment, moral motivation and commitment, and moral character and implementation—a far more eclectic agenda than other moral psychologists.

Kohlberg's stage and sequence theory uses *steps*, and is fairly rigid. Rest and his colleagues are more interested in *schema*, in the shifting distributions among/between stages and variables of moral development.

The DIT is a pencil-and-paper test of moral development; Kohlberg and Gilligan used lengthy interviews. Rest argues that the DIT overcomes some of the problems of Kohlberg and Gilligan. Data from more than 20,000 individuals indicate that he is correct.

Their four-component schema focuses on:

1. **Moral Sensitivity**: How do our actions affect others? How aware are we of the consequences of our behavior? How much empathy do we display? How sophisticated are our "role-taking" skills as we put ourselves in the shoes of others?
2. **Moral Judgment**: Faced with choices, which line of action is more morally justifiable?
3. **Moral Motivation and Commitment**: How do various values compete with one another? Can we effectively sift and sort through the competing moral and non-moral values?
4. **Moral Character and Implementation**: What kind of job do we do in walking the walk, having ego strength, perseverance, backbone, toughness, strength of conviction, and moral courage? (Rest & Narvaez, 1994; Bebeau, 1998)

Because Rest's schema is so much more comprehensive than the theories of the other moral psychologists introduced above, we conclude this chapter with a closer look at the four components. We will connect Rest's theories to the blogging and PR case studies, looking at both the reasoning processes and the behaviors that may result from different arguments.

Moral sensitivity involves the awareness of how our actions affect others. It involves being aware of different possible lines of action and how each line of action could affect all parties concerned. It involves imaginatively constructing possible scenarios, and knowing cause-consequence chains of events in the real world. It requires empathy and role-taking skills. It also involves seeing things more abstractly—from legal, institutional, and national perspectives—to develop interpretive abilities needed in life and work settings. It means being able to accurately and appropriately figure in one's emotional responses to repugnant situations. All this is learned from sensitivity training, through real or hypothetical situations that require us to identify and "make vivid" the situations of others, and through peer mediation and conflict resolution.

The Freedonia blogger and PR person demonstrate low levels of moral sensitivity when they argue from self interest—as in the first five arguments. Most of the 18 arguments demonstrate an increasing degree of empathy, role-taking skills, and abstract reasoning. The final few arguments show the blogger and PR practitioner downplaying their personal agendas in the calculus, using insights that incorporate various theories of moral philosophy. Rest and his colleagues would applaud your efforts to look at these hypothetical cases from a variety of perspectives; they would say you have been working on your moral sensitivity when you go beyond the simple, pat answer to the cases.

Moral judgment entails being aware of possible lines of action and how different stakeholders would be affected by each decision. It then judges which line of action is more morally justifiable. Young people learn to distinguish right from wrong—society's rules.

Older people are generally able to:

- learn pertinent rules and professional codes
- state the criteria for judging the adequacy of a moral argument
- distinguish a well-reasoned argument from weaker ones
- make morally defensible decisions
- apply the ideals of great moral thinkers to current moral problems
- distinguish the premises and conclusions of an argument
- understand the distinctions between truth and validity in logical argument
- uncover unstated premises in an argument
- test hypotheses systematically
- identify the moral assumptions of various moral theories
- apply moral theories to specific cases.

Have you weighed the pros and cons of various resolutions to the case studies, or were you satisfied with your initial thoughts about what you would do as the blogger and PR person? In retrospect, do the arguments at the beginning of the list seem less justifiable than the arguments near the end of the list? Do the latter arguments motivate you to think of an expanding number of stakeholders, and the interests each of them might have in a final decision you would make? Do the professional codes of ethics help you choose, or do you have to make some of your own decisions, based on moral philosophy? Have you noted logical and moral weaknesses in any of the arguments on the list?

Moral motivation and commitment deals with the importance given to moral values in competition with other values. Problems occur when one ranks moral values lower than other values, such as when values such as winning, meeting a deadline, or making a profit become more important than treating all people with respect, keeping promises, or telling the truth.

Young people do well to develop an individual moral identity and a sense of rootedness in a community. More mature people distinguish between and prioritize values, develop a professional moral identity, clarify the social contract that undergirds their profession, and clarify beliefs that lead each individual to be an autonomous moral decision maker.

Even before exploring moral and non-moral values—detailed in Chapter 6—you've undoubtedly had to sort through competing values when playing the role of the blogger and PR person. Some of those values are unabashedly moral, such as truth telling/honesty, keeping promises/loyalty, or standing up for your beliefs/courage. Others tend to be non-moral, pragmatic, or craft-based values, such as beating the competition, or earning more money, or living a comfortable life, or gaining social recognition.

As you look at the 18 arguments, which values motivated you? How did you resolve the conflicts between multiple values—in particular, the values of loyalty and honesty, or honesty and money? It's important to remember that these are all values with worthwhile claims to make, and it's up to us to choose among them. Indeed, it wouldn't be a dilemma if it didn't entail a values clash.

Moral character and implementation involves ego strength, perseverance, backbone, toughness, strength of conviction, and courage. People may be morally sensitive, may make good moral judgments, and may place high priority on moral values. But people who wilt under pressure, are easily distracted or discouraged, or are weak-willed wimps ultimately fail because of deficiency in this fourth component of morality. Young people develop this ideal trait by focusing on impulse control, self-discipline, self-efficacy, persistence, and resistance to peer pressure. More mature people develop self-regulation and implement abilities needed for effective moral action. They develop skills in conflict resolution, develop interpersonal skills, practice active listening, and have strong written and oral communication skills.

Now the rubber meets the road. No matter which argument we posed, no matter which theory or values had the most appeal, no matter how sophisticated our reasoning process, the whole thing has just been a theoretical exercise if we don't do *ethics. Our actions speak louder than our words.*

SUMMARY AND CONCLUSIONS

This chapter has introduced perspectives on how we grow morally, intellectually, professionally, and personally. The perspectives vary but have interesting commonalities. The progression from pre-conventional to conventional to post-conventional thinking and decision making is neither absolute nor immutable. There are substantial reasons for our thinking and behaving to reflect each of the phases, stages, and sequences described in this chapter. Many of those judgments and actions are individualistic, but most occur in the pressures of a workplace and community environment.

Tracing our decision making as the blogger and PR practitioner may help us test different models and justifications for thinking what we think, doing what we do. The following practical applications and case studies may help us refine our moral reasoning skills and our willingness to walk the moral walk when facing the struggles we inevitably will undergo in our professional lives as we seek to become independent thinkers and autonomous decision makers. Those struggles will help us in refining, articulating, and acting upon notions of empathy, justice, and care. The theories of moral psychology may help us discern which lines of reasoning are morally justified, based on higher levels of moral development, and which are morally problematic.

When we do a good job with this, we go a long way toward answering the important question: "Who wins, who loses?"

Chapter 5 applies this chapter's theoretical insights into moral development and empathy when it considers two extremely important issues in the media ethics environment: loyalty and diversity.

CHAPTER VOCABULARY

Note: Definitions are available at this book's companion website.

- contextual relativism
- conventional phase of moral development
- Defining Issues Test (DIT)
- dualism
- empathy
- epistemology
- moral development

- moral psychology
- morality of care
- morality of justice
- post-conventional phase of moral development
- pre-conventional phase of moral development
- social contract

PRACTICAL APPLICATIONS

1. Think about a "reality" television show you watch on a regular basis, such as *Survivor*. At what stages of moral development do most of the characters act? What stages of development seem to work best for players to survive? What stages are more likely to lead to players being voted off the show?

2. Consider how journalists, bloggers, and talk show hosts report and critique politics. What stages of moral development do they tend to reflect? Why? What changes might you propose in political discourse?

3. Take another look at a code of ethics that is most pertinent to your mass media specialty. At what levels of moral development does the code seem to be written? Do you think that level is appropriate? Why or why not? How would you improve it?

4. If you did the "Practical Application" in Chapter 2 and wrote your own code of ethics, go back and consider it through the prisms of moral development presented in this chapter. At what level did it seem to be written? You might want to rewrite your code so it captures different (and perhaps more sophisticated) levels of moral development and "voices."

5. How feasible does it seem for you to reason and act at the post-conventional level? What realities in the workplace and in your personal life may have impeded you from reaching that stage?

■ ■ ■

CASE STUDIES

The case studies that follow do not ask you to reach conclusions. The purpose is to let you see how loyalties—and decisions—can change based upon your level of moral development and the extent to which you identify with "others" in your society. Answer the questions by focusing on Tables 4.1 through 4.4, which show levels of moral development as described by Kohlberg, Gilligan, Perry, and Belenky.

■ ■ ■

Table 4.1 How Kohlberg's levels of development affect ethical decision making

	Level	Description*	Who wins	Who loses	Your decision	Your justification
Pre-conventional	Stage 1	• ego • fear of punishment				
Pre-conventional	Stage 2	• individualism • "use and be used"				
Conventional	Stage 3	• conformity • "being a good girl/boy"				
Conventional	Stage 4	• rule-following • following organizational or societal norms				
post-conventional	Stage 5	• law abiding • social contract • individual rights				
post-conventional	Stage 6	• universal principles • justice seeking • conscience-driven				

* Refer to the book for a more complete description of this level of development

Table 4.2: How Gilligan's levels of "ethics of care" affect ethical decision making

	Description*	Who wins	Who loses	Your decision	Your justification
1—Pre-conventional					
2—Conventional					
3—Post-conventional					

* Refer to the book for a more complete description of this level of development

Table 4.3: How Perry's levels of development affect ethical decision making

	Level	Description*	Who wins	Who loses	Your decision	Your justification
Pre-conventional—Modifying dualism	Position 1	Black and white				
	Position 2	Uncertainty as fraud, or an academic exercise				
	Position 3	Uncertainty is temporary				
Conventional—Relativism	Position 4	It's all about opinions				
	Position 5	Everything is relative				
	Position 6	Orientation to a relativistic, uncertain world				
ostte-conventional—Evolving of Commitment	Position 7	Commitment is begun				
	Position 8	Implications of commitment are explored				
	Position 9	Commitments are lived				

* Refer to the book for a more complete description of this level of development

Table 4.4: How Belenky's "women's ways of knowing" affect ethical decision making

	Level	Description*	Who wins	Who loses	Your decision	Your justification
Silence	Stage 1	We live at the behest of people around us				
Received knowledge	Stage 2a	We listen to authorities who provide answers				
Subjective knowledge	Stage 3a	Inner voice: We see truth as subjective and personal				
	Stage 3b	Quest for self: We work to shape and direct our own world				
Procedural knowledge	Stage 4a	Voice of reason: Like 3b, but we see that gut-level reasoning is not sufficient				
	Stage 4b	Separate and connected knowing: Merge both critical thinking and empathy				
Constructed knowledge	Stage 5	Integrating voices: Our own voice emerges as we deal with ambiguity and conflicting roles and responsibilities				

* Refer to the book for a more complete description of this level of development

CASE 4.1 **Journalism: Publish or Not: Changing Stages, Changing Sides?**

You are an editor with Freedonia Media International (FMI), your nation's largest wire service with 1,000 domestic clients. Freedonia has long been at war with a smaller nation thousands of miles away, and FMI has long had reporters and photographers embedded with Freedonia military units to document the action for the 1,000 newspapers that are your clients.

A week ago, an FMI photographer was on a routine mission with the Freedonia military, for a magazine-length story about difficulties encountered by such units. The unit was hit by an ambush, and your photographer captured photos of an enlisted man receiving first aid by fellow soldiers minutes after being hit by a rifle shot. The photos show a slight hint of blood, but you've seen worse watching PG-rated war movies.

The soldier died on an operating room table a few hours after the photo was taken. You followed military protocol, which forbids publishing photos until the next of kin are notified. Moreover, you made sure an editor showed a photo to the family before releasing it to your clients.

The family says it does not want you to publish the photo, and both military public affairs personnel and high-ranking Freedonia Department of Defense officials have called you to ask that you respect the family's wishes.

➤ **You feel pulled by both sides. You appreciate the point of view of the military and the family—your father was an officer for ten years, although you never served. But you also feel the need to tell the story.**

Questions to Answer

1. For each stop along Kohlberg's list of moral development stages (Table 4.1), describe the competing interests, your decision if you acted at that stage, and the justification.
2. Now consider the same case study, this time using Gilligan's "ethics of care" orientation (Table 4.2) to defend decisions both to publish the photo and not to publish the photo.
3. At what point do the Kohlberg and Gilligan developmental approaches intersect?
4. Which approach felt more comfortable to you?
5. Imagine that you were the editor of the hometown newspaper of the soldier who died: How might this affect your decision?

■ ■ ■

CASE 4.2 **New Media: Paying to Reveal a Product**

At www.freedonialive.com, you are always on the lookout to write about happenings at Mango Inc., a maker of high-tech equipment. The company is very secretive about its highly sought-after products, which draw a great deal of consumer and media interest. You know a new version of its popular device is in the works, but the company won't say anything about it.

One day you receive an email asking you whether you'd be willing to pay to take possession of what the writer claims is the next version of its new device, which a Mango employee accidentally left behind in a public place. The cost is $5,000.

The law suggests that it's a misdemeanor for failing to return lost property when you know its owner. A crafty prosecutor may also be able to make a case that you acted as a "fence" by receiving stolen property. And the company could file a legal claim that you stole their intellectual property.

On the other hand, you know that news about the product will drive millions of people to your site—and if "news" is defined as what people want to know about, you'll be breaking news.

➤ **What do you do?**

Questions to Answer

1. For each stop along Kohlberg's list of moral development stages (Table 4.1), describe the competing interests, your decision if you acted at that stage, and the justification.

2. Now consider the same case study, this time using Gilligan's "ethics of care" orientation (Table 4.2) to defend decisions both to pay for access to the phone or not to take the offer.

3. At what point do the Kohlberg and Gilligan developmental approaches intersect?

4. One of the arguments that might be made in your defense is that you are a journalist, so some rules about "theft" might not apply to you. Do you agree? How does your answer fit into a discussion about moral development?

■ ■ ■

CASE 4.3 **Public Relations: A Stealthy Way to Cause a Scoop**

As a public relations representative for TinyPhone Inc., you want free media to write about an upcoming cellular phone you plan to release on the market. Your company runs a distant second in the phone business, which means you have to try harder to generate media attention for your phones, which are technically as good but just don't have the "sex appeal" of your key competitor's phones.

You have an idea: A key tech journalist is coming to your office next week for an interview on a different subject. You could make sure your desk is fairly clean, except for a few family photos and a folder labeled "Project Zeta." You could have someone call you, so you'd have an excuse to leave the room for a few minutes.

During that time, you can hope that the nosy journalist opens the folder and reads all the details and insight into the upcoming cell phone. You know the journalist could take notes, take a picture of the information on his cell phone, and give the information to someone else at his office to post online.

You know that the stealthiness of the information would make it seem like a "scoop" for the journalist, which raises the news value. The journalist would be praised for driving the additional traffic to the site, because other media outlets would quote the original source.

Moreover, it would be a "win–win" because both of you could deny being the source of the information.

➤ **Does this seem like a good idea?**

Questions to Answer

1. For each stop along Perry's list of moral development stages (Table 4.3), describe the competing interests, your decision if you acted at that stage, and the justification. Not all levels may have a position.

2. Now consider the same case study, this time using Belenky's "ways of knowing" orientation (Table 4.4) to defend decisions both to go through with the plan or not to do that because you think it's wrong.

3. Which approach felt more comfortable to you? Why?

4. What would you do if the journalist asked you: "Why did you leave this on your desk so I could see it? Were you trying to trick me?"

■ ■ ■

CASE 4.4 **Advertising: Drop the Pitchman?**

You are in charge of advertising for an athletic apparel company that sells billions of dollars of products to both men and women. Your multiple advertising campaigns rarely cross gender lines; that is, you hire famous male athletes to represent the company in ads aimed at men and broadcast during programming aimed at men. The same goes for women who endorse products aimed at women.

One of your key male athletes is famous because he has led his team to championships while winning individual honors. He's been terrific as a pitchman, doing everything you've asked him to do. You have a new campaign focusing on him set to start in six weeks, at the start of the sport's new season.

But then you receive news reports that he has been accused of boorish behavior toward women. No arrests have occurred, and no charges are pending, but there's an undercurrent of negative stories and comment about him. On one hand, you may be worried that keeping him could affect sales of women's products, if groups protest his continued use. On the other hand, your campaigns were designed to keep him away from women's products (and, therefore, mostly female audiences) long before the news broke.

➤ **Do you keep him as a pitchman, hide him until it blows over, or continue plans for the new campaign?**

Questions to Answer

1. For each stop along Kohlberg's list of moral development stages (Table 4.1), describe the competing interests, your decision if you acted at that stage, and the justification.

2. Now consider the same case study, this time using Gilligan's orientation (Table 4.2) to defend decisions about whether to use the athlete as planned, to delay the campaign, or to dismiss him.

3. As mentioned in the text, Kohlberg and Gilligan differ about how men and women develop morally. What, if any, key differences do you see when using these different approaches to tracking moral development for this case, which may cross gender lines in significance?

4. Which approach felt more comfortable to you? Why?

5. If you choose to keep this athlete as a pitchman, what legal or moral line must he cross in order for you to drop him?

■ ■ ■

CASE 4.5 **Entertainment: Send Adolescents to Fly Island?**

You are a new assistant for a production company that makes fairly tame reality television shows, and the boss calls a staff meeting to describe plans for a new show that puts a new twist on an old idea: Select 30 adolescents, ages 9 to 14, put them on a deserted island, and film them building a new community and governing themselves.

The participants would be shown working, cooking, and making decisions about their lives. While adults (the film crew, plus medical personnel and a child psychologist) would be there, they would not appear on camera and would give participants as much latitude as possible to make their own decisions. While parents would sign legal agreements to absolve the company (including you) of liability, participants could go home at any time with no questions asked.

The boss figures that the show will attract viewers who include both youngsters and adults, since nearly all of them read *Lord of the Flies* in school. In fact, the proposed name of the show—*Fly Island*—pays homage to the William Golding novel.

The boss tells you that, in order to meet state laws regarding the use of children in productions, the series will be filmed not in Freedonia (which has strict child-labor laws) but in nearby Sylvania, which has fewer restrictions on the hours and working conditions for people younger than 17. Simply put, the show's production would be legal.

The boss predicts that thousands of children will apply to be a cast member, even though they would miss school and go nearly six weeks without seeing their parents. A child psychologist would be included in cast selection.

You have concerns, and not just because you've also read *Lord of the Flies*. In the back of your mind you wonder about the mindset of parents who would let their children participate, as well as whether this would be good for the children involved. You also wonder what lessons it might teach viewers. You wonder whether the show will exploit the children for your company's profits, or whether it could teach them (and viewers) lessons about human interaction.

Before you can express these concerns, your boss says you will be part of the crew on the island hired to help the children. (You have no training in taking care of others; you don't even have a goldfish.) If all goes well, you are promised a shot at moving up in the company.

➤ **Do you say anything? What do you do about your conflicting concerns related to the job, the children, yourself, and society?**

Questions to Answer

1. For each stop along Perry's levels of intellectual and moral development (Table 4.3), describe the competing interests, your decision if you acted at that stage, and the justification.

2. Now consider the same case study, this time using Belenky's "women's ways of knowing" orientation (Table 4.4) to defend decisions both to take part in *Fly Island* and to decide not to take part.

3. How do the Perry and Belenky developmental approaches intersect?

4. Which approach felt more comfortable to you?

5. What would you ultimately do in this situation? What would you do if your 12-year-old sibling wanted to take part?

6. What, if any, special ethical complications exist because children are involved? Would your thinking change if the participants were adult? Why or why not?

■ ■ ■

Loyalty and Diversity

INTRODUCTION

THIS CHAPTER links two issues of increasing import-ance in mass communication: loyalty and diversity. These philosophical issues have pragmatic ramifica-tions as we ask and try to answer the question, "Who wins, who loses?"

Loyalty and diversity cause us to ask: Who deserves our allegiance and respect, and to whom are we obligated? The simple answer is that *everyone* deserves to be treated with respect. Regardless of our media specialty, we owe allegiance to our sources, subjects, audiences, employers, and co-workers.

Of course, because simple answers often lead to overly narrow, gut-level responses, we should ratchet up the discourse by asking and answering tougher questions: What does respect by media personnel look like, and what does disrespect look like? Do all sources, subjects, audiences, employers, and co-workers deserve *equal* respect? If not, how do we morally justify showing more loyalty to one than to another? Do the under-represented segments of society—the "voiceless"—deserve special treatment? If not, why not? If so, how do we make those judgment calls?

This chapter argues that:

- throughout history, loyalty has been defined as a somewhat problematic virtue; we draw distinctions among loyalty, values, and principles
- we deal with many objects of loyalty: sentimental and non-sentimental loyalties; reciprocal and non-reciprocal relationships
- when loyalty is tested, it may be appropriate to shift loyalties
- loyalty is related to moral development and the expansion of empathy
- concerns over diversity and stereotyping are, at their base, concerns over loyalty and empathy
- media struggle with ways to portray an increasingly diverse world accurately and respectfully.

This chapter explores the issues through case studies and a combination of philosophic and practical reasoning. The diversity section was written by Eric Deggans, veteran *St. Petersburg Times* media critic and author of the popular blog, "The Feed."

ON LOYALTY

What do we mean by loyalty? Some scholars limit discussions of loyalty to "what we owe one another." They talk in terms of "allegiance" or "commitment" or "obligation." They are concerned primarily about loyalty to people and secondarily about loyalty to institutions. The stakeholders include (but are not limited) to ourselves, our family and friends, our colleagues, our local community, our professional community, our country, and to the individuals and groups that compose all of humanity.

Other scholars define loyalty much more broadly. In addition to the just-mentioned stakeholders, these scholars also embrace commitments to brands, principles, ideas, ideals, ideologies, and values—almost "anything to which one's heart can become attached or devoted" (Konvitz, 1973, p. 108). This view says we have loyalty not only to human stakeholders, but also to a business, craft, or profession; to religious or political or socioeconomic bodies and to the theories underlying them; and to abstract moral and non-moral values such as truth, happiness, freedom, competition, and success. Along the way we should be loyal to the very notion of loyalty (Royce, 1908). In short, loyalty can be owed to every one and every thing.

The authors of this textbook prefer the former perspective. We find it helpful when "doing ethics" to separate personal loyalty from notions of principles and values. That preference reveals itself in three of our six guiding questions, as we sift through "Who wins, who loses?" "What's it worth?" and "Who's whispering in your ear?" When we ask who wins or loses, we think of loyalty as a matter of our obligations "to whom" rather than "to what." When we ask what something is worth, we are engaged in values inquiry. When we defer to the tribal elders whispering in our ears, our focus is on understanding and applying moral principles. "Doing ethics" becomes a more manageable enterprise when we don't conflate these three lines of inquiry.

A Brief History of Loyalty

Loyalty has always been an important consideration, but only lately has it attracted the attention of moral philosophers. History's earliest plot lines are filled with stories of loyalty and disloyalty, of fidelity and infidelity, of relationships sealed and broken. The Old Testament includes case studies on loyalty and fidelity. Loyalty to God was non-negotiable and rewarded, disloyalty was punished, and loyalty to one's family and tribe was demanded. Similarly, Socrates' choice to accept the death sentence imposed by the fathers of Athens was a matter of loyalty: The philosopher remained loyal to his discipline and his fellow philosophers and to his God, even if it meant he was signing his own death warrant by appearing disloyal to Athenian lawmakers. Through the Middle Ages, the emphasis on single-minded loyalty continued unabated in the Western world, as seen in tales of King Arthur and other knights and vassals, and Robin Hood and his merry band. Similarly, in China, stories of second-century military general Guan Yu's loyalty are told in *Romance of the Three Kingdoms*, written in the 1400s. He is still revered today, and his stories remain in print (Guanzgong & Roberts, 2005).

Among philosophers, Thomas Hobbes (1588–1679) may have broken the tradition of seeing loyalty as a single-minded devotion, when he claimed that people should have multiple loyalties. In his 1651 work, *Leviathan*, Hobbes said developing a social contract based on loyalty is the only way to establish and maintain a society. Without loyalty, people would resort to their natural and base instincts—selfishness, competitiveness, aggressiveness, etc.—and exist in a state of "war of every one against every one." (The most famous quote from *Leviathan* is Hobbes's description of life as "solitary, poor, nasty, brutish, and short.") His bottom line: "Laws of nature" or moral imperatives dictate various kinds of cooperative behavior, and self-preservation has to be factored into the equation.

Other and more refined perspectives on loyalty have emerged in the past century. One of the most influential writers on the subject was theologian Josiah Royce (1855–1916). The Harvard professor described loyalty as the "willing and practical and thoroughgoing devotion of a person to a cause" (Royce, 1908, p. 17). In his famous book, *The Philosophy of Loyalty*, he said a loyal individual should be so possessed by a cause that he or she would be able to say, "I am the servant of this cause, its reasonable, its willing, its devoted instrument, and being such, I have neither eyes to see nor tongue to speak save as this cause shall command." This single-minded devotion seems reminiscent of Biblical and medieval writings, but Royce saw it as a complex virtue that promoted self-realization. However, the obedience demanded by Royce implies that true loyalty works best in a closed-minded, authority-driven society governed by hierarchical role relationships. Such a system would seem to minimize individual autonomy, despite Royce's insistence that loyalty is essential to morality.

Alasdair MacIntyre (1984) built upon Royce's argument in maintaining that the "good life" is possible only when we focus on notions of community, virtues, narrative, traditions—and loyalty. Patriotism was high on MacIntyre's list of "loyalty-exhibiting virtues," although numerous philosophers have called patriotism a "dubious virtue" (Kleinig, 2007; Baron, 2001, p. 1028).

Evolutionary biologist James Q. Wilson described loyalty as a genetically transmitted adaptive mechanism, a felt attachment to others that has survival value (1993). In this sense, loyalty—even self-sacrificial loyalty—is directed primarily to group survival.

While it appears that loyalty is a virtue, a deeper look at the literature suggests this is not necessarily the case. Much of the recent discussion of loyalty focuses on how problematic loyalty can be. We praise the faithful friend but wonder about someone who protects a criminal. We admire the loyal worker but are conflicted about the whistleblower's motivations. We credit people who work to support their professional community but worry when their loyalty undercuts the greater public interest. And so it goes. As the *Encyclopedia of Ethics* says, loyalty is not innocuous (Baron, 2001, p. 1027). Misplaced loyalty, the absence of loyalty, disloyalty, and fickleness may be vices, but loyalty in and of itself is not necessarily a virtue.

The claims of some ancient and modern thinkers—Biblical and medieval writers, Royce, and to a lesser extent, MacIntyre—can be challenged for their seemingly arbitrary nature. Should we ever choose a cause, or show loyalty, that demands single-minded devotion? Is it healthy? Can we be loyal to a bad cause? Nazi official Albert Speer, for instance, ultimately concluded that he had abdicated moral responsibility for his evil actions because he had been so absolutely devoted to Hitler (Baron, 2001). If we have blind loyalty, can we ever be open-minded enough to question that loyalty or to consider alternatives? Can we be so deeply rooted into our family, friends, workplace, university, community, or nation-state that we fail to recognize alternative and generalized loyalties? If we're in the majority, does that mean the minority is disloyal? How much are we permitted to do in the name of loyalty, and how much are we morally required to do?

> When an organization wants you to do right, it asks for your integrity; when it wants you to do wrong, it demands your loyalty.
> —Anonymous, cited by Kleinig, 2007

We ponder these questions when exploring loyalty dilemmas in everyday life and in the media ethics environment. We wonder how much of a virtue loyalty is, or whether it can lead us into conflicts of interest. We wonder whether loyalty is unconditional or relative. We wonder who deserves our loyalty, and when it is morally permissible or morally mandatory to shift loyalties.

Objects of Loyalty

The real world provides plenty of reasons to make deals, exchange favors, and build special relationships. Most of us feel the need to care for, and care about, our families, friends, and others who care about us. Professionals have contractual obligations to clients. Subordinates have obligations to their bosses different from obligations to the general public, and bosses owe their subordinates considerations that do not extend beyond the office arena. Lobbyists and politicians make deals supposedly in the interest of citizens. If more good than harm emerges from these special relationships, many moral arguments can justify reciprocity. But those justifications should be clear, rational, and transparent.

Political consultant James Carville put a tantalizing twist on the egoistic theory of loyalty, calling it a zero-sum game of winners and losers. In *Stickin': The Case for Loyalty*

(2000), he argued that "sticking with" one person means "sticking it to" another. The argument makes some sense in the political world, but it strikes us as somewhat warped and out of sync with professional ethics (Scanlon, 1998).

It may be helpful to distinguish between sentimental and unsentimental loyalty. We show sentimental loyalty when we bond with individuals or groups simply because we like them, or in gratitude because they have been good to us. Voluntary associations based on genuine affection can lead to strong and enduring feelings and commitments. Violations of personal trust, infidelity, and fickleness can harm those relationships.

On the other hand, loyalty can be unsentimental and practical. Media ethicist Louis Day, who interchanged the words "loyalty," "obligation," and "allegiance," wrote that marketplace loyalty "is not always based on genuine affection but is more often a reflection of a feeling of obligation" (Day, 2006, p. 180). Those obligations, which philosophers would call "particularistic," tend to be conditional and transitory. Doctors go to great lengths to care for individual patients; lawyers zealously argue for their clients. These practical behaviors come with the professional territory. In a broader sense, the medical community is trying to improve health across the board, and lawyers are trying to maintain a professional advocacy system in which justice is expected to prevail. In short, while professionals may display loyalty to specific stakeholders, their more enduring commitment is to their professional calling. When they do so they are kindred spirits with Socrates, who chose hemlock over disloyalty.

The world of mass media appears driven by both sentimental and unsentimental loyalties. Individual journalists and their news organizations frequently demonstrate how much they care for and care about individual stakeholders—the child who needs an organ transplant, the students at impoverished schools desperate for good textbooks, the unemployed, the homeless, crime victims, etc. Public relations and advertising personnel, talk show hosts, and producers of documentaries often display genuine affection toward individuals and groups whose causes they embrace. Do we doubt the sincerity of Oprah Winfrey, Glenn Beck, Rush Limbaugh, or Keith Olbermann? While this sentimental loyalty may be admirable and might lead to some good results, it can be problematic. Sentimental loyalties have been misplaced if resources and public attention are focused on quick-fix individual cases rather than systemic problems that cannot be resolved without demanding sustained efforts and resources. And are sentimental loyalties virtuous when they are based on prejudices?

Medical and legal professionals rely on unsentimental loyalties to see "the big picture," and so should media practitioners. Of course advertisers and public relations people promote the causes of their individual clients, and journalists try to minimize harm and to protect their anonymous or vulnerable sources. Advertisers and PR practitioners work diligently for clients who want their messages to trump competitors' messages in the battle for public opinion. They are saying, "So long as you've signed on as a client, you will receive the unsentimental loyalty of this agency." Reporters and editors show unsentimental loyalty to their news sources and subjects. They are saying, "Our relationships are not based on friendship, but on a certain utility: You tell me what you are trying to promote or what you are willing to reveal, and I'll decide whether to put your story out for public consumption." The bigger picture reveals that they are advocating loyalty to a system—the adversarial system of competing persuasive messages in advertising and PR; the system or definitions of news.

Mass communicators' ultimate loyalty should be to the public, because high-quality competitive promotions and well-told stories on important topics will enhance public opinion and collective decision making. Moreover, the systems created by mass communicators should focus on values that show loyalty to the public. Box 5.1 shows what mass media codes of ethics say about loyalties.

Loyalty and Moral Development

Loyalty, like empathy and moral development, expands in an ever-widening arc. It begins with loyalty to ourselves, then to people in a position to directly punish or reward us (bosses, colleagues, subordinates, sources, subjects, clients), then to our professional and local communities, then to society and posterity in general. The lists by two leading media ethicists reflect this arc, as they describe loyalty to individual conscience, loyalty to "objects of moral judgment," loyalty to financial supporters, loyalty to the institution, loyalty to professional colleagues, and loyalty to society (Christians et al., 2008; Day, 2006). In this sense the development of loyalty mirrors the development of morality, as described in Chapter 4. However—and this is a crucial point—loyalty can be morally justified at each and every step along the way.

There is little to criticize about being loyal to yourself, especially if you are driven by self-awareness, self-respect, and an articulated conscience that considers the needs of others. Conscience is not the same as egoism, as seen in the quote: "I couldn't live with myself if I had done such-and-such!" This is akin to what philosopher Ayn Rand had in mind in her novels *The Fountainhead* (1943) and *Atlas Shrugged* (1957), and in her essay *The Virtue of Selfishness* (1964), in which she argued that it is generally ethically justifiable when people act in their own self-interest. On the other hand, it is hardly morally justifiable when people are totally self-interested, self-centered, and act with hedonistic loyalty that disregards the needs of anyone and everyone else.

Similarly, it is appropriate to demonstrate loyalty to your peer group, boss, and people you rely upon to do your job well, so long as you have more than a non-moral "use and be used" or "tit-for-tat" relationship.

A fixation on reciprocal loyalty—"If you take care of me, I'll take care of you"—reflects a pre-conventional stage of moral development. (Remember Kohlberg's Level 2 from the previous chapter?) Nevertheless, it is frequently obvious in the contemporary media business world. Many of this book's case studies raise the issue: When your bosses aren't loyal, why should you be? If you are typical of today's college students and young adults, you'll likely have many employers, sets of bosses, and colleagues throughout your career. Indeed, you are likely to work in more than one profession. Given this, why make permanent commitments, and why expect others to be committed to you? Why shouldn't your loyalties be tentative and conditional?

Box 5.1 | EXAMPLES FROM MEDIA CODES ON LOYALTY

Journalism

From the Society of Professional Journalists' Code of Ethics:

Journalists should be free of obligation to any interest other than the public's right to know.

Journalists should:

- avoid conflicts of interest, real or perceived
- remain free of associations and activities that may compromise integrity or damage credibility
- deny favored treatment to advertisers and special interests and resist their pressure to influence news coverage.

Public Relations

From the Public Relations Society of America Member Code of Ethics:

Advocacy. We serve the public interest by acting as responsible advocates for those we represent.

Independence. We provide objective counsel to those we represent.

Loyalty. We are faithful to those we represent, while honoring our obligation to serve the public interests.

Advertising and Marketing

From the American Association of Advertising Agencies Standards of Practice:

We hold that a responsibility of advertising agencies is to be a constructive force in business.

We hold that, to discharge this responsibility, advertising agencies must recognize an obligation, not only to their clients, but to the public, the media they employ and to each other.

From the American Marketing Association's Ethical Norms and Values for Marketers:

As marketers, we recognize that we not only serve our organizations but also act as stewards of society in creating, facilitating and executing the transactions that are part of the greater economy. In this role, marketers are expected to embrace the highest professional ethical norms and the ethical values implied by our responsibility toward multiple stakeholders (e.g., customers, employees, investors, peers, channel members, regulators and the host community).

FIGURE 5.1 | Concentric circles of loyalty

A pragmatic answer is that the more loyalty you show, the more likely it is that others will be loyal to you. However, the pragmatic answer is not always the morally mature one. Tough as it may be, the better option is to display—and to feel—loyalty to something greater than your immediate surroundings. It is praiseworthy to demonstrate loyalty, even in the abstract, to people you may never meet and from cultures distinct from your own: "I want to leave my campsite better than I found it, out of loyalty to my grandchildren and people around the world who might be remotely affected by my carbon footprint."

WHEN LOYALTIES COLLIDE IN FREEDONIA

The question is not merely whether we should be loyal. The answer is obvious: We should factor loyalty somewhere in our moral decision making. It is a key to finding out who wins, who loses, and where on the win/loss continuum the best resolution might lie. The problem occurs when multiple parties have a legitimate moral claim on our loyalty.

This is seen very clearly in the two cases from Chapter 1. If you own www.freedonia live.com or are public affairs officer for the Freedonia National Paper Corp., to whom do you owe primary loyalty, and to whom do you owe secondary loyalties? It is important to define the conflicting loyalties before reaching a conclusion about your professional and personal dilemma. What is expected of you by virtue of needing to put food on your table and a roof over your head, or by being a parent, sibling, friend, and member of a wider community? Similarly, by virtue of being an independent blogger or an NPC employee, what explicit and implicit promises have you made to be a "good worker"? As a blogger, what loyalty do you owe MarketingMarx, your readership, or patrons of the restaurants and other establishments you will cover? As a PR person, what loyalty do you owe other workers at the plant, or the journalist from the newspaper with whom you have had a solid working relationship? How do you prioritize those loyalties?

It is tempting to answer these questions with an eye toward short-term commitments and temporary consequences. When doing so, you'll find yourself concerned with how close the individuals have been to one another, and what temporary effects a given decision might have on those relationships. Will your website incur any immediate benefits or setbacks because you have made nice with a particular restaurant? Will your readers think any more or less of you tomorrow? Will you and the folks from MarketingMarx have a better relationship? As a PR practitioner for a plant that may be closing, what immediate good derives from doing what your boss tells you to do? What do your children and your sister's family gain or lose if you keep quiet about the plant's closing, or if you tell only them? What difference does it make in your relationships, tonight or tomorrow?

Loyalty, however, takes a different hue when you use a wider lens when asking and answering these questions. What do all bloggers and public relations people—any mass communicator, for that matter—owe all of their audiences? In general, how do professionals balance self-interest against public interest? What would happen to notions of trust if all communicators blurred the lines between information and persuasion and withheld crucial information from stakeholders?

More specifically, media practitioners should ask themselves whether their loyalties impede their ability to serve the needs of the general community. Are reporters showing more loyalty to their news sources than they are to the subjects and audiences? Are they inevitably biased by their political/religious/gender/demographic characteristics—even their sense of patriotism? Do public relations spokespersons "spin" their internal and external communications to ignore data or claims by anyone except the clients who pay them? Are market-driven news and entertainment media ignoring minority interests, pandering to the lowest common denominator? Are advertisers promoting products and causes in ways that overstate their good qualities and ignore the potential for harm? Are entertainment media more focused on ratings and money than on the effects their programming might have on children? And how tightly must you feel loyal to people you deal with regularly—such as sources, bosses, or clients—in order also to have loyalty to the general community? (Put another way: If a journalist does not show some degree of loyalty to a source, that journalist may not be in a position to report a story that's important to the public. Or if a PR practitioner doesn't show some loyalty to a client, then that client will likely find another firm.)

When considering the nature of loyalty, a reasonable set of conclusions for media practitioners might be that:

1. Loyalty, like patriotism and fidelity, is good if properly tempered. It should be based on a correct (or at least adequate) vision of what is worthwhile. It also should not be so single-minded as to blind us to conflicting moral claims. Thus, loyalty requires caution and independent judgment.

Box 5.2 | EXAMPLES FROM MEDIA CODES AND GUIDELINES ON DIVERSITY

The Poynter Institute, a Florida "think and do tank" for journalists, has done some excellent work helping individual journalists and their organizations to cover race. The ethics team has assembled a number of ideas on how to achieve diversity "in staff and story." One constant is the notion that the only way a news medium can be successful in its diversity efforts is through deliberate, thoughtful processes that focus on the goals of inclusiveness, knowledge, acting with integrity, reaching out, and embracing complexity. For each of the variables, they propose an idea, an action plan, and some key questions that need to be asked.

Keith Woods, until 2010 the Poynter Institute's dean of faculty, notes that for decades the media used racial identifiers to single out people who were not white. The practice helped form and fuel stereotypes and continues today to push a wedge between people. Woods says journalists can handle this delicate material better by flagging every racial reference and asking these questions:

1. Is it relevant?
2. Have I explained the relevance?
3. Is it free of codes?
4. Are racial identifiers used evenly?
5. Should I consult someone of another race/ethnicity?

The Poynter Institute says that the following questions should be asked by journalists seeking to cover race fully and fairly. They are the blended product of a variety of sources, ranging from the *Seattle Times*' Race Awareness Pilot Project (RAPP) to suggestions from Sandy Rivera at KHOU-TV, Houston; Mervin Aubespin, the *Louisville Courier-Journal*; and Sherrie Mazingo, University of Minnesota. They were developed at the Poynter Institute and appeared in the Society of Professional Journalists' handbook, *Doing Ethics in Journalism*.

*   Have I covered the story with sensitivity, accuracy, fairness, and balance to all of the people involved?
*   What are the likely consequences of publishing or broadcasting this story? Who will be hurt and who will be helped?
*   Have I sought a diversity of sources for this story?
*   Am I seeking true diversity or using "tokenism," allowing one minority person to represent a community or a point of view?
*   Have I allowed preconceived ideas to limit my efforts to include diversity?
*   Am I flexible about the possibility that the focus of the story may change when different sources are included?
*   Am I being realistic? Are there stories that cannot be diversified? Is there reasonable effort to balance the story and avoid exclusion?

continued

Box 5.2 | *continued*

- Have I developed a meaningful list of minority sources to bring perspective and expertise into mainstream daily news coverage?
- Have I spent time in minority communities and with residents to find out what people are thinking and to learn more about lifestyles, perspectives, customs, etc.?
- If I am writing about achievements, am I writing about them on their own merits rather than as stereotype-breakers?
- Am I letting place names (south side, inner city, Watts, etc.) become code words for crime or other negative news?
- As I seek diversity, am I being true to my other goals as a journalist?
- Will I be able to explain clearly and honestly, not rationalize, my decision to anyone who challenges it?

From The Society of Professional Journalists' Code of Ethics:

Journalists should:

- Tell the story of the diversity and magnitude of the human experience boldly, even when it is unpopular to do so.
- Examine their own cultural values and avoid imposing those values on others.
- Avoid stereotyping by race, gender, age, religion, ethnicity, geography, sexual orientation, disability, physical appearance or social status.
- Give voice to the voiceless; official and unofficial sources of information can be equally valid.

From Al Jazeera's Code of Ethics:

6. Recognize diversity in human societies with all their races, cultures and beliefs and their values and intrinsic individualities in order to present unbiased and faithful reflection of them.

From CyberJournalist.net's model Bloggers' Code of Ethics:

Minimize Harm. Ethical bloggers treat sources and subjects as human beings deserving of respect. Bloggers should: Show compassion for those who may be affected adversely by Weblog content.

From The Society of News Design's Code of Ethical Standards:

Inclusiveness. We will remain vigilant in our quest to combat prejudice and lead needed reforms. We will avoid stereotypes in reporting, editing, presentation, and hiring. Diversity, broadly defined, will be a hallmark of our work. We accept the responsibility to understand our communities and to overcome bias with coverage that is representative of the constituent groups in the community. Over time, all groups, lifestyles, and backgrounds should see themselves and their values represented in the news.

continued

Box 5.2 | *continued*

From the American Marketing Association's Ethical Norms and Values for Marketers:

Responsibility—to accept the consequences of our marketing decisions and strategies. To this end, we will:

- Recognize our special commitments to vulnerable market segments such as children, seniors, the economically impoverished, market illiterates and others who may be substantially disadvantaged.

Respect—to acknowledge the basic human dignity of all stakeholders. To this end, we will:

- Value individual differences and avoid stereotyping customers or depicting demographic groups (e.g., gender, race, sexual orientation) in a negative or dehumanizing way.
- Make every effort to understand and respectfully treat buyers, suppliers, intermediaries and distributors from all cultures.

2. Loyalty to the majority, or to the movers and shakers, impedes the development of genuine empathy with minorities or people who are unrepresented or misrepresented in media.
3. Loyalty is important, if only to maintain good working relationships, but it is more important to be good. And our loyalty has probably been misplaced if our loyalty and our sense of doing the right thing are at odds. If pressures on the job to remain loyal (to our boss, our company, our co-workers, or to unchallenged traditions) make it impossible for us to do the right thing, or to have a legitimate "voice" in how our workplace makes choices, then it could be time to find another job. Or perhaps we should become a whistle-blower, recognizing that whistle-blowers are not universally loved (Hirschman, 1970).

ON DIVERSITY

If clarifying our loyalties helps us expand our worldview, it is only natural that we will expand it to include people who are not like us—people different in race, ethnicity, physical ability, religion, sexual orientation, age, economic class, etc. That expanding view will cause us to question our stereotypes, our tendencies to make snap judgments, and our habits of lumping people and situations into dogmatic categories. Awareness of the world's rich tapestry should lead us to doing better journalism, better public relations, better advertising, better entertainment. Meanwhile, we become better citizens if we seriously attend to media that reflect the rich tapestry of life.

Several media organizations have drafted guidelines to help their personnel meet the challenge.

ERIC DEGGANS, ON DIVERSITY

St. Petersburg Times TV/media critic Eric Deggans writes a popular blog, "The Feed," about television, media, and modern life. He describes himself as "possibly the most critical guy at the Times." He has served as music, media, and TV critic for more than a decade. He wrote this essay specifically for this textbook.

■ ■ ■

Diversity: The Gateway to Accuracy and Fairness in Media

Often in the media world, there are two notable reactions to the notion of working hard to ensure ethnic and gender diversity.

The first and more gratifying response—especially for a person of color seeking allies while advocating on these issues—is a sense that diversity is required as a means of social justice. The second, and less gratifying, is the fear that diversity is a scam.

Diversity and Social Justice

Media people know as well as anyone how completely the white male culture dominates and controls American society. Try covering a professional football game, bird-dogging news in a state legislature, or doing time as a crime reporter in a decent-sized city without noticing how often race and gender issues shape who wins and loses in our society.

Careful observers also know that media can quite effectively pass along distorted images of a minority group to the masses, affecting how that group is treated. For proof, look no further than the massive 1994 massacre in Rwanda, where newspapers and radio stations operated by the Hutu-controlled government spread so much bile about the Tutsis, a rival ethnic group, that the population tolerated a genocide in which Hutu militias killed more than 800,000 people (BBC, 2008).

In a less dramatic example, I often quiz students in classes I've taught about racial imagery and media on their own ideas about different groups of people. Invariably, I find students have exaggerated ideas about certain groups—overestimating what proportion of the nation's poor are black or how many professional athletes are African American—indulging attitudes they later realize are fed by media coverage.

Given the possible consequences, it only seems fair to work hard at hiring a fair proportion of racial minorities and women, with the idea that a media workplace mirroring the nation's demographics would be better equipped to represent all issues in news, entertainment, and persuasive media enterprises.

That concept extends to all media. In a nation where one-third of its residents are Hispanic or non-white (US Census Bureau, 2008), one of the surest guides to how well a culture has blended into the great American melting pot is how it is depicted in movies and television—the instruments of fantasy and distraction we allow into our homes and now carry with us everywhere, thanks to mobile media technology.

Almost since their inception, movies and television have struggled with how to depict people of color and women. It started with the clearly racist stereotypes embedded within the 1915 film *Birth of a Nation* (an innovative work hailed as the first Hollywood blockbuster as well as a movie so stereotypical the Ku Klux Klan used it as a recruiting tool for 60 years). It continued with *Amos 'n' Andy*, which began on radio in the 1920s and made the jump to television in the 1950s.

Half a century later, critics continue to voice concern over modern-day programs, from the Fox-TV show *24*'s depiction of Arabs as terrorist villains to the unrelenting picture of poverty, rape, and personal dysfunction in the 2009 film about an abused black teenager, *Precious*.

What is Diversity in Entertainment?

The story of diversity in twenty-first century media has been one of change: the journey from struggling to fill a slice of the mainstream media pie to staying visible in a sea of niche-oriented products, all targeting a different, profitable audience.

That means the diversity debate has shifted from tracking how many TV shows feature characters of color and how many wide-release movies feature female or minority stars. Now, media critics watch as middle-aged female movie stars move from film to cable TV (Glenn Close in FX's *Damages*, Holly Hunter in TNT's *Saving Grace*, Kyra Sedgwick in TNT's *The Closer*), and moguls such as Tyler Perry earn millions focusing film and TV projects on a loyal niche of African-American women.

Even the dynamics of media loyalty and diversity have changed as the country has grown more diverse. When film and TV producers first tackled ways to present fairer images of black people, they found African-American audiences responding loyally and enthusiastically to landmark work by performers such as Sidney Poitier, Bill Cosby, and Diahann Carroll. The resulting ratings and box office revenue provided a powerful argument that diversity equals good business.

But such equations grew more complicated when producers moved to other ethnic groups. Though critics hailed ABC-TV for building a predominantly Asian-American cast around comic Margaret Cho's 1994 sitcom *All American Girl*, some Asian-American commentators noticed that the show's Korean star was surrounded by non-Korean actors, while the program's mostly white writing staff struggled to handle the racial issues embodied in an Asian girl torn between her parents' immigrant culture and the American mainstream (Park, 2009).

Producers of Hispanic-centered TV shows discovered similar problems. Even though ABC's sitcom featuring Mexican comic George Lopez was successful for years, it often wasn't among the top ten most-watched English language shows in Hispanic households. Series such as Fox's blockbuster singing competition *American Idol* and NBC's gross-out stunt competition *Fear Factor* scored higher.

It seems Spanish-language shows united a diversity of Hispanic viewers across a common language in a way that casting a particular Hispanic actor in a show could not match.

Diversity in Advertising: Making the Offices Match the Product

The advertising world faces different diversity challenges. Look at most major American marketing campaigns. You'll see an admirable attention to onscreen diversity, from McDonald's commercials starring a black family to Old Navy commercials featuring a crop of youthful mannequins that seem to reflect a wide array of ethnicities and both genders.

Indeed, clothing store Benetton's advertisements are so diversely cast (using the tagline "United Colors of Benetton") that the company's name has become an irreverent shorthand for media diversity among the pop culture savvy. Some experts, such as Georgia State University sociologist Charles Gallagher, even criticize these ads for displaying too much diversity—evoking a world where people mix among friends and neighbors of varying ethnicities in a way that most Americans never experience (Lewan, 2009).

But the attitudes of the advertising industry behind the scenes have not been so progressive. According to 2008 data from the US Bureau of Labor Statistics, 5 percent of the advertising workforce was African American, 3 percent Asian, and 8 percent were Hispanic or Latino (Newman, 2008). That isn't much change from 40 years ago, when federal officials found that just 5 percent of the nation's advertising workforce was black and Hispanic.

And the industry's diversity problems reached beyond employment numbers. One study found that black college graduates in advertising earned 80 cents for every $1 earned by equally qualified white counterparts; they were one-tenth as likely to earn a salary over $100,000 annually (Bendick & Egan, 2009). Small wonder that some civil rights groups and experts say there are few industries in America as indifferent to their own diversity issues as the advertising industry.

The real fallout from this lack of diversity may be in spending. Of particular concern is the occasional dictate from media advertising buyers—the companies that buy air time for commercials on behalf of advertisers—that no "urban formats" or "combo" formats blending urban sounds and other styles be included. This is widely viewed as shorthand for excluding radio and TV outlets targeting black consumers—something the Quiznos subs sandwich chain declared in 2004 (Green, 2004) and BMW automobiles declared in 2009 (Marcellus, 2009). The process was considered so unfair that the FCC banned the practice (Smikle, 2007).

Diversity as a Scam?

The second response to a call for attention to diversity in media is darker, though in an odd way more pragmatic and cynical: the fear that this is mostly an unfair scam.

This is odd, because few people of color in media can name a single job they earned because of affirmative action or other diversity initiatives. One is rarely tapped on the shoulder and told, "Hey, you're the black guy we decided to hire this week. Regale us with tales of your childhood watching *Soul Train* and doings at the cool hip hop club of the moment." The FCC keeps track of diversity levels at TV stations, but I have never heard of a station losing its license or being fined for a lack of staff diversity. And, in fact, the diversity figures are not even made public.

In the eyes of some, diversity initiatives designed to expand hiring for people of color will never be more than a misguided attempt to gain political correctness points. These impulses, they feel, have been exploited by the cynical or ambitious to gain jobs they did not earn requiring talent they don't have leading to job security they don't deserve.

Accuracy and Fairness

Seeing diversity initiatives mostly as a means for social justice or as window-dressing misses the point. Diversity in media—especially for newsrooms and news content—is important because it enables two other vitally important ethical values: accuracy and fairness.

These are lessons the national press corps learned the hard way during the 2008 campaign and election of Barack Obama as America's first non-caucasian president. As issues arose intertwining race, class, and gender politics, pundits and political reporters accustomed to reporting on a field of white male candidates found themselves at a loss to describe the situations accurately.

When discussion arose about whether black people would consider candidate Obama "black enough" because of his interracial heritage; when longtime Obama minister Jeremiah Wright's controversial sermons raised questions about how much parishioners in black churches subscribe to their pastors' views; when questions arose about the moment young Barry Obama in Hawaii began calling himself by the African name bestowed by his absent biological father—each of these stories required knowledge of black culture and sources who could explain it all.

The initial drive to diversify the nation's newsrooms was rooted in an even more important need for truth. Back in 1968, as American cities were wracked by race riots, then-President Lyndon B. Johnson tasked the 11-member National Advisory Commission on Civil Disorders, better known as the Kerner Commission (for its chair, Illinois Governor Otto Kerner, Jr.), to investigate the causes.

In addition to identifying tensions over housing segregation, unequal schools, and lack of economic opportunity, the group also faulted the news media for inaccurate reporting that inflamed race tensions and exaggerated the damage done by riots.

The report said:

> The news media must publish newspapers and produce programs that recognize the existence and activities of the Negro, both as a Negro and as part of the community. It would be a contribution of inestimable importance to race relations in the United States simply to treat ordinary news about Negroes as news of other groups is now treated.

(Moyers, 2008)

Box 5.3 | HOW DO MEDIA TEND TO COVER RACE?

News media struggle to cover matters of race. Scholars Clint Wilson and Felix Guiterrez describe five evolutionary patterns of race coverage in American media:

1. The exclusionary stage, in which ethnic minority groups are not covered.
2. The threatening issue stage, in which ethnic minorities are covered as threats to society's "normal order."
3. The confrontation phase, in which media focus on physical conflicts stimulated by the majority group's fear of minorities.
4. The stereotypical selection phase, in which reporting neutralizes white majority apprehension of minority groups by emphasizing themes that conform to majority attitudes toward minorities.
5. The integrated coverage phase, in which news is reported from a perspective that includes all citizens. (Wilson & Guiterrez, 1985, p. 135).

Individual journalists as well as their publications or broadcast outlets can evolve through these five stages, but the transitions are not pain-free. It may be the pain imposed by outraged minorities, or pain from lost revenues, or pain from an emerging self-awareness about justice, equity, and community. Whatever the cause, the journey from blind ignorance to fully open, integrated news coverage is slow. Not everyone has made the whole trip.

—Jay Black

Of course, smart news organizations were already learning this lesson.

As riots occurred in black neighborhoods in New York, Los Angeles, Philadelphia, and elsewhere, some news organizations found the situation too dangerous for white reporters to tackle. So they turned to staffers of color working in their marketing departments, classified sales, or even in janitorial services to join the ranks of journalists chronicling this landmark level of unrest.

These pioneers faced serious challenges in navigating newsrooms unused to their presence. By the early 1970s, journalists such as Connie Chung, Lesley Stahl, Ed Bradley, and Geraldo Rivera had begun working for the news divisions at big TV networks, as the industry took the Kerner Commission's words to heart and began diversifying newsrooms.

Picturing the World as it is Versus the World We'd Like to See

TV and movies in the 1950s and 1960s faced a similar struggle over accuracy and ethnicity.

Back then, TV especially was a land of escapism. Family comedies featured squeaky-clean nuclear households where kids still worshipped their parents, dads wore jackets and ties to the dinner table, and the newly burgeoning suburbs were a middle-class promised land. The Vietnam War and open warfare over civil rights may have been roiling the country, but on the small screen, Andy Griffith helped his friends in mostly white Mayberry handle much smaller problems and misfit Marine Gomer Pyle never went anywhere near a real war.

Critics often say controversial content on television creeps behind popular mores, because the programs find people inside their homes, welcomed into their living rooms like an honored guest. To make money, their advertisements must persuade viewers to buy goods and services, which is never a good time to challenge people on their personal prejudices or misconceptions.

Watching images of minorities on TV and movie from the 50s to the 70s was like watching a slow parade toward reality, starting with the dimwitted, childlike caricatures of Amos and Andy in the 1950s, progressing to the accomplished but solitary black characters played by Bill Cosby on *I Spy* and Diahann Caroll on *Julia* in the 1960s, and continuing through to a black family surviving in a Chicago ghetto on *Good Times* in the 1970s.

These images taught viewers of all ethnicities what was possible and desirable. A young black child could dream of life as a secret agent after watching Cosby's Alexander Scott dispatch bad guys on *I Spy*, while a white voter could wonder what politicians were doing to help the poor after watching James Evans's family struggle on *Good Times*.

The progression became a familiar dance. At first black people fought to be shown at all. Then the struggle continued for more realistic and respectful depictions, forging a slow, steady movement that would be duplicated by other ethnicities.

But while critics pressed TV shows and movies to portray people of color more realistically, the struggle over advertising was a struggle to become part of America's dreams.

The issue was embodied in an insurance company advertisement that ran in black-focused magazines such as *Ebony* and *Black Enterprise* many years ago. In it, a young black boy gazed into a bathroom mirror, a towel pinned to his back in obvious emulation of a square-jawed superhero.

But the face looking back at him in the mirror was that of a white man. Even in his dreams, this young boy couldn't imagine anyone who looked like himself as a hero.

This is what the naysayers about too-perfect diversity images in advertising seem to miss: by including a range of people, viewers are shown an ideal picture in which everyone is included.

For cultures legally barred from such acceptance for so many years, it is an important and gratifying goal.

Conclusion: The Obstacles that Remain

These efforts at equality have not met with uniform acceptance. Moving the needle on diversity numbers often requires significant attention and hard work, leading some to wonder if media organizations aren't favoring minority candidates at the expense of others. Such sentiments surfaced in the early days of the 2003 scandal involving *New York Times* reporter Jayson Blair, a young African-American reporter who was unmasked as a liar and plagiarist after working on several high-profile stories for the Grey Lady.

Other critics maintained the focus on diversity initiatives distorted news reporting itself, creating a "politically correct" prism in which coverage reflecting the mores of minority pressure groups was preferred. One of the strongest advocates of this view has been William McGowan, an author and fellow at the conservative Manhattan Institute think tank, who crystallized his critique in the 2001 book *Coloring the News: How Political Correctness Has Corrupted American Journalism* (McGowan, 2001).

"I wrote about a climate that allowed activism and ethnic and racial cheerleading to eclipse neutral observation," McGowan said in a later essay published in the *Wall Street Journal*. (Full disclosure: he also criticized me in the piece for my negative review of his book.) He called such attitudes "a kind of wishful thinking that caused too many journalists to see a world where 'what ought to be is substituted for truth itself,' as *Washington Post* columnist Richard Cohen has phrased it."

Critics of McGowan's work—including me—note that mistakes in covering some stories or ham-handed diversity initiatives do not invalidate the idea that diversity produces better journalism. Instead, McGowan's analysis seems to assume that the only cultural attitudes that can distort news coverage are those belonging to racial minorities—dissecting the many instances when big media outlets handled race and culture stories badly without allowing that diversity may also have led to some good coverage, as well. Books such as *Coloring the News* mostly prove that getting to the bottom of such thorny ideas as race, culture, gender, and class conflict is a difficult matter. It isn't always handled well by media outlets, big or small.

Likewise, the entertainment media continue to struggle with equal representation issues, occasionally offering a fall crop of new network TV shows in which no people of color are featured in starring roles, as happened in 2008 (Deggans, 2008). Or creating a landscape in which all seven talk shows airing on network TV during weeknights are hosted by middle-aged white men.

The *Los Angeles Times* noted the dearth of quality roles for black women in film and television by exploring the BBF syndrome, or Black Best Friend dynamic. Citing projects ranging from *The Nanny Diaries* and *The Devil Wears Prada* to *The New Adventures of Old Christine* and *Private Practice*, the newspaper noted how talented black actresses were constantly playing characters "whose . . . principal function is to support the heroine, often with sass, attitude and a keen insight into relationships and life" (Braxton, 2007).

That such dynamics can surface years after movies and television have featured black and Hispanic presidents—seemingly, as a preparation for President Obama's real-life election—only demonstrates how persistent stereotypes can be in media.

The bottom line: As audiences are shrinking and communities are becoming more diverse, the last thing media outlets can afford is to lose touch with audiences or provide a false echo of their lives.

—Eric Deggans

■ ■ ■

SUMMARY AND CONCLUSIONS

This chapter linked two issues that should concern all media practitioners and consumers: loyalty and diversity. We concluded that comprehensive and honest media performance should demonstrate respect to one and all. Being realistic, we don't sidestep the problem of sifting and sorting through competing loyalties, through legitimate and less legitimate claims by everyone seeking to have a story told, an image presented, an argument made. Doing good journalism, public relations, advertising, or entertainment means making choices between and among the competing claimants.

■ ■ ■

CHAPTER VOCABULARY

Note: Definitions are available at this book's companion website.

- adversarial system
- communitarianism
- loyalty

- particularistic loyalty
- sentimental loyalty
- unsentimental loyalty

PRACTICAL APPLICATIONS

1. Make a list of your loyalties—personal (family and friends, including Facebook friends or other social media relationships) and others (professional, academic, etc.). Rank order them. Ask: Who deserves and receives your strongest loyalty, and whose loyalty is negotiable? Which loyalties are sentimental, and which are unsentimental?

2. What conditions would cause you to quit a job and walk away from colleagues, a boss, or your line of work? How much trouble would you go through to preserve any of those relationships?

3. In your own experience, what (if anything) does loyalty have to do with moral development? Do you accept the text's argument that we expand our arena of loyalty as we develop morally?

4. Make a case for or against the idea that being loyal primarily to yourself is morally inappropriate.

5. Look for examples of diversity in different media over the course of a week: news, online, public relations, advertising, or entertainment. Which media seem to be doing the best job of capturing and reflecting the diversity of contemporary society, and which are doing a poor job? Why do you think this is the case?

6. Research the definitions of "stereotype," "prototype," and "archetype." Why are the distinctions important? How can a communicator use these distinctions in portrayal of others?

■ ■ ■

CASE 5.1 Journalism: The Harsh Out-of-Town Story

You are an editor at *The Freedoniaville Times*, a 6,000-circulation daily newspaper in a small town. Part of your job is to choose the stories from national and international news services that are printed in the paper.

At 6 p.m. you see the story budget of *The Daily Metropolis*, one of the nation's largest daily newspapers, with the list of stories it will publish the next day. The paper makes its stories available to other newspapers at 9 p.m., and it's not uncommon for *The Freedoniaville Times* to publish a story or two each day written by *The Daily Metropolis*.

The list of stories for the next day includes one about the habits of child molesters. The budget line says the story focuses on John Smythe of Freedoniaville. You know him as a member of a prominent Freedoniaville family, and you know he moved to Metropolis seven years ago and has been rarely seen in Freedoniaville.

The budget line says Smythe was arrested two days ago in Metropolis on child molestation charges. The budget line says that Smythe acknowledges that he molested a child but blames his problem on his upbringing in Freedoniaville, including his claim that an unnamed uncle molested him when he was a child there. Your quick look at the newspaper's archives show that Smythe had two uncles. Both are dead, but their widows still live in Freedoniaville. One widow is head of the city council, and the other is prominent on the hospital board, two organizations you cover on a regular basis.

The story will not be available for a few hours, but you need to make a quick decision about whether to run the story in tomorrow's edition of *The Freedoniaville Times*.

➤ **What do you do?**

Questions
- **What's your problem?**
- **Why not follow the rules?**
- **Who wins, who loses?**
- What else do you need to know?

Thinking it Through
1. Is this an ethical issue? Why or why not?
2. Make a list of the people (including yourself) and groups who are stakeholders in your decision.
3. Organize that list in order of who you consider most important to least important.
4. Which sets of stakeholders are most in conflict with one another? How, if at all, can these conflicts be reconciled?
5. Do the considerations from Chapter 4 (about moral development) play a role in your decision? To what extent?

6. What responsibility, if any, does a local news organization have to protect its community from out-of-town journalists who write about your community without really understanding it?

7. To what extent, if any, is your decision influenced by the fact that the story will be published by *The Daily Metropolis* and be available online?

8. To what extent, if any, would your decision be different if you knew you likely would run across one of those living relatives on a regular basis in your community?

9. If you're inclined to run the story, do you have an obligation to let family members know that the story will be published and to seek comments from them? Why or why not?

10. If you're inclined to run the story, do you have an obligation to "localize" the national story by pointing out what you know, such as the names of the two uncles? Why or why not?

11. Do you wait a day to write a story? Put another way: Do you write a story about the story?

■ ■ ■

CASE 5.2 **New Media: Is the Nominee Gay?**

The president of Freedonia has just nominated Leslie Smith for a lifetime appointment to the Supreme Court, which is big news in the nation and on your www.freedonia live.com site. Leslie has very little name recognition, and your first online post as head writer is about that lack of name recognition and judicial experience. You learn that Leslie is middle-aged and never married. Given that 95 percent of Freedonia adults marry at least once, this is peculiar.

It's not peculiar, then, that there are Internet rumblings about Leslie's sexual orientation. You have no evidence about the nominee's sexual orientation. Smith is not giving media interviews, and even asking the president's spokesperson or Smith's colleagues and friends about the issue seems troubling.

Your site is known as a "Fifth Estate" site because of its criticism of the "Fourth Estate," i.e., mainstream media. You have noticed that few, if any, mainstream news organizations in Freedonia have touched the topic in print or in their broadcasts. Whether or not sexual orientation is relevant to Smith's appointment, it is a topic that is floating through cyberspace yet scarcely mentioned in mainstream media and is not a question that has been directly asked of the president's spokesperson.

➤ **The question: What, if anything, do you write about the fact that mainstream media aren't writing about Smith's sexual orientation?**

Questions
- **What's your problem?**
- **Why not follow the rules?**
- **Who wins, who loses?**
- What else do you need to know?

Thinking it Through
1. Is this an ethical issue? Why or why not?
2. To what extent, if any, is this issue related to privacy? To diversity?
3. How relevant is Leslie Smith's sexual orientation to Smith's court nomination?
4. How do your personal feelings about homosexuality play into your decision?
5. Is it ethically possible to write meta-criticism—how journalists are/are not covering a sensitive story related to privacy and diversity—without falling into the same ethical traps as the journalists you write about?
   A. If you choose to write about the topic:
      a. How do you justify your decision?
      b. What do you write? (Write an outline with topic sentences of the points you would make?)

    c. How do you deal with the question about Smith's sexual orientation? (Write the sentences you would post to handle that question.)

B. If you choose not to write about the topic:

    a. How do you justify your decision?

    b. Would you change your mind if you could find an ethically justifiable way to answer Question 5?

    c. How can you stay relevant if you do not write about topics that are clearly ones that people (rightly or wrongly) are talking about?

6. Would the nominee's gender—note that the case doesn't say whether Leslie is male or female—have any bearing whatsoever on your decision?

■ ■ ■

CASE 5.3 **Public Relations: Wrestling with Your Conscience and a Friend Bound to Fail**

You are ten months into your new job as an account executive with MarketingMarx, a public relations and marketing firm based in Freedonia's biggest city. You're under a great deal of pressure to bring home a new account, because the company tends to dump new employees who have not brought in any new business (regardless of size) within their first year. The economy is in a downturn, and you have few if any other job prospects.

One day you get a call from Casey Smith, a fairly close college friend whose parents died in an accident two years ago. Casey was the lone survivor and spent nearly a month in the hospital. You haven't seen each other since the funeral, but you have stayed in touch online since you took this job.

Casey received $20 million to settle claims involving the accident. You are both single and in your early 20s, and after sharing some memories Casey mentions plans to use the money and go into the sports entertainment business.

Casey's plan is to introduce Freedonia to "alysh"—a form of wrestling in which contestants must hold onto their opponents' belts at all times and throw their opponents onto the mat.* Casey saw the sport while on vacation in Turkey and thinks it would appeal to a wide Freedonia audience, since both sexes can wrestle.

Casey describes a proposal for the "Freedonia Alysh Independent League" (FAIL) and a $10 million marketing campaign to introduce Freedonians to the sport. The plan includes spending money on advertising, a public relations campaign, efforts to obtain citizenship for "alysh" wrestlers, and (of course) your fees.

Casey was a sociology major who knows little about business, much less your business, but is insistent on the $10 million ad campaign. Casey says you are the perfect person to handle the campaign, calling you a long-time, trustworthy friend.

It's clear to you that Casey's idea is half-baked and doomed, and you believe that Casey isn't thinking straight after the stress of the accident. In fact, you believe that Casey may have suffered a brain injury from the accident.

You think Casey will quickly burn through that money and have nothing to show for it but memories of a bad idea. At the same time, this account means you keep your job.

When you take the "FAIL" idea back to your bosses at MarketingMarx, they start making the "baa" noises of sheep as they crudely describe making easy money by fleecing Casey. They tell you that your task is to take as much money from Casey as

---

* Learn more about the sport at http://alysh.com or www.wrestling-belts.org.

possible and do the best creative work you can, but you will not be held responsible when FAIL wrestling league lives up to its acronym.

➤ **More importantly, you are told that your job is safe once you've signed Casey to a contract.**

Questions

- **What's your problem?**
- **Why not follow the rules?**
- **Who wins, who loses?**
- What else do you need to know?

Thinking it Through

1. Is this an ethical issue? Why or why not?

2. Make a list of the people (including yourself) and groups who are stakeholders in your decision.

3. Organize that list in order of who you consider most important to least important.

4. Which sets of stakeholders are most in conflict with one another? How, if at all, can these conflicts be reconciled?

5. Do the considerations from Chapter 4 (about moral development) play a role in your decision? If so, to what extent?

6. What moral and pragmatic arguments can you make for either taking or not taking the account?

7. In making your decision, how much does it matter to you that the key wrestlers come from Turkey? Is that national flavor a good thing or a bad thing? How can you develop marketing plans that can both promote and deflect the international flavor of the sport? Is there a moral issue in both promoting and deflecting the same issue?

8. What obligation, if any, do you have to determine whether Casey suffered a brain injury? If you learn that Casey has a brain injury, what (if any) impact might it have on your decision?

9. The bottom-line question: Would you take Casey's money to develop the campaign?
   A. If you choose to take the account:
      a. Why? Who wins and who loses?
      b. What loyalties were most important to you in your decision?
      c. Is there a middle ground you can strike with Casey, so the entire $10 million won't be eaten away? What if Casey still refuses to listen to you argue against spending so much, saying "you've got to spend money to make money"?
      d. How can you deal with bosses who see "shearing sheep" as a legitimate business practice?

    e. What sort of ad campaign would you create?

    f. How would you explain your decision to Casey once the money is gone (with little if anything to show for it)?

B. If you choose not to take the account:

    a. What loyalties were most important to you in your decision?

    b. What if Casey takes the account to another ad agency?

    c. Do you "tell off" your bosses for trying to make you take advantage of a friend?

    d. How do you explain your decision to Casey?

    e. Will you talk about your decision in any job interviews you might have if you lose your job at MarketingMarx?

■ ■ ■

CASE 5.4 **Advertising: Using Stereotypes to Sell Soda**

You are an account executive for an international advertising agency whose clients include a soft drink company that wants to increase sales in Sylvania. The company knows its sales are hurt by Sylvania's well-known bias against all things Freedonian, so its solution is "Sylvania Smooth," a new soft drink brand it will sell only in that country.

The soda company hires a Sylvania native as its in-house marketing executive for the brand. You are her liaison at your ad firm.

The soda company's in-house ad team has a plan that centers on an animated series of ads depicting a goofy-looking Freedonia expatriate living in Sylvania. The ad portrays him—in a good-natured, over-the-top way—as what Sylvania natives would see as a stereotypical Freedonian living in their country: He mangles the language in funny ways, dresses funny compared to Sylvania natives, and clearly isn't as cool and sophisticated as a Sylvanian native. But when he pulls out a can of "Sylvania Smooth" and sips it, he morphs from a doofus Freedonian into a suave man who has facial features that are unmistakably Sylvanian. What's more, this man transformed by the soft drink could grace the cover of any Sylvania magazine. The ad campaign's tag line: "Be Sylvania Smooth."

➤ **The Sylvania-born marketing executive with the soft drink company comes to you with her plan, hoping for your insight. What do you say?**

Questions
- **What's your problem?**
- **Why not follow the rules?**
- **Who wins, who loses?**
- What else do you need to know?

Thinking it Through
1. Is this an ethical issue? Why or why not?
2. Make a list of the people (including yourself) and groups who are stakeholders in your decision.
3. Organize that list in order of who you consider most important to least important.
4. Which sets of stakeholders are most in conflict with one another? How, if at all, can these conflicts be reconciled?
5. Do the considerations from Chapter 4 (about moral development) play a role in your decision? To what extent?
6. What moral and pragmatic arguments can you make for developing or refusing to develop the advertising campaign?
7. Do you agree that the ad could be interpreted as reinforcing the stereotype of Freedonians being inferior to Sylvanians? Should advertisers be concerned about such stereotypes?

8. How can you justify (or, not justify) the use of cultural stereotyping?
9. The bottom-line question: Would you recommend that the advertising campaign go forward?

■ ■ ■

CASE 5.5 **Entertainment: Misdirection for Fun and Profit**

You are head of a film distribution company in Freedonia, and much of your success has come from helping television stars make the move to film. On your meeting schedule is a semi-famous television comedian, Byron Coen, whose "Golly Gee" character has been a huge success interviewing politicians and celebrities who don't necessarily know they're being spoofed. The humor comes from asking such strange questions and doing such outrageous things that the people on the receiving end of his antics end up saying funny things or looking bewildered. It's not everyone's favorite type of humor, but it has worked well on cable television to a limited audience. Although Coen is well known to his niche but not a national name, you are not alone in thinking that he could be a worldwide star (and make a lot of money for everyone) if he finds the right role.

Coen comes to you with what he hopes is that right role, and with the expectation that you will financially back a movie in which he introduces a new character, Tarob. In the title role, he would play a foreigner from Sylvania who comes to Freedonia to learn about Freedonian culture and maybe find a new wife. Some of the movie would be scripted, but much of the humor would come from non-scripted interactions Tarob would have with real people who actually think they are dealing with a foreign person unfamiliar with Freedonian customs. By asking the right questions the right way, he can lead participants to say things that might be interpreted as racist, sexist, and homophobic. With good acting, he can lead participants to behave in bizarre and foolish ways—sometimes by using the graciousness of people who put up with buffoonery they may attribute to their belief that Tarob simply doesn't know any better because he's not familiar with their nation's culture and mores.

To solve the legal issues, participants would sign a release form granting the filmmakers the right to use their image—but participants would not be told that Tarob is a fictional character or that the film is a comedy and not a documentary. Participants also would not be compensated for appearing in the movie. Your lawyers tell you that you are on solid legal ground, since the participants are old enough and aware that they are being filmed—and many of them would be politicians or celebrities who are used to being in the media.

You have seen some video shot by Coen's production company and find it hilarious—even as you wince at the fact that the participants were tricked into taking part. You know it would cost little to produce but could make Coen an international star, and earn millions at the box office.

➤ **Coen tells you that you have the right of first refusal on the project, but another film distribution company is waiting in the wings. You have 48 hours to decide.**

Questions

- **What's your problem?**
- **Why not follow the rules?**
- **Who wins, who loses?**
- What else do you need to know?

Thinking it Through

1. Is this an ethical issue? Why or why not?
2. Make a list of the people (including yourself) and groups who are stakeholders in your decision.
3. Organize that list in order of who you consider most important to least important.
4. Which sets of stakeholders are most in conflict with one another? How, if at all, can these conflicts be reconciled?
5. Do the considerations from Chapter 4 (about moral development) play a role in your decision? To what extent?
6. The bottom-line question: Do you financially back Coen's film proposal?
   A. If you're inclined to support the film project:
      a. Why? Who wins and who loses?
      b. What loyalties were most important to you in your decision?
      c. What moral and pragmatic arguments can you make for producing the film?
      d. How persuasive is the lawyers' statement that you are legally protected?
      e. How would you deal with the inevitable criticism that will arise once the film is released and participants see themselves being spoofed?
   B. If you're inclined not to support the film project:
      a. Why? Who wins and who loses?
      b. What loyalties were most important to you in your decision?
      c. What moral and pragmatic arguments would you make for refusing to do the film?
      d. How persuasive is the lawyers' statement that you are legally protected?
      e. What if Coen peddles the proposal to another film company, which makes a great deal of money from it?

What's It Worth?

Now that we have framed ways of defining our moral problems, understanding formal and informal rules, and developing empathy for stakeholders, it is appropriate to do some values inquiry.

Values are part and parcel of the mass media environment. Because values are standards of choice through which individuals and institutions seek meaning, satisfaction, and worth, it's easy to see how often media decision making involves values choices. Some values are routine, craft-based, and non-moral in nature; others are inescapably moral. Values are often in conflict, the choices frequently subtle and nuanced. In the public arena we call the media ethics environment, values selections should be relatively transparent, and media practitioners should be held accountable for those choices.

> Prioritize your values—both moral and non-moral values—and decide which one(s) you won't compromise.

The fourth section of this textbook is the longest, because the "values turf" is expansive. We devote four admittedly selective chapters to a topic that admittedly deserves a book-length treatment. In deciding what to include in a discussion of "What's it worth," we have chosen to focus on philosophers' and social scientists' insights into the nature of personal and professional values (Chapter 6) and some specific values important to media: truth telling (Chapter 7), privacy and public life (Chapter 8), and the values dilemmas arising in media persuasion and propaganda (Chapter 9).

In Chapter 6 we tussle with insights from moral philosophers and moral psychologists who have explored the nature of values and value systems, and we apply these insights to mass media. By reviewing media ethics codes and media behavior, we come to appreciate the complicated mix of individualized and collective values driving the media machines. We also note how media practitioners constantly juggle their own—and their institutions'—values with those of their clients, sources, subjects, and audiences.

Almost all media value truth telling—some entertainment media being the understandable exception to the rule. In Chapter 7 we investigate the philosophic and pragmatic nature of truth telling. We also consider some limits to getting it right: how inherently elusive truth is, how it is gathered and disseminated selectively, how it is balanced against equally compelling values, and how general semantics can help us understand the use and abuse of truth claims.

Privacy, the value we discuss in Chapter 8, entails a never-ending balancing act in media: How much personal information is there a legal right to know, how much do we need to know, and how much are we merely interested in knowing? Have social media and ubiquitous marketing irrevocably altered our expectations of privacy? Encroachment upon individual moral autonomy continues to highlight today's arguments about balancing the value of privacy against other prima facie values.

Finally, this section treats persuasion and propaganda as matters of value. Chapter 9 recognizes the significant role of advertising, public relations, and other forums for advocacy—and information—in contemporary life. It offers a model for ethical advocacy, recognizing the legitimacy of selective truth telling and loyalty to clients. It approaches propaganda as an inevitable component of the media landscape, and suggests that sophisticated consumers and producers of persuasive messages should be wary of closed-minded, propagandistic advocacy.

As we will see, "value" is both a noun and a verb. It is the collective conception of what we find desirable, important, and morally proper. It also is the criterion by which we evaluate our own actions and those of others (American Marketing Association, 2009). These four chapters attempt to help media practitioners, consumers, and citizen-critics make informed values choices.

---

1. **What's your problem?**

2. **Why not follow the rules?**

3. **Who wins, who loses?**

4. <u>**What's it worth?**</u>

5. **Who's whispering in your ear?**

6. **How's your decision going to look?**

CHAPTER 6

Personal and Professional Values

INTRODUCTION

WE HAVE said it before, but it bears repeating: Ethics is more than simply choosing right from wrong. When we make a complex decision, we are really choosing between different, competing priorities. Some of those priorities are moral; others are routine, craft-based, and non-moral. Often the choices are between—or among—equally compelling "right-versus-right" options, as Rushworth Kidder explains in *How Good People Make Tough Choices* (1995). When we make these decisions, we apply judgments that reveal something of our personal values. When our profession makes decisions, its institutional values are in play.

Our values help determine our loyalties. In Chapter 5 we presumed loyalty toward people was a value worth holding, and we explored the ramifications of specific questions about who deserved our loyalty and under what conditions. That may have left us with the problem of deciding how to balance our loyalties against our values, such as honesty and transparency. This chapter should help us understand the balancing act.

The discussion of values is particularly important in mass media, because it is clear that media shape as well as reflect a society's values. Media critics have commented that "Those who tell the nation's stories control the nation's values." Research concludes that mass media affect different people in different ways at different times. This "mixed-model" theory of media effects suggests that media practitioners can never be sure of the power their messages will have in affecting the values and—either directly or indirectly—

This chapter:

- turns to various social science and humanities disciplines and media codes of ethics for help in defining values

- considers the extent to which values are relative or universal

- discusses the basics of systematic values inquiry, an exercise that can help you determine your values

- uses these insights to assess values in media ethics codes and policy statements, taking special note of the values embedded within journalism

- invites you to resolve values issues found in media cases.

behaviors of their audiences. At the least, media practitioners should understand the values that they bring into their decision-making processes, even as they decide what role those values should play in helping shape the values of their audiences.

It is also worth noting that different media types have different values that often compete. Journalists, advertisers, and public relations practitioners all say they value "truth," but the definition of truth often depends upon their viewpoint and who's paying their salaries.

Moreover, the seeming disconnect between the values of the mass media and the professed values of a community also come into conflict. For example, journalists who value truth might find themselves under attack in a community that values harmony and privacy. Or someone in the entertainment industry who values gaining an audience might use "shock value" that grabs attention but turns off potential viewers who value self-respect and wouldn't want to be seen watching that sort of show.

DEFINING VALUES

Values have been discussed and debated for millennia. Plato, Aristotle, and Kant are among the many philosophers who have weighed in on questions about what values are, where they come from, and how they impact our lives. More recently, social scientists—particularly psychologists and sociologists, but also political philosophers and economists—have studied the nature and ramifications of individual and institutional values. Philosophic investigations have dealt with the nature of good, right, obligation, virtue, moral and aesthetic judgment, beauty, truth, and validity. More recent investigations by social scientists have considered the nature of individual belief systems and the foundations of social-political-economic structures. Values—both moral and non-moral—are at the heart of such inquiries (Frankena, 1967; Black et al., 1992; Viall, 1992).

The term originates from the Latin *valere*, meaning "to be of worth." It is no surprise that scholars specializing in values inquiry have generated hundreds of definitions. The *Encyclopedia of Ethics* says a value "is a thing or property that is itself worth having, getting or doing, or that possesses some property that makes it so," and that a value "belongs to anything that is necessary for, or a contribution to, some living being or beings' thriving, flourishing, fulfillment, or well-being" (Bond, 2001, p. 1745). Social psychologist Milton Rokeach defines a value as "an enduring belief that a specific mode of conduct or end-state of existence is personally or socially preferable to an opposite or converse mode of conduct or end-state of existence" (1973, p. 5). Another social psychologist, Shalom Schwartz, defines values as "conceptions of the desirable that guide the way (people) select actions, evaluate people and events, and explain their actions and evaluations" (1999, p. 24). Others have said values are standards of choice through which individuals and groups seek meaning, satisfaction, and worth.

If the definitions in the preceding paragraph seem overly broad, it may be because the word "values" is highly elastic: "Sometimes it is used narrowly as a synonym for 'good'

Box **6.1** | **"VALUE" AND THE PARTS OF SPEECH**

"Value" is both a noun and a verb. The distinction is seen in the American Marketing Association's statement of ethical norms and values (2009):

> Noun-sense: "Values represent the collective conception of what communities find desirable, important and morally proper."

> Verb-sense: "Values also serve as the criteria for evaluating our own personal actions and the actions of others."

It is therefore correct to say that something has value, and that we value something.

or valuable, and sometimes it is used broadly for the whole scope of evaluative terms, ranging from the highest good through the indifferent to the worst evil" (Pojman, 1990, p. 56). For instance, some philosophers approach values by discussing abstract things that appear to be intrinsically good, such as happiness or truth. Others—particularly social scientists and lay commentators—merely define what it means to say something *has* value. They also make descriptive generalizations of what is regarded as worthwhile in a culture and theorize about those values (Frankena, 1967). Some describe values as metaphysical, unobservable, and unmeasurable (Brecht, 1959), while others maintain that ultimate values such as "desire" can be scientifically validated and measured (Perry, 1954).

Psychologist Meg Rohan has said that research studies and theories of values have suffered "because the word *values* is open to abuse and overuse by nonpsychologists and psychologists alike." She has pointed to politicians' "moaning" about family values as merely one example of the semantic abuse that has made the study of values difficult (2000, p. 255). Journalists, bloggers, talk show hosts, advertisers, entertainers, and public relations practitioners have contributed to this semantic abuse.

Values are not the same as ideologies, worldviews, beliefs, or attitudes. It is helpful to think of our values system as the underlying foundation for these other constructs. Rokeach (1968; 1973) has said that values help determine virtually all kinds of behavior that could be called social behavior—of social action, attitudes, ideology, evaluations, moral judgments and justifications of self and others, comparisons of self with others, presentations of self to others, and attempts to influence others. He concludes that values help guide and determine social attitudes and ideologies on one hand, and social behavior on the other.

In keeping with Rokeach's framework, many social scientists conclude that our general beliefs about the world, and our opinions and attitudes about specific situations, emerge from our core values or personal value system. At the same time, each of us has a cluster of "value priorities" that may subtly shift in relation to one another in different situations.

While people disagree about the subtle meanings of the term, few "dissent from the principles that values are important in behavior, they concern standards of choice and the normative, and they involve some degree of commitment" (Barrett, 1961, p. 2).

Philosophers, meanwhile, focus on the moral dimensions of values. In Louis Pojman's view, values are central to the domain of morality. He argues that they are prima facie (Latin for "at first sight") variables that undergird principled judgments, decisions, and actions (1990, pp. 64–66).

Media ethicist Clifford Christians and his colleagues point out that any decision involves "a host of values that must be sorted out," because these values "reflect our pre-suppositions about social life and human nature" (Christians et al., 2001, p. 2). They add that moral values play a role even as we judge something by aesthetic, professional, logical, and sociocultural values.

Obviously, not all values deal with morality. We value many non-moral (not the same as "amoral" or "immoral") things: independence, financial security, a nice place to live, friendship, sex, good health, a meaningful job, etc. In the world of media, these non-moral values include beating competitors, garnering audiences, selling products, meeting deadlines, influencing public opinion, creating art, winning accounts, etc. Some of these values are means to an end, such as gaining an audience in order to entertain or persuade them. Other values are ends in and of themselves. When we talk about values in the world of media, therefore, we must consider both moral values and craft-based, institutional, non-moral values.

Regardless of whether we focus on moral or non-moral values, specific values obviously relate to one another, and multiple values can compete for priority at any given moment. While these specific values provide reasons to take or avoid taking action, we also are motivated by a more deeply held "system" of core values. The Public Relations Society of America code calls its core values "the fundamental beliefs that guide our behaviors and decision-making process." This "system" of values, described by Rohan (2000) as a cognitive structure, is a fundamental mental system that helps us make sense of the world. Once formed, our cognitive structures are relatively impervious to change.

Summing up the definitional issues, philosophers and social psychologists—who frequently disagree about motivation and behavior—seem to agree that:

- values are agents of our own thinking, acting, and choosing
- values may be selfishly or societally oriented; rooted in ideals or in practicality
- some values are moral; others are non-moral
- some values are specific; others are abstract
- values underlie our attitudes, beliefs, and opinions, which in turn underlie our behavior
- we seek consistency/balance in our values, either consciously or unconsciously.

Although it may be splitting semantic hairs, the varied efforts to define values have several common features. They show that values are (a) concepts or beliefs, (b) about desirable end states or behaviors, (c) that transcend specific situations, (d) guide our selection or evaluation of behavior or events, and (e) are ordered by relative importance (Schwartz & Bilsky, 1987; 1990). Simply put, what we value goes a long way in determining how we act. A moral dilemma results when values conflict; the conflicts should be resolved if moral action is to occur.

VALUES INQUIRY

We probably do not spend much time pondering our values—where they came from, how they influence our behavior, and how they may clash or coincide with those of other people. It is not the sort of topic discussed around the office water fountain or on Facebook, even though those topics of conversation often are framed by our political or socioeconomic or personal values. Indeed, if we ever consciously explored the nature of values, we most likely did so in a religious or educational setting.

Box 6.2 | DID MEDIA FAILINGS LEAD TO VALUES EDUCATION IN PUBLIC SCHOOLS?

The debate about values-based character education in schools seems to hinge on questions such as "Whose values are being taught?" or "Why don't we just leave this stuff to the family or religious environments?" Values education was considered a natural (however didactic) component of the public school curriculum for most of American history. It slipped off the radar screen in the 1960s, a time of declared open-minded tolerance of all perspectives (a.k.a. relativism) in which colleges of education and public schools grew increasingly concerned about "imposing" values on students.

The resurgence of values exploration and character-based education, starting in the 1990s, has been attributed to concerns that this "stuff" just isn't being taught effectively at home or through religious education—and certainly not over the wide-open Internet, on television, in popular music, or through other mass media.

Therefore, educators thought, why not do it carefully and systematically in a school setting? Why not explore myriad opportunities to have youngsters recognize and operationalize commonly accepted, non-political civic values and virtues? What's not to like about honesty, respect, responsibility, caring, fairness, citizenship, etc.?

To avoid having our "values inquiry" be random and superficial, and to make it more systematic and scholarly, consider these pointed questions:

1. Where and how did we learn or gain our values? Did they spring upon us without our being aware of them, or was it a conscious process? Have we been brainwashed or propagandized into accepting certain values, or has it been the result of commonly accepted education—in the home, the church or synagogue, the school?
2. Does it matter whether these values were developed rationally or irrationally, imposed upon us by authority figures or self-selected?
3. What is the most appropriate arena for the inculcation of values—religious setting, home, classroom, on the street, through mass media, from societal consensus, from laws or court decisions? Serious inquiry should show how these value-forming institutions are frequently in conflict, causing the contents of our value system to ebb and flow.

If we agree that ethics demands decision making, and that decision making is based on values, then we must understand values to understand ethics. If we understand the different values that underlie our approaches to ethical decision making, then we will better recognize our own priorities.

ARE VALUES RELATIVE OR UNIVERSAL?

Despite the different ways values have been defined, many social scientists over the past half century have concluded that people share the same values—to different degrees, of course. The debate over "core values" is far from settled, and evidence demonstrates that while we say we value something, we don't always walk our talk. The debate nevertheless provides interesting fodder for discussions about the media ethics environment.

Consider the United Nations' Universal Declaration of Human Rights, drafted when the UN was founded in 1948. In essence, the UN said that to belong to the world community a nation-state had to defend the core values of life; liberty; freedom from personal attack; freedom from slavery; recognition before the law and the presumption of innocence until proven guilty; freedom from torture; freedom of conscience and religion; freedom of expression; the right to privacy, family, and correspondence; freedom to participate freely in community life; education; and a standard of living adequate for maintaining health and well-being. The "freedom of expression" value is particularly important for mass media practitioners, because our attitudes and behaviors are often based upon that value.

Kidder (2004) concluded that when thoughtful people were asked what values they would include in a global code of ethics, there was consensus about love, truth, fairness, freedom, unity, tolerance, responsibility, and respect for life.

A survey of 272 global ethicists, convened in 1996 by former Soviet leader Mikhail Gorbachev, identified five core moral values as universal: compassion, honesty, fairness, responsibility, and respect. Those values helped frame the Josephson Institute's character and community ethics programs.

A 2004 analysis of "citizen ethics" in a global context, by Clifford Christians of the University of Illinois and Kaarle Nordenstreng of Finland, led to a short list of "proto-norms," or universal values, that emerge from the sacredness of human life: respect for human dignity, respect for truth telling, and respect for nonviolence (or nonmaleficence/ no harm to the innocent). They said all communications media codes of ethics should reflect those universals, and critics of media can use the protonorms when holding media accountable. "The socially responsible press is brought to judgment before the ultimate test," the authors say, when these questions are asked: "Does it sustain life, enhance it long term, contribute to human well-being as a whole?" (p. 25).

Closer to home, social scientists have described American or national values as a subset of universal values. James Christenson and Choon Yang (1976) listed what they called the "dominant values in American society." Their rank-ordered list consisted of moral integrity, personal freedom, patriotism, work, being practical and efficient, political democracy, helping others, achievement, rational progress, material comfort, leisure, racial equality, individualism (non-conformity), and sexual equality.

Sociologist Robert Bellah and his colleagues, in their best-selling 1985 social analysis *Habits of the Heart*, expressed concern that a self-defined American value system is typified by emphasis on success, freedom, and justice—what they called a self-centered, relativistic set of motivations. (Bellah's book was a motivation for the communitarian movement of the 1990s, which in turn led to "civic" or "public" journalism efforts that sought to include public participation in defining issues for journalists.)

Frances Lappé offered a rebuttal to Bellah's pessimism. *Rediscovering America's Values* (1989) defined values as the foundation for a common identity—in America's case, the "common language of our commonwealth, without which we could not talk to each other and be understood" (p. 3). She suggested that Americans' fundamental and enduring values include freedom, democracy, fairness, responsibility, productivity, community, family, and work itself.

Many other scholars and pundits have tried to describe universal, national, institutional, and personal values. Some lists are more positive than others, seemingly reflecting an ideal world; others are less so, even bordering on the pessimistic. Some lists are descriptive, a simple compilation of what people say they value; others are normative, telling us what we ought to value so we can live well and flourish. Some are based on rigorous social science or philosophic inquiry; others are impressionistic and "popularized."

But you get the point. As Betty Sichel put it, "A society or nation cannot survive and progress without some common basic values and common moral principles" (1982, p. 11).

MEASURING VALUES

Many researchers have tried to systematically analyze and even to quantify values. By empirically studying these phenomena, social scientists have entered what previously had been the relatively subjective philosophic realm of valuation.

The social scientists making the biggest impact in values research have been Rokeach and Schwartz, whom we discussed earlier in this chapter. Rokeach's research concluded that all people "everywhere possess the same values to different degrees" (1973, p. 3). Reminding us that values underlie beliefs, attitudes, and behaviors, he concluded that values are easier to uncover and study than other variables because "an adult probably has tens or hundreds of thousands of beliefs, thousands of attitudes, but only dozens of values" (1968, p. 124). He said these values are identifiable components and measurable in relation to one another as part of a "value system," which he defined as "an enduring organization of beliefs concerning preferable modes of conduct or ends states of existence along a continuum of relative importance" (1973, p. 5). This structure helps individuals choose between alternatives, resolve conflicts, and make decisions (p. 14).

Rokeach's research tool consisted of 36 values—two parallel lists of values that people were asked to rank in order of relative importance to themselves. He identified:

- "Instrumental" values that help us reach our desired goals: being ambitious, broad-minded, capable, cheerful, clean, courageous, forgiving, helpful, honest, imaginative, independent, intellectual, logical, loving, obedient, polite, responsible, and self-controlled.
- "Terminal" values, or goals that we would like to reach during our life: a comfortable life, an exciting life, a sense of accomplishment, a world at peace, a world of beauty, equality, family security, freedom, happiness, inner harmony, mature love, national security, pleasure, salvation, self-respect, social recognition, true friendship, and wisdom.

The Rokeach inventory has been used thousands of times on hundreds of thousands of people and is the most frequently cited means of conducting values research. However, it has been faulted for being Rokeach's own intuitive assessment of what we value, and it fails to include values relating to physical well-being, individual rights such as privacy and dignity, and others. Rohan concluded that because Rokeach offered no theory about the underlying value system, the inventory is "essentially a list of unconnected value words" (2000, p. 260).

Rokeach seemed to anticipate the criticism and suggested that the framework of our values systems, and how those values are formed, is a more interesting research question than the actual content of such values. However, we need to study both the structure and content of values systems because a course exploring professional ethics is interested in (1) where our values, and those of our clients, sources, subjects, audiences, and various institutions come from, (2) how these values change over time, and (3) how to use our communications skills to effectively deal with values clashes.

Box 6.3 | VALUES IN MEDIA CODES OF ETHICS

Codes of ethics are often framed by general value statements and filled with lists of specific values. As the American Marketing Association's code says: "Values represent the collective conception of what communities find desirable, important and morally proper. Values also serve as the criteria for evaluating our own personal actions and the actions of others."

These are some of the many values found in 15 media codes of ethics.

Journalism: Nine Codes

The Society of Professional Journalists frames its code by four broad value statements. Beneath each broad statement are specific value terms:

1. Seek truth and report it (honesty, fairness, courage, care, diligence, openness—and the proviso to "examine their own cultural values and avoid imposing those values on others")
2. Minimize harm (non-maleficence, respect, compassion, sensitivity, good taste, judiciousness, humility)
3. Act independently (free of obligation, avoid conflicts of interest, be courageous, resist pressure, be wary, avoid compromise)
4. Be accountable (clarify, explain, invite dialogue, voice grievances, admit mistakes, correct mistakes, expose unethical practices).

The CyberJournalist bloggers' code borrows from the SPJ, listing as its values:

- being honest and fair (reliability)
- minimizing harm (compassion, sensitivity, no arrogance, good taste)
- accountability (explain, disclose, expose colleagues).

Kuhn's proposed code for bloggers advocates interactivity (being entertaining, interesting, and/or relevant), free expression (accountability), transparency, minimizing harm, promoting community/ relationships.

The American Society of Newspaper Editors (ASNE) has six articles in its statement of principles, all of which are value statements:

1. Responsibility (serve, inform, enable, scrutinize)
2. Freedom (be alert, vigilant)
3. Independence (avoid impropriety/appearance of impropriety, avoid conflict of interest/appearance of conflict)
4. Truth and accuracy (free from bias, fair, correct errors)
5. Impartiality
6. Fair play (decency, accountability, honor pledges).

The ASNE code concludes with this statement:

These principles are intended to preserve, protect and strengthen the bond of trust and respect between American journalists and the American public, a bond that is essential to sustain the grant of freedom entrusted to both by the nation's founders.

continued

Box 6.3 | *continued*

The Radio Television Digital News Association (RTDNA) stresses public trust, truth seeking (accuracy, context, completeness, without distortion), fairness (impartiality, emphasis on significance and relevance, respect, compassion, diversity), integrity (decency, avoiding conflicts of interest, dignity and intelligence), independence (includes avoiding undue influence from ownership and management), and accountability (to the public, the profession, and themselves).

Public Radio News Directors Inc. (PRNDI) has three basic values:

1. Truth (accuracy, balance, comprehensiveness, diversity)
2. Fairness (context, clarity, compassion, decency, respect, thoroughness, timeliness)
3. Integrity (independence, guarding against conflicts of interest, accountability).

Al Jazeera states that it values honesty, courage, fairness, balance, independence, credibility, diversity, truth, accuracy, respect, and transparency.

The National Press Photographers Association (NPPA) values being faithful, being comprehensive, truths (not manipulating), exposing wrongdoing, inspiring, understanding, connecting people, being accurate, resisting being manipulated, being complete, providing context, avoiding stereotyping, right of access, diversity, independence, unobtrusiveness, and being humble.

The Society for News Design (SND) lists five values:

1. Accuracy (do not mislead, "deliver error-free content")
2. Honesty (attribute content, be free of special interests, transparency)
3. Fairness (minimize harm)
4. Inclusiveness (combat prejudice, avoid stereotypes, promote diversity, overcome bias)
5. Courage.

SND concludes with a strong values statement: "Logic and literalness, objectivity and traditional thinking have their important place, but so must imagination and intuition, responsible creativity and empathy."

Public Relations/Public Affairs: Two Codes:

The PRSA frames its code by six broad values:

1. Advocacy (responsible advocacy)
2. Honesty (accuracy and truth)
3. Expertise (specialized knowledge, professional development, research, education)
4. Independence (objective counsel, accountability)
5. Loyalty ("faithful to those we represent, while honoring . . . public interest")
6. Fairness (respect all opinions, right of free expression).

The PRSA's code also lists six specific provisions that are value statements:

1. Free flow of information ("accurate and truthful . . . contributing to informed decision making in a democratic society," honest, correct errors)
2. Competition (healthy and fair competition)

continued

Box 6.3 | *continued*

3. Disclosure of information (open communication, investigate, reveal, disclose)

4. Safeguarding confidences ("privacy . . . of clients, organizations, and individuals," "protect privileged, confidential, or insider information")

5. Conflicts of interest ("avoiding real, potential or perceived conflicts," earn trust, disclose conflicts)

6. Enhancing the profession ("strengthen the public's trust in the profession," professional development).

The International Public Relations Association has a code that respects the United Nations charter's "faith in fundamental human rights, in the dignity and worth of the human person" and the UN Universal Declaration of Human Rights. It then lists 12 principles/values public affairs people should have in working with public authorities:

1. Integrity (honesty and integrity, securing the confidence of people with whom they work)
2. Transparency (openness and transparency in declaring who they are/work for)
3. Dialogue (rights of all parties to state case and express views)
4. Accuracy (truth and accuracy of information provided to public authorities)
5. Avoiding falsehood (don't intentionally disseminate false/misleading information; correct such acts)
6. Avoiding deception (don't obtain information by deceptive or dishonest means)
7. Confidentiality (honor confidential information)
8. Influence (don't improperly influence public authorities)
9. Inducement (don't offer or give financial or other inducement to public authorities)
10. Conflicts of interest (avoid professional conflicts of interest; disclose them when they occur)
11. Profit (don't sell to third parties documents obtained from public authorities)
12. Employment (abide by authorities' rules).

Advertising and Marketing: Three Codes:

The American Association of Advertising Agencies standards of practice hold that:

It is recognized that keen and vigorous competition, honestly conducted, is necessary to the growth and health of American business. However, unethical competitive practices in the advertising agency business lead to financial waste, dilution of service, diversion of manpower, loss of prestige, and tend to weaken public confidence both in advertisements and in the institution of advertising.

The code concludes with: "sound and ethical practice is good business. Confidence and respect are indispensable to success . . ." in business. Value terms within the code include competing on merit and that ". . . in addition to supporting and obeying the laws and legal regulations pertaining to advertising . . . " they "will not knowingly produce advertising that contains":

1. "False or misleading statements"
2. "Testimonials that do not reflect . . . real opinion"
3. "Price claims that are misleading"
4. "Claims insufficiently supported or that distort the true meaning"

continued

Box 6.3 | *continued*

5. "Statements, suggestions, or pictures offensive to public decency or minority segments"
6. "... poor or questionable taste ... that is deliberately irritating."

The American Advertising Federation (AAF) has eight "principles" in its statement of principles:

1. Truth (significant facts)
2. Substantiation (of claims)
3. Comparisons ("refrain from making false, misleading, or unsubstantiated statements")
4. Bait advertising ("shall not offer products or services ... unless ... bona fide")
5. Guarantees and warranties (must be explicit)
6. Price claims (avoid those that "are false or misleading")
7. Testimonials ("competent ... real and honest")
8. Taste and decency ("free of" matter that is "offensive to good taste or public decency").

The American Marketing Association's (AMA) Ethical Norms and Values promote "the highest standard of professional ethical norms and values."

Its ethical norms include:

1. "Do no harm."
2. "Foster trust in the marketing system."
3. "Embrace ethical values."

Its ethical values include:

1. Honesty (be truthful, "offer products that do what we claim," stand behind products, honor commitments)
2. Responsibility (avoid coercion, acknowledge social obligations, recognize "... special commitments to vulnerable market segments," "consider environmental stewardship")
3. Fairness (balance needs of buyer with needs of seller; avoid "false, misleading and deceptive promotion;" reject manipulations; "refuse to engage in price fixing, predatory pricing, price gouging or 'bait-and-switch' tactics;" "avoid knowing participation in conflicts of interest;" protect private information)
4. Respect (value difference, avoid stereotypes, listen, "understand and respectfully treat [those] from all cultures," acknowledge others' contributions, "treat everyone ... as we would wish to be treated")
5. Transparency (communicate clearly, "accept constructive criticism," "explain and take appropriate action," disclose)
6. Citizenship ("fulfill the economic, legal, philanthropic and societal responsibilities that serve stakeholders," protect the environment, "give back to the community," "ensure that trade is fair for all").

A section on "Implementation" then notes that the AMA expects members to be courageous and proactive.

continued

Box 6.3 | *continued*

Entertainment Industry: One Code of Ethics

The Free Speech Coalition is the trade association for many companies in the adult entertainment industry in the United States. The industry's code of ethics lists six values:

1. Respecting self determination (give adults the right to make their own decisions about sex and viewing sexual information, but respect the rights of people and groups that choose to block access to such material; create sexual health policies for performers and give them the right to stop an activity during a video shoot)

2. Protecting minors (make sure performers are of legal age and do not give the impression that performers are underage; do not market products to underage people)

3. Safeguarding privacy (of consumers and people in the industry)

4. Implementing professional business practices (to make sure performers are treated properly, that intellectual property rights are protected, and that contracts are fair and understood)

5. Promoting social responsibility (by providing accurate information about sex, by making sure sex products are safe, by working with groups outside the industry, and being sensitive to others in marketing)

6. Enhancing the industry (by doing the right thing, advocating First Amendment principles and sharing information).

Schwartz worked to resolve some of the concerns raised about Rokeach. Schwartz looked at the origination of values—what motivates us to prioritize one value over another —and how our value systems are structured. He and colleague Wolfgang Bilsky concluded that values emerge from our need to resolve fundamental conflicts between (1) either being open to change/opportunity, or holding fast to the status quo/ organization, and (2) either being motivated by self-interest, or by the interests of others. These two conflicts are captured in ten broad value types: power, achievement, hedonism, stimulation, self-direction, universalism, benevolence, tradition, conformity, and security. Each value type is represented by several specific values. For example, "achievement" is reflected in the values of success, capability, ambition, and influence; "universalism" is seen in broadminded, wisdom, social justice, equality, a world at peace, a world of beauty, unity with nature, and protecting the environment; "conformity" is found in politeness, obedience, self-discipline, and showing respect.

The ten value types and 44 specific values cluster in meaningful ways. If we place a high value on self-direction, stimulation, and thinking outside the box (change/opportunity), for example, we probably place less value on conformity, tradition, and security (organizational/conservative values). Another example: If we place a high value on achievement, power, and ambition (self-interest/self-enhancement), then we likely place less value on social justice, equality, being helpful, honesty, and loyalty (social context/ universalism/benevolence). As Rohan describes Schwartz and Bilsky's clusters of values, "The relative importance people place on each value type reflects their choices about what they are prepared to lose a little of to gain a little more of something else" (2000, p. 262).

Our values may influence the line of work we enter, including the myriad jobs in the mass media business. An advertising executive, or a "new media" worker, or someone in the entertainment business, may place a high value on achievement, power, and ambition (self-interest/self-enhancement), but lower value on social justice, equality, being helpful, honesty, and loyalty (social context/universalism/benevolence). A journalist might be more likely to place a high value on social justice, equality, and being helpful.

Drawing from Schwartz and Bilsky's research, we can look more closely at the values systems and specific values within the media ethics environment. One way to do this is to analyze media ethics codes and policy statements, because organizations use these vehicles to proclaim what they deem to be of worth—what they value.

SOME CONCLUSIONS ABOUT VALUES IN MEDIA ETHICS CODES

Three key sets of values emerge from the codes of ethics considered in Box 6.3. In descending order, those values are:

1. Social responsibility: minimizing harm; demonstrating care and respect; being fair, balanced, truthful, honest, and accurate; and being transparent and accountable. These specific values mesh nicely with Schwartz and Bilsky's category of values that transcend self-interest—social values of universalism and benevolence. As such, they are fundamental claims about the interdependent web of media, society, and the environment; working and playing well with others; and demonstrating empathy.
2. Freedom and the avoidance of real, perceived, or potential conflicts of interest. These values, which stress "thinking outside the box," coincide with Schwartz & Bilsky's "opportunity" values—self-direction and openness to change. Media practitioners whose codes describe professions that enjoy negative freedoms (such as freedom from governmental control) make value statements about creative and courageous use of their independence.
3. Focus on tradition, conformity, and security: humility, good taste, decency, obeying the Golden Rule or standards set by authorities, and being good citizens. Such statements appear occasionally in codes drafted by public relations and advertising associations, and rarely in codes for the news media.

It should come as no surprise that the media codes make no specific reference to Schwartz and Bilsky's fourth general category of values—those that focus on self-interest, ambition, power, and achievement. A profession's code of ethics would not endorse social status and prestige, control over people and resources, individual achievements, and sensual satisfaction. (The adult entertainment industry's code might be the exception, as the industry seeks social status.) Such values are part of many people's views of the world but are not evident in professional value statements. Highlighting these values would be at odds with the public relations function of such codes.

Eyeballing the codes, the SND and the AMA seem the most oriented to "openness to change/opportunity and self-transcendence/social context outcomes." These codes are phrased in positive, idealistic, and morally philosophic terms. Many of the news media codes also describe positive values, along with admonitions against conflicts of interest and plagiarism. Meanwhile, the IPRA and AAAA codes are the most oriented to "conservatism/organizational and self-enhancement/individual outcomes." The PRSA and advertising codes are a mixed bag of positive and negative value statements; most

Box 6.4 | COMPARING VALUE WORDS IN MEDIA ETHICS CODES

Media codes of ethics are filled with words that reveal what code writers believe are the values of their organization and craft. One analysis (Roberts, 2010) found interesting similarities and differences in the "values" words scattered across 11 media codes of ethics: five news-focused codes, two PR codes, three advertising/marketing codes, and a blogger code.

Matching the codes' value words with Shalom Schwartz's 44 representative values inside his ten value types showed that:

- The codes focus on social context outcomes such as truth, fairness, diversity, and public service. Benevolence and universalism values make up half the values in every code, although news/blogging codes are more focused on universalism themes than PR codes, which are more focused on benevolence themes.
- The codes value "truth" but have different definitions. News codes define truth in terms of what they deliver to audiences. The PRSA's code says its members adhere to truth and accuracy "in advancing the interests of those we represent," which suggests a selective truth-telling model.
- For PR and ad practitioners, the codes are more likely to mention obedience to rules, and power/prestige themes, than news codes.
- For journalism, the codes place a higher value on "self-direction" than others, because journalists say they need independence to do their jobs correctly.
- Rarely, if ever, do the codes move into the Schwartz categories of stimulation, hedonism, or security—which are opposites of benevolence and universalism values.

Table 6.1 below shows how values stack up in those codes.

of those values espouse social responsibility, and several remind practitioners to enhance their organizations, to behave decently and respectfully, and to obey existing law.

Most codes refer to the values of truth and honesty and conflicts of interest; while some of them do so in the affirmative ("seek truth," "be honest," etc.), others do so in negative terms (don't intentionally produce or disseminate false or misleading information). The difference in wording may be significant, as was suggested in the Chapter 2 discussion of codes—we would expect to see positive idealistic moral philosophy in codes that advocate "openness to change/opportunity and self-transcendence/social context outcomes." On the other hand, we could safely predict that codes tending toward "conservatism/organizational and self-enhancement/individual outcomes" would be phrased in minimalistic and legalistic terms. Our brief content analysis supports this hypothesis.

Table 6.1 Percentage of values by Schwartz's general value type and types of ethics codes

Value category/ Larger focus	News	Public Relations	Advertising/ Marketing	Blogging
Social context outcomes				
Universalism	38	15	27	67
Benevolence	32	48	23	25
Individual outcomes				
Achievement	–	15	3	–
Power	–	3	–	–
Organization				
Conformity	13	9	43	8
Tradition	2	–	–	–
Security	–	–	–	–
Opportunity				
Self-direction	15	9	3	–
Stimulation	–	–	–	–
Hedonism	–	–	–	–

Source: Roberts (2010)

NEWS VALUES—A SPECIAL CASE

Students of mass media have learned, often by rote, how to define news. Something is deemed newsworthy if it entails some of the following characteristics:

- Proximity (the closer to the audience, the more newsworthy)
- Timeliness (the more recent the event, the more newsworthy)
- Prominence (the better known the newsmakers, the more newsworthy)
- Impact (the greater the potential consequences, the more newsworthy)
- Novelty (the more unique the story, the more newsworthy)
- Conflict (the greater the conflict, the more newsworthy).

Other qualities that turn up on some lists include currency, magnitude, personality, mystery, adventure, and the like. (Some say news is anything the editor says is news, or anything that happens within ten feet of an editor.) There is no magic formula for what makes news, but these terms are most likely to be invoked.

Although journalists often maintain that news is objectively gathered and reported, these traditional definitions show that news is value-laden. An editor or reporter makes decisions about all of these criteria: Does a story about a tsunami in Asia or earthquake in Haiti override the bias toward proximity, and therefore earn a front-page spot instead of a local weather story? Do some stories have a long shelf-life and get milked day after day even if there's little new to report? How prominent must someone be to become newsworthy? How much guesswork is involved in deciding that one story will have a greater impact than another? How novel must a story be to become newsworthy? How does the gatekeeper decide which of many global and local conflicts—military, political, religious, etc.—are more deserving of media time and space?

> Try to engage a roomful of journalists in a discussion about values and the discomfort is palpable; you can see the necks stiffening, hear the teeth grinding in emotional overload . . . The tradition that says journalists should not deal in the realm of values blinds us to the fact that other people do. It is another of those "trained incapacities" that our culture foists on us.
>
> The people we seek to inform filter virtually everything they learn through their own value systems. By reporting and writing as if that does not happen, we create yet another major disconnection between us (and our product) and citizens at large.
>
> —Davis "Buzz" Merritt (1995, pp. 93, 95)

More than three decades ago, sociologist Herbert Gans challenged the notion that news is—or could be—a value-free enterprise. His study of gatekeeping decisions made at CBS Evening News, NBC Nightly News, *Newsweek*, and *Time* led to the book, *Deciding What's News* (1979), which has had a major impact on the discussion of news values.

He maintained that most news stories consciously or unconsciously reflect several cultural values and biases, or "para-ideologies." His list of values:

- Ethnocentrism—our country is superior to others; democracy is superior to dictatorship.
- Altruistic democracy—politics should follow a course based on public service and the public interest; citizens should be participants.
- Responsible capitalism—news is optimistic about competition and prosperity, and decries unfairness and exploitation.
- Small town pastoralism—news reflects a romanticized world of cohesive community and environment; bigness is bad, impersonal, and inhuman.
- Individualism—news focuses on rugged individualists and heroes who fight against encroachments of the nation and society.
- Moderatism—news emphasizes the need to maintain the social order; excess or extremism are discouraged.

Building upon Gans and other social scientists, recent critics have concluded that since news is inherently a values-based enterprise, it should be driven by moral values that transcend routine, craft-based values.

Deni Elliott (1988; 2009) has maintained that contemporary journalism has three "essential shared values": (1) Publishing news that is balanced, accurate, relevant, and complete; (2) avoiding preventable harm; (3) giving citizens information they need for self-governance.

Bill Kovach and Tom Rosenstiel argued in *The Elements of Journalism* that the purpose of journalism is to "provide people with the information they need to be free and self-governing" (2007, p. 5). Journalists must make continuous values choices in order to do their job properly.

Former *Chicago Tribune* publisher Jack Fuller (1996) described how "intellectually honest" news values must play out when journalists routinely resolve tensions between truth and loyalty to sources; the push for diversity and the need for coherence; the responsibility to reflect and sometimes oppose the communities they serve. (Fuller's list of tensions is reminiscent of *How Good People Make Tough Choices*, in which Kidder said most values choices are not between right and wrong, but between two rights: truth vs. loyalty; justice vs. mercy; individual vs. community; long-term benefits vs. short-term benefits.)

A recent gathering of media ethics scholars defined journalists as skilled communicators who gather and distribute information with professional commitments to truthfulness, accuracy, comprehensiveness/thoroughness, proportionality, authenticity, fairness, skepticism, objectivity, verifiable reporting, articulated and appropriate loyalties, a watchdog function, minimizing harm, diversity, accountability, transparency, social responsibility, independent judgment, and autonomy (Black, 2010, p. 107). If this list sounds familiar, it may be because all these values appeared in the news media codes of ethics we analyzed elsewhere in this chapter.

Meanwhile, some say the traditional lists of definitions of news should be expanded to move beyond craft-based non-moral values and to reflect a broader, systems theory. "Proximity" would go beyond physical closeness and include larger frames of reference to include society as a whole. "Timeliness" would take in larger spans of time, and consider gradual changes. "Prominence" would include ordinary people and the community as a whole. "Impact" would look at subtle, indirect consequences on the system as a whole, rather than on a few individuals. "Novelty" would be redefined to include the status quo, or "business as usual." And "conflict" would be refocused to consider examples of cooperation within communities and institutions (Hendrickson & Tankard, 1997, p. 43).

A popular media ethics textbook asks students to expand their definitions by asking news to be accurate, withstand scrutiny, be based on tenacious reporting, leave the subjects with a sense of dignity and self-respect, emerge from a reciprocal partnership with audiences, receive sufficient resources so the product is thorough, seek justice and equity for all stakeholders, value social cohesion, and reflect diversity (Patterson & Wilkins, 2008, pp. 35–36).

The bottom line is that news is not value-free. Journalists and their institutions constantly make values choices, many of which are fundamentally moral in nature. The public is better served when journalists recognize and deal openly with matters of values than when journalists pretend there are few if any values in the news business.

REVISITING FREEDONIA

Let's return again to Freedonia, this time to consider the values clashes in the case studies in which you are a blogger and a public relations practitioner (Cases 1.1 and 1.2).

The title of Case 1.1, in which you run www.freedonialive.com and can make more money by serving a marketing company, hones in on a values question: Can you "keep the money—and your self-respect?" Other values in the case study are explicit or implied: achievement, influence, credibility, enjoyment in life, independence, creativity, honesty, loyalty, obedience (to law and/or codes of ethics), reciprocation of favors, and transparency. There may be others, but this is a pretty heady list to work through.

Do any of the above represent your essential core values? Where is the dynamic tension? For instance, do some of them speak to who you are as an individual seeking self-enhancement (achievement and power) or as someone primarily concerned about others (benevolence and universalism)? Do some of them reflect your openness to change and opportunity, and others your concern about security, conformity, and tradition?

Which of the values are the most superficial?

You might find it helpful to array these values systematically according to the priority you would place on each one: How much are you willing to give up to get what you most value? Which values are "throwaways"?

We can ask the same questions about Case 1.2, in which you are the PR manager of the Freedonia paper plant that is soon to close. You will recall that in this case your loyalty is being tested: Do you abide by the management's request to remain silent about the plant closure, or do you tell any of the numerous stakeholders? You may have already reached a tentative conclusion about your conflicting loyalties, based on insights into codes of ethics and rules (Chapter 2), moral development (Chapter 3), and loyalty (Chapter 5). Regardless of your specific choice of loyalties, you have to add the general notion of loyalty to the list of values in the case: a comfortable life, family security, responsibility, courage, obedience, independence, self-respect, true friendship, equality, social justice, honesty, reciprocation of favors, transparency. Again, there may be others, but this is a tough list to work through.

Ask yourself the same questions you asked in the blogging case. Cluster the values by general types and then more specifically. Which values do you put at the top of your list, and which ones are of lesser importance? How does your value selection help you make a final decision?

Obviously, there is no single correct answer to these questions, but how you rank these values is an important part of doing ethics. You are attempting to answer one of our basic "5Ws and H" questions: "What's it worth?"

One more thing to consider: You probably answered the "What's it worth?" question from your own personal and professional perspective. Think about how values clash when you ask the question from someone else's perspective ("projective" inquiry). If you are the Freedonia blogger, you may have the same basic value system as the readers of your blog, but you are likely to choose different options based on your personal values. Likewise, different values priorities will emerge among National Paper Corporation's top management, your sister Elizabeth and her husband, a potential buyer of one of Elizabeth's homes, a company stockholder, the plant employees, and community residents.

In these and other cases, different stakeholders will likely make different choices. This does not necessarily mean that one choice is morally superior to another. Neither does it mean that values are completely situational or relative. The most important question is whether any given stakeholder made a rational choice based on clearly articulated values.

SUMMARY AND CONCLUSIONS

All the values described by scientists and philosophers represent two basic conceptions: the *desirable* (what people ought to do) and *desired* (what people want to do). These values therefore serve as guides for survival, guides for "goodness," and guides to what Aristotle called "eudaimonia," or the best possible living. They represent basic human survival requirements: biologically based needs, interpersonal social needs, and group/institutional needs.

Values clashes, and values changes, are to be expected. Different individuals, different members of professional or cultural groups or communities, and different dilemmas lead to values clashes. And as we undergo life changes, our concept of "best possible living" changes. As our experiences evolve within the media ethics environment (whether working for or consuming media), so too do our values.

We seek consistency in our values, and we try to meld our personal/social (or "personal/ tribal") values, and make them conform to one another. Those reconciliations may be instantaneous and relatively painless, or ponderous and somewhat painful—especially when our profession or peer groups and colleagues display values that strongly conflict with our own.

Reconciling the personal and the tribal (Allport, 1955) may be a life's work, but it cannot begin until we have articulated our own value system and values priorities. Otherwise, it becomes a vague, abstract, and uncomfortable "sense" that something is amiss. We cannot "fix" it until we "understand" it.

A relevant question to ask when dealing with values disconnects is: How do we bridge the values gaps? A glib answer would be to try to be sensitive to the fact that while we differ significantly on how we prioritize individual values, we nevertheless have all the same values somewhere on our radar screens. That should give us some talking points. For instance, to improve communication between environmentalists and people in a position to harm nature, both parties must seek commonality and talk about what they both value, such as being responsible, or loving, or self-controlled.

People preparing for careers in media would do well to recognize that their personal and institutional values may not jibe fully with those of their sources, subjects, clients, or audiences. Nevertheless, there are ways to bridge values gaps. Consider the investigative journalist who values honesty, responsibility, and being broadminded, ambitious, and independent. She may find herself sparring with a reluctant source who places a higher value on obedience, politeness, and self-control . . . but who also values honesty and responsibility. They might connect by defining their overlapping needs for honesty and responsibility rather than by shoving the other values in one another's faces. Or consider advertising practitioners who value truth but run up against the need to find a unique selling proposition to differentiate their products from others, even though their product is a commodity (like a can of corn) that is essentially no different from the others on the market.

At this point it is tempting to make some preliminary value judgments about values in media ethics, and values of media ethicists. Here's a short list.

Media ethicists and media reformers are generally motivated by a value system centered on social context/universalism/benevolence. Specifically, they value social responsibility, attention to the interdependent web of stakeholders, honesty, open-mindedness, and loyalty. While holding and advocating these values, media ethicists are unlikely to place a premium on values that reflect individualism/egoism/self-enhancement. There is very little promotion of the need for individual media practitioners to be at the "top of the heap" (social power, authority, wealth) or to live a hedonistic life ("it's-all-about-me," success, ambition, influence, pleasure, enjoyment of life).

Media ethicists and critics are also far more likely to have value systems that focus on opportunity and openness to change ("thinking outside the box," freedom, independence, curiosity, creativity) than on organizational and personal security (holding fast to tradition, conformity, obedience).

The authors of this textbook are consciously in alignment with the dominant value systems in the field of media ethics. We are driven more by social responsibility than by individualism, and more by openness to change than by organizational and personal security. This is who we are as individuals, scholars, professionals, teachers, parents, and members of our communities. We cannot help it. (But at least we admit it, unlike many scholars who claim their work is value-free.) Significantly, we relied upon objective social science to reach the conclusion that we are biased moral philosophers!

Therefore, the astute readers of media criticism in general and this book in particular should be aware of the value biases they are encountering.

■ ■ ■

CHAPTER VOCABULARY

Note: Definitions are available at this book's companion website.

- amoral
- civic journalism
- cognitive structure
- communitarianism
- eudaimonia
- hedonism
- immoral
- instrumental values

- metaphysical
- non-moral
- prima facie
- protonorm
- public journalism
- terminal values
- values

PRACTICAL APPLICATIONS

1. Herbert Gans's content analysis of major news media concluded that journalists were motivated by several values—whether they knew it or not. Do a small-scale study similar to the one Gans did, but instead of looking at news media, do a content analysis of your favorite blog, magazine, or video game; an advertising or public relations campaign; or a TV show or popular film. What moral and non-moral values do your media reflect? Do you think the producers were making conscious values choices, and did they expect to influence the audiences with those choices?

2. In your values analysis, compare the values you observed in the media with the values statements found in any of the pertinent media codes of ethics. How do the "real" values align with the "professed" values? If there is a disconnect, try to explain it.

3. Write a values statement for each of the media you studied. Can you prioritize that medium's moral and non-moral values?

4. Milton Rokeach developed a values inventory of 18 instrumental and 18 terminal values (see page 182). For each of the two lists, what do you personally "value" the most, and what the least? What does your personal inventory tell you about where you might fit best in the media workplace?

5. From this chapter's discussion "Are Values Relative or Universal?" make your own short list of what you think would be the essential shared valued held by your ideal circle of friends, neighborhood, university, or nation. What's at the top of your list? Why? Compare your list with the lists composed by your classmates or colleagues, and with the list you imagine would be drafted by someone with whom you seem to clash politically, socially, religiously, or in other ways.

6. Think about the "character words" or values you likely were taught in elementary or secondary school. How much did those words stick with you? Was that focus on "character education" useful, boring, a waste of time, inspiring, or something else?

■ ■ ■

CASE STUDIES

Rather than working through an entirely new set of case studies for this chapter, let's analyze the values dimensions in several of the cases we have previously encountered. (Alternatively, your instructor might send you to different case studies.) For each of the following we have already asked and answered three questions: "What's your problem?" "Why not follow the rules?" and "Who wins, who loses?" Now, however, our focus is on the fourth question, which concerns values: "What's it worth?"

Shalom Schwartz and Wolfgang Bilsky concluded that values emerge from our need to resolve fundamental conflicts between (1) either being open to change/opportunity, or holding fast to the status quo/organization, and (2) either being motivated by self-interest, or by the interests of others.

As you revisit each of the cases, make a list of all the moral and non-moral values you see within them. Then use the Schwartz-Bilsky framework to categorize those values: openness to change/status quo; self-interest/altruism. Which values do you think should prevail as you try to resolve the problems within the case studies? Are they the same values you think would actually prevail in the workplace?

When you and your classmates tried to resolve the cases the first time you encountered them, how much attention did you pay to values? Which values caught your attention at the time? Now, having read this chapter, do you work through the values issues any differently?

Use the following set of cases to answer the values questions:

- **Journalism:** Chapter 3, Case 3.1: Can you show readers what the fuss is about? (page 94)

- **New Media:** Chapter 3, Case 3.2: When in Sylvania, do you do as the Sylvanians? (page 96)

- **Public Relations:** Chapter 2, Case 2.3: Public relations: The truth of "left to pursue other interests" (page 63)

- **Advertising:** Chapter 5, Case 5:4: Using stereotypes to sell soda (page 168)

- **Entertainment:** Chapter 5, Case 5.5: Misdirection for fun and profit (page 170)

Truth and Deception

INTRODUCTION

THIS CHAPTER explores one of the most important values in the media ethics environment: truth telling. Truth is the coin of the realm whether our concern is news reporting, blogging, advertising, public relations, photography or videography, documentary filmmaking, or non-fictional memoir publishing. At least, that's what you'd think after perusing the ethics codes drafted by major media organizations. (See Box 7.1, "Media Codes of Ethics Call for Truth Telling," on page 207.)

It would be nice to say the matter is settled, because media practitioners by and large have advocated truth telling. But we cannot be that naïve. Even a passing awareness of contemporary media issues tells us that truth is often elusive. We all must decide how to seek the truth, how to tell the truth, when to balance truth telling against other compelling values, when to be a selective truth teller, and when it may be ethically justifiable to deceive for a greater good. Unfortunately, when media practitioners cross the line and out-and-out lie, they drive deep chinks into media credibility.

SOME PERPLEXING TRUTH-TELLING ISSUES

Several examples will set the stage. First we explore the problem of photo manipulation in general and in fashion magazines more specifically. Next are examples that appear to display blatant disregard of truth telling: a recent flurry of faked memoirs—books

---

This chapter:

- provides a broader perspective of truth by considering the basic nature of "truth" as a philosophic and pragmatic concept. We'll discuss "objectivity" and problems of semantics as touchstones in truth telling

- shows how some contemporary ethicists and media organizations have developed justification models and public statements to help practitioners and critics understand the challenge and do a better job of thinking their way through dilemmas

- presents several practical applications and case studies about truth telling and mass media. We'll note immediately that some choices are fairly tough for media practitioners hoping to fulfill their truth-telling mission while remaining faithful to other role-related obligations, such as minimizing harm and remaining relatively free of censorship.

that have been marketed as non-fiction—and a governmental disinformation campaign that manipulates the media. The fourth case deals with a form of deception frequently practiced by broadcast news when conducting undercover or surreptitious reporting.

Photo Manipulation

At some point in history, people came to recognize that it was incorrect to say "the camera never lies." Since the 1800s, shortly after the invention of the still camera, photographs began to lie. They were manipulations of reality when they were posed, when they were dodged and burned in the darkroom, when they were cropped, when they were printed, when they were distributed. A famous 1860s photo of Abraham Lincoln was contrived in the darkroom, where Lincoln's head was attached to John Calhoun's body. Many of Civil War photographer Matthew Brady's iconic battlefield scenes were not what they appeared to be: Brady frequently rearranged bodies and weapons—and even switched Union and Confederate uniforms on dead soldiers—to make powerful visual statements. Throughout the twentieth century, people were added to or deleted from parades and staged events depending upon the whims of those in power. Joseph Stalin, Adolf Hitler, Benito Mussolini, Mao Tse-tung, and Fidel Castro were not the only leaders to move friends into—and enemies out of—sight.

Photographs could lie before the 1980s, but the film negative of the original photo made it relatively easy to catch the liars. Then digital photography changed everything. As everyone who has ever played with Photoshop or other imaging software knows, it's not too tough to make something of nothing, or nothing of something. *National Geographic* did it a couple of times to satisfy layout demands in the early years of digital, once by moving pyramids around and another time by moving a tree, horse and rider, and moon closer together. *TV Guide* put Oprah Winfrey's head atop Ann-Margret's body. Both magazines' contrivances became food for public and media debate, and for a while it seemed a new set of standards was about to be created. And in the meantime, fashion magazines were electronically airbrushing models, giving them flawless skin, smiles, and bodies.

However, in 1994 the digital manipulation controversy went well beyond mass circulation and entertainment magazines. Traditional news media, it appeared, were also crossing the digital divide. New York's *Newsday*, a major newspaper, splashed a composite photo across its front page, depicting warring Olympic ice skaters Nancy Kerrigan and Tanya Harding practicing alongside one another. The same year a *Time* magazine cover showed a digitally darkened face of murder suspect O.J. Simpson. One thing set these two photos apart from the other news photos that had been manipulated: The public was well aware that these were not the real thing. It was widely reported that Kerrigan and Harding had not been skating together, and anyone who had seen Simpson's mugshot in *Newsweek* or elsewhere knew that in the original photo he had not been as dark or sinister as *Time* made him appear.

The controversy has continued unabated, as evidenced in the National Press Photographers Association's online report, "Ethics in the Age of Digital Photography" (2009). The association reports that in dozens of noted cases, media "caught" manipulating images either dismissed the accusations as trivial or apologized to critics and pledged to change their policies. Nevertheless, the trend continues, in coverage of wars and major international news events and in the routine presentation of news.

There seems to be little consensus among photographers, editors, advertisers, and the public about the ethics of the matter. Tom Wheeler (2002) once described cosmetic retouching as the most perplexing topic in photojournalism ethics. Meanwhile, in the commercial world, advertising practitioners and critics remain uncertain about where to draw the line. Many continue to think the practices are harmless and insignificant, even as others have pointed out the very strong likelihood that some harm occurs when certain types of images are digitally manipulated.

A troubling case in point is the digital manipulation of fashion photography in fashion magazines. The practice has been correlated to magazine fans' low self-esteem and dangerous eating disorders. The problem is yet another of those values clashes, this one aided by new technology: artistic freedom and the right to make a profit on one hand, and probability of harm to consumers on the other (Reaves et al., 2004).

Several research studies, and numerous commentaries, have argued that when magazines electronically distort models' bodies to make them unnaturally thin, the youthful readers of the magazines grow increasingly dissatisfied with their own bodies and go to great lengths to emulate the "thin ideal" models. The vicious cycle even includes a degree of addiction to the magazines themselves, and it doesn't matter whether the magazine readers know that the photos are highly contrived (Bush Hichton et al., 2008; Bissell, 2006; Reaves et al., 2004; Harrison & Cantor, 1997).

Is it ethical to digitally manipulate photographs? Should different standards be applied for news photos and advertising photos? Do news photos have to appear precisely as the event would have been perceived by an impartial onlooker, or is it permissible to do minor re-touching, such as removing a distracting sign or pole from the photo? In advertising, how much visual enhancement is appropriate? Does creative and commercial license permit impossible contrivances? For instance, if it is OK for ads to show people flying through the air, then why isn't it OK to show unrealistically slinky and cosmetically flawless fashion models? What should fashion magazines do—if anything—about the evidence that digitizing their models contributes to a major health hazard?

Faked Memoirs

The world of literature has a long and mostly honorable history of blending historical facts with fiction, in a genre appropriately known as "historical fiction." Most readers know when they're reading fiction. However, when they pick up a personal memoir or autobiography, they expect to be reading non-fiction. Lately, we cannot be sure, because the lines have gotten terribly blurred.

In 2008, the *New York Times* and other publishers gushed over a memoir by a part white, part Native American named "Margaret B. Jones." *Times* book reviewer Michiko Kakutani said Jones wrote a "humane and deeply affecting memoir" about being orphaned and coming of age in gang-infested south-central Los Angeles; the scenes Jones recreated from her youth "can feel self-consciously novelistic at times" (Kakutani, February 26, 2008). Two days after the review, the *Times* devoted 33 paragraphs in its House & Home section—a major commitment of space—to another story about the "refugee from gangland." Reporter Mimi Read tracked "Margaret B. Jones" to her four-bedroom suburban bungalow in Eugene, Ore. Read also gushed over the incredible story—a memoir that was "an intimate, visceral portrait of the gangland drug trade of Los Angeles" (Read, February 28, 2008).

Less than a week later, beneath a bold headline that screamed "Gang Memoir, Turning Page, Is Pure Fiction," the *Times* took it back. The article explained:

> The problem is that none of it is true.
>
> Margaret B. Jones is a pseudonym for Margaret Seltzer, who is all white and grew up in the well-to-do Sherman Oaks section of Los Angeles, in the San Fernando Valley, with her biological family. She graduated from the Campbell Hall School, a private Episcopal day school in the North Hollywood neighborhood. She has never lived with a foster family, nor did she run drugs for any gang member. Nor did she graduate from the University of Oregon, as she had claimed.
>
> Riverhead Books, the unit of Penguin Group USA that published "Love and Consequences," is recalling all copies of the book and has canceled Ms. Seltzer's book tour . . .
>
> (Rich, March 4, 2008)

Margaret Seltzer's mendacity was revealed by her older sister, who called Riverhead Books after seeing the February 28 *Times* profile. In her defense, Seltzer said she thought she had "an opportunity to make people understand the conditions that people live in and the reasons people make the choices" they are forced to make. Her editor, who said she had been fed a consistent, but fictitious, line for the three years the book was under development, said, "There was a way to do this book honestly and have it be just as compelling" (Rich, March 4, 2008). In another article, the *Times* quoted the publisher of Riverhead Books as saying:

> . . . the author went to extraordinary lengths: she provided people who acted as her foster siblings. There was a professor who vouched for her work, and a writer who had written about her that seemed to corroborate her story.

Not only that, but Seltzer signed a contract in which she promised to tell the truth (Rich, March 5, 2008). Even the fact checkers and copy editors for the *New York Times* were bamboozled by the trail of deception.

Love and Consequences was just one in a recent series of truth-bending memoirs. At about the same time, a gripping Holocaust memoir had been revealed as a fake. The author,

"Misha Defonseca," wrote in 1997 about a horrific childhood in which between the ages of six and ten she escaped from the Nazis, killed a German soldier in self-defense, and lived with wolves while scouring Europe for her deported parents. The highly successful memoir, *Misha: A Mémoire of the Holocaust Years*, was translated into 18 languages and made into a film in France. But there was no Misha; author Monique DeWael grew up as a Catholic in Brussels. Her parents had been killed by the Nazis for being resistance fighters. "There are times when I find it difficult to differentiate between reality and my inner world," DeWael said. "The story in the book is mine. It is not the actual reality—it was my reality, my way of surviving." The French film being made from the book was described by a spokeswoman for the director as "a fiction from the book. No matter if it's true or not—she believes it is, anyway—she just thinks it's a beautiful story" (Mehegan, 2008).

Probably the best known literary fraud in recent years was James Frey's *A Million Little Pieces*. Touted by Oprah Winfrey in 2005, the book about Frey's struggles with drug addiction sold 3.5 million copies and shot to the top of the non-fiction bestseller list. After Thesmokinggun.com revealed significant discrepancies between Frey's real life and Frey's memoir, the backlash was instant and severe. Oprah, who initially defended Frey, brought him back to her show and excoriated him. "I don't think it's a novel. I still think it's a memoir," Frey told Oprah. "I don't feel like I conned you. I still think the book is about drug addiction and alcoholism, and no one is disputing that I was a drug addict and an alcoholic, and it's about the battle to overcome that" (CNN.com, 2006). Some of Frey's claims were questioned as early as 2003, when the book was first published. Frey said he had never denied altering small details in the book, and that he stood by the book as being the essential truth of his life. On the Oprah show, however, he said the same demons that addicted him to drugs and alcohol made him fabricate significant parts of his memoir.

It is not the only time Oprah was tricked, either. Herman Rosenblat appeared on her show twice involving the story that became *Angel at the Fence: The True Story of a Love that Survived*. His memoir involves his life with Roma, a woman he met while in a Nazi concentration camp and married 15 years later after a blind date in New York. The story was fake, and the book was canceled. After being caught, he released a note through his agent that said: "In my dreams, Roma will always throw me an apple, but I now know it is only a dream" (Rich & Berger, 2008).

Other recent literary frauds were traced by the *New York Times'* Motoko Rich in an article titled "A Family Tree of Literary Fakers" (March 8, 2008). They included a novel and story collection by "J.T. LeRoy," who passed himself off as a West Virginia truck stop prostitute but who was, in reality, a Brooklyn woman named Laura Albert, who used a friend to impersonate LeRoy in interviews and public appearances. Another well-known case was that of ersatz journalist Clifford Irving, who wrote a fake autobiography of billionaire Howard Hughes in 1972. Irving, who got a $765,000 advance from his publisher, spent 17 months in jail for his hoax. (Irving called *The Hoax*, the 2006 Richard Gere movie version of his case, "a hoax about a hoax.")

Some key questions about these incidents: Are these stories "lies"? What harm is caused by fiction passed off as non-fiction? Who gets hurt? Who benefits? Could the same powerful stories be told without the fictional embellishments? Could the problem be resolved if the stories were labeled as fact-based fiction?

Government Disinformation

Truth is said to be the first casualty of war (Knightley, 2002). It is sacrificed not only by totalitarian or communist regimes, but by democratic states. The United States is no exception.

During the recent war in Iraq, the US engaged in an "information offensive" closely aligned with its military offensive. The US government secretly paid Iraqi newspapers large sums of money to plant pro-American articles, written in Arabic and disguised as coming from Iraqi sources, in Baghdad newspapers. A *Los Angeles Times* investigation (Mazzetti & Daragahi, 2005) said the "basically truthful" but one-sided articles were produced and distributed by a Washington-based firm called the Lincoln Group. Its operatives, posing as freelance writers or advertising executives, would show up at financially strapped Iraqi newspapers with a wad of currency—sometimes as much as $1,500—and give an editor or staff member a "news article" ready for publication. Many of the articles were published "as is," while some were published as paid advertisements, although the distinction between the two forms was never clear.

According to the *Los Angeles Times*:

> The military's effort to disseminate propaganda in the Iraqi media is taking place even as U.S. officials are vowing to promote democratic principles, political transparency and freedom of speech to a country emerging from decades of dictatorship and corruption. It comes as the State Department is training Iraqi reporters in basic journalism skills and Western media ethics, including one workshop titled "The Role of Press in a Democratic Society."
>
> (Mazzetti & Daragahi, 2005)

The propaganda campaign worried some military officers and civilians, who said that undermining the news media would damage America's credibility at home and overseas. Lines were growing more and more blurred between legitimate public affairs operations of the military (providing truthful information to the media) and the kinds of overt and covert propaganda produced by the Pentagon and companies it hired to plant stories. Among the Pentagon's overt propaganda efforts: buying an Iraqi newspaper and taking control of a radio station to channel pro-American messages, without identifying them as military operations. It is against US laws to do this kind of "psychological operation" within the American borders, but there is some question about the legality of doing it overseas.

If truth is the first casualty of war, and if propaganda emerges naturally as a political and military instrument, what can the conscientious citizen do? Where do we turn to get full, unvarnished facts about our government, our military operations, and the operations of those we are fighting? Or, during wartime, is it appropriate to set aside such unrealistic expectations and accept the stories and versions of reality produced by those with special agendas—even if the producers are on "our side"? Is selective truth telling, or deception, or outright lying permissible under these special circumstances? What are the short-term and long-term consequences of such actions?

Journalistic Deception

Charter Behavioral Health Systems is a major provider of mental health in the United States. CBS News's *60 Minutes II* broadcast an investigative report about Charter, involving undercover surveillance and a hidden camera. The broadcast documented patient deaths, physical injury, unsafe conditions, falsification of records, untrained staff, and physical restraint of patients in dangerous and abusive ways (CBS, 1999). In narrating the report, newsman Ed Bradley said the only way to know what goes on behind the scenes was to work there. CBS recruited Terrance Johnson—a recent graduate of a master's program in social work at the University of Pennsylvania—to apply for a job at the Charter facility in Charlotte, NC. Johnson, recommended by Penn faculty, was neither a journalist nor a regular employee of CBS. Producers equipped him with hidden camera equipment and instructed him about the investigation, especially that he was not to lie and that his first duty was to protect patients in his care and fulfill his job assignments for Charter.

CBS producers worked closely with lawyers throughout the investigation. When stories such as this end up in court, the costs are high. (In the 1990s, ABC News spent millions in legal fees to fight charges that its workers trespassed and broke other laws when they went undercover to film a story about sanitary conditions at Food Lion grocery stores in the Carolinas.) Following the CBS broadcast, US Department of Health and Human Services and the US Department of Justice were among federal agencies that conducted their own investigations of the entire Charter system and took various actions against Charter. The company then closed or sold more than 50 installations.

This case is of special importance in the ethics of journalism, in part because of continuing controversy related to undercover investigations by news organizations. Critics of such investigations are concerned about the inherently deceptive nature of undercover work and excessive use of the technique. Proponents suggest that in many situations—nursing homes, mental institutions, prisons, businesses—going undercover is often the only effective way to discover what goes on behind closed doors and to document it in ways that eliminate deniability by wrongdoers. The debate continues.

CBS said of the piece: "'Unsafe Haven' demonstrated that most of the terrible things that happen inside private mental hospitals are shrouded in secrecy." The Society of Professional Journalists gave "Unsafe Haven" and producers Helen Malmgren and David Gelber special recognition for excellence in investigative reporting (Hodges, 2000).

STOP!

Before proceeding, compare and contrast these examples. The photo examples describe a popular but problematic distortion of reality, using readily available technology available on almost every home computer. The next examples involve high levels of deceptive storytelling and psychological warfare. The fourth involves deceptive newsgathering techniques. Can you justify any of the media actions in these examples? On what basis? How do any of the behaviors mesh with the statements in the various codes of ethics cited in Box 7.1?

This chapter presents justification models intended to help us resolve these types of cases. For now, however, see what you come up with when relying upon some basic, tried-and-true thought processes about "doing ethics" when tempted to commercialize distortion, blend fact and fiction, produce propaganda, or use surreptitious reporting techniques.

SOME THEORIES OF TRUTH

An old joke about baseball umpires reminds us about different theories of truth:

> Three umpires are arguing. The first umpire says, "Some are balls and some are strikes, and I call them as they are."
>
> The second umpire replies, "Some are balls and some are strikes, and I call them as I see them."
>
> The third umpire says, "Some are balls and some are strikes, but they ain't nothing until I call them."

It is easy to dispense with discussions of truth by uttering any number of bromides: "Truth is absolute; based on reality. There are no ifs, ands, or buts about it." "Truth is revealed." "Truth is based on hard facts; it emerges from scientific inquiry." "Truth mirrors reality." "There's Capital-T Truth and small-t truth." "There is no such thing as Capital-T Truth." "Truth is a matter of context." "Truth is in the eye of the beholder." "Truth is what I say it is." "There's truth, and then there's truthiness." "There's no such thing as truth. Period."

Actually, each bromide has some philosophic and historical basis. Good people, attempting to make sense of their world, have developed a wide range of perspectives about the nature of truth. Students interested in digging deeply into these perspectives will find arguments saying truth is epistemological; truth is moral; truth is based on either realism or idealism; truth is either discovered or revealed; and that truth emerges from either scientific naturalism or subjective relativity. Three of those perspectives highly pertinent to the media ethics environment are the correspondence theories, coherence theories, and pragmatic theories.

Box 7.1 | MEDIA CODES OF ETHICS CALL FOR TRUTH TELLING

Regardless of the media specialty, truth is an overarching value. These codes of ethics all call for communicators to be truthful.

Society of Professional Journalists: The first principle of the SPJ code is: "Seek truth and report it. Journalists should be honest, fair and courageous in gathering, reporting and interpreting information." Seven specific examples of how to carry out these duties are listed in the code, which says journalists should:

- Test the accuracy of information from all sources and exercise care to avoid inadvertent error. Deliberate distortion is never permissible.
- Make certain that headlines, news teases and promotional material, photos, video, audio, graphics, sound bites and quotations do not misrepresent. They should not oversimplify or highlight incidents out of context.
- Never distort the content of news photos or video. Image enhancement for technical clarity is always permissible. Label montages and photo illustrations.
- Avoid misleading re-enactments or staged news events. If re-enactment is necessary to tell a story, label it.
- Avoid undercover or other surreptitious methods of gathering information except when traditional open methods will not yield information vital to the public. Use of such methods should be explained as part of the story.
- Never plagiarize.
- Distinguish news from advertising and shun hybrids that blur the lines between the two.

National Press Photographers Association: The preamble to the NPPA code says "Our primary goal is the faithful and comprehensive depiction of the subject at hand." The code notes that "photographic and video images can reveal great truths," and that news photographers should "be accurate and comprehensive in the representation of subjects," to "resist being manipulated by staged photo opportunities," to "maintain the integrity of the photographic images' content and context," and not to "manipulate images or add or alter sound in any way that can mislead viewers or misrepresent subjects."

The Radio Television Digital News Association: The code says professional electronic journalists should "seek the truth, report it fairly and with integrity and independence, and stand accountable for their actions." RTDNA members are told to "pursue truth aggressively and present the news accurately, in context, and as completely as possible." Specifically, the code says its members should "continuously seek the truth," "resist distortions that obscure the importance of events," and "clearly disclose the origin of information and label all material provided by outsiders." Members should not "report anything known to be false," "manipulate images or sounds in any way that is

continued

Box 7.1 | *continued*

misleading," "plagiarize," or "present images or sounds that are reenacted without informing the public."

The Society for News Design: Its code of ethics focuses on accuracy, honesty, fairness, inclusiveness, and courage. Under "accuracy" SND says "We must ensure that our content is a verifiable representation of the news and of our subjects." Under "honesty" it says "Our work will be free from fraud and deception—that includes plagiarism and fabrication." Under "fairness" it says "Even when it is impossible to avoid harm in the pursuit of truth telling, we will work hard to minimize that harm."

CyberJournalist.net: A Bloggers' Code of Ethics proposed by CyberJournalist.net adapts the SPJ framework; its guidelines tell bloggers to "be honest and fair in gathering, reporting and interpreting information," to "never plagiarize," to "identify and link to sources whenever feasible," to "make certain that Weblog entries, quotations, headlines, photos and all other content do not misrepresent . . . not oversimplify or highlight incidents out of context," to "never distort the content of photos without disclosing what has been changed," to "never publish information they know is inaccurate," to "distinguish between advocacy, commentary and factual information," and to "distinguish factual information and commentary from advertising and shun hybrids that blur the lines between the two."

Public Relations Society of America: One of the six statements of professional values listed at the outset of the PRSA code is: "Honesty: We adhere to the highest standards of accuracy and truth in advancing the interests of those we represent and in communicating with the public."

American Advertising Federations: The first line in the AAF advertising principles of American business is: "Truth—Advertising shall reveal the truth, and shall reveal significant facts, the omission of which would mislead the public."

The American Association of Advertising Agencies: The AAAA standards of practice says:

> We will not knowingly produce advertising that contains a) false or misleading statements or exaggerations, visual or verbal; b) testimonials which do not reflect the real opinion of the individual(s) involved; c) price claims that are misleading; d) claims insufficiently supported, or that distort the true meaning of practicable application of statements made by professional or scientific authority; e) statements, suggestions or pictures offensive to public decency or minority segments of the population.

Free Speech Coalition: Even the adult entertainment industry makes passing reference to truth telling, in its provisions about "promoting social responsibility." The first clause under that provision says its members "promote dissemination of accurate information about responsible adult sexuality to both industry performers and consumers."

Correspondence Theories

Correspondence theories are also known as theories of conformity, congruence, or agreement. They are tied to metaphysical realism, holding that truthful propositions correspond to or mirror objective reality. For instance, consider these quotes from the *Stanford Encyclopedia of Philosophy* (2005):

> Aristotle: "To say of what is that it is not, or of what is not that it is, is false, while to say of what is that it is, or of what is not that it is not, is true."

> Thomas Aquinas: "Truth is the equation of thing and intellect . . . A judgment is said to be true when it conforms to the external reality."

> Bertrand Russell: "Thus a belief is true when there is a corresponding fact, and is false when there is no corresponding fact."

> Rene Descartes: "I have never had any doubts about truth, because it seems a notion so transcendentally clear that nobody can be ignorant of it . . . the word 'truth,' in the strict sense, denotes the conformity of thought with its object."

> Immanuel Kant: "The nominal definition of truth, that it is the agreement of (a cognition) with its object, is assumed as granted."

And, baseball umpire No. 1: "Some are balls and some are strikes, and I call them as they are."

John Milton and later Enlightenment scholars challenged the Medieval view that truth existed "out there" and is revealed by God or other authority figures—an argument against "tenacity" as a way of fixing our beliefs, as discussed in Chapter 1. Rather, Enlightenment scholars advocated using intellect, judgment, and basic senses (touch, taste, smell, etc.) to discover what is true and what isn't. They gave birth to ideas of democracy and rational government, and to the scientific method—truths are perceived by senses and intellect; they are discovered, rational, verifiable, recorded, and replicable.

In the media ethics environment, correspondence theories of truth have led to the notion of objectivity in journalism and truth-claims in advertising. Based on the scientific method, objectivity holds that journalists can make factually true statements about the real world. The more carefully they observe that world, the more truthful their reports can be. In another media arena, when advertisers are told to make factual statements or truth claims about their products, they speak in terms of verifiable evidence. The government demands long, scientifically based "disclaimers" on prescription drugs. And we might also note the permissible "puffery," those fuzzy generalizations ("Whiter than white," "fresher than springtime," "always low prices," "be all you can be") that cannot be scientifically proven and are therefore not held to standards of correspondence. And, in the world of autobiographies and memoirs, readers have a reason to expect the stories to be based on events that actually happened.

Before we say, "This enlightenment perspective makes perfectly good sense; how could anybody argue against systematic, scientific reasoning?" we should note some problems with correspondence theory. To begin, some philosophers' definitions are extremely broad; the definitions seem either to be so intuitively obvious that they are trivial platitudes, or so obscure that they seem meaningless. Although they may be readily applied to science and some other fields, they don't work as well on matters of morality, as there are no "moral facts." (We should be aware, however, that critics concede there are "moral truths," for instance, that it is wrong to cause harm to innocent and help-less persons. But that's a somewhat different matter, given that such statements don't necessarily correspond with a specific body of facts.) Finally, one who accepts corres-pondence theory of truth must necessarily be skeptical about the external world. Consider the difficulty of "stepping outside our mind" to do a reality check: How do we compare our minds with mind-independent reality? We would have the impossible task of encountering reality on its own terms, independent of what we think of it.

Coherence Theories

Coherence theories of truth hold that the truth of propositions, assertions, or beliefs must connect logically and directly with other propositions, assertions, or beliefs that we think are true. Such theories hold that our propositions, assertions, or beliefs are false if they are inconsistent with or contradict other beliefs that we believe are true. Put another way, it's a matter of language, in which the goal is to make systematic and rigorously consistent connections between the assertions. This contrasts with correspondence theories, which focus on systematic and proper connections between our assertions and objective reality. The basic question about coherence theory is whether our propositions cohere to one another, not whether our propositions cohere to external reality.

A problem with coherence theories is that we can believe something because it is consistent with other things we believe, but never have any independent evidence to support those beliefs. Someone who is extremely closed-minded or dogmatic is likely to have an extremely coherent and logical view of the world, with few of those beliefs based on reality. (Remember Misha, the Holocaust survivor discussed above? She had created her own reality—a logical but not fact-based reality—that constituted her life story. Her quote—"There are times when I find it difficult to differentiate between reality and my inner world"—is an operational definition of a coherence theory of truth.) Coherence theory allows people to be sincere in their beliefs—but sincerely wrong when compared to reality.

We encounter the coherence theory continuously in the media environment.

Advertisers, public relations practitioners, and producers of entertainment fare often engage in word play or symbolic manipulation. As they produce a highly creative campaign or a story line, they may find themselves relying upon truth claims that have a tenuous correlation with external reality. Effective advertising is often reduced to a slogan about a slogan, when a 30-second spot is focused on a selling proposition that can be reduced in a few seconds to a single rhetorical claim. The presumption is that if consumers accept the longer proposition they also will respond when the core claim is repeated. A similar principle holds for public relations campaigns seeking to solidify or shift public opinion: Once the essential concept is laid out, it needs to be effectively reinforced by slogans or other symbolic manipulations. Entertainment producers who deal in myths and stereotypes also make effective use of the coherence theory of truth. In the process of piling truth claims upon truth claims, the creators of media fare may have come to believe their own rhetoric. When that happens, they are still "speaking truth," according to coherence theory.

Coherence theory motivates many stakeholders in the world of journalism. Investigative and political reporters attempt to cut through the self-serving or evasive rhetoric, the hyperbole, the claims and counter-claims of individuals and institutions. The defense mechanism of the journalistic "targets" may be to remain consistent in their claims —regardless of whether those claims have any basis in objective reality. Journalists and news consumers often find this to be extremely aggravating. If a leader insists that the economy is going well, the war is being won, the environment is in good shape, and all of our tomorrows will be glorious, it is likely that these truth claims are coherent or consistent with the leader's view of the world ... regardless of hard evidence to the contrary. To expect that leader to give opinions to the contrary would be to ask the leader to make false statements, according to the coherence theory. It also follows that journalists who accept sources' questionable truth claims and repeat them verbatim may also be abiding by the coherence theory.

As umpire No. 2 said: "I call them as I see them."

Pragmatic Theories

Pragmatic theories come in many varieties; some theorists put them under the coherence theories umbrella. Basically, they combine umpire No. 2's subjectivity with umpire No. 3's "they ain't nothin' until I call them." In other words, these are theories about statements that are true if they let us get on with the business of interacting with the real world, a world "out there" and a world partly of our own making.

Not all pragmatic theories approach the subject similarly. One view, akin to coherence, is that we assert that a statement is true merely by asserting the statement itself: "It's true because I say so."

Pragmatic theories of truth are concerned with the semantics of assertions but go beyond that perspective. They suggest that we interpret the world, we give the world meaning, and we recognize the limits of our observational powers and the power of our truth statements. As postmodern theorists suggest, truth is in the eye and mind of the beholder, and each of us is entitled to different truths because each of us is an individual with unique values, biases, and perspectives. Given this "standpoint epistemology," each of us is a truth maker.

Obviously, pragmatic theories butt heads with correspondence theories of truth. The battle lines are significant in the media ethics environment. Whereas notions of objectivity emerge from correspondence theories, which suggest that systematic inquiry and fair-minded reporting are achievable (Figdor, 2010), the modern criticisms of objectivity spring from pragmatism. How, the pragmatist asks, can we expect objectivity from a flawed human, working in a flawed institution, where observations are nuanced by individual points of view, values, and even the simple matter of where stakeholders are standing when observing something? The best to be hoped for, according to the pragmatist, is an open-minded and ongoing commitment to accuracy and fairness. When the Society of Professional Journalists rewrote its ethics code in 1996, traditionalists decried the absence of the word "objectivity." It is safe to say traditionalists accepted the premises of correspondence theory, whereas the SPJ ethics committee tended toward the pragmatic.

> Objectivity means giving all sides a fair hearing, but not treating all sides equally . . . So objectivity must go hand in hand with morality.
> —Christiane Amanpour, in "Just the facts?" *The Washington Monthly*,
> Jan/Feb, 1999, p. 23
>
> Anybody who's ever interviewed five eyewitnesses to an automobile accident knows there's no such thing as objectivity.
> —Molly Ivins, quoted in Navasky, 2005

In entertainment media, is it OK to rearrange or ignore what really happened in order to save money, save time, not bore the audience, or to state a larger truth? If so, are there lines that cannot be crossed? At what point does a lack of verisimilitude become ethically troublesome?

Is it fair for public relations or advertising practitioners to communicate their own version of "truth" when their idiosyncratic version ignores other versions of what truth might be—or that they have come to their version of truth because they were paid to believe it? (We explore the difficult nature of "selective truth telling" in Chapter 9.)

As is the case with other theories of truth, pragmatism has its problems. There's a good possibility that pragmatism leads to relativism and the belief that what's right for one individual, institution, or community may not necessarily be right for all. Several people in the examples at the start of this chapter seemed to have created their own unique realities; a couple of them didn't appear to understand how out of sorts they were with mainstream perspectives on truth telling. Because truth is "constructed" under the pragmatic (and coherence) theories, all sorts of semantic and political mayhem may occur. Meanwhile, it is easy for an adherent of pragmatic theories to conclude that there are varying degrees of truth, and that some beliefs are more "effective" than others.

If you think about this stuff too hard, you may not know how to answer when the bailiff asks you to promise to tell the truth, the whole truth, and nothing but the truth . . .

THE SEMANTICS OF TRUTH TELLING

If there is a growing disconnect between media practitioners and their audiences over matters of truth, part of the problem may be due to the careless use of language. We have considered various philosophic and pragmatic explanations of truth, but there is more to be said about the everyday use and abuse of truth claims. The field of general semantics provides some additional ideas about how to connect language and truth in ways that improve the media ethics environment (Black, 2001; 2009).

General semantics, a field of study framed by Alfred Korzybski in *Science and Sanity* (1933/1948), assesses human's unique symbolic behavior by studying the relationships between words and what we do with them and what they do to us. At its heart is the argument that unscientific or "Aristotelian" assumptions about language and reality result in semantically inadequate or inappropriate behavior. In short, general semantics goes beyond simple matters of grammar or language style, and encompasses the broader semantic and symbolic environment.

General semanticists' descriptions of sophisticated language behavior include—but are not limited to—awareness that:

1. Our language is not our reality, but is an inevitably imperfect abstraction of that reality.
2. Unless we're careful, our language usually reveals more about our own biases than it does about the persons or objects we're describing.
3. People and situations have unlimited characteristics. The world is in a constant process of change; our perceptions and language abilities are limited.
4. A fact is not an inference, and an inference is not a value judgment.
5. Different people perceive the world differently, and we should concede that all viewpoints are the result of imperfect human perceptual processes, and not as absolute truth.
6. People and situations are rarely if ever two-valued. Propositions do not have to be either "true" or "false," specified ways of behaving do not have to be either "right" or "wrong," "black" or "white." Thinking along a continuum or an infinite-valued orientation is a more valid way to perceive the world than an Aristotelian two-valued orientation (Bois, 1966; Chase, 1938, 1954; Hayakawa, 1949, 1954, 1962; Johnson, 1946; Korzybski, 1948; Lee, 1941; Postman, 1985. See also *Etcetera: A Review of General Semantics*, a quarterly published by the Institute for General Semantics).

The general semantics literature suggests a series of patterns that typify either the semantically sophisticated or unsophisticated communicator. The insights should be of value to any media that purport to be truth tellers. (Entertainment and fiction-based media are held to somewhat different semantic standards, because they make fewer truth claims.) These semantic "behaviors" concern not only the *process* of gathering and presenting information that is used to produce news, advertising, and public relations, but also the media *products*. Furthermore, they address the needs of consumers of media, who use media to help them make sense of the world.

Specific semantic problems for the communicator can be identified, and semantic solutions to those problems can be proposed. Although presented in polarized form, they are best understood in terms of a continuum:

1. Problem: The Blurring of Abstraction Levels. Problems arise when media carelessly jump within and among different levels of abstraction, when they leave the impression that "that's the way it is," when they draw inferences and value judgments without sharing with their audiences the hard data (if any) used to move to those higher levels of abstraction.

Alternative: Truth tellers should know, and show, the differences between objects, statements of fact, inferences, and value judgments. They should remember that abstraction is the inevitable process of narrowing and reducing data from the real world and from humans' limited ability to observe it; they should be aware of what they are leaving out and what they are adding. Fact statements can be verified by impersonal means, and they are used to apply to particular people or situations at a particular time and particular place. Inferences and value judgments should emerge from fact statements.

Truth tellers would do well to tell what someone or something "does" rather than what it "is." They should encourage their audiences to draw their own conclusions rather than doing all their thinking for them. When media people do draw conclusions in their news reports, editorial opinion columns, ads, or PR campaigns, those conclusions should be based on verifiable evidence that is shared with the audiences. That way, audiences can "check it out" for themselves.

2. Problem: The Tendencies Toward "Allness." Problems arise when communicators act as though they have seen all they need to (or could possibly) see, have described all they need to (or could possibly) describe, and have concluded all they need to (or could possibly) conclude. Their language is replete with terms such as "all," "every," "none," "never," "nobody," "everybody," "unanimous," "absolutely," "positively," "forever," "always," "finally," etc. "Allness" writing appears dogmatic, and appears to presume that all the evidence is in and has been duly considered, and that people, situations, and problems are generally alike in most respects.

Alternative: Media practitioners and consumers should be conscious of "etcetera," aware that descriptions may be adequate yet incomplete: People can never see, or say, everything that needs to be seen or said about an individual or situation, so they shouldn't pretend they're doing otherwise. Semantically sophisticated communication is characterized by "etc." terms that alert everyone to the reality that most generalizations are problematic: "perhaps," "some," "several," "sometimes," "however," "on the other hand," "maybe," "not always," "usually," "generally," "often," "most," "majority," "plurality," "minority," "indefinitely," and other such qualifying words. Media that seek alternatives to "allness" are filled with answers to "how much" and "to what extent" questions. To achieve this, practitioners are driven by boundless curiosity and dissatisfaction with simplistic explanations of complex issues. As many general semanticists have explained, "The map is not the territory."

3. Problem: The "Two-Valued Orientation.**"** Semantic and ethical problems arise when the world and all its subsets of data are arbitrarily divided into mutually exclusive, polarized opposites.

"Two-valued" communicators say that "on the one hand ... on the other hand" (there are only two hands?); they seek out spokespersons who confirm these perceptions of mutual exclusivity (some journalists seem to "balance" their coverage by interviewing an "articulate idiot from each ideological pole"); their adjectives describe stereotypical types, such as "hot/cold," "tall/short," "black/white," "liberal/conservative," "you're with us/you're against us."

To hold such a static view demands that belief-discrepant information be avoided or downplayed, dissonance quickly reduced. Granted, it is easier to view the world in this way, but it is ethically problematic.

Alternative: To demonstrate a multi-valued orientation, the use of "etcetera" is helpful. It reminds media practitioners and audiences that persons and situations are rarely if ever two-valued; that propositions do not have to be either "true" or "false," specified ways of behaving do not have to be either "right" or "wrong," "black" or "white," that continuum-thinking or an infinite-valued orientation is a more intellectually honest way to perceive and communicate about the world than an Aristotelian two-valued orientation.

Hyphens, rather than "either/or," are the stylistic tool of choice, to describe mind-body, secular-religious, socio-economic, and other relationships. The semantically mature communicator displays awareness that people and situations have unlimited characteristics, that the world is in a constant process of change, that human perceptions are limited, and that language cannot say all there is to be said about a person or situation.

Indeed, a multi-valued media practitioner relishes subtlety in sources, subjects, and stories, and processes dissonance with a certain level of comfort.

4. Problem: The "Is of Identity.**"** When people ask "What is?" or "Who is?" the answers tend to be stereotypes. The questions, and answers, may make reporters and other story tellers—along with their audiences—appear unconscious of myriad individual differences among individuals, situations, problems, etc.

Truth claims can emerge from observation and scientific evidence, or from unverifiable bases such as faith, aesthetics, authority, intuition, or philosophy. Problems arise when communicators fail to recognize which source is which.

When "to be" verbs are used as an equal sign ("He *is* a terrorist"; "She *is* a freedom fighter") they suggest that language is equated to reality. To do so is to set up false-to-fact relationships, resulting in stereotypes, labels, name-calling, and instant classification of individuals, groups, and situations. Such behaviors ignore that language is only an imperfect abstraction of reality.

Alternative: Semantically sophisticated truth tellers seek nuances. They use verbs of "non-identity." They separate nouns with qualifying verbs (if only in their heads) such as "may be classified as," "goes by the name of," "is referred to as," "calls himself/herself/itself/themselves," "so-called," or any other terms that answer the question "How do you classify?" They differentiate among people, situations, and problems.

5. Problem: The "Is of Predication." When people use "to be" verbs between nouns and adjectives ("He is stupid," "She is beautiful"), or when they carelessly employ adjectives to affirm qualities, they may falsely assume that everyone else sees the qualities in the same way. That is, unsophisticated communicators are ignoring their own selectivity processes. Their language reveals more about their own biases than it does about what they are describing; they may unconsciously be projecting their own biases onto their audiences.

Alternative: Communicators should be aware of their selectivity and projections by qualifying problematic noun/adjective relationships. They can use "to me," or "according to . . . ," or "in . . . opinion," or "from . . . point of view," or "as . . . sees it," or "perhaps," or "one school of thought is," or "possibly." Instead of asking "What is . . . ?" the communicator asks, "What do you think is . . . ?"

6. Problem: Being Time-bound. The time-bound communicator apparently fails to understand or appreciate the interconnectedness of time and development, the inter-relationship of past, present, and future. Some manifestations of this trait: When communicators fixate on the past, they put "new information into old bottles," because it is more understandable and predictable that way. When they fixate on the present, information seems void of context. When they fixate on the future there's little value in taking note of precedents—prognostication is the coin of the realm. (Aside: Why do the talking heads, the speculators and prognosticators, prevail in our sports, business, political, and other media? And who calls them to account when they are wrong, as they so often are?)

Alternative: Change is the constant companion for the semantically sophisticated media practitioners. Life is gestalt—anything is the cause and result of everything. Subtle forces from the past influence the present media environment, and the future is a multifaceted mystery affected only partly by what is known of past and present. Conscientious communicators need not be obsessed by past/present/future inter-relationships, but do well to appreciate them. They should be curious about their heritage, learn from their mistakes, and remain guardedly optimistic.

Summing Up: As many general semanticists have maintained, "The map is not the territory." With that in mind, all the stakeholders in the media ethics environment should be better at making and reading maps.

A TRUTH CONTINUUM

A helpful approach to understanding varying shades of truth was proposed by now-retired University of Alabama journalism professor Frank Deaver (1990). He sketched a continuum of truth telling that ranged from capital-T "truth" at the top to "blatant lies" at the bottom. His continuum was divided into four broad categories, each of which necessitated a different type of ethical justification.

At the top of the list are conscientious attempts to present information correctly, accurately, fully, and without bias—as far as is humanly possible. This is the goal of communicators who gather and process facts and information. Deaver distinguished between elusive TRUTH and small-t truth, admitting to the pragmatists' view that the best we can do is perceive, view, and describe honestly and to the best of our ability.

Drawing from Plato's allegory of the cave (in which prisoners confuse shadows on the cave wall with objective reality) and Walter Lippmann's classic *Public Opinion* (1922), Deaver observed that we should make a clear distinction between "news" and "truth."

Items in continuum	Group characteristics
TRUTH/truth	*Intent to inform*
facts and information	*accurately, fully;*
journalistic "news"	*no apparent bias.*
public relations copy	*Intent to persuade*
editorials/columns	*by using selective*
advertising copy	*information; truth*
propaganda	*but not whole truth.*
parables and allegories	*Non-truths told*
fiction	*without intent*
honest error	*to deceive.*
deceit	*Intent to deceive,*
"white lies"	*even if for purpose*
BLATANT LIES	*claimed to be justifiable.*

FIGURE 7.1 | Truth continuum

Facts and information are not the same as truth. At best, a collection of facts can lead to a body of information, but it does not necessarily equate to truth.

The second group of items along the continuum entails some aspects of persuasion. Deaver says it is significant that persuasion does not permit the telling of untruths. Public relations copy, editorials and columns, advertising, and even propaganda are intended to persuade, but do so via selective truth telling, bias, and expression of opinions. Propaganda—a complex topic discussed in Chapter 9—is at the bottom of this second category in Deaver's continuum, because some types of propaganda stretch the truth to the breaking point.

The third group of items deals with untruths that are not intended to deceive people. Parables and allegories by tribal and religious leaders actually intend to tell "greater truths" than might be produced by "objective" writers of non-fiction. Information is shared to illustrate or entertain, or is simply erroneous even if thought to be true. Some characters in this chapter's opening examples slipped into this category when they said their memoirs contained some accidental untruths. But the uproar over these cooked autobiographies makes it clear that we're bothered by fiction posing as non-fiction. By definition, fiction is untruthful. We're looking to be entertained when we go to the fiction section of our favorite bookstore, so we are not being deceived. But we're less tolerant of non-fiction authors whose works are "reality based," and we don't accept the fakers' arguments that they committed honest errors. Likewise, we expect fact checkers and copy editors to keep honest errors out of news reports. And we hope bloggers who claim to be reporting truths are not inventing facts.

The fourth group of items in Deaver's continuum represents conscious efforts to deceive by communicating false information. Two of the three items in this group may be rationalized as justifiable for a defined purpose (deceit and "white lies"), but the final one is by definition without any redeeming value (blatant lies). According to Deaver:

> Deceit is a broad category of misinformation that may be communicated without culpably "telling a lie." However, deceit broaches ethical justification in that it is intentionally deceptive communication. Nevertheless, a communicator may loudly proclaim that a message contained no specific untruths, no outright lies.
>
> (p. 175)

Several categories of deceit are discussed: "deceit by omission," "deceit by generalization," and "deceit by over-specificity or cardstacking." As we saw in the broadcast example at the top of this chapter ("Unsafe Haven"), journalists sometimes justify such deceit for a "greater good." In a moment we will consider such justifications.

Next, we find white lies or untruths that are justified as being for a good purpose, such as not hurting someone's feelings. Philosophers who insist that we follow moral rules and duties—deontologists—would not excuse white lies, but utilitarians and other consequentialists—teleologists—would conclude that there are times when the ends justify the means. Media ethicists clearly distinguish between passive deception (letting someone assume you are something that you are not) and the kind of active deception that occurs when you tell a white lie to gain admission to some event, or actively misrepresent yourself or fib a bit in order to get a good story.

At the bottom of the heap are blatant lies, untruths with no redeeming purpose. We find the occasional blatant lie in the media ethics environment, but once exposed, the consequences are swift and severe, and usually very public. Clifford Irving's totally faked "autobiography" of Howard Hughes comes to mind, as do the behaviors of Janet Cooke of the *Washington Post*, Stephen Glass of *The New Republic*, Jack Kelley of *USA Today*, and Jayson Blair of the *New York Times*. These cases of plagiarism and blatant lying were so egregious that some media ethicists don't find them philosophically interesting; however, they provide important moral lessons for media practitioners. University of Maryland professor Carl Sessions Stepp once told a journalism class that Jayson Blair spent lots of time in his office while as a student, but it never occurred to Sessions Stepp to tell Blair not to lie or make up stuff. That was Sessions Stepp's closing comment to those students: "If no one has ever told you, let me be the one: Don't make up stuff. And don't lie."

ON DECEPTION AND LYING: IS IT EVER JUSTIFIED?

Introduction

Deception is broadly defined to include concepts of intentionality, commission, and omission. Sissela Bok's book *Lying: Moral Choice in Public and Private Life* defines a lie as "any intentionally deceptive message which is stated" (1978, p. 14). She said deception occurs:

> when we undertake to deceive others intentionally, we communicate messages meant to mislead them, meant to make them believe what we ourselves do not believe. We can do so through gesture, through disguise, by means of action or inaction, even through silence.
>
> (p. 13)

Lou Hodges (1988) said deceit refers to acts that intentionally seek to make others believe what we ourselves do not believe. It may take the form of lying, concealment, or misrepresentation.

Others, casting a broader net, refer to deception as any action or inaction that is intended to mislead the receiver of the communication. And to stretch the issue even more, some have argued that deception can be unintentional and occur in the mind of people who feel themselves deceived, regardless of the intent of the communicator or creator of the message so understood.

Deception in Mass Media Practices

Deception is frequently used in mass media—by journalists, advertisers, public relations practitioners, and others. For example, a journalist's sources may lie or obfuscate about whether they have information, or what information exists. Similarly, journalists may mislead in attempting to induce sources to part with information, or they may pose as people they are not in hopes that sources will relax their guard. Deception often seems a useful and easy strategy to obtain information that journalists think readers and/or viewers have a right to receive. Public relations and advertising practitioners are admonished against deception, but a candid appraisal of their daily practice would have us conclude that they often deceive. When acting as advocates they engage in selective truth telling, as they pick and choose which characteristics of a product or service or client should be emphasized and which should be overlooked or downplayed. Deception, be it innocent or egregious, seems to go with the territory.

Yet by its very nature, deception is a destructive force both for individuals and for society. It should be rare. Nevertheless, it is recognized that situations arise in which other moral rules or goals should override the reluctance to deceive.

As Hodges put it:

> Deceit is sometimes justifiable if it is required to achieve important goals or to obey moral rules that are even more important than the rule against deception; e.g., to save a life or to protect someone from certain and serious harm.
>
> (1988, p. 28)

The questions are: When do we justify deceit, and by what manner, so we have some confidence the justification is valid? In journalism, say you are a reporter who attends a public meeting of college students who had been incest victims/sexually abused. You don't identify yourself as a reporter, but you write a full story, with quotes and identification. Have you done the right or wrong thing? You could argue that the speakers knew the meeting was open to the public, and that speakers might not have told the "truth" had they been aware a reporter was there.

Reasonable responses to this question might include these arguments:

1. You should let people know they'll be identified in print.
2. People should know when they are talking on the record.
3. While there was no counterbalancing of good over harm, it could have been justified on utilitarian grounds had the story not identified or quoted the incest victims.

These are prima facie journalistic duties or rules (that is, all else being equal, these rules should be followed). However, in some cases these rules might be set aside.

A classic case of media deception centered on the Mirage Tavern, operated by reporters from the Chicago *Sun-Times* newspaper in the late 1970s. The reporters observed and recorded policemen, firemen, building inspectors, and other public officials who followed their standard practices of accepting bribes from bar owners to overlook legal/structural flaws in the bar. It was deceptive, obviously, because the reporters never revealed that they were reporters. However, was the deception justified? If there was a prima facie duty not to deceive, was there not some other duty to let the public know what sorts of criminal behavior their public officials were engaged in? Could the story have been told another way without deception? Who wins, who loses? What's it worth?

Questions could be raised about departing from prima facie rules of reporting to reach a greater good. In such cases, it seems OK to break the rules. To rephrase the rationalization, it's OK to break a rule if we are willing to pay the consequences and/or if we can justify doing so by citing some greater or more important rule.

Consider other examples from the world of mass communication:

- Advertising and public relations are fields in which the temptation always exists to make products, services, and individuals something bigger or better than reality. For instance, an advertising department tries to make its products look as good as possible on television. Unfortunately, TV lights ruin such things as ice cream. So is it OK to use mashed potatoes instead of ice cream, or put clear marbles at the bottom of a bowl of soup so the meat and vegetables will show up better?
- Should fashion models have absolutely flawless skin and 17-inch waistlines?
- Is there any problem with "planting" commercial products in Hollywood entertainment films, given that such products are used in daily life, and placing them in movies helps underwrite the expensive production costs?
- In public relations, is it justifiable to put words in the mouth of one's client? There was quite a flap when President Ronald Reagan's press secretary, Larry Speakes, attributed to Reagan certain statements that the president had never made (Cases and Commentaries, 1988).
- Is it justifiable to manipulate data and perhaps over-represent the amount of support for your particular cause, to engage in "Astroturf" campaigns by artificially creating public opinion?
- Is it appropriate to stonewall the press and public when they demand to know whether your football coach has decided to take another job? Is it OK for the coach to deny—up until the moment he departs for a greener gridiron?
- Should an administrator mislead the public by saying, "No member of the faculty has been arrested for a felony," when the answer would be different had the reporter thought to ask: "Have any members of the faculty or staff been arrested for a felony?"

From Bok and others, we learn about the nature and consequences of lying, and some systematic "justification models" or means of deciding whether such acts are ethically defensible or whether they are not.

Sissela Bok's Justification Model

In her book, *Lying,* Bok offered a strong utilitarian/consequentialist objection to lying. She claimed that lying rips the social fabric, and that liars usually underestimate the harm and overestimate the good caused by their lies. Liars who are caught lose credibility and trust. To avoid detection, more lies may have to be told. When victims of lies learn that they have been deceived, they naturally feel betrayed. Even when the deceptions are minor, as with a glowing letter of recommendation about a mediocre job candidate, the social fabric is torn.

Bok concluded that we should accept what she calls the principle of veracity. This principle, while not condemning all lies, holds that a negative weight should be attached to every lie. At the very outset, the liar bears a burden of proof that the lie is necessary as a last resort. Acceptable alternatives to lying that accomplish the same end are to be sought and, if discovered, chosen. Bok made several major points about lying that mass communicators (and nearly everyone else) should consider when tempted to use ruses, deception, or lies:

- The practice of lying comes dressed in many varieties of sheep's clothing, and lies are excused supposedly because they avoid harm, produce benefit, assure fairness, and even foster a faith in truthfulness! But beware of easily invoking these excuses, most of which will not stand critical examination (pp. 77–94).
- Liars and deceivers tend to "overestimate the forces pushing them to lie" (p. 25). Moreover, the "need" to lie often expands beyond the scope of lying originally intended (pp. 126–127).
- Crises in some professions are frequent; therefore, doctors, lawyers, journalists, police, and soldiers constantly face ethical dilemmas. Yet "there is, in fact, rarely a clear professional standard or open discussion of the unspoken standards in professional organizations" (p. 127).

Chapter 7 of *Lying* presents a three-step justification model for anyone to use when tempted to lie. (You encountered Bok's model in this textbook's second chapter.) Like most good justification models, she presents a series of decision points, where our answers to each question branch logically to the next query.

- First, are there alternative forms of action that will resolve the difficulty (dilemma) without the use of a lie?
- Second, what might be the moral reasons brought forward to excuse the lie, and what reasons can be raised as counter-arguments?
- Third, as a test of these two steps, what would a public of reasonable persons say about such lies?

"Most lies will clearly fail to satisfy these questions of justification," she concludes (pp. 111–112). With the first question, we see that we should pursue other available options beyond lying. If we're stymied and conclude that deception is necessary, we move to the second question and imagine a debate among moral philosophers.

If there are moral reasons to excuse the lie, we should be willing to make them public. Her "test of publicity" is a request for transparency, akin to the sixth question in our "5 Ws and H" approach to doing ethics: "How's your decision going to look?" She argued that "publicity" is a moral principle, and that justifications must be capable of being publicly stated and defended. She further argued that this publicity should be directed to reasonable people, so the test is made outside the narrow and selfish view of the potential liar.

The question, then, is: "Which lies, if any, would survive the appeal for justification to reasonable persons?" The reasonable persons would include people who are likely to be lied to. How will our decision look when it goes global, instantaneously, on Facebook or other social media? Although many people create false identities, use anonymity, and actually get away with "lying" on social media, do "reasonable persons" feel ripped off by the practice? Will the decision to deceive withstand scrutiny by objective judges, the court of public opinion, and the "cleansing light of publicity?"

Lou Hodges's Justification Model

Hodges (1988) offered a justification model for the news media that asks a journalist contemplating deception to answer three questions sequentially. He said deceptive tactics are not justified unless the particular circumstances of a proposed deceit pass all three:

1. The information sought must be of overriding public importance. It is not sufficient to be merely interesting information that readers would want to know. It must be information readers need to know in order to achieve important goals or to avoid serious harm.
2. There must be no reasonable likelihood that comparably accurate and reliable information could be obtained as efficiently without deception.
3. The deception contemplated must not place innocent people at serious risk. This test would ordinarily rule out posing in a role the journalist could not reasonably fulfill (such as a firefighter or doctor), but it would not rule out posing in roles the journalist is equipped to play (such as a nursing home orderly or factory worker).

SUMMARY AND CONCLUSIONS

This chapter continues our investigation of the question, "What's it worth?" Truth is one of the most important values in the media ethics environment. Media practitioners and media consumers have made an implicit agreement: Media that inform and persuade have a special obligation to be truth seekers and truth tellers. Truth has a high value, and when it is diminished all of us suffer to some extent.

Truth telling is not a simple matter in the media world. All too often, it must be balanced against other compelling values, such as the value of minimizing harm, or the value of sustaining relationships with sources, clients, subjects, and audiences. In such cases it is helpful to have a reliable moral compass and to employ a valid justification model. Truth telling also has a pragmatic justification: It is good business.

When it comes to truth telling, the commitments to do the right thing, for the right reasons, are invaluable. "What's it worth?" Telling the truth is priceless.

■ ■ ■

CHAPTER VOCABULARY

Note: Definitions are available at this book's companion website.

- coherence theories
- consequentialist
- correspondence theories
- deception
- implicit agreement

- intentionality
- objectivity
- omission
- pragmatic theories

PRACTICAL APPLICATIONS

1. Given these checklists and theories of truth, it should be possible to revisit—and resolve—the examples presented at the outset of this chapter. Ask yourself what you would do if you were one of the decision makers, either as authors/photographers, or editors/gatekeepers, or public stakeholders in each of the four examples. Would the behaviors in question be morally permissible, according to any of the justification models or theories? If not, what alternative behaviors would you recommend?

2. Do a content analysis of fashion magazines or body-building magazines. Can you tell if the models have been digitally manipulated? Ask yourself and your friends whether it matters. (You might find it interesting to see whether males and females have different opinions.)

3. Do a semantic analysis of some newspaper or news magazine articles, or a television newscast. Do you see any violations of general semantics principles? What examples can you find that show gatekeepers are semantically sophisticated?

4. Apply Hodges's justification model to the example of reporters not identifying themselves when writing a story from a public meeting of college students who had been incest victims/sexually abused. Do the same for the Mirage Tavern example in the text.

5. Have social media such as Facebook changed the rules about truth telling as a value in the media environment? If so, does it matter?

■ ■ ■

CASE 7.1 **Journalism: How Much Deception Do You Need to Nail the Story?**

You are an editor at *The Freedonia Times* newspaper with 15,000 subscribers and a website that encourages reporters to record video and audio with their stories.

Your star reporter, Ellie Blight, comes to you wanting to document what she says are abysmal conditions at the government-run mental hospital. At the very minimum, the story will rely heavily upon public records such as inspection reports, audits, and lawsuits. She will also interview experts, hospital administrators, patients' families, and others.

But will that be enough to tell the story, especially for the web? As you sit and discuss ways to get the story, you come up with five reporting choices in which the paper could:

1. ask administrators to give Blight access to the hospital, and let her bring along a staffer to record images

2. ask patients' families to record conditions in the hospital

3. use video shot by hospital workers to show the conditions (you could use video shot on their cell phones, or provide better equipment to them); you would not reveal the names of those workers

4. let reporter Blight go to the hospital (without identifying herself as a reporter) and take a look at conditions, since she'd be more likely to see conditions as they are; she likely could use small cameras to record the sights and sounds

5. let reporter Blight go undercover by taking a job at the institution, which would give her even wider access to describe the conditions as well as surreptitiously record sound and images.

➤ **Your task: You must recommend to your boss and to the reporter what, if any, level of deception might be required to nail the story.**

Questions
- **What's your problem?**
- **Why not follow the rules?**
- **Who wins, who loses?**
- **What's it worth?**
- What else do you need to know?

Thinking it Through

1. Make a list of the people (including yourself) and groups who are stakeholders in your decision. How big of a concern might patient privacy be?

2. As was noted in this chapter, ethicist Hodges said that deceit may be justifiable "if it is required to achieve important goals or to obey moral rules that are even more important than the rule against deception." His model said that deceit may be justifiable if the information to be obtained is (a) of overriding public importance, (b) there's no other way to get the information, and (c) the deception does not put people at risk. Decide whether each choice in the case study would be justifiable and how it could be justified.

3. Are there possibilities beyond those choices that might meet Hodges's standards?

4. Would this discussion be different if the news organization were a television station and not a newspaper?

5. This case study is loosely based on Nellie Bly, who feigned mental illness and spent ten days in a New York institution in 1887. Go online to read more about what she did, and then go back and apply Hodges's guidelines to decide whether her deception was justifiable. What might have changed in the decades since then that might change your mind?

CASE 7.2 **New Media: Are You Using, or Being Used by, a Sock Puppet?**

You are a contributing writer to www.freedonialive.com and part of your compensation is based upon the number of hits you receive for the posts you write.

You've been writing a lot lately about a controversial bill that would eliminate smoking in nearly all public areas of Freedonia. The bill is to be considered in Freedonia's next legislative session, and you've been writing about it for weeks. You've come out (slightly) against the ban, saying the bill is too restrictive even though some limits on smoking may be needed.

Each time you write, the comment section below each post takes on a life of its own. You notice that a particular reader who calls himself "TobaccoJoe" is front and center in the debate, criticizing you for your lukewarm opposition to the ban and forcefully arguing that it's simply not fair to restrict any activity that's legal for adults. It seems as if every other post is from TobaccoJoe, arguing with people in favor of the ban or making his own comments. His comments have driven a huge debate online, and each comment adds to your bottom line because of the online traffic it brings.

You are curious about TobaccoJoe, so you learn more about him. Freedonialive.com does not require users to list their real names or addresses, but the site's tools keep up with the IP addresses of users. When you track TobaccoJoe through his IP address, you quickly discover that TobaccoJoe's IP address belongs to the "Institute for Tobacco Freedom," an organization funded by cigarette companies to fight laws such as the one being considered by your legislature. You've linked to that group's site a few times, just as you have for anti-smoking groups.

Simply put, you figure TobaccoJoe is a "sock puppet," the term for someone who assumes a false identity online in order to discuss an issue in which they have a self-interest.

➤ **Now that you know, what do you do? TobaccoJoe is driving lots of traffic (and therefore, more money) for you, but at what cost to you or your readers?**

Questions
- **What's your problem?**
- **Why not follow the rules?**
- **Who wins, who loses?**
- **What's it worth?**
- What else do you need to know?

Thinking it Through

1. Is this an ethical issue, especially since Freedonialive.com did not require its users to register with real names and affiliations?

2. Do you invade TobaccoJoe's privacy by tracking his IP address to discover more about his identity? Why or why not?

3. Did TobaccoJoe lie to you and others by not stating that he was working for a pro-tobacco lobby? What would Bok say?

4. The bottom line: What, if anything, do you tell your readers about TobaccoJoe?

    A. If you decide to say nothing:

        a. How do you justify your decision?

        b. How much of your decision is based upon the concern that you'll start losing traffic (and therefore, money) when you write on the topic again?

        c. What, if anything, do you tell TobaccoJoe?

    B. If you decide to write about TobaccoJoe:

        a. How do you justify your decision?

        b. How do you justify your work to uncover TobaccoJoe's identity?

        c. Do you give TobaccoJoe a chance to comment before publishing your blog post?

        d. What do you tell readers about TobaccoJoe?

5. Is there another choice in this case? If so, what is it and how do you justify it?

6. If you were in charge of Freedonialive.com, would you require users to reveal their real identities before being allowed to post? Would you make those real identities available for all to see? Why or why not?

7. How different would the discussion be if every commenter were required to list a real name and affiliation when posting?

8. Have you ever posted something anonymously in an online forum that furthered your self-interest? How do you justify your action?

9. Consider TobaccoJoe's activities through Bok's justification model and determine whether his activities are justified. Then run your decision (about whether to "out" TobaccoJoe) through that model.

■ ■ ■

CASE 7.3 **Public Relations: When the Boss Lies to You**

You are press secretary to Freedonia's governor. You are quoted in newspapers and seen on television many times a week, making you the most visible person in the executive branch after the governor.

You come to work on Monday, and there is nothing listed on the governor's weekly public schedule of events. By late Monday, reporters are calling to ask what he is doing that week, since several public events had been on the schedule late last week. You ask the governor's chief of staff, who tells you to tell reporters that the governor is on vacation. You dutifully relay that to reporters nearly every day for a week.

As it turns out, the governor wasn't on vacation at all. He was in the neighboring state of Sylvania, where he and the Sylvanian governor were secretly negotiating a treaty related to water rights for a river between the two states' borders.

The chief of staff calls you in at 11:30 a.m. Friday, telling you that the governor wants you to call a media conference at 3:30 p.m. to announce the agreement. You ask the chief of staff why you were told to tell reporters that the governor was on vacation. The chief tells you it was better that you not tell the truth so the governors could freely negotiate. You press further by telling the chief of staff that reporters won't trust you (and by extension, the governor) if you lie to them. The chief of staff sniffs and again says you were kept out of the loop for the reason stated. Then you're dismissed from the office.

You wait until 12:40 p.m.—after the noon newscasts—and send an email to reporters telling them of the press conference in less than three hours. Then the emails from reporters start coming: "Why did you lie to us and to the public? Did you know the governor was working on the agreement, or were you lied to, too?" Another reporter asks: "Why should we trust you anymore?"

➤ **What do you do?**

Questions
- **What's your problem?**
- **Why not follow the rules?**
- **Who wins, who loses?**
- **What's it worth?**
- What else do you need to know?

Thinking it Through

1. Is this an ethical issue? If so, how do you make that clear to the chief of staff and governor?

2. Work through these options involving:

   A. What you do about your job:

      a. Quit on the spot. Make sure reporters know you quit because you were misled.

      b. Quit on the spot, but don't talk to reporters about the reason.

      c. Keep working that day, but start putting out resumes on Monday.

      d. Stay on the job, but make it clear to the governor and chief of staff that you'll quit if it ever happens again.

      e. Stay on the job, knowing that there are times when the governor needs to misdirect staffers (and the public) for a greater good.

      f. Do something else. Explain.

   B. What you do at the press conference:

      a. You're not going, because you quit.

      b. You stay on the job, but you tell the chief of staff that you won't be at the press conference, since your credibility might become an issue. Let the governor clean up the mess.

      c. Attend the press conference but not answer questions. Again, let the governor clean up the mess.

      d. Simply not answer questions from reporters who ask about the deception, saying you don't have an answer.

      e. Let reporters know off the record that you didn't know you were misled, so they understand that you had no control over the incident.

      f. Answer the reporters' questions on the record. Tell the truth: "I was misled and I'm not happy about it."

      g. Answer reporters' questions on the record. Tell them that sometimes the governor needs to misdirect staff (and the public) for a greater good, and you agree with the decision (even though you don't).

      h. Same as (f), but tell them you agree with the governor's decision (because you really do).

      i. Do something else. Explain.

3. Are there times when it's OK for leaders to mislead their staff? If so, was this one of those times? If not, when might it be legitimate?

4. Are there times when it's OK for a public relations practitioner to mislead journalists (and, by extension, the public?) If so, was this one of those times? If not, when might it be legitimate?

5. What if the governor took an afternoon that week to play golf? Could you then say that the governor actually was on vacation?

6. Be the governor: Would you have made the decision not to tell your spokesperson what you were doing? Or would you have told the spokesperson about the negotiations and included orders not to talk about it to reporters?

7. Be a reporter (or, by extension, a member of the public): What, if anything, would you write about the governor's decision to keep his spokesperson out of the loop? If you write about it, does it become a paragraph deep in the story or a full-blown story? How much could you trust that spokesperson in the future? Whom would you trust more: A spokesperson who was misled, a spokesperson who lied to you, or one who simply would not talk about the governor's whereabouts?

8. Consider Bok's three-pronged test involving the justification of lies. Does this one pass her test?

■ ■ ■

CASE 7.4 **Advertising: In-text Ads***

You are an advertising manager for a magazine, and your boss orders you to make more money with online ads. One way to do that is by introducing "in-text" ads that tie into the content published on the site.

Simply put, advertisers buy keywords that might appear in your stories. When one of those words appears in a story, a double line is inserted under the word. When a user scrolls over the word, an ad pops up with a small display ad and a link to a larger ad. The newspaper is paid when a user clicks on that ad.

A software company will run the project. All you do is sit back and share the revenue.

When you mention the possibility, your boss asks you to come up with a list of concerns.

1. It may be seen as blurring the line between advertising and journalism, since ads appear in the text of stories.

   On the other hand, writers don't know what the keywords are, so they won't be writing stories in order to get those keywords online. What writers don't know actually helps in this case.

2. Because the links come from stories, some readers might be confused. Because some stories come with links chosen by writers, some readers might think that the magazine is responsible for ad placement. Moreover, federal rules say that it is improper to deceive readers into thinking that editorial content is actually advertising content.

   On the other hand, the ad company has tried to avoid the confusion by placing ad links in double-lined green, not the single-line blue that is common with a traditional link.

3. Ads may appear in the wrong places. For example, it would be problematic to have an in-text ad for Freedonia Used Cars pop up in a story about ways not to be ripped off when buying a car.

   On the other hand, the company that runs the system says it has ways to make sure that ads that might potentially embarrass advertisers won't appear.

4. A reader can log in to the magazine's website and change the settings so the ads will not appear.

   On the other hand, it's a four-step process to remove those ads, and readers may feel like they are giving up their privacy because they must register to remove the ads.

---

* This case study is based upon a "Cases and Commentaries" discussion from the *Journal of Mass Media Ethics*. For more information, see: Craig, D.A. (2007). In text ads: Pushing the lines between advertising and journalism. *Journal of Mass Media Ethics* 22(4), 348–349.

5. The ads seem out of context in many cases.

    On the other hand, readers may not expect ads to have much context compared to magazine stories.

6. Some readers may be turned off by the imposition of ads in stories.

    On the other hand, readers should know that information is not free, and magazines are an advertising-driven enterprise, even as people read online without paying.

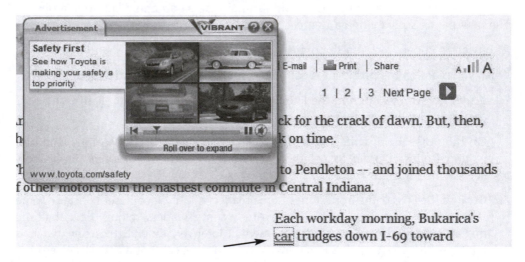

FIGURE 7.2 | Scroll over the word "car" in this July 2010 news story about interstate gridlock published in a regional newspaper, and a video ad for a car manufacturer pops up and begins to play.

Questions
- **What's your problem?**
- **Why not follow the rules?**
- **Who wins, who loses?**
- **What's it worth?**
- What else do you need to know?

Thinking it Through
1. Is this an ethical issue? Why or why not?
2. The case study lists six concerns. Can you think of other concerns not listed here?
3. Go through each of the concerns and decide which of each argument for each concern is more persuasive.
4. To what extent, if any, do concerns about truth and deception play into your discussion?

5. The bottom line: Would you recommend to your boss that your magazine start selling "in-text" ads?

   A. If you said "yes":

      a. How do you justify your decision?

      b. would you rank the six concerns listed in the case study, from most troublesome to least troublesome?

      c. What ethical lines should not be crossed between editorial and advertising?

      d. Is there some sort of content that should not be exposed to in-text ads, such as editorials or obituaries?

   B. If you said "no":

      a. How do you justify your decision?

      b. How would you rank the six concerns listed in the case study, from most troublesome to least troublesome?

      c. If your concern is that stories might be watered down, then what sorts of websites might you say could use in-text ads?

      d. Is there some sort of editorial content that could be exposed to in-text ads?

■ ■ ■

CASE 7.5 **Entertainment: Based on a True Story**

One of the most-talked-about events of the decade occurred a few months ago, when a Freedonia Airlines airplane made a crash landing after a lightning strike crippled its electronic controls and blew out an engine. The skilled pilot and co-pilot managed to put the aircraft into the ocean, about two miles from shore but near a ship that quickly rescued the 175 passengers. The lone casualty was a man in his early sixties with a weak heart who died of a heart attack during the landing.

A national television network wants to create a made-for-TV movie that will recreate the event in dramatic form. The network will sell it as "based on a true story," including the use of real names of participants.

But the network wants to make a few changes. The script calls for the following:

1. The co-pilot will be played by an African-American woman. The network notes that the actual crew was not racially diverse, so adding a woman of color would draw more non-white viewers.

2. The heart-attack victim will be portrayed as dying because he did not follow the flight crew's directions. The network notes that this will be more dramatic and will be a public service in reminding people how important it is to obey crew instructions.

3. The airline name will be fictitious. The real Freedonia Airlines does not want to be involved.

4. Much of the dialogue differs from what actually was said at the time.

5. A passenger will be invented. The network says this "composite" passenger will reenact some of the events and conversations of five actual passengers on the flight, because it takes too much effort by viewers to keep up with the five actual people and will make the movie seem faster-paced. (It's also true that the network will save money by hiring one actor with speaking lines instead of five, since actors without lines are paid less than actors who speak.)

Questions
- **What's your problem?**
- **Why not follow the rules?**
- **Who wins, who loses?**
- **What's it worth?**
- What else do you need to know?

Thinking it Through

1. Is this an ethical issue? Why or why not?

2. Assuming all of the changes are made, where would you place this movie along Deaver's truth-telling continuum?

3. For each of the changes, ask:

    a. Is this change ethically justifiable?

    b. Is this change worth the loss in truth?

    c. Would the change bother you if you were the principal involved (such as the co-pilot or family of the heart-attack victim)?

    d. If you were the movie producer, would you make this change?

4. How much freedom should moviemakers have in being able to change events in order to tell a story? What's more important: sticking to facts in artistic endeavors based on true stories, or "creative license" that can let entertainers and artists tell a higher "truth"?

5. Search Wikipedia for the 2008 movie *Frost/Nixon*. Read the "noted fiction and inaccuracies" section, and follow a few of the footnoted links to criticisms about how the movie did not follow reality. Do you agree with the criticisms?

6. If moviemakers change the truth in "based on a true story" movies, do they have an obligation to tell the audience (perhaps online) what changes they made?

■ ■ ■

CHAPTER 8

Privacy and Public Life

This chapter:

- reviews numerous issues that show the complexity of privacy in today's mediated world, and how privacy almost always involves a values choice

- traces the evolution of the term "privacy," drawing from philosophers, political theorists, and legal scholars

- looks closely at what various media institutions and organizations have told the public and their own practitioners when it comes to matters of privacy. Media codes of ethics tell us much about how privacy must be delicately balanced against other, equally compelling media values. We will assess some of these codes, noting that privacy is

continued

INTRODUCTION

SOME OF the most vexing issues in today's media ethics environment involve the notion of privacy. For society to function effectively, how much personal information should we have the legal right to know, the need to know, or merely an interest in knowing? What's the difference between "the public interest" and "what the public is interested in?" What are we to make of mediated voyeurism, which might be relatively useful (televising Katie Couric's colonoscopy may have saved some lives) or useless (knowing the contents of Anna Nicole Smith's refrigerator hours before she died)? Does everyone deserve equal protection from the prying eyes of journalists, "big brother," and market researchers? Do the ubiquitous social media contribute to the social need for civic engagement, public participation, and public record? How much control should we have to create and maintain our own reputations, let alone our physical space? Is the loss of privacy inevitable in this fast-paced, 24/7, interdependent, crowded world? When can mass communicators or everyday users of social media justify taking away a person's privacy to serve a greater good? Is privacy a completely relative term—significant in a liberal-democratic environment with its focus on individualized citizens, but far less relevant elsewhere, where community and relational identities differ? Is it more important to older generations than it is to so-called millennials?

Framed as a values question: What is privacy worth, and what are the consequences of giving up a little of it—or all of it?

PRIVACY: THE BALANCING ACT

Governments, health professionals, and financial institutions are among the many non-media groups that seek to balance individual privacy against competing interests. Meanwhile, mass media practitioners must balance individual privacy with competing interests that include making money, reporting the news, adhering to government regulations, and trying to provide new and useful information online. This section looks at the balancing act of privacy issues for non-media and media organizations.

General Privacy Issues

To appreciate how concerned some people have become over invasions of privacy and (real, potential, or imagined) threats to civil liberties, look at the balancing act related to issues being discussed in the popular and specialized media and by the Electronic Privacy Information Center (EPIC), a public interest research center in Washington, DC (www.epic.org, 2009):

US troops in Iraq have used mobile scanners to take fingerprints, eye scans, and to collect other personal data from Iraqis at checkpoints, workplaces, the sites of attacks, and door-to-door canvasses.

The balancing act: Biometric IDs may help troops protect themselves and innocent civilians from potential harm, but they may intrude upon law-abiding citizens' sense of self-worth and could fuel ethnic cleansing or other reprisals if the data fell into the wrong hands.

The US Department of Homeland Security and governmental domestic surveillance activities include using "whole-body imaging" at airports, "fusion centers" or large intelligence databases that collect information on ordinary citizens, closed-circuit TV surveillance, and "Suspicionless Electronic Border Searches." On the books is a controversial proposal for a national ID card. "National Security Letters" compel banks, telephone companies, Internet service providers, and others to disclose customer records to the FBI. The federal government and companies such as Facebook, Yahoo (Flickr), MySpace, Google (YouTube), Blist (which sells "social data delivery" information combined from government and other sources), and other social networks have engaged in "cloud computing" or information sharing agreements.

The balancing act: Domestic surveillance by federal agents in the US is a constant and delicate tradeoff between expectations of national security and fears that an intrusive "big brother"—a "conspiracy" between governmental and corporate interests—will erode civil liberties.

continued

constantly pitted against values such as the short-term and long-term considerations of truth telling, accuracy, and fairness in all media; benefits and costs of comprehensive, free flowing information; need for respect and public decency; and the pros and cons of knowing all that can be known about media consumers and audiences of advertisers

- offers five practical applications and five case studies for further exploration of the topic.

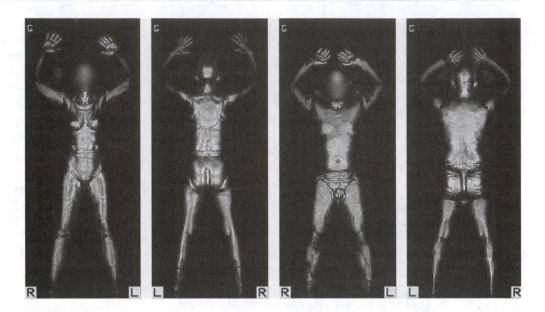

FIGURE 8.1 | The US government has introduced technology at airport security checkpoints that essentially "sees" through clothing. Some see the whole-body imaging technology as an invasion of privacy, while others see it as a reasonable tradeoff to be safe.
Source: Transportation Security Administration

As health records go electronic, several proposals would assure comprehensive safeguards for US medical information, including patients' prescriptions.

The balancing act: Protecting medical records may assure patients that they won't be deluged with unwanted advertising and promotional items, and that their medical histories won't lead to discrimination when seeking employment. But too much secrecy will impede medical research and could contribute to a pandemic if people are unknowingly exposed to someone who is highly contagious.

Just as government and private institutions gather record amounts of personal, private data, identity theft has gone global: credit card numbers are readily available in bulk, online, for as little as 40 cents. Names, Social Security numbers, addresses, and birthdates sell for $2 a crack. Security experts say the problem is that "the world's ability to collect data has far outstripped its ability to protect it" (Marks, 2008).

The balancing act: Identity theft certainly harms its victims, but it also encourages government and security experts to create more sophisticated means of protecting privacy.

Mass Media Privacy Issues: Advertising, Marketing, and Social Media

Media organizations and software developers have similar issues as they try to balance individual privacy with competing interests that include the enhancement of public life, making money, reporting the news, adhering to government regulations, and trying to provide new and useful information online. Some recent issues include the following.

Search engines continue to use "cookies," raising concerns over the collection, retention, and disclosure of information relating to Internet Protocol (IP) addresses that show where we are (and where we have been) on the Internet. Major Web companies track what we do online in order to deliver ads tailored to our interests. Billions of times each month, Americans collectively reveal personal information to researchers and advertisers. Five companies—Yahoo, Google, Microsoft, AOL, and MySpace—record at least 336 billion transmission events monthly. Yahoo alone gathers data more than 2,500 times a month for each visitor to its sites.

Meanwhile, social media blur the definitions between "public" and "private"—for example, a "private" Facebook page is published for others to see. Facebook in 2009 ended "Beacon," a controversial advertising technique that broadcast user purchases in public profiles. It paid $9.5 million to settle a lawsuit, with proceeds going to a fund focusing on online privacy (Brodkin, 2009). But Facebook users who rented videos from Blockbuster have had to seek federal privacy protections. And Facebook has been criticized for overly complicated privacy settings on its site, which has led to lawsuits

---

Box 8.1 | FACEBOOK'S CHANGING PRIVACY STANDARDS

In 2005, Facebook had 5.5 million members on college campuses. Its privacy policy said, "No personal information that you submit to Facebook will be available to any user of the website who does not belong to at least one of the groups specified by you in your privacy settings."

In 2010, it topped 400 million members worldwide. Its privacy policy said:

When you connect with an application or website it will have access to General Information about you. The term General Information includes your and your friends' names, profile pictures, gender, user IDs, connections, and any content shared using the "Everyone" privacy setting . . . The default privacy setting for certain types of information you post on Facebook is set to "everyone."

Facebook founder Mark Zukerberg, responding to lawsuits and confusion by Facebook users, in 2010 announced revisions to the company's privacy policies, giving more control to users.

—Horiuchi, 2010; Zukerberg, 2010

and stern letters from lawmakers (Helft, 2010). A legal settlement between Google Books and authors and publishers may have created a single digital library, operated by Google, but it permits the collection of personal information from "Google Library Project" patrons, including the right to read anonymously.

The balancing act: Personal computers customize materials to serve our social interests and make money for advertisers, and conveniently downloaded books and articles may satisfy our values of thrift, comfort, and wisdom. But we may be revealing more about ourselves than we would prefer, since Google and its competitors seem to see all, know all, remember all, and share all. Whether we know it or not, our Internet browsing tells researchers what we like, what we worry about, what we aspire to become. The data help advertisers produce persuasive messages carefully tailored to each of us—even if data are gathered crumb by crumb, without our awareness. Although the corporations say they are gathering information from computers and not individuals, each of us is being monitored hundreds of times a month as we browse the Internet (Story, March 10, 2008). The bottom line is that while a great deal of information about millions of us is conveniently and centrally available for a multitude of uses, do we want corporations and government to know this much about us?

Advertisers are trying harder to break through the clutter and produce carefully targeted ads. They are using biometric tools to measure consumers' brain waves, galvanic skin response, eye movements, pulse rates, and nearly anything else neuroscience can measure. Companies such as NeuroFocus and EmSense track consumers' attention second by second and gauge their emotional involvement in programs and commercials (Elliott, 2008).

Brain scans using magnetic resonance imaging (MRI) are becoming digital mind readers. They can reveal whether people are telling the truth, in love, or altruistic; what they intend to buy; what they're afraid of; what they recall; and when they know they've made a mistake. The day may come "when others—the government, employers, even your spouse—might turn to technology to determine whether you are a law-abiding citizen, a promising new hire or a faithful partner" (Wise, 2007, p. 66).

The balancing act: Biometric research, including brain scans, can help advertisers, political campaigners, private investigators, law enforcement, employers, and others make informed decisions about people who are potential consumers, voters, employees, lovers, security risks, or sophisticated liars. But involuntary biometric research, including MRI scans, raises questions about privacy, about illegal search and seizure, and about the loss of Fifth Amendment rights regarding self-incrimination.

Some of the most sophisticated research is conducted for strictly commercial purposes:

- The Nielsen Co., which partially owns NeuroFocus, has tracked television viewing habits for decades. It wants to do more than just tell producers which programs are popular; it also wants to tell advertisers which commercials are effective. To get more data than it gets from diaries and "people meters," Nielsen has asked its sample households to share their web surfing, cell phone use, and their specific shopping habits. Many "Nielsen Households" objected to the latest privacy intrusion, so Nielsen scaled back its plans (Story, February 26, 2008).

- The direct mail marketing firm Valpak sends 520 million envelopes to households each year, to 45 million different addresses. The envelopes contain coupons Valpak believes will entice us to shop. Those coupons are not randomly produced, on the off chance we might be persuaded by them. They are based on careful research by major marketing research companies. Valpak's research *per se* is not an invasion of privacy; tens of thousands of adults serve as willing research subjects, completing detailed telephone and mail surveys about personal finances, use of technology, diet and health, travel habits, and more. However, the data provide almost eerily intrusive insights into the minds and behaviors of Valpak's target consumers (Oleary, 2008).

The balancing act of all this marketing and advertising: Sharing personal information with private businesses may seem a reasonable cost for receiving specific goods or services, but we don't want to be pawns in the hands of businesses that collectively know more about us than we may know about ourselves.

Mass Media Privacy Issues: Entertainment/Citizen Journalism

Reality-based entertainment programs such as *America's Most Wanted* and *To Catch a Predator*, and all manner of "citizen journalism" efforts that encourage non-professionals to submit video, have attracted large audiences and activist citizens interested in seeing that justice is done. But while the programs promote public life, they have brought inappropriate attention to innocent people who are judged guilty without a formal trial.

The balancing act: While these shows can alert viewers to potential dangers and may catch a perpetrator every once in a while, they also pander to audiences' voyeuristic tendencies, engender paranoia, and occasionally stigmatize innocent parties. As for "citizen journalism" efforts, the concern is that people who are not trained as journalists might be invading privacy or taking risks to capture images of what they think is news.

Mass Media Privacy Issues: News

State laws and a liberal reading of federal standards suggest that news media have the right to name victims of sex crimes, but victims' rights groups and others maintain that unwarranted publicity re-injures people who have been assaulted and does little to elevate public discourse on an incredibly significant social issue (Black, 1995, 1996; Gartner, 1990, 1992; King, 1994; Margolik, 1990; Overholser, 1989; Shaw, 1991a, 1991b; Ticker, 1994). Also, while some states forbid law enforcement officials to identify minors who have been arrested, it is not illegal for the media to identify those people.

Box 8.2 | VALPAK KNOWS MORE ABOUT US THAN WE SUSPECT

Valpak, a Florida-based direct marketing company, delivers more than 20 billion coupons and sales offers per year to more than 45 million households across the United States. It leaves little to chance when deciding what coupons it sends to whom.

Valpak relies upon hundreds of variables when customizing its millions of coupons, clustering under categories such as automotive, financial, beverages, business decisions, computers, demographics, drug/grocery store, health care, home improvement, household shopping, lifestyles, media, retail shopping, telephone, travel, and voting.

Valpak also uses research data from Claritas, which offers behavioral research it calls "PRIZM"—an acronym for "Potential Rating Index by ZIP Markets." It breaks the US into ZIP + 4 neighborhoods of six to 15 households, profiling us by social rank, household composition, mobility (length of residence), ethnicity, urbanization, and housing.

There are 66 PRIZM clusters, revealing more about ourselves than we may suspect. Two very broad categories of interest to Valpak are social groups and "LifeStage" groups. Among social groups, the most affluent suburban social group, the "Elite Suburbs," have six-figure incomes, post-graduate degrees, single-family homes, and managerial and professional occupations. They are stereotyped by the terms "upper crust," "blue blood estates," "movers and shakers," and "winner's circle." Middle-class homeowners in small towns and remote exurbs constitute another social group. These members of "Middle America" are profiled by the terms "simple pleasures," "red, white and blues," "heartlanders," "blue highways," "kid country, USA," and "shotguns & pickups."

In addition to social groups, PRIZM also classifies us by LifeStage groups, based on two variables that predict consumer behavior: the age of each segment's residents and the presence of children. The "younger years," "family life," and "mature years" groups are further subdivided by affluence.

Opinion is divided over whether all this sophisticated research is an invasion of privacy or merely an attempt to overcome the lament of yesteryear's marketers, who are said to have said that "Half the money I spend on advertising is wasted, and the problem is I do not know which half." In truth, it is both—yet another values clash, this time between the right or perceived psychological need to be free from unwarranted intrusion on one hand and the right or perceived economic need to communicate one's goods and services effectively on the other.

—Oleary, 2008

The balancing act: Publicity about sex crimes balances the rights of vulnerable individuals to avoid being "revictimized," against the right (or "desire") of the public to satisfy its idle or prurient curiosity coupled with the desire of news media to attract audiences and make money. Viewed from another perspective, the balancing act is between First Amendment absolutists intent on publishing everything they think the public "needs to know," and others who tend toward censorship, prior restraint, or ethical concerns.

Summing Up

In short, the examples above are values conflicts that boil down to balancing the need for information that lubricates social, economic, and political institutions against the need to protect people from unwarranted intrusion into their private lives.

WHAT IS PRIVACY?

Philosophers, political theorists, and legal scholars have long grappled with the notion of privacy and distinctions among what is public, what is private, and what is both public and private. The blurry line has resulted in a never-ending series of controversial definitions of privacy (Schoeman, 2001, p. 1382). The struggles for definitional clarity point out how often privacy conflicts with other values.

Our understanding of privacy has emerged from several interrelated concepts, including the concept of distinct public and private "spheres" of life, natural rights, liberty, property, individuality, intimacy, secrecy, autonomy, and human dignity (Winch, 1996, p. 198). Debates over these concepts have continued for millennia: public and private roles—*polis* and individuality—were rhetorical and pragmatic fodder for ancient Greeks; natural rights and property rights were roundly argued as long ago as the 1300s and have continued into today's democratic-/socialistic-/market-driven economic debates. Moreover, philosophers and pragmatists have articulated concepts of intimacy, secrecy, autonomy, and human dignity over the past several centuries.

In the late 1800s, Thomas Cooley described privacy as merely "the right to be let alone" (Cooley, 1888; Hodges, 1983, 1994, & 2009). Around the same time, Boston lawyers Samuel Warren and Louis Brandeis (1890) built on Cooley's definition in an influential *Harvard Law Review* article that called for a constitutional right to privacy from unwarranted and sensationalistic journalistic intrusion into private affairs. They wrote during a time of urbanization and a recognized loss of "personal space" and physical privacy. It was also the era of yellow journalism, when gossip was the mainstay of newspapers.

By the mid-twentieth century, philosophers and commentators were concerned with more than intrusion into personal space and hurtful gossip. Secrecy and circles of intimacy became part of the privacy rhetoric. Alan Westin called privacy the:

... claim of individual, groups, or institutions to determine for themselves when, how, and to what extent information about them is communicated to others ... The claim is not so much one of total secrecy as it is of the right to define one's circle of intimacy—to choose who shall see beneath the quotidian (daily) mask. Loss of control over which "face" one puts on may result in literal loss of self identity.

(1967, p. 7)

Morton Levine called privacy the "maintenance of a personal life-space within which the individual has a chance to be an individual, to exercise and experience his own uniqueness" (1980, p. 19). Sissela Bok called it the "condition of being protected from unwanted access by others—either physical access, personal information, or attention" (1984, pp. 10–11).

One source frequently cited by media ethicist Lou Hodges (1983; 1994; 2009) is A.C. Breckenridge, who defined privacy as the:

... rightful claim of the individual to determine the extent to which he wishes to share of himself with others and his control over the time, place, and circumstances to communicate to others. It means his right to withdraw or to participate as he sees fit. It is also the individual's right to control dissemination of information about himself; it is his own personal possession.

(1980, p. 1)

A distinguished scholar in the field of privacy, Ferdinand Schoeman, tried to settle the definitional problem. His conclusion:

When privacy embraces some aspects of autonomy, it is defined as control over the intimacies of personal identity. At the broadest end of the spectrum, privacy is thought to be the measure of the extent to which an individual is afforded the social and legal space to develop the emotional, cognitive, spiritual, and moral powers of an autonomous agent.

(2001, p. 1382)

Encroachment upon individual moral autonomy highlights today's arguments about the value of privacy. Helen Nissenbaum's 2009 book, *Privacy in Context*, maintains that people are not concerned over the sharing of information *per se*, which they understand is essential to make societies function. She says people are disturbed when personal information is shared inappropriately or improperly, as noted in chapter titles such as "Keeping Track and Watching Over Us" and "Knowing Us Better than We Know Ourselves: Massive and Deep Databases." She argues that information should be protected or revealed in keeping with the general social norms and values we expect within the workplace, at school, when we seek health care, or when we gather with family and friends.

Our bottom line is that privacy is an important value, but it is just one in a panopoly of often conflicting values. As Joseph Grcic (1986) wrote, privacy is not an absolute right, and it can be trumped by more compelling rights.

MEDIA CODES OF ETHICS AND THE VALUE OF PRIVACY

Most codes in media address the dynamic tension between society's need to be told the truth (about some people, events, goods, or services), while simultaneously protecting individuals from undue harm. The word "privacy" does not appear in all media codes, but many codes—particularly in journalism—suggest that the innocent, or naïve, or disenfranchised members of society have a particular need to be physically and psychologically protected. The Society of Professional Journalists and many other journalism codes lay it out succinctly: seek truth and report it; but minimize harm.

Other news media codes make the same point, calling for:

- truth and fairness (RTDNA and PRND)
- truth and respect (Al Jazeera)
- honesty/fairness and minimizing harm (CyberJournalist)
- accuracy/comprehensiveness and respect/dignity (NPPA)
- accuracy/honesty and fairness (SND).

Strikingly similar phraseology appears in public relations and advertising codes. The PRSA tells members to be honest advocates while assuring fairness, and to support the free flow of information while safeguarding confidential information. The IPRA calls for dialogue and accuracy but also protection of people's dignity and worth, and confidentiality. The AAAA tells advertisers to avoid false and misleading statements, while also avoiding statements, suggestions, and pictures offensive to public decency; it also encourages truthfulness and tastefulness. The AAF seeks truth and taste/dignity, and the AMA wants marketers to have honesty and fairness/respect. The Better Business Bureau (BBB) code of business practices lists "safeguard privacy" as one of its eight standards; the BBB's privacy standard focuses on protection of consumer data. The Free Speech Coalition (adult entertainment industry) devotes a hefty share of its code to safeguarding the privacy of customers and employees.

The values listed here seem reasonable for media professions to fulfill. It is inherently good for communicators to rely upon honesty and truthfulness as they help us become informed citizens or consumers. Likewise, there's little to criticize when media practitioners tell one another to value privacy, dignity, fairness, and respect. We doubt, however, that most of the code writers recognized the dynamic tension they created when drafting their professional codes.

Quite simply, you cannot have it both ways: Regardless of the media institution for which you work, you cannot truthfully disclose all you know without doing some harm to stakeholders, and you cannot bend over backward to protect all the stakeholders unless you limit release of some information you know to be true.

Invasions of privacy will inevitably cause harm. Advertisers and public relations people cannot succeed in their advocacy work unless they accumulate and massage data about consumers, voters, or other stakeholders. Yet they must be careful not to use data in ways that would unfairly manipulate or otherwise harm individuals.

Journalists must be particularly sensitive about privacy. Reporters and editors say their primary ethical obligation is to inform the public by seeking truth and reporting it as fully as possible, but they must balance that obligation against the obligation to respect individuals and their privacy. The challenge for journalists is to be courageous in seeking and reporting information, while being compassionate to people they cover.

It is not an impossible challenge. Most journalists make the right ethical calls daily, even on deadline, when facing this challenge. For instance, consider the self-imposed ethical checklist proposed by Garry Bryant, a now-retired nationally award-winning news photographer from Utah. His "soul-searching" took place at the moment he came upon a news story with his camera. Within seconds he would ask, and then answer, four simple questions:

1. Does the private moment of pain and suffering I find myself watching need to be seen? Should this moment become public? If so, does it tell the story or part of the story of this event?
2. Are the people involved in such shambles over the moment that being photographed will send them into greater trauma?
3. Am I at a distance trying to be as unobtrusive as possible?
4. Am I acting with compassion and sensitivity? (1987, p. 34)

Bryant developed his checklist after years of professional work. It would be a healthy exercise in moral philosophy for media practitioners in all fields to create similar checklists that they can turn to when balancing privacy and other values.

Some Codes Capture the Delicate Balance

The following statements recognize that the issues are complex, and no simple rules will resolve them. They call for ethical reflection and reasoning, which should lead to making principled decisions. They ask practitioners to be philosophers, to consider the nature of their obligations to others, and to think about the short- and long-term consequences of their decisions. As noted above, however, the code writers may not have fully recognized that they were proposing some fairly complicated values choices.

The Grand Forks (North Dakota) *Herald* tells its reporters to remember that:

> . . . many people place a high value on their privacy, and we should honor that basic interest unless there are compelling reasons to the contrary. When people thrust

Box **8.3** | EXAMPLES FROM MEDIA CODES ON PRIVACY*

Journalism

Society of Professional Journalists and Cyberjournalists.net:

- Be sensitive when seeking or using interviews or photographs of those affected by tragedy or grief.

- Recognize that private people have a greater right to control information about themselves than do public officials and others who seek power, influence or attention. Only an overriding public need can justify intrusion into anyone's privacy.

Radio Television Digital News Association:

- Exercise special care when children are involved in a story and give children greater privacy protection than adults.

Al Jazeera:

3. Treat our audiences with due respect and address every issue or story with due attention to present a clear, factual and accurate picture while giving full consideration to the feelings of victims of crime, war, persecution and disaster, their relatives and our viewers, and to individual privacy and public decorum.

National Press Photographers Association:

4. Treat all subjects with respect and dignity. Give special consideration to vulnerable subjects and compassion to victims of crime or tragedy. Intrude on private moments of grief only when the public has an overriding and justifiable need to see.

Australian Journalists' Association:

At times of grief or trauma, always act with sensitivity and discretion. Never harass. Never exploit a person's vulnerability or ignorance of media practice. Interview only with informed consent.

Philadelphia Inquirer:

Most of the people mentioned in the news columns are public officials, whose official activities are legally the subject of scrutiny, or public figures, who often seek out publicity. However, private citizens who have not sought public notice are frequently surprised, and sometimes upset, when they are approached by reporters or find themselves written about. This is especially true in tragic situations. Staff members should approach stories with both a desire to inform the public and compassion for the individuals involved.

A private citizen who is thrust unwittingly and unwillingly into a public situation is likely to be unfamiliar with news-gathering practices. Staff members should clearly identify themselves when approaching such inexperienced people and treat them with courtesy.

continued

Box 8.3 | *continued*

Relatives of public officials and public figures are sometimes newsworthy solely because of their family position. Such stories can, however, be overdone. They should be handled thoughtfully and not be simply voyeuristic.

When it is decided that a person in a news story should not be named, such as a rape victim or a witness in possible danger, care should be taken not to identify the person through other specific references, such as home address, place of work or school attended.

A person's mental or physical infirmities, sexual preference or the like generally should not be referred to unless it is relevant to the story.

San Jose (Calif.) Mercury News:

The Mercury News is sensitive to the privacy of victims of rape and child molestation, or of subjects who clearly would be in physical danger by publication of their names and addresses. Exceptions to this rule may be made in some circumstance, but they must be approved by the executive editor or editor.

Ordinarily, consent is implied if a photographer approaches a subject, indicates that he/she is a newspaper photographer and asks for names and other facts. In some circumstances, written releases may be required (at mental health institutions or orphanages, for example).

Spokane (Wash.) Spokesman-Review and Chronicle:

There are inevitable conflicts between the privacy of individuals and the public good or the public right to know about the conduct of persons in regard to public affairs. Newsworthiness, common sense, humanity, and the law are factors which should be considered in each case.

Legality Only One Measure:

The legal standard, however, is not the only standard by which to measure a story or a picture. What is legal, in other words, is not necessarily what is ethical or what is in good taste.

It is perfectly legal to identify rape victims, for instance. But these newspapers do not identify rape victims, even when they testify in open court. It is legal, too, to publish pictures of victims of fatal accidents or pictures of persons displaying any number of private emotions as long as they are in public situations. But good taste may dictate against the use of such shots.

There can be few hard-and-fast rules governing the use of stories and pictures that have the potential to be offensive to great numbers of readers. There are exceptions to every rule. Even the rape rule has exceptions: We do identify rape victims in some instances, such as when a woman sues her convicted rapist for civil damages, or when a wife charges her husband with rape.

continued

Box 8.3 | *continued*

In the absence of specific rules, the important point is to consider the implications of using material that might prove objectionable to many of our readers.

National Victim Center (Texas):

Victim's Rights and the Media

Never feel that because you have unwillingly been involved in an incident of public interest that you must personally share the details and/or your feelings with the general public. If you decide that you want the public to be aware of how traumatic and unfair your victimization was, you do not automatically give up your right to privacy. By knowing and requesting respect for your rights, you can be heard and yet not violated . . .

You have the right to grieve in privacy.

Grief is a highly personal experience. If you do not wish to share it publicly, you have the right to ask reporters to remove themselves during times of grief.

Advertising/Marketing

Better Business Bureau:

7. Safeguard Privacy.

Protect any data collected against mishandling and fraud, collect personal information only as needed, and respect the preferences of customers regarding the use of their information.

An accredited business or organization agrees to:

A. Respect Privacy

Businesses conducting e-commerce agree to disclose on their Web site the following:

> what information they collect,
> with whom it is shared,
> how it can be corrected,
> how it is secured,
> how policy changes will be communicated, and;
> how to address concerns over misuse of personal data.

B. Secure Sensitive Data

Businesses that collect sensitive date online (credit card, bank account numbers, Social Security number, salary or other personal financial information, medical history or records, etc.) will ensure that it is transmitted via secure means. Businesses will make best efforts to comply with industry standards for the protection and proper disposal of all sensitive data, both online and offline.

continued

Box 8.3 | *continued*

C. Honor Customer Preferences

Businesses agree to respect customer preferences regarding contact by telephone, fax and email, and agree to remedy the underlying cause of any failure to do so.

Entertainment

Free Speech Coalition:

3. Safeguarding Privacy: Consumer and employee trust requires that confidential behavior and information be steadfastly protected. FSC members:

3.1. Safeguard the identities and billing records of present, former and prospective consumers of adult material.

3.2. Alert consumers to any surveillance or other activities that would alter a reasonable expectation of privacy.

3.3. Keep secure all confidential employee and independent contractor records, such as legal names, contact numbers and medical information.

3.4   Make clear to employees and independent contractors that an unreasonable breach of confidential consumer information, or confidential information about employees or independent contractors, is grounds for dismissal and/or legal action.

* Note: Numbers in these excerpts are as they appear in the original codes.

---

themselves into the public spotlight, either momentarily or over time, to some degree they forfeit their right to privacy. In many other circumstances, the public's legitimate right and need to know must take precedence. Because it is vital that we reserve to ourselves the authority to make such decisions, it is equally vital that we make them carefully and responsibly.

The Norfolk (Va.) *Virginian-Pilot* code says:

There are inevitable conflicts between an individual's desire for privacy and the public good or the right to know about the conduct of public affairs. Reporters and photographers should make judgments in the light of common sense, decency and humanity, keeping in mind that we do not encourage them to badger a person who has made it clear he does not want to be interviewed or photographed.

The *Philadelphia Inquirer* reminds its reporters that

. . . public officials' official activities are legally subject to scrutiny, but private citizens who have not sought public notice should [be] approached with both a desire to inform the public and compassion for individuals involved.

It should be noted that this has a legal parallel, as the *New York Times v. Sullivan* decision makes it easier for private citizens to win libel lawsuits than public figures.

The San Jose *Mercury-News* code says its journalists should be "sensitive to privacy of victims of rape and child molestation, or of subjects who clearly would be in physical danger."

SUMMARY AND CONCLUSIONS

This chapter includes an array of concepts related to the importance of privacy. Among them are biometrics, behavioral profiling, whole body imaging, brain scans, domestic surveillance, a national ID, the smart grid, cookies, cloud computing, digital libraries, NeuroFocus, Valpak, PRIZM, identify theft, reality-based entertainment, sex crime victims, medical records, citizen journalism, voluntary and involuntary public figures, personal space, and autonomy.

Many of these concepts assist marketers, journalists, and government agencies in their ever-expanding quest for information about citizen-consumers and those who may threaten social stability. The same concepts trouble civil libertarians who see incremental encroachments into personal space and moral autonomy. In the midst of it all, of course, are media that constantly seek to inform, entertain, and persuade.

The chapter suggests that privacy should be defined as more than just our right to be left alone. To survive—let alone flourish—in contemporary society, we have voluntarily relinquished that right. We give up any claims to absolute privacy when we use a post office or street address, Social Security card, driver's license, student ID, library card, credit card, ATM card, or when we go on the Internet. Meanwhile, we have implicitly permitted "big brother" to photograph us when we shop or stroll down the street or sit in the park, or board a commercial plane, or enter many governmental and private offices. The list goes on, but the point is that contemporary society chops away at our presumed right to be let alone.

Philosophers have long talked about the public and private "spheres" of life, natural rights, liberty, property, individuality, intimacy, secrecy, and human dignity. Some (see Shoeman, 2001; Nissenbaum, 2009) describe privacy in broader terms, such as the extent to which any of us is given the social and legal space to develop the emotional, cognitive, spiritual, and moral powers we need in order to be autonomous agents. Encroachment upon individual moral autonomy continues to highlight today's arguments about the value of privacy.

Most media organizations have tacitly recognized the difficulty of making sweeping generalizations about privacy, preferring instead to couch it as one of many prima facie ("at first glance") values that must be balanced against competing claims. Not surprisingly, journalists and photographers have had the most to say about privacy in their ethics codes, but other media take note of the need for respect, dignity, minimizing harm, fairness, and confidentiality—all, to some extent, synonyms for privacy.

When media ethicists inquire, "What's it worth?" they often are asking about privacy. It has long been a bone of contention in the media ethics environment, and we see no signs of its disappearance. Thus it behooves every student of media ethics, every media practitioner, and every media consumer to give careful thought about how to balance privacy against other values.

■ ■ ■

PRACTICAL APPLICATIONS

1. Over a given week, how much private information have you willingly or unwillingly shared? How did you leave a trail, who received the information, and how could any of it be used to make you a more (or less) vulnerable consumer or citizen?

2. Write a set of privacy standards for a blogger's code of ethics. Include some specifics.

3. Look at photographer Garry Bryant's four-point checklist and adapt it for the deadline world of public relations or advertising.

4. The law lets journalists and others gather and share all sorts of private information about people. Should there be one set of standards for celebrities and public figures, and another set for private citizens? Why or why not?

5. As a way to limit libel or privacy cases, many movies include a disclaimer along these lines: "All characters appearing in this work are fictitious. Any resemblance to persons living or dead is coincidental." Think about movies you have seen and consider how often that disclaimer is true.

CASE STUDIES

Note: The first three case studies have different perspectives on the same situation. You may find it instructive to consider the other cases once you've worked through the case specific to your communication discipline.

■ ■ ■

CASE 8.1 **Journalism: Publish the Name or Not?**

You cover student government for the student newspaper at Freedonia University. A big story on campus this week is a ballot-box "stuffing" effort that led to sanctions against Gabba Gabba Hey, a social organization. Apparently, Gabba Gabba Hey members were able to create extra votes for the Student Government Association presidential candidate backed by their organization.

University officials say disciplinary action has been taken against the organization, but it will not say what. Officials cite student privacy rules when refusing to say whether additional action has been taken against any individuals, and they will not provide specific names of Gabba Gabba Hey members. The president of Gabba Gabba Hey has no comment.

But you are a solid journalist who does more than rely on official sources. An acquaintance, who is friends with some Gabba Gabba Hey members, tells you that the fraternity members will be required to spend a week scrubbing university floors as punishment. Your friend also tells you that the instigator behind the plan was a member named Sidney Bracey, an 18-year-old political science major. Your source says Bracey will either be suspended or will be required to work a month cleaning floors.

When you talk to Bracey, he will neither confirm nor deny that he instigated the ballot box stuffing. But he pleads with you not to print his name in the paper in connection with the incident. "It could ruin my life," he said, but he wouldn't explain what he meant by that.

The student paper publishes weekly, and before the next print edition a local blog, www.freedonialive.com, breaks the news about the election issue. The blog post has no named sources, but it names the group and describes its punishment. It also calls Bracey the instigator, although it does not say whether Bracey was punished and has no indication whether the blog attempted to reach Bracey for comment.

Your writing deadline is tomorrow. The paper's lead story will be your story about the apparent election fraud, and you plan to mention Gabba Gabba Hey's involvement. But you're not sure whether to print Bracey's name. You feel fairly sure he's the one and feel comfortable with your source. But in the back of your head you still hear Bracey's plea. And you wonder whether it's big enough news on campus that you need to print his name.

➤ **What do you do?**

Questions

- **What's your problem?**
- **Why not follow the rules?**
- **Who wins, who loses?**
- **What's it worth?**
- What else do you need to know?

Thinking it Through

1. Is this an ethical issue? Why or why not?

2. To what extent, if any, is this issue related to privacy?

3. Do the privacy, loyalty, or truth-telling statements in any media codes of ethics come into play here? How do you decide which variable trumps the others?

4. Does this have to be a win–lose resolution, or can you make it a win–win?

5. Philosopher Ferdinand Schoeman called privacy "the measure of the extent to which an individual is afforded the social and legal space to develop the emotional, cognitive, spiritual, and moral powers of an autonomous agent." Given that definition, how much protection should college students have when it comes to having their names publicized in connection with a disciplinary hearing? At what point should students lose their privacy?

6. Is there a difference between printing Bracey's name in a student publication and publishing it in a "real" news publication? Why or why not?

7. Do you print Bracey's name or not?

   A. If you choose to print the name:

      a. How do you justify your decision?

      b. How do you respond to Bracey's fear that publication could ruin his life?

      c. How concerned were you that you did not receive the name from an official source?

      d. How much were you influenced by the blog's decision to print the name?

      e. What do you say to Bracey if you end up face-to-face one day?

      f. Do you also print a photograph of Bracey?

   B. If you choose not to print the name:

      a. How do you justify your decision?

      b. How influenced were you by Bracey's plea?

      c. What do you say to people who argue that Bracey's name became public once it was printed on the website?

      d. Would you have printed his name had it been given to you by university officials?

■ ■ ■

CASE 8.2 **New Media: Choosing Among Privacy, Loyalty, and the Truth**

You've been running www.freedonialive.com for a decade, and your archives remain up to date and searchable. As owner of the longest-running blog in Freedonia, your archives are used by thousands of people to read about events that are now history. Nearly a tenth of your Web traffic comes from people reading what was published months and years ago, which means your archives make money for you.

Four years ago, you broke the news about students stuffing the ballot box in student government elections at Freedonia University. You wrote that a Gabba Gabba Hey member named Sidney Bracey, then 18, led the scheme that let other members of the group vote multiple times for their favored presidential candidate. While university disciplinary committee's proceedings are private, you reported that the entire Gabba Gabba Hey organization was required to spend a week scrubbing the floors as punishment. You named Bracey as the instigator but did not report whether he received individual punishment because you could never find out.

Again, that was four years ago. Today you received a call from Bracey, nearly in tears when telling you that he has lost another job because of what's published on your website. It seems that when someone types "Sidney Bracey" in any search engine, one of the top-ranked results is a link to your coverage in www.freedonialive.com.

Bracey tells you that a mean-spirited rival at work showed the boss your story, and the boss apparently used it as the "tie-breaking" factor when deciding who would be the final worker to be laid off.

"It's just not fair," Bracey tells you. "It happened when I was a kid in college, and it's ruining my life." He says his wife is two weeks away from giving birth to their first child, and he needs another job. He tells you that your website's old stories are a Sword of Damocles hanging over his head, since he never knows when it might hurt him again and might cost him a chance at another job if a prospective employer finds the story online.

He asks that you remove the story, since it wasn't very important four years ago and is doing nothing but harm today.

➤ **What do you say?**

It appears that you have three choices: remove the entire post from four years ago, edit the archives to remove Bracey's name, or keep the post as it is. (We'll assume you wouldn't be so mean as to write about Bracey calling you today to talk about losing his job because of your website.)

Questions
- **What's your problem?**
- **Why not follow the rules?**
- **Who wins, who loses?**
- **What's it worth?**
- What else do you need to know?

Thinking it Through

1. Is this solely an ethical issue, or might there be a legal issue, too?

2. What are your loyalties in this case? What are your values?

3. How do your loyalties and values conflict with Bracey's?

4. Do the privacy, loyalty, or truth-telling statements in any media codes of ethics come into play here? How do you decide which value trumps the others?

5. What do you decide to do? Does it have to be a win–lose resolution, or can you make it a win–win?

   A. If you remove the entire post from the archives:
      a. What loyalties did you decide were more important than others?
      b. If privacy trumped loyalty, how did you decide which was more important?
      c. Would removing Bracey's name mean you were compromising your truth-telling goal?
      d. Would you write a note for readers to tell them that you removed the post? Why or why not? Would you explain the reason?
      e. At what point would you refuse to remove a post when asked?

   B. If you choose to remove Bracey's name but keep the story in the archives:
      a. What loyalties did you decide were most important?
      b. If privacy trumped loyalty, how did you decide which was more important?
      c. Would removing Bracey's name mean you compromised your truth-telling goal?
      d. Would you write a note telling readers that you removed the name from the original post? Why or why not? Would you explain the reason?
      e. Would you be willing to make it a practice to edit posts on a regular basis? What would you tell people who accuse you of "rewriting history?"
      f. Is there a point at which you would remove posts in order to help someone who asks?

   C. If you choose not to remove the post from the archives:
      a. What loyalties did you decide were more important than others?
      b. Did truth telling trump privacy when making your decision? Why or why not?

c. Is there a point at which you would go back and edit your archives to help someone who asks?

d. Is there a point at which you would remove posts in order to help someone who asks?

e. Might you write something about Bracey's request to remove the post?

f. How much of your decision is based upon the concern that you'll start losing traffic (and therefore, money) when you write on the topic again?

CASE 8.3 **Public Relations: "Hiding" Behind a Fuzzy Law?**

You are a junior majoring in public relations at Freedonia University, and you work 15 hours a week with its media relations staff.

When you go to the office Tuesday morning, the university's chief spokeswoman tells you to expect reporters to start calling soon with questions about claims that a student organization stuffed the ballot box in recent student government elections.

She tells you that Gabba Gabba Hey members managed to vote multiple times for the presidential candidate of their choice. When confronted with evidence, the group quickly pleaded guilty to the dean of student life. Group members were sentenced to a week of scrubbing floors across campus. She also tells you that member Sidney Bracey, 18, confessed to leading the vote-stuffing scheme and received an additional three weeks of clean-up work.

She also tells you to keep quiet about what you know and to refer questions to her.

You ask her whether you ought to prepare a press release about the incident. "No," she says. "It's not our job to tell others about bad news. We let reporters come to us."

Sure enough, a reporter from the student newspaper drops by later that day, and you are in the room during the interview.

The spokeswoman won't name the fraternity involved and won't confirm that it was Gabba Gabba Hey when the reporter asks if that was the group involved. The spokeswoman also will not confirm the length of punishment.

When the reporter asks whether any individual students received further discipline, the spokeswoman won't say. When the reporter says he heard that a student named Sidney Bracey received a two-week suspension, the spokeswoman will neither confirm nor deny that any individual student was disciplined.

When asked to summarize, the spokeswoman offers the talking point she hopes the reporter will use: "Freedonia University was quickly in control of the situation and took care of the matter in the appropriate and proper manner."

When the reporter asks why the university won't offer more details, the spokeswoman cites FERPA, the Federal Educational Rights and Privacy Act*—the law that protects the records of any student enrolled at a school that receives federal funds. The student reporter seems grudgingly to accept this explanation at face value.

When you go home that evening, you look up the law that the spokeswoman cited. It's complicated, but it seems unclear the extent to which disciplinary proceedings are private, and it doesn't say much about whether entire organizations, such as fraternities, would be exempt.

➤ **You wonder what you'd do if you were the spokesperson and the questions came to you.**

---

* Federal Educational Rights and Privacy Act of 1974, 20 U.S.C. § 1232g.

Questions

- **What's your problem?**
- **Why not follow the rules?**
- **Who wins, who loses?**
- **What's it worth?**
- What else do you need to know?

Thinking it Through

1. Make a list of the people (including yourself) and groups who are stakeholders in your decision. How much privacy does each of the stakeholders deserve? Does an organization like Gabba Gabba Hey deserve privacy in an issue like this?

2. Should the spokeswoman have told you the name of the student or the group involved, and then told you not to tell anyone? Why or why not?

3. Is it ethical for a spokesperson to tell the media that the university "took care of the matter in the appropriate and proper manner" without providing evidence? Why or why not?

4. The university sends many media releases highlighting good news among faculty, staff, students, and administrators. Does the university have an obligation to send similar releases when newsworthy events occur on campus that aren't as positive, or is it OK to keep quiet until a media member asks?

5. If you were the university spokesperson, would you have written a press release explaining what happened? Why or why not?

6. Would you have identified Gabba Gabba Hey? If not, would you have confirmed it had a reporter asked for confirmation? Consider the same thing for the precise punishment for the group.

7. Would you have released the student's name? If not, would you have confirmed it had a reporter asked for confirmation? Consider the same thing for the precise punishment for the student.

8. In this example, the student reporter's information about the punishment was incorrect. Does the spokeswoman have an obligation to correct the information, or at least say that it is incorrect?

9. By refusing to answer specific questions, it could be argued that the university's lack of candor fuels rumors. What responsibility does the university have to stop rumors, and how does it balance that task with the need to protect student privacy and to maintain a favorable image?

10. What if the student journalist, whom you have had in a couple of classes, asks you later to confirm some information confidentially? What would you do?

For more information see *The Columbus Dispatch* newspaper, which published a May 2009 series that looked at how universities used privacy laws to keep athletic information secret. Go to www.dispatch.com/live/content/local_news/stories/2009/05/31/FERPA_MAIN.ART_ART_05-31-09_A1_VFE0G7F.html to learn more.

■ ■ ■

CASE 8.4 **Advertising: Mining the Data**

As head of advertising for a general-merchandise retailer, you have an appointment with a marketing company that collects and "mines" data that let you know more about your customers and their buying habits. The marketing company assures you that it can mix and match data mining solutions to produce double-digit increases in sales. There is no up-front payment, since the marketing company earns its fees by taking a percentage of the sales it can prove it increased through its techniques.

The options the marketing company offers:

- Create "loyalty cards" for your store. Shoppers who sign up provide their phone number, home address, email addresses, and other information that can track buying habits of individual consumers. In exchange, customers with loyalty cards receive discount coupons, and people who use their cards in the store pay less for certain items than people without loyalty cards.

- Ask customers to give their phone numbers at the point of purchase, and use that information to track their purchases over time. (You'll still sell to customers who do not give a number, but your sales force will make it sound more like a requirement than a request.)

- Target ads to neighborhoods that spend the most, offering discounts that are not offered to others. (As a practical matter, this means that people in wealthier neighborhoods will pay less for products than people in poorer neighborhoods.)

- Mix information from your stores' sales with information from other stores, so you can learn even more about what individuals buy.

- Allow information about sales at your stores to be used with information from other stores, so other stores can learn even more about customer shopping habits. (Options include "aggregated" data by store or shoppers' neighborhoods, or individualized data by customer.)

- Run credit reports on shoppers, so direct mail can be tailored to people with higher credit scores (but not to people with lower credit scores.)

- Create a free email service for customers. In exchange for a state-of-the-art email experience, users allow you to search through the content of their messages so you can tailor ads to them, recommend products they might want to buy, and even offer money-saving coupons for those products.

Questions

- **What's your problem?**
- **Why not follow the rules?**
- **Who wins, who loses?**
- **What's it worth?**
- What else do you need to know?

Thinking it Through

1. For each of the seven options described in the case, ask:
   A. Is this an invasion of the customers' privacy?
   B. Would you feel comfortable providing this information if you were a customer?
   C. How would you explain to customers this use of their information?
   D. Would you choose this option for your company?

2. Make a list of the people (including yourself) and groups who are stakeholders in your decision. Do any of them have any special privileges, or deserve special protection?

3. Is it fair to offer lower prices to people who give up some of their privacy? Or, put another way, is it unfair not to offer the same prices to people who value their privacy?

4. Should retailers be required to explain to potential shoppers how individual information is used to track their buying habits? Why or why not?

5. Even if none of these options seems ethically wrong individually, is there a point when if combined they could become ethically troublesome?

CASE 8.5 **Entertainment: Which Syndicated Shows to Buy?**

You are the young and newly appointed general manager of a low-budget local television station. Among your responsibilities is choosing the syndicated shows that will appear on your station. Those shows generally appear during the afternoon and early evening. You travel to a national convention where you choose the shows you want to broadcast and make deals with the syndicators.

The convention floor has dozens of companies with scores of shows to sell, including a variety of "entertainment news magazines" that use TV news techniques in telling stories about celebrities. Other available shows are "reality-based," using dramatic video captured by law enforcement and other sources.

You are interested in ratings but also want to broadcast shows that will not make you uncomfortable when you are asked about your choices.

Ignoring the legal issues revolving around privacy, consider the following types of shows and go through the questions that follow:

1. An entertainment news show that pays paparazzi for video and images showing actors and other celebrities in unflattering situations. The hottest celebrities are seen climbing in and out of cars, eating in restaurants, walking down streets, relaxing on the beach, and in other situations when they may or may not know they have been photographed. The show's producers say they are careful not to break laws, such as trespassing, when shooting celebrities.

2. An entertainment news show that asks for video or photos of famous people, taken by its viewers. Viewers who send along images are usually rewarded with a show T-shirt, and the best viewer-provided image of the week receives $500.

3. An entertainment news show with segments about under-18 actors and musicians. These children are famous, but the show pays paparazzi for video and images showing the young stars in unflattering situations, such as underage drinking and when they're misbehaving on dates.

4. An entertainment news show that once a week produces a "children of celebrities" segment. Viewers see paparazzi-provided images of the children of celebrities, generally as they walk down the street or go to amusement parks with their famous parents. The show's announcers comment on the looks, clothes, and behaviors of the children.

5. A reality show dealing only with police chases, with video taken from in-dash recorders on police vehicles and television news helicopters. While each show closes with a reminder to viewers that it's best to obey traffic laws, the repeated viewings of crashes (including slow motion) suggest that the show really is more about voyeurism. Sometimes, people are killed in those crashes.

6. A reality show that uses police surveillance video of public streets. It shows crime but also random acts of cruelty, public displays of affection, or goofiness of ordinary people who likely did not know that "big brother" was watching them. The show blurs faces of some people, but it includes the date and location of where it was shot.

Questions

*   **What's your problem?**
*   **Why not follow the rules?**
*   **Who wins, who loses?**
*   **What's it worth?**
*   What else do you need to know?

Thinking it Through

For each of the six show examples (1 through 6), ask and answer:

1. Is this an ethical issue? Why or why not?
2. To what extent, if any, is privacy an issue for each of these shows?
3. All other things being equal, would you choose to broadcast this show? Why or why not? How do you justify your decision?
4. If you were sure that ratings for this show would be higher than the ratings for the show currently broadcast in its place, would you choose this show?

Other questions

5. Do you know any famous people? How do they seek to balance their private lives with their public persona?
6. How much privacy would you be willing to trade in order to be famous?
7. Go to www.posh24.com/celebrity_children* to see paparazzi photos of celebrities and their children. As the site says, "Celebrity children are always beeing [*sic*] watched." Do these sorts of images seem ethically justifiable to you? Why or why not?
8. Many celebrities spend a great deal of time and attention to creating images of themselves that may not match reality. How much privacy should celebrities have when living lives that may be hypocritical?

■ ■ ■

---

* This website and its "celebrity children" tag were active as of July 2010. A similar site is www.celebrity-gossip.net/category/celebrity-kids, which declares: "The hottest kids in Hollywood! They're famous because of their parents or they've made a name for themselves—either way they're HOT! Fashion, Money, Toys, Excess.. [sic] they live fabulous lives in the spotlight."

CHAPTER 9

Persuasion and Propaganda

This chapter:

- reviews examples of persuasion and advocacy in the mass communication environment that demonstrate the increasingly complex moral domains of advertising, public relations, and marketing

- considers the case for ethical persuasion and selective truth telling

- tries to put propaganda in an appropriate perspective as an inevitable component of contemporary society

- presents a new model for making moral decisions about persuasion

- presents several practical applications and five new case studies on persuasion.

INTRODUCTION

PERSUASION IS inherent in most realms of life. It is part and parcel of intrapersonal, interpersonal, organizational, professional, social, political, corporate, religious, and other relationships. We invest an enormous amount of time, energy, and resources in trying to persuade one another to change or reinforce beliefs, prejudices, and behaviors. We act as advocates and selective truth tellers when we go on dates, apply for jobs, request a pay raise or promotion, outline our political or cultural or religious ideologies, and do business. We expect the same from others: Do our dates willingly reveal all of their faults, or do they display their best attributes? Do our potential employers tell us the working conditions might not be ideal, or do they use selective information to recruit us? Do they automatically give us whatever raise or promotion we request, or do they expect us to negotiate? Do others accept without question our views on politics, culture, or religion, or do the subjects automatically lead to debate? Do we think the marketplace is balanced in our favor, or do we know we are entering a competitive arena that may favor the sellers?

Many critics think we commit too much private and public money peddling ideas, goods, and services to one another: Why vote for one political party instead of another, when pragmatic pressures will force candidates to break their campaign promises? Why use one brand of face soap—or line of clothing, computer, or automobile—instead of another, when each does essentially the same job? Why mount public service campaigns against air pollution, smoking, or hollow calories when people will keep doing what they already know is harmful?

In this fourth chapter committed to answering the question "What's it worth?" we focus on the values of persuasion in contemporary society. In particular, we are interested in the moral and non-moral components of advertising, public relations, and a whole slew of persuasive activities. We believe these fields play an important role in informing and persuading us citizen-consumers. Furthermore, we believe that all of us benefit when the enterprises are carried out responsibly, but little good accrues when advocates act unethically.

SOME ISSUES OF PERSUASION

To launch our discussion of advertising, public relations, marketing, and propaganda, we start by defining what we mean by persuasion and how it can be ethical or unethical. Persuasion is designed to "move" people (Rogers, 2007, p. 5)—that is, to affect beliefs and behaviors that individuals have about products, services, political candidates, or public issues. Advocacy is a type of persuasion designed to address issues, including public health, governmental, and socioeconomic matters. When persuasion is employed ethically, it involves sharing credible evidence through rational and emotional appeals. It is when that evidence is skewed, manipulative, or harmful the persuasion can become an unethical activity.

Consider several issues that deal with persuasion in the modern media environment. They are not the most important examples of advocacy or persuasive ethics, they merely represent thousands of potential cases that would demonstrate the complexity of morality in these arenas. Some of them show the blurring of the lines between and among media of information, entertainment, and persuasion. Collectively, they reveal the delicate nature of selective truth telling and the need to minimize harm, the difficulty of balancing loyalties between clients and consumers, and the importance of transparency and accountability.

Commercials Inside "News" Content

As traditional mainstream media are increasingly stressed financially, threatened by new media's usurpation of audiences and advertising revenue, we have seen a corresponding increase in morally questionable behavior. Motivated by the need to deliver eyeballs to advertisers, scrambling for a diminished share of the fragmenting mass audience, and competing against new media forms, commercial media have been part of a multi-billion dollar a year global business known as "product placement" or "embedded advertising." The problems include traditional product placement in commercial films, concept placement in entertainment TV, the planting of branded products and services (embedded advertising), an increase in advertorials and infotainment, payola and plugola, and the misuse of video news releases.

Critics have long gnashed their teeth over video news releases (VNRs)—public relations packages that look like traditional TV news stories and are given to TV news outlets

(Wulfemeyer & Frazier, 1992). PR practitioners say the VNRs are a modern version of printed press releases, which have long been staples in the media environment. In fact, studies say nearly half of a newspaper's content is related to information from press releases (Berkowitz, 1990; Cobb & Elder, 1983; Turk, 1986). VNRs describe an event, product, idea, or candidate in a visually appealing way. Their visuals are usually good enough to meet the news stations' production demands, and their contents are interesting and relevant enough to meet stations' definitions of newsworthiness. Besides, they don't cost the local stations a dime. Some news organizations use VNRs in their entirety, while others may incorporate portions of these packages in broader news stories.

Critics are concerned, however, that TV stations often show the VNRs intact, without identifying the source of those materials and without augmenting them with any balance or "localized" reporting.

For example, over a ten-month period in 2005 and 2006, the Center for Media and Democracy documented 77 cases of local television stations' use of VNRs produced by PR firms for corporate clients including General Motors, Intel, Pfizer, and Capital One. While their sponsors may have been identified when the VNRs were sent to the stations, the center was concerned that news stations did not identify what information came from a corporation so audiences could make informed decisions about the material presented (Farsetta & Price, 2006).

The center's report, titled "Fake News," received a thorough airing in the nation's press, providing the public with new insights into not only how corporate America was selling itself, but how the US government was doing likewise. Under the Bush administration in the first few years of the 2000s, at least 20 federal agencies used taxpayer dollars to produce VNRs that touted the administration's Medicare prescription-drug benefit program, free after-school tutoring, curbing childhood obesity, preservation of forests and wetlands, fighting computer viruses, and fighting holiday drunken driving. The Health and Human Services department spent more than $124 million to produce VNRs. Many of the VNRs, hosted by pseudo-journalists Karen Ryan and Alberto Garcia who looked and sounded like TV reporters, ran unedited and with nothing to identify the source (Barstow & Stein, 2005).

Once the public heard the debate, the Federal Communications Commission and PR and broadcast organizations responded (Aiello & Proffitt, 2008). The FCC reminded broadcasters of their obligation to identify VNRs when they were being shown. The PRSA reminded its members that their code of ethics says: "Open communication fosters informed decision making in a democratic society" and members should "reveal the sponsors for causes and interests represented." The ethics committee of the Radio Television News Directors Association (which in 2009 changed its name to Radio Television Digital News Association) developed the set of guidelines reproduced in Box 9.1.

The point: There's nothing wrong with persuasion *per se*. However, those who pass along the persuaders' messages should be transparent. Audiences deserve to know whether

Box **9.1** | **RTDNA GUIDELINES FOR USE OF NON-EDITORIAL VIDEO AND AUDIO**

Television and radio stations should strive to protect the editorial integrity of the video and audio they air. This integrity, at times, might come into question when stations air video and audio provided to newsrooms by companies, organizations or governmental agencies with political or financial interests in publicizing the material. News staffs should find answers to the following questions when making decisions to broadcast video or audio produced and/or supplied by non-editorial sources.

RTDNA's Code of Ethics and Professional Conduct states that professional electronic journalists should clearly disclose the origin of information and label all material provided by outsiders. The following guidelines are offered to meet this goal.

- News managers and producers should determine if the station is able to shoot this video or capture this audio itself, or get it through regular editorial channels, such as its network feed service. If this video/audio is available in no other way but through corporate release (as in the case of proprietary assembly line video), then managers should decide what value using the video/audio brings to the newscast, and if that value outweighs the possible appearance of product placements or commercial interests.

- News managers and producers should clearly disclose the origin of information and label all material provided by corporate or other non-editorial sources. For example, graphics could denote Mercy Hospital video and the reporter or anchor script could also acknowledge it by stating, This operating room video was provided by Mercy Hospital.

- News managers and producers should determine if interviews provided with video/audio releases follow the same standards regarding conflicts of interest as used in the newsroom. For instance, some releases might contain interviews where subjects and interviewers are employed by the same organization. Consider whether tough questions were asked and if the subject was properly questioned.

- Before re-voicing and airing stories released with all their elements and intended for that purpose, managers and producers should ask questions regarding whether the editorial process behind the story is in concert with those used in the newsroom. Some questions to ask include whether more than one side is included, if there is a financial agenda to releasing the story, and if the viewers and/or listeners would believe this is work done locally by your team.

- Producers should question the source of network feed video that appears to have come from sources other than the networks news operation. Network feed producers should supply information revealing the source of such material.

- News managers and producers should consider how video/audio released from groups without a profit or political agenda, such as nonprofit, charitable and educational institutions, will be used in newscasts, if at all. Can this material add valuable insight to local stories? Has it been issued to be aired locally and credited to the issuing organizations. Will viewers find it to be useful information.

—RTDNA Ethics Committee (2010)

they're receiving objective news or persuasion (or some combination thereof). In the long run, the most-effective means of regulating VNRs may not come from government or professional associations, but from market forces—audiences who are aware that their news is slanted, and who suspect the slanting is done by unidentified sources (Nelson et al., 2009).

New Media, New Persuasion

At the same time, the relatively unregulated world of evolving new media has experimented with even more creative ways to garner audiences and income.

Advertorials, in-text ads, kick-through ads, contextual link ads, pop-ups, pop-unders, fake dialogue boxes, interstitial or prestitial ads, and overlays—these are all relatively new terms in the communications lexicon. But they are central to online communications media's efforts to make money. As Martha Spizziri (2009) says, while they are not inherently unethical, they all come with ethical hazards.

Advertorials are ads that are intentionally made to look like news articles. In-text advertising is a generic term describing several ways that readers of online news items are lured into reading promotional messages (Craig, 2007a). Kick-through ads are display ads that take users to a site when they merely pass their mouse over the ad. Contextual link ads are words or phrases within editorial copy that are linked to pop-up ads; users don't even have to click on the key words for the ads to appear. Pop-up ads appear in small windows in front of the main browser windows; pop-unders are similar, but don't appear until users close the window. Interstitial or prestitial ads appear prior to the editorial content the browser is searching. Overlay ads appear over existing content, but in the same window rather than in a new window (they're usually Flash windows.)

Professional and academic authors of a *Journal of Mass Media Ethics* "Cases and Commentaries" discussion were mixed in their criticism of in-text ads: The pros invoked tradition and media freedom to experiment, while the academics, who described the practices as morally troubling, called for clear standards in ethics codes as well as moral theory and the principles of truth telling and transparency (Craig, 2007a).

The Internet has become the brave new world of not just product placement and clever ways of luring users to commercial messages, but also of stealthy concept placement. One of the best-known cases of concept placement on the Internet was Wal-Marting Across America (Burns, 2008; Craig, 2007b; Jordan, 2009). Two bloggers described their cross-country trip in an RV, which they parked nightly in Wal-Mart parking lots. Their blog, sponsored by "Working Families for Wal-Mart," was filled with heart-warming stories and photos about Wal-Mart employees. So far, so good—a bit of Americana on the Web.

However, the blog was not a spontaneous collection of stories about Wal-Mart families. It was created by employees of Wal-Mart's public relations agency, Edelman, in response to negative PR the quarter-trillion dollar corporation had been receiving for its wages and benefits policies, working conditions, and aggressive lobbying. "Working Families for Wal-Mart" paid the expenses of the freelance reporter and photographer. Even more troubling: the photographer was a *Washington Post* staffer working on his own time, and Richard Edelman's PR firm helped write the Word of Mouth Marketing Association's code of ethics. That code included the policy statement: "Honesty of identity: You never obscure your identity."

The trip across America's parking lots lasted two weeks before other bloggers "outed" the campaign. The posts came down, the photographer repaid what he was paid for his work (Kurtz, 2006), and Richard Edelman, who caught fire from numerous corners, took the high road and apologized.

Summing Up the Cases

These cases are not necessarily horror stories. They merely describe some recent uses of persuasion. Certainly we could have chosen examples in which advocacy and persuasion are altruistic, put to unquestionably good purposes, and are fully transparent. In fact, the media ethics environment is filled with many examples of ethical persuasion practices. What makes the above cases morally interesting is that they nearly cross—or actually cross—some moral benchmarks. They may have been initiated with the best of motives: a conviction that the public needed the information, the sponsor had the right to be heard, and the media wanted the income. But the cases became morally problematic because of the manner in which the campaigns were carried out, the potential for harm, and the lack of transparency.

ETHICAL ADVOCACY, SELECTIVE TRUTH TELLING, AND TRANSPARENCY

The debates in this chapter may make more sense if we use a continuum of beliefs while considering the pros and cons of persuasion. Which comes closer to your view—A or B?

Type A:

- Everyone deserves to have a voice in the marketplace of ideas—including advertisers, PR practitioners, and propagandists.
- People are generally rational and motivated by self-interest and tend to make competent decisions in an open, competitive marketplace of ideas.
- Advertisers, PR practitioners, propagandists, and other special pleaders stimulate the economy and political discourse. They deserve legal protection in the marketplace unless they are shown to be causing specific harm—particularly to the most vulnerable consumers.
- Truth and social value will ultimately emerge if the marketplace is allowed to operate relatively free of government restrictions.

Or Type B:

- Advertisers, PR practitioners, and special pleaders dominate the marketplace of ideas, goods, and services. They have the money to set the agenda. They drive up prices, promote a lot of relatively worthless products, and force weaker advocates off the playing field.
- Consumers are by far the disadvantaged party in these transactions.
- Professional advocates are smarter but less moral than consumers; they know more about our needs, wants, and weaknesses than we know about ourselves, and they capitalize on those weaknesses.
- Government should protect us from manipulative persuasion to ensure social justice and a level playing field.

How you respond to these statements says a lot about your worldview, your model of humanity, and ultimately, your concept of ethics. All things considered, do you tend to think humans are rational or irrational? Are they autonomous agents or victims? Should persuaders have complete access to the marketplace of opinion, or should their actions be tightly controlled? Do you think persuaders are motivated by public interest and long-term social benefit, or by self-interest with little if any concern for consumers' economic or mental health or welfare?

The first set of assumptions is an overstatement of classical liberal theory, and the second is an overstated view of modern social responsibility theory. Some scholars might call the first argument the "professional entitlement" or "laissez-faire" ("government should not interfere") perspective, and the second the "professional responsibility" or "communitarian" perspective (Baker, 1999; Christians et al., 2008; Fitzpatrick & Gauthier, 2001; Fitzpatrick & Bronstein, 2006; Freeman, 2009; Wilkins & Christians, 2001). As discussed in Chapter 3 and elsewhere, these are complex theories that rarely, if ever, fully reflect the real world. On most issues we likely avoid extremes and come down somewhere in the middle.

Moral Confusion in Persuasion

Outsiders often misunderstand the fields of advertising and public relations (A/PR), and one suspects that A/PR practitioners themselves are somewhat unsettled about their significant role in society. Given widespread criticism by the public, special interest groups, governmental watchdogs, and scholars, it is little wonder A/PR practitioners struggle to explain the moral and pragmatic foundations of their enterprises.

Traditionally, there have been key distinctions between advertising and public relations, although the lines between the two have grown blurry in an era dominated by the new era of electronic media and "integrated marketing." Both fields engage in selective truth telling, and both appear to be as loyal to their clients as to their audiences. Whether "in your face" or "behind the scenes," the products of advertisers and public relations practitioners are readily criticized by lay critics and ethicists.

Some ethicists find it difficult to apply an objective moral theory to industries that rely upon selective truth telling and for which loyalties are narrow rather than general. The argument is supported by such influential deontologists as Immanuel Kant (trans. 1953), Sissela Bok (1979), Bernard Gert (1998), and others, who suggest that deception and narrow loyalties are inherent in professions founded to tell only one side of a story. By implication, they say, the act of persuading through the mass media victimizes vulnerable innocents, who are left with a diminished capacity to test for and base actions on truth. From this perspective, A/PR seems to be little more than a morally underdeveloped "use-and-be-used" enterprise, valuing individuals primarily as means to selfish ends rather than as ends in and of themselves. However, most practitioners do not manipulate or deceive their audiences merely by providing persuasive messaging.

Classical liberal markets are supposedly subject to certain self-correcting "natural laws" that come into play when there are deficiencies or inequities. One of the natural laws, as John Locke, Adam Smith, and others saw it, is that people are instinctively wired to trade, barter, and persuade (Maciejewski, 2003). Another is Smith's argument that self-interest does not run amok but leads to a sense of justice; it causes people to follow the rules, because each person knows that every other person is also self-interested (Maciejewski, 2003). Yet another is the claim that "the market, as a self-contained, self-repairing, complex mechanism, must be left alone (laissez-faire) to follow its natural course" (Rotzoll & Haefner, 1996, p. 26).

Alas, the theory does not always work. Some people, even rational ones, aren't competent at trading, bartering, or persuading. Advertisers can be more effective appealing to emotions than to intellects. Self-seeking individuals often cheat or otherwise manipulate the system to benefit themselves, and to heck with the rules. In short, the "invisible hand" that supposedly guides an open marketplace may not have the firm grip its exponents expected it to have.

If the classic liberal marketplace does not function precisely as promised, what is the alternative? As we said in Chapter 3, calls for social responsibility arose when the libertarian model proved to be problematic and not always realistic. Some critics began to see advertising not merely as a means to beneficial self-fulfillment, but as "reinforcing materialism, cynicism, irrationality, selfishness, anxiety, social competitiveness, power-lessness and/or loss of self-respect" (Polley, 1968, p. 18, cited by Rotzoll & Haefner, 1996, p. 185). Although guilt is not generalizable throughout the profession, in American advertising's case, the government and other agencies of accountability have stepped in, and court rulings have given commercial speech less protection than political, news, or artistic speech. The Food and Drug Administration, Federal Trade Commission, Securities and Exchange Commission, and dozens of other federal and state agencies serve as official watchdogs. Non-governmental watchdogs include the Better Business Bureau, National Advertising Review Board, AAAA, AAF, and myriad other trade and institutional groups. (Scores of other nations have hundreds of similar agencies and groups.) Codes of ethics—some more substantive than others—have been drafted by and/or imposed upon advertising practitioners. Most of these interventions into the business have occurred in the name of social responsibility; if the business won't regulate itself, the government may step in to protect its citizens.

Meanwhile, the multifaceted public relations industry has had its own growing pains. PR practitioners engage in a wide range of activities, such as conducting opinion research, press agentry, product promotion, publicity, lobbying, public affairs, fundraising, membership drives, and special event management. Traditionally, several of these activities are asymmetrical, or unbalanced in the clients' favor: PR "sells" the organizations' points of view or activities to carefully selected "target" audiences. The asymmetrical model has little expectation that the organizations and clients will change. When organizations using the asymmetrical model conduct public opinion and behavioral research, they use the data to improve the clients' persuasive appeals.

As an alternative to the asymmetrical model, scholars and practitioners such as James Grunig (1993) advocate two-way symmetrical communications as potentially more ethically sound. Under this model, PR uses research to negotiate and manage conflicts among organizations and strategic publics. The goal is not merely to persuade, but to assist the public and the organizations in being more responsive and responsible. This "counseling" model seeks win–win resolutions in the PR process. Of course, the model does not fit with the goals of many organizations and clients, especially those who enter the marketplace of ideas with goals of persuading various publics. It is of little value to those who think they need no research data to help them plan events or develop video news releases or launch a viral marketing campaign.

As Genevieve McBride (1989) has explained, in part the ethical challenges in public relations exist because PR practitioners have not decided whether they are heirs to the journalism/objectivity/informationalist ethic espoused for public information specialists/journalists in residence early in the twentieth century by Ivy Lee, or the persuasion/advocacy/cheerleader ethic espoused by Edward L. Bernays, whose book *The Engineering of Consent* (1955) argues that people should not know they are being manipulated. Most public relations texts, for example, when describing the moral goal of the practitioner, avoid the objectivity/advocacy dilemma by recommending some version of "corporate social responsibility" (Bivins, 1989, p. 49).

To resolve some of the confusion over A/PR's moral heritage, we suggest that the persuasion ethic is not only defensible, but laudable in a participatory democracy. The role of persuasion should not be confused with the client counseling role that many A/PR people undertake; each has its own special place in the media environment.

The Advocacy Model

Debates over A/PR ethics seldom include the baseline argument that persuasion is not only socially acceptable, but perhaps even socially necessary in a democratic, participatory society. Advertising and public relations practitioners play important roles in distributing important information—highly selective or not—which consumers can choose to accept or reject. Some place A/PR practitioners in roles somewhat similar to lawyers, lobbyists, and other special pleaders who provide selective information that the judiciary, legislatures, and courts of public opinion rely upon to make decisions.

The most persuasive description of the A/PR role revolves around recognizing that American public philosophy is founded on advocacy and adversarial relationships (Barney & Black, 1994). Whether intentionally or not, we seem to have decided over the past 200 years, and particularly since World War I, that social benefits emerge when people arrive at collective judgments about public issues through public debate. It is likely that more goods or truths are peddled through techniques of debate and advocacy than through calm, rational, objective discourse in the open marketplace of public opinion. This is not to say everything is debatable, that we polarize every issue and argue vehemently for our side and demonize the other sides (Washington, DC, in recent years notwithstanding). On the contrary, we should applaud calm, rational discourse when considering human progress. In the marketplace of ideas, however, there is ample evidence that advocacy prevails: Imagine salespeople, for example, who extol the virtues of competing products as more desirable than the products off which they make their living. A "search for truth" between the salesperson and the customer is subverted to the sales mandate—the language of commerce. Likewise, it is a rare marriage proposal in which a supplicant lists self-deficiencies in anything more than a sympathetic way.

The advocacy system "encourages the adversaries to find and present their most persuasive evidence" (Landsman, 1984, p. 4). Lawyers are advocates for their clients— with an overriding obligation to the interests of that client in an adversary society. Therefore an advocate arguing a reverse position (prosecutor, defense attorney, etc.) must identify and disclose the weaknesses in the opposition's case. Each participant in the process has a specific assignment.

The task of participants in an adversarial climate is not easy. It creates serious stresses between the advocate and society, because an advocate must relegate society's immediate interest to a secondary position behind that of the client. Just as a lawyer serving a client has conflicting duties imposed by society and profession, so does an A/PR practitioner confront conflict between society and client. As Chapter 5 discussed, choosing one's personal and professional loyalties is sometimes complicated. Nevertheless, making good choices about loyalty is essential to become an ethical advocate or persuader.

Public relations practitioners, in the role of advocates, accept roughly the same obligations to their clients as lawyers. The analogy is not original. Public relations pioneers Edward Bernays and Ivy Lee, nearly a century ago, both claimed that public relations practitioners should serve as lawyers in the court of public opinion (Bernays, 1923, 1928; Hiebert, 1966). Lawyers are adversaries/advocates in the formalized courts of law, and public relations people argue their cases as advocates/adversaries in the informal courts of public opinion. They can do this at a high level of moral development, as they endeavor to keep a participatory democracy viable. They should not have to apologize for playing this role in society—until or unless they violate their role-related moral expectations, at which point they would not be principled advocates (Baker, 2008, 2009; Fitzpatrick & Bronstein, 2006).

Selective Truth: A Moral Stickler

Media ethicist Tom Bivins, when describing the future of public relations and advertising ethics, insisted that truth telling is the centerpiece of the moral equation—the default position for all serious media:

> What will carry the most precious parts of the mass media ideal of the last millennium into the new millennium? What will protect us as increasing sophistication of message delivery vehicles breeds an increasing sophistication in the techniques of deceptive persuasion? It if will be anything, it will have to be *truth*—in all its manifestations.
>
> (Bivins, 2008, p. 233)

Under the adversary system, selective telling of truth is generally acceptable behavior. At the same time, it intuitively raises serious ethics questions relating to fairness, equity, and justice. This is particularly pressing when no adversary is guaranteed in the arena of public opinion, as it is in a court of law. An adversarial society assumes that spokespeople with alternative views will emerge to balance the advocate. If that doesn't work, some will argue that the journalist, the independent blogger, or some other consumer advocate, motivated by an objectivity and stewardship ethic, will assure some balance in the public messages.

The "PR-practitioners-are-like-lawyers" comparison ultimately fails, however. "Discovery" rules require lawyers to provide evidence to their opponents; no such rule exists in public relations. The reality is that the court of public opinion has no guarantee that adversaries will square off and exchange comprehensive truths or that an impartial judge will oversee the process. Just as a lawyer has no obligation to be considerate of the weaknesses of his courtroom opponents, so the public relations person can clearly claim it is another's obligation to provide countering messages. The egoistic public relations professional will likely cherish the situation in which opposition remains silent; the more socially conscious one will welcome fair competition.

Some would create ethical and even legal obligations of balanced presentation for both journalists and the persuasive communications professionals. When they do so, they intuitively condemn the persuasive arts as unethical on their face. Yet, under the First Amendment, moral suasion is the only tool available to those who cry out for balance. As the late Mr. Justice Potter Stewart of the United States Supreme Court noted, the First Amendment only makes possible free discussion; it does not guarantee the discussion. Put another way, the First Amendment only makes it possible for the adversary to emerge in a given case; it doesn't necessarily guarantee an open marketplace of price-controlled information and persuasion.

Such a position calls on relevant parties to provide their own advocates to balance the message. It would also suggest that consumers must exercise due diligence when sifting through persuasive messages, to do their own "discovery" in gathering and evaluating of information, and even to become active adversaries to counter unopposed views. In short, an advocacy culture assumes both *caveat emptor* and *caveat venditor*—let the buyer as well as the seller beware (Wakefield & Barney, 2001).

Clearly there must be moral limits. Under an injunction that one has a moral obligation to society that sometimes transcends obligation to one's client, it is reasonable to suggest that A/PR practitioners will avoid doing harm by omitting critical truths or fabricating truth claims. It is a tough balancing act to employ selective truth telling that incorporates critically important truths, while avoiding truths or un-truths that could harm vulnerable populations. It demands moral maturity and competence.

In short, we should expect our persuaders to be truthful and to avoid unnecessary harm, particularly to vulnerable populations.

Transparency, Accountability, Social Response-ability, and Loyalty: More Moral Sticklers

To enfranchise the public fully and ensure that the marketplace of persuasion pitches its tents on a level playing field, communicators must treat people with respect. As Kant would argue, each person ought to be regarded as an end in and of himself or herself, rather than merely as a means to somebody else's ends. Kant's admonition applies to vulnerable as well as fully alert audiences, to clients and sponsors, and to fellow professionals.

To encourage respect for one another, the marketplace should provide a way for all stakeholders to be held accountable for their communications. This is a premise of Chapter 13. If a persuader unjustly manipulates the public, all those affected should have the motivation and capacity to respond—hence our term "social response-ability." The system needs to be transparent to enfranchise all participants in the communications chain.

Media ethicist Patrick Plaisance reminded us that transparency refers to much more than merely letting people see what the persuader's real message is; it refers also to the openness of the process by which messages are made, and the motivations of the messenger. Paraphrasing Kant, Plaisance concluded that "Transparency, or truthful forthrightness . . . defines what it means to live an ethical life" (2007, p. 204; and 2009, p. 59). A commitment to transparency respects the rationality, worth, and dignity of all parties. Systemic transparency should curtail dogmatic and authoritarian power plays, and should advance a participatory democracy by holding persuasion and advocacy in check.

In the world of A/PR, transparency and accountability are in dynamic tension with practitioners' independence and loyalty to their clients. When they think in these terms, advocates are pushed to think beyond their "particular" loyalties and expand their sense of "general" loyalties.

This process is particularly problematic in the Internet era, "the PR and advertising vehicle of choice in the future" (Bivins, 2008, p. 235). On the net, persuaders can readily hide their real identities and agendas; terms that describe such actions include "astroturf," (fake grassroots organizations), "flogging" (fake blogging), "false flagging" (a term derived from the military in which you pretend to represent another entity), and "sock puppetry" (pretending to be a different person online, often for promotional purposes).

Transparency is not a simple solution to media credibility problems. While helping revise the SPJ code in 1996, one of this book's authors suggested that asking journalists to hold themselves accountable (the fourth general principle in the code) by letting the public in on some of the secrets about how news is manufactured probably would have short-term negative consequences. After all, if skeptical audiences see more media airing their dirty laundry, running corrections columns, and opening themselves up to public criticism, wouldn't this confirm their prejudices that the media are badly flawed institutions? The SPJ ethics committee countered, optimistically, that it might cause a drop in credibility in the short run but in the long run would improve public under-standing and trust. (Nobody seemed to be able to define "the long run.") Some news organizations meet this standard through ombudsmen, who are given free rein to critically assess the quality of the work done by the news organization that hired them. They publish their work for audiences to see.

It could be argued that ethical journalism is transparent by definition, since its messages (almost always) define sources and provide balance. Can the same be said about ethical advocacy? Can advocates be ethical without identifying their sources, their paymasters, or providing balance? Bivins tried to answer these questions:

> One of the primary differences between journalism and the "consulting professions" of advertising and public relations is that we expect the latter two to be biased in their point of view. As consumers of information, we go into the melee knowing this. However, this does not absolve either public relations or advertising professionals of the obligation to treat us with respect by honoring our autonomy as decision makers.
>
> (p. 234)

In short, persuaders ought to be transparent and accountable, and they have a moral obligation to consider who deserves their loyalty.

ON PROPAGANDA

> Why, then, is "propagandist" an epithet in our society? Almost any other name sounds sweeter to most people. If a man is not called an educator, he seems to prefer to be known as a publicity agent, a public relations counsel or officer, an advertising agent or account executive, a salesman, a promoter, a barker, a preacher, a lecturer, or even a politician.
> —L.W. Doob (1948, p. 231)

[W]e need more propaganda, not less. We need more attempts to influence our opinions and to arouse our participation in the democratic process . . . We need more propaganda about issues of universal concern to all human beings . . . We need more propaganda to counter the hate-inspired propaganda of certain factions attempting to undermine peaceful co-existence between peoples.

—P.M. Taylor (2003, p. 320)

Why Worry About Propaganda?

There is no end to debates over propaganda. What is it? Who does it? How does it affect us? Is it necessarily evil? Could it possibly be ethical?

This discussion begins with the premises that propaganda:

- has been hard to discuss because it's been hard to define. How we define propaganda most assuredly determines whether we perceive the enterprise to be ethical or unethical. It is not just a semantic game, although we must pay more than a little attention to the semantics of propaganda analysis.
- is inevitable in today's media mix. It is not a question of "if" our society and its institutions engage in propaganda; it is rather a question of "how." It is not just what the "bad guys" do; modern media systems are perfectly honed to be agents of propaganda, with modern media audiences its willing recipients.
- has become problematic in part because the lines have blurred among the information, persuasion, and entertainment functions of media. The fragmentation of the mass audience implies that we seek out and absorb propaganda that reinforces our individual prejudices. Propagandistic media cater to closed-mindedness, to willing and uncritical recipients. The ethical implications are striking, for people who would be successful propagandists, for people who would avoid being propagandists, for people who are targets of propaganda, and for students of propaganda.
- can lead to serious repercussions for public opinion, community building, and self-governance if we are not careful and sophisticated consumers and producers of media fare.

Early History of Propaganda

"Propaganda" originates from the Latin *propagare*, meaning the gardener's practice of pinning the fresh shoots of a plant into the earth in order to reproduce new plants that will later take on a life of their own. An implication of the term, when it was first used in the sociological sense by the Roman Catholic Church, was that the spread of ideas brought about in this way is not one that would take place of itself, but rather through a cultivated or artificial generation. In 1622, the Vatican established the *Congregatio de Propaganda Fide*, or "The Congregation of Propaganda," or "The Propaganda," a committee of cardinals that had, and still has, charge of the church's foreign missions. Naturally, this effort to reach non-Christians was regarded as a good thing.

The word's negative connotations appeared in the nineteenth century. One definition of propaganda, published in the 1842 *Dictionary of Science, Literature and Art*, called it something "applied to modern political language as a term of reproach to secret associations for the spread of opinions and principles which are viewed by most governments with horror and aversion" (Wreford, cited by Qualter, 1962, p. 4).

During the early 1900s, Americans were concerned that Axis powers were using propaganda and psychological warfare deviously. Propaganda played important military and political roles in both world wars. We feared that propaganda and brainwashing went hand in hand and therefore had no part to play in a democratic society, unless that society was fighting a war for survival. Thus the word "propaganda" came to be known for the Machiavellian manipulation of opinion toward political, religious, or military ends.

Not surprisingly, propaganda analysts during World War II took a great deal of trouble to define and categorize the ways propagandists manipulated public opinion. The American Institute for Propaganda Analysis at Harvard set out to defend America from propaganda. It gave us guidelines to use in determining whether a message aimed at us was propaganda (Institute for Propaganda Analysis, 1937; Lee, 1952).

Some Definitions of Propaganda

An interesting array of terms has been used over the years to describe propaganda: organized persuasion, manipulation, lies, deceit, mind control, brainwashing, spin, news management, info-mercials, info-ganda, fake news, truthiness, public relations, and advertising. (Yes, even advertising and public relations have fallen under the propaganda umbrella.) Some scholars take a relatively objective stance and others an extremely judgmental stance when appraising propaganda:

- "The art of influencing, manipulating, controlling, promoting, changing, inducing, or securing the acceptance of opinions, attitudes, action, or behavior" (Martin, 1958).
- "Any word or deed, short of the use of physical force, designed to make others think or act the way the initiator wants them to think or act" (Joyce, 1963).
- "The deliberate and systematic attempt to shape perceptions, manipulate cognitions, and direct behavior to achieve a response that furthers the desired intent of the propagandist" (Jowett & O'Donnell, 2006).

Some see propaganda as Machiavellian manipulation of symbols by powerful and deceitful and unethical political groups. Others see propaganda as inevitable in any technologically driven culture. Some see propaganda as inherently evil and immoral. Others see it as morally neutral. We often use the term rather loosely to cast aspersions on ideas put out by anyone whose motives we suspect. (We have the US Information Agency; our ideological "enemies" have propaganda agencies.)

The fear of propaganda has lessened in the past decades, as social scientists have realized that communication in and of itself doesn't have the absolute mind-molding power once attributed to it. But the word has taken on broader meanings, as it has come to be associated with most arenas of social and economic and political life, and not just military life or psychological warfare.

Propaganda and Modern Society

Jacques Ellul, whose book *Propaganda: The Formation of Men's Attitudes* was translated into English in 1965, did much to revise the world's thinking about what propaganda is and how it works. He defined it not necessarily as something a political party or religion or someone purposively creates to manipulate the helpless masses, but as something inevitable in a democratic or technological society. He called it a sociological phenomenon, built into and carried out through the mass media.

When Ellul said propaganda is inevitable in a democratic society, he meant that propaganda makes society work. It is seen in nearly all of the institutions that have helped to create the social environment, the economic system, the political theories, and regional and national values systems.

Ellul described two broad categories of propaganda: agitation propaganda and integration propaganda; or put another way, "political" propaganda and "sociological" propaganda.

The first—agitation/political—is typified by revolutionary movements, efforts to make massive shifts in public opinion, frequently accompanied by force and control over the channels of communication so those channels speak as one authoritarian voice.

The second—integration/sociological—is more typical of post-revolutionary societies that are making various efforts to stabilize public opinion through various instruments of mass communication. Through integration propaganda modern society "holds itself together," as it creates and maintains public opinion.

When Ellul says propaganda is everywhere, he's describing the phenomenon of integration or sociological propaganda. To Ellul and other recent scholars, modern people need propaganda to live in a technological society. People need to be "integrated into society" by means of the mass media; they seek and then suffer from information overload; they need media to help make sense out of this confusing world; the news and the advertising and the public relations messages become forms of propaganda. J. Fred MacDonald wrote in Smith's book, *Propaganda: A Pluralistic Perspective*:

> Mass man is educated and controlled through propaganda. His civic values are filtered through school boards, party committees, state legislatures, courts of law, and other forums intending to preserve orthodoxy. The communications media

through which daily he is informed—whether via formal news broadcasts or through the many formats of popular entertainment—frame the world to complement the historic national understanding that he has learned. Little he usually hears, sees, or reads, has not been prepared by experts committed to the system and familiar with its language.

(MacDonald, 1989, p. 30)

MacDonald calls public relations a "modern fine art" that is key in the political process. So is advertising, in which candidates are hawked in ads in the same way (and by the same people) who peddle fried chicken or perfume. In short, Ellul and MacDonald argue that we need propaganda to survive in a technological and informational society. Surprisingly, Ellul argues that the people most vulnerable to propaganda are intellectuals—people with the greatest need to know, to have opinions, to be able to influence others—the very people too busy to experience life firsthand and therefore those most reliant upon mediated information. Given Ellul's argument, it would appear that our hunger for truth, half-truth, limited truth, and truth out of context gives rise to propaganda machines (a.k.a. mass media) that fulfill our appetites to know, to be informed, to be entertained, to be persuaded, and often to reinforce our beliefs.

> In an open society, such as the United States, the hidden and integrated nature of the propaganda best convinces people that they are not being manipulated.
>
> —Nancy Snow (2003, p. 22)

If we agree with Ellul, we recognize that one of the greatest problems of modern propaganda is that it panders to closed minds.

Propaganda and Modern Media

In a democratic society, consumer-citizens need to be open-minded as they encounter the marketplace of ideas: curious, questioning, unwilling to accept simple answers to complex situations. "Mental freedom" comes when people weigh numerous sides of controversies and reach their own decisions, free of outside constraints.

Milton Rokeach, in *The Open and Closed Mind* (1960), concluded that the degree to which a person's belief system is open or closed is the extent to which the person can receive, evaluate, and act on relevant information received from the outside on its own intrinsic merits, unencumbered by irrelevant internal and external factors. Open-minded people seek out mass media that challenge them to think for themselves, rather than media that offer easy answers to complex problems. Open-minded media consumers seek "free" (i.e., independent and pluralistic) media because they themselves want to remain free.

There is one constant in contemporary mass media criticism: The mass media in general, and television and advertising and public relations more specifically, tend to inculcate a close-mindedness in audiences. Media, by their commercial nature, can weaken people's sense of discernment, heighten stereotypical thinking patterns, and create tendencies toward conformity and dependency.

Media propaganda in general, and the efforts of articulate advocates in particular, furnish an explanation for all happenings—a key to understanding the whys and wherefores of social, economic, and political events. The great force of propaganda lies in giving people all-embracing, simple explanations and massive, doctrinal causes, without which they could not live with the news, Ellul argued. He added that we are doubly reassured by propaganda because it tells us the reasons behind developments and it promises solutions for seemingly intractable problems.

It is easier to go through life closed-minded than open-minded, according to social psychologists. It is difficult to hold two contradictory ideas at the same time; cognitive dissonance theories say when we receive a message that doesn't match our preconceived notions, then we must take action (accepting the message, rejecting it, or finding a middle ground) to regain "harmony" in our thought lives. Propaganda—especially propaganda that matches a person's already-held beliefs, which is readily available given society's wide range of media choices—meets media audiences' needs for predigested (closed-minded) presentations.

Propaganda and the News

News organizations are not simply the gatekeepers who reject, accept, or filter the messages they receive from the "usual suspects" of advertisers, PR practitioners, and politicians. Whether they know it or not, news organizations can create propaganda of their own.

Propagandists and propaganda analysts have known for many years that the most effective means of manipulating public opinion through the news media is not through advertisements and editorials, but, in Nazi propaganda minister Joseph Goebbels's terms, in slanted news that appears to be straight. Qualter (1962) argued that, with the growing recognition of the extent to which opinion governs the selection and manner of presentation of news, any division between editorial opinion and straightforward presentation of facts on the news pages is an artificial division.

Thus, students hoping to better understand contemporary media propaganda need tools to discern the mindsets and techniques used by propagandists. This is easier said than done, however, because many forms of propaganda do not actually reflect the conscientious efforts of the special pleader. Even journalists who fancy themselves as objective—or at least fair—can fall into propagandistic patterns:

> The temptation is great, under the pressures of daily journalism, to leap to conclusions, to act as an advocate, to make assumptions based on previous experience,

to approach a story with preconceived notions of what is likely to happen. To give way to such tendencies is to invite error, slanted copy, and libelous publications for which there is little or no defense. An open mind is the mark of the journalist; the propagandist has made up his mind in advance.

(Hohenberg, 1969, p. 330)

John Merrill said journalists act as propagandists when they spread their own prejudices, biases, and opinions—whenever they attempt to affect the attitudes of their audiences. They, and others, are manipulative when they use stereotypes to simplify reality or present opinion disguised as fact. The process of information selection becomes a propaganda technique when a pattern of news selection of a viewpoint is exercised with some consistency (Merrill & Lowenstein, 1971, pp. 188–201).

Several analysts have commented that public relations press releases are highly propagandistic elements of news media: persuasion or advocacy disguised as news. Nelson and Hulteng, for example, noted that public relations can be delayed propaganda if audiences do not recognize that many of the stories they consume originated from "interested sources." Hence the reason media professional codes of ethics insist that journalists indicate what information has been provided through news releases.

"Not that the PR man minds," they wrote. "He knows that the credibility of the information about his client is enhanced if the reader believes that a working journalist rather than a propagandist originated the story and wrote it. It is better to have a friend tell others how good you are than for you to do it yourself" (Nelson & Hulteng, 1971, p. 278). Indeed, implied third-party credibility is a goal of public relations.

While not all propaganda techniques apply to the news pages of the mass media, most have been used by the media and by public relations practitioners and advertisers. Robert Cirino (1971) concluded that bias and propaganda are inevitable because of the great volume of news, how it must be processed, and the public's need to make some kind of order out of the chaos of news events.

Propaganda Redefined

Many authors distinguish between propaganda and education, or between propaganda and any other means of inculcating values and changing beliefs and attitudes. Some authors distinguish between pernicious propaganda and honest persuasion. This seems speculative in that often the only distinction between pernicious propaganda and honest persuasion is whether "they're" doing it or "we're" doing it.

Students of ethics should be struck by certain commonalties among most of the traditional and some of the contemporary definitions:

- A presumption of manipulation and control, if not outright coercion, that dehumanizes the audiences or intended "victims" of propaganda.

- A power imbalance—rhetorical, political, economic, etc.—between propagandists and propagandees.
- A presumption that principles of science, rhetoric, semantics, and enlightened or open-minded education serve as powerful antidotes to propaganda.
- More subtle, but perhaps as intriguing, are recent suggestions that propaganda is systemic in a democratic, technological, post-industrial information society and that instruments of mass media (advertising and public relations, entertainment outlets, and news journalism) are every bit as propagandistic as are totalitarian dictatorships.

The central thesis of this chapter deserves repeating: In a politically competitive democracy and a commercially competitive free enterprise system, mass communication functions as an arena where advocates can battle. Propaganda therefore becomes part of that open marketplace of ideas; it is not only inevitable, but it is probably desirable that there are openly recognizable and competing propagandas in a democratic society. People who define propaganda as inherently evil or unethical appear to be coming from the "society-as-victim" school. The authors of this book tend generally to hold to the "society-as-rational-beings" perspective. Well, maybe not completely rational, but capable of rationality, and certainly not always victims.

Therefore, let us redefine the enterprise:

While the people or groups who create propaganda may or may not have demonstrably closed minds, propaganda contains characteristics associated with dogmatism or closed-mindedness. While the messages may or may not be intended as propaganda, this type of communication seems non-creative, with the goal of short-circuiting critical thinking on the part of audiences. While creative communication accepts pluralism and assumes that receivers should investigate the message's claims, propaganda does not. Rather, propaganda:

1. includes heavy or undue reliance on authority figures and spokespersons, rather than empirical validation, to establish its truths or conclusions
2. uses unverified and perhaps unverifiable abstract nouns, adjectives, adverbs, and physical representations, rather than empirical validation, to establish its truths, conclusions, or impressions
3. offers a finalistic or fixed view of people, institutions, and situations, divided into broad, all-inclusive categories of in-groups (friends) and out-groups (enemies), situations to be accepted or rejected in whole
4. reduces situations into readily identifiable cause-and-effect relationships, ignoring multiple reasons for events
5. creates its own sense of time by focusing too much or too little on the past, present, or future as disconnected periods, instead of a demonstrated consciousness of time flow.
6. places more emphasis on conflict than on cooperation.

This description lets both practitioners and observers of media and persuasion investigate their own and their media's behavior. It applies to the news as well as to entertainment and persuasion functions in the media. Audiences willing to accept distorted pictures of reality, simple explanations for complex issues, and other propagandistic perspectives provided by mass communicators will find no shortage of these propaganda elements in their media.

It is possible to be an advocate, or a journalist, without being unduly propagandistic. Democracy requires this skill set.

But democracy also needs pluralism in its persuasion and information, and not the narrow-minded, self-serving propaganda some communicators inject—wittingly or unwittingly—into their messages. Open-mindedness and mass communications efforts need not be mutually exclusive.

Propaganda: Some Conclusions

We are not suggesting that propaganda results every time anyone merchandises ideas, goods, and services. Far from it. But we suggest that message creators engage in propaganda when they repeatedly jump to dogmatic conclusions, rely unduly on authority, base assumptions on faulty premises, and otherwise engage in inappropriate semantic behavior. They may be doing it unconsciously. It may just be that their view of the world, their belief systems, their personal and institutional loyalties, and their semantic behaviors are propagandistic.

But that's no excuse.

Some ethicists say we should never attribute to malice what can be explained by ignorance. That certainly applies to propaganda, which too many observers call an inherently immoral enterprise that corrupts all who go near it. If we consider propaganda in less value-laden terms, we may recognize ways all participants in the communications exchange can proceed intelligently through the swamp, and we can make informed judgments about the ethics of particular aspects of our communications rather than indicting the entire enterprise.

In a politically competitive democracy and a commercially competitive free enterprise system, mass communication provides the competitive arena where advocates of all sides can do battle. What many call "propaganda" therefore becomes part of that open marketplace of ideas; it is not only inevitable, but may be desirable that there are *openly recognizable and competing propagandas* in a democratic society that challenge all of us— producers and consumers—to sift and sort through them wisely.

SOME TENTATIVE CONCLUSIONS ABOUT PERSUASION

Chapter 2 showed that the "seek truth and report it" requirement for ethical journalism is in moral tension with the need to "minimize harm." We also showed how "be independent" juxtaposes with "be accountable." We can draw somewhat similar models for moral decision making in the worlds of advertising, public relations, and other arenas of persuasion.

Recognizing the particular moral roles of advocates and persuaders, we can conclude that they are obligated to communicate truth, to minimize harm, to be loyal, and to be accountable. As was the case with journalists, the truth-telling mandate (even if it entails *selective* truth telling) is in dynamic tension with the need to minimize harm to vulnerable populations. Also, the need to act out of particular as well as general loyalties is in dynamic tension with the need to be accountable and transparent.

Truth claims made by advocates are admittedly selective, but they should not cause unnecessary harm. Persuaders' loyalty is initially to their clients, with the expectation that the clients are interested in the welfare of audiences and consumers. When messengers recognize that their clients may cause undue harm to vulnerable populations, the professional persuaders' loyalties should shift to the public. The entire process should be relatively transparent, but not to the point that transparency needlessly stifles business. Paid advocates should not disclose their clients' trade secrets, but they ought to acknowledge that they are accountable to the public, professional peers, and regulatory agencies for their messages. As Chapter 13 discusses, also in play is the question of "How's it going to look?" if the information becomes public.

The principles are not absolute, but they should serve as moral weigh stations en route to making good choices. They often collide with one another. Resolving the conflicts requires some use of moral philosophy.

The models in Figure 9.1 encourage persuaders to avoid the either/or polarization of ethical decision making. Instead, they present four guiding principles on a set of horizontal and vertical axes.

"Bad" persuasion occurs when practitioners do an inadequate job of truth telling and when vulnerable populations are put at risk for no justifiable reason. Telling lies and hurting people is morally unjustifiable, even in an open marketplace of ideas. ("Low truth telling/low effort to minimize harm"—the lower-left quadrant on the horizontal and vertical axes.)

Somewhat "better" persuasion might occur when some harm occurs as a result of communicating very important truths ("High truth telling/Low effort to minimize harm"—the lower-right quadrant). People may feel harmed if they are taken out of their comfort zones when forced to confront persuasive messages that run counter to their basic beliefs, even if those messages are for a good cause. Warning us about climate change may cause discomfort about our carbon footprints; anti-smoking commercials may create dissonance if we use tobacco; showing us photos of oil spills and earthquake victims may stir our repressed generosity. Beyond bringing on discomfort, some truthful persuasion may cause us to make major life-changing choices—actual pain.

Likewise, it is somewhat defensible to use messages that are not totally true if they cause no harm ("Low truth telling/High effort to minimize harm"—the upper-left quadrant).

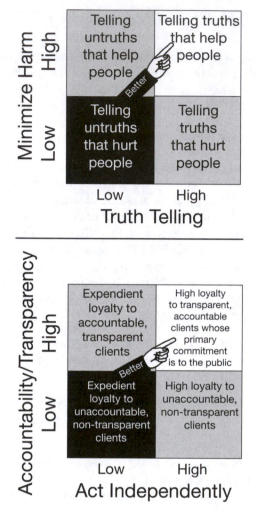

FIGURE 9.1 | A model for moral persuasion

Little harm comes from creative commercials that portray the physically impossible. In the real world, ducks and geckos don't sell insurance, horses don't play football, cars don't fly, and sprinters don't outrun rockets.

Ethical and excellent persuasion maximizes the amount of truth and makes the greatest effort to minimize harm ("High truth/High effort to minimize harm"—the upper-right quadrant). Important truths are told, and no one is harmed.

At the same time ethical persuaders strive to communicate truths and minimize harm, they also must balance the moral tension of how to be loyal and how to be accountable. The second chart describes this.

"Bad" persuasion occurs when the persuader remains tentatively and expediently loyal to a client who refuses to be transparent or accountable for the persuasive campaign ("Low loyalty/Low accountability"—the lower-left quadrant). Loyalty is misplaced if the persuader remains loyal to clients whose self-interest overrides any sense of social responsibility and continues to persuade just because the job pays well. This dubious loyalty is compounded by unwillingness to be transparent or accountable. For example, a PR person should exit any relationship with a client whose business is based exclusively on the profit motive and who refuses to respond to calls for openness.

Somewhat slightly "better" persuasion would exist when A/PR people have an intense but narrow loyalty to clients or businesses that refuse to be held accountable ("Low accountability/High loyalty"—the lower-right quadrant). This might occur when A/PR people work for self-interested clients who are so certain of their ideas or products that they see little need for openness or feedback; the campaigns would be arrogantly asymmetrical.

Likewise, it is only marginally justifiable for A/PR practitioners to have expedient loyalty for clients or businesses that try to be transparent and accountable ("High accountability/Low loyalty"—the upper-left quadrant). The problem is that the persuaders have more loyalty to the client/business than to the public or any other stakeholders—a mindset that does not bode well for the persuaders' future work products. The effort may be transparent, but the persuader is not really committed to the greater good.

The ideal, of course, is to loyally serve clients or businesses that are genuinely transparent, accountable, and committed to serving the public interest ("High accountability/High loyalty"—the upper-right quadrant). In these cases the persuaders are displaying dual loyalties: to the clients and all other stakeholders. All parties hold one another accountable for the greater good.

As with most models, these depictions of ethical persuasion have some limitations. Sometimes truth telling and loyalty are in tension, and other times minimizing harm and transparency are tested. A more-comprehensive model would probably be an eight-by-eight, three-dimensional depiction of the dynamic tensions in this complicated media ethics environment. In this model, as suggested above, the principled persuader would display a high degree of truth telling, a constant goal of minimizing harm, a realistic sense of when to shift loyalty from client to public, and a strong commitment to transparency and accountability.

SUMMARY AND CONCLUSIONS

"What's it worth?" This is the fourth chapter to address the question of worth. Again we ask and attempt to answer a question about what society values, and how our media create or reflect those values. We have maintained that society finds a great number of things to be valuable, including truth telling and respect for privacy. In most cases, these and other values must be balanced against one another. History and current events tell us that society also values persuasion—a system providing individuals and institutions a forum that permits them to influence one another.

The introduction to this chapter outlines two perspectives on persuasion. Regardless of where we put the needle on the continuum, we have every right to ask our persuaders to abide by fundamental principles of morality. Whether they operate in an unregulated market or one that is tightly controlled, they should take care when they make "truth claims" or use their power in ways that could harm weaker parties. For idealistic as well as crassly pragmatic reasons, they should opt for truth over falsehood, care over harm, and compassion over indifference. Whether from self-interest or the highest level of moral development, they ought to use their talents and treasures to build up, rather than destroy, institutions that are of value in a community or culture.

One ethicist has concluded that professional persuaders need "elbow room to work their persuasive magic in the competitive environment fostered by a free enterprise, entrepreneurial society" (Barney, 2001, p. 73). Thoughtful media critics are almost universally concerned about audiences who are targets of persuaders/advocates/propagandists, and they encourage persuaders to act morally. However, these critics generally fall into two camps: One advocates morality because vulnerable audiences need to be protected, and the other advocates morality that "enlists audiences as morally culpable participants in the process, who should develop the analytical skills that would help them contend with the myriad of conflicting messages they encounter" (Barney, 2001, p. 77). Our challenge as consumers of media messages and students of media ethics is to understand the morality of persuasion, regardless of the theoretical perspective we prefer.

Fundamentally, this textbook reflects the rational/autonomous model of humanity. If we didn't believe students and other consumers are capable of rational thought, and if we didn't believe media practitioners can trust audiences to be rational, why would we write this kind of book?

■ ■ ■

CHAPTER VOCABULARY

Note: Definitions are available at this book's companion website.

- advertorials
- asymmetrical model of public relations
- *caveat emptor*
- *caveat venditor*
- implied third-party credibility
- political propaganda

- propaganda
- social response-ability
- sociological propaganda
- transparency
- two-way symmetrical communications
- video news releases (VNRs)

PRACTICAL APPLICATIONS

1. School persuasion: Assuming that you went through a college-sponsored tour and/or orientation, think about the persuasive techniques that university officials used on you. Think about what was said—and left unsaid—about the positive things of your school. Think about the people who were chosen to lead the tours. Think about the places you visited on the tour, and places where you were not taken.

    Answer these questions:

    *   How persuasive was the tour/orientation?

    *   How close did the tour/orientation reflect what you've found to be the reality at your school?

    *   How might you change the tour if you were in charge?

    *   Did the tour/orientation focus more on the students or the parents?

    *   If you happen to be a student who leads the tours, how much latitude do you have to veer from the script?

    *   Is your campus's diversity accurately reflected in the literature given to new and prospective students?

    *   If you took several tours at different schools, how did they compare in their persuasive efforts?

2. Do an informal content analysis of several newscasts and your local newspaper, and try to determine the percentage of stories that resulted from public relations efforts—video news releases, press releases, or events that were pre-planned by individuals or organizations other than the news media. Do the media explicitly indicate when the stories include information from these sources?

3. Do a critical analysis of various campaigns, including editorial campaigns, according to the discussion of "Propaganda Redefined" in this chapter.

4. Use "A Model for Moral Persuasion" in Figure 9.1 to analyze the two Freedonia case studies we first encountered in Chapter 1: the blogger and the PR practitioner. What resolutions would produce the most morally defensible examples of advocacy, and which the least defensible? Explain.

■ ■ ■

CASE 9.1 **Journalism: Taking Sides During Battle**

War has come to your nation of Freedonia—or, at least a skirmish with the neighboring nation of Sylvania in the remote mountainous region that is the border between the two nations. Fighting began yesterday morning, yet it's still unclear which side started it, whether it's continuing this morning, and precisely in whose territory it happened. At least a dozen Freedonia troops have died in action, as well as 30 from Sylvania. Both sides are rushing soldiers and weapons to the region.

Your locally owned television station, where you are news manager, carried live coverage of the Freedonia president's speech last night. The president called for fellow Freedonians to be filled with prayer and patriotism in the coming days, but he offered few specifics beyond accusing Sylvania of "naked aggression" against freedom-loving, peace-loving Freedonia.

Your station also had later coverage of the Sylvania president's speech, in which he also told his people to be filled with prayer and patriotism, but he offered few specifics beyond accusing Freedonia of "naked aggression" against freedom-loving, peace-loving Sylvania.

It's morning, and you attend the daily morning meeting of managers at your TV station. The events of the past day dominate talk of the meeting. The station manager suggests the station should take up the president's plea and show its Freedonian patriotism. He says the station should:

- put the national colors in the bottom of the screen at all times

- change the station's logo from its current colors to the Freedonia national colors

- create a visual "signature" for all news about the conflict, with a logo that includes a map of the two nations and the Freedonia flag waving

- create an overarching label for all news about the conflict: "Freedonia's Freedom Fight"

- make sure news anchors wear lapel pins of the Freedonia flag.

"The president says we should show our patriotism, so we should take him at his word," the manager says. "Besides, I'm getting lots of calls from viewers and politicians asking us what we're going to do. And it probably wouldn't hurt our ratings to be seen as patriotic, either."

As news manager, you are responsible for nearly six hours of news coverage daily. Your news ranks tops among Freedonia viewers, and you have few viewers in Sylvania. The station has long had a four-person staff in Sylvania to cover that nation's news.

➤ **As you sit in the meeting, you wonder to yourself: "Can I be patriotic and still do objective news? What do I say to the boss?"**

Questions

- **What's your problem?**
- **Why not follow the rules?**
- **Who wins, who loses?**
- **What's it worth?**
- What else do you need to know?

Thinking it Through

1. Is this an ethical issue? Why or why not?
2. Do you agree with the station manager's patriotism plans?
   - A. If you agree:
     - a. How do you justify your decision?
     - b. Would you change your mind if your station had a bigger audience in Sylvania?
     - c. What if it turns out that Freedonia was the aggressor?
     - d. How much do ratings affect your decision?
     - e. What would you do if a news anchor won't wear the flag pin, saying she "won't participate in jingoism?"
     - f. What would you do if one of your reporters uncovers evidence that Freedonia's military committed war crimes, killing and raping people in a Sylvania village along the border?
     - g. What if your station's four news staffers in Sylvania were arrested by Sylvanian officials for being spies, and Sylvania's government says your station's obvious support of Freedonia is proof of the spying?
   - B. If you disagree:
     - a. How do you justify your decision?
     - b. Would you change your mind if ratings began to fall?
     - c. Would you change your mind if it is learned that Sylvania actually did the invading?
     - d. Respond to this argument: Since it's your nation's freedom that gives you the right to broadcast, why don't you support your nation?
     - e. Respond to this argument: Why aren't you supporting the troops?
3. Is there another choice you could make? If so, how do you defend that choice?
4. What if this were an election year, and opposing parties accuse the president of whipping up war frenzy in order to stay in office?
5. Let's say you've got two key news competitors and they do the exact opposite of what you do. What do you do then? How do you defend your actions?
6. Regardless of your decision, what might it take to change your mind?
7. What if the Freedonia military instituted wartime censorship rules that required your station to submit its news to the government for approval before it could be broadcast?

CASE 9.2 **New Media: To Link, or Not to Link?**

As the leader of www.freedonialive.com, you learned early on about the importance of providing hyperlinks within blog entries. In fact, you require your bloggers to include hyperlinks. A typical posting might include a dozen links inside the text; for example, a posting that mentions the Freedonia Chamber of Commerce would include a hyperlink to the chamber's website. You do this to provide transparency and evidence for your posts, so people can click on those sites if they choose and make up their own minds about your conclusions.

One of your writers has just submitted a potential blog post about an upcoming protest march in your town sponsored by the Freedonia Fanatical Folk, better known as the "FFF." The group's key purpose is to promote policies that oppose every race and religion that is not the dominant one in Freedonia. FFF members wear capes and hoods, and some have been charged with violent acts related to their views.

Included in the posting are details about the march, a little about the FFF's history and beliefs, as well as comments from an FFF spokesman and comments from groups opposed to the FFF. In all, the posting is balanced and neither a diatribe against the FFF nor a free ad for the FFF.

➤ **The question: Do you include a hyperlink to the Freedonia Fanatical Folk's website?**

You could choose:

A. not to link and provide no explanation

B. not to link and explain why

C. to include an intermediate step: when people click on the link, they would go to a screen that warns them that the site has content that most people would find objectionable; people would have to click a second time to go to the link

D. to provide a link, but include a warning within the link

E. to provide a link with no explanation or warning.

Questions
*   **What's your problem?**
*   **Why not follow the rules?**
*   **Who wins, who loses?**
*   **What's it worth?**
*   What else do you need to know?

Thinking it Through

1. Is this an ethical issue? Why or why not?
2. What do you do?
   A. If you choose not to link and provide no justification:
      a. How do you justify your decision not to link?
      b. How do you justify your decision not to explain why you had no link?
      c. Should you let people who comment on the blog posting include a link to the FFF site? Should you allow comments at all, since they may quickly turn nasty?
      d. Since finding the FFF site is as easy as going to a search engine, why exclude the link?
      e. Do you include links to sites that are opposed to the FFF? Why or why not?
   B. If you choose not to link and explain why:
      a. How do you justify your decision not to link?
      b. How do you justify your decision to explain why you had no link? Write a few sentences that you would post on your site to explain why there's no link.
      c. Should you let people who comment on the blog posting include a link to the FFF site? Should you allow comments at all, since they may quickly turn nasty?
      d. Since finding the FFF site is as easy as going to a search engine, why exclude the link?
      e. Do you include links to sites that are opposed to the FFF? Why or why not?
   C. If you choose to include the link, but with a warning screen that requires people to click a second time:
      a. How do you justify your decision to include the link?
      b. How do you justify your decision to require readers to take the extra step to go to the FFF site? Write a few sentences that you would post on the warning screen.
      c. Since finding the FFF site is as easy as going to a search engine, why is it necessary to include the link?
      d. Do you include similar warnings in links to sites that are opposed to the FFF? Why or why not?
      e. Should you let people who comment on the blog posting include a direct link to the FFF site? Should you allow comments at all, since they may quickly turn nasty?
   D. If you choose to include the link, but include a warning within the link:
      a. How do you justify your decision to include the link?
      b. How do you justify your decision to include that warning? Write an example of the warning you would include.

      c. Since finding the FFF site is as easy as going to a search engine, why is it necessary to include the link?

      d. Do you include similar warnings in links to sites that are opposed to the FFF? Why or why not?

      e. Should you let people who comment on the blog posting include a direct link to the FFF site? Should you allow comments at all, since they may quickly turn nasty?

   E.   If you choose to provide a link with no explanation or warning:

      a. How do you justify your decision to include the link?

      b. How do you justify your decision to include no warning?

      c. Since finding the FFF site is as easy as going to a search engine, why is it necessary to include the link?

      d. Should you let people who comment on the blog posting include a direct link to the FFF site? Should you allow comments at all, since they may quickly turn nasty?

3. Is there another choice you could make? If so, how do you defend that choice?

4. When a site links or fails to link to another site, does that imply endorsement? What ethical considerations enter into that question?

5. Google and other search engines consider the number of external links from "credible" sites when ranking websites. Does that consideration enter into a decision—and an ethics discussion?

6. How helpful would it be to create "rules" about linking for your site to make it easier to answer Question 2 ("Why not follow the rules?") in your decision making? Where do you draw the line? Do you refuse links to "illegal" content, such as to child porn or copyrighted material? What sorts of content would you refuse to link to for ethical reasons?

■ ■ ■

CASE 9.3 **Public Relations: Responding to a Smelly Crisis**

You work in public relations for the National Paper Corp. plant in Freedonia. The plant makes lots of paper—and odors that waft across town. The sewer-and-petroleum smell has been an issue for as long as the plant has been open. While newcomers and visitors notice it immediately, long-time residents call it "the smell of money" because the plant is Freedonia's largest employer.

As part of your job, you've long dealt with calls and complaints about the smell. One of your talking points is to remind people that the company voluntarily files reports that detail discharges that cause odors, never surpasses the maximum discharges allowed by law, and has never received a penalty from the government.

At 9 a.m. Wednesday you receive a phone call from a *Freedonia Times* reporter seeking comment on an upcoming story that will say the company's top management for five years refused to spend $10 million on new filtering technology that would have cut the smell by 20 percent. The reporter says the paper has records showing that the plant wouldn't spend the money because it was not tax-deductible.

You are taken aback by this charge, and you cannot comment until you learn more. You ask that the reporter email a list of questions and main points of the story, and you seek 48 hours to be able to gather information and respond. The reporter agrees, and you guess correctly that the story is scheduled to be published on Sunday, the largest paper of the week.

Management holds a crisis meeting to decide what to do. Your boss emerges with this plan: call a press conference for 2 p.m., Thursday, when the company will announce plans to install a $12 million filter that will cut the odor by 25 percent. (The money was in the long-term capital budget over three years, but the plan calls for a way to install the filter a year earlier than planned.)

The boss also says to invite only the local television news stations and not the *Freedonia Times*.

As for responding to the *Freedonia Times*: you are told that at 9 a.m., Friday, at the end of the 48-hour window, you are to release a general statement that does not respond to the paper's specific questions or accusations, says the company has new management in place that is "looking forward to the future," and highlights the plans for the filter.

Your boss says the plan is elegant. National Paper Corp. can announce a solution and be seen as a good corporate citizen. The timing means TV will announce the good news that you hope will mitigate the impact of the negative *Freedonia Times* story. You kept your word to respond in two days to the paper, and even if their feelings are hurt they'll still have to deal with you because you are such a large entity. Your boss says it'll blow over soon, because the newspaper's rapid personnel turnover means a new reporter will be covering the plant in the next year or so anyway.

➤ **The boss asks you what you think. What do you say?**

Questions

- **What's your problem?**
- **Why not follow the rules?**
- **Who wins, who loses?**
- **What's it worth?**
- What else do you need to know?

Thinking it Through

1. Is this an ethical issue? Why or why not?
2. Do you agree with the plan?
    A. If you agree:
       a   How do you justify your decision?
       b. What do you say to the *Freedonia Times* reporter who calls to complain? What if the reporter calls on Thursday evening, after seeing a TV news story about the filter?
       c. How do you think the paper will respond next time it has questions regarding the company?
       d. Public relations practitioners often use "embargoes," in which they provide information to journalists only after journalists agree to hold their stories until an agreed-upon time. Should journalists seek a "reverse embargo," that requires that targets not discuss the story with other media in exchange for providing time to properly respond to questions?
    B. If you disagree:
       a. How do you justify your decision?
       b. What specific parts of the plan do you disagree with? Why?
       c. What would you propose to do instead? (A reminder: Bosses want you to come to them with solutions, not just problems.)
       d. How do you balance loyalties to yourself, your company, the reporter, and the community?
3. Should the company have announced plans to cut the smell long before the paper forced its hand? Why or why not?
4. This case study was based on a pair of true-life occurrences involving charges against the military and the Central Intelligence Agency (Roberts, 2007–2008). Some questions:

A. Can there be justifiable differences in ethical standards of public relations between a for-profit corporation, a non-profit, a government entity, and a religious organization?

B. It can be argued that the newspaper "played fair" with the target of its investigation. Does the target have the ethical obligation to "play fair" in return, even when there's not a promise involved beyond responding within 48 hours?

5. Would this case study be an example of "spin"? Why or why not?

■ ■ ■

CASE 9.4 **Advertising: The Not-so-Accidental Tourist**

You are a senior in advertising at Freedonia University, which is in a cosmopolitan area and is a tourism destination. A rite among tourists is to have their picture taken at the Learning Tower of Freedonia, a site that draws hundreds of thousands of people each year for its architectural beauty and flawed physics.

A friend who graduated a few years before you, who now works at an advertising agency, calls you one day and offers you a part-time job.

Your friend's client is an electronics company that is releasing a new line of cameras aimed at the consumer market. The media campaign will include television and print ads, but your friend has another idea: Why not let people see those new cameras in action?

The job is for you to dress like a tourist and hang around the Learning Tower for several hours a day. You are to look for actual tourists who have old cameras, approach them and ask them to take a picture of you with the tower as a backdrop. As you pose and give directions about how to use the camera, you also are to talk about how terrific the camera is, about its key features, its cost, and where it can be bought. By the time the tourist has taken your photo, you essentially will have given the photo-taking tourist an advertising pitch for the camera. You never have to tell anyone that you're working on behalf of an ad company.

Your friend at the agency says it's a terrific way to give consumers a product demonstration, and by focusing on the right people you'll find people who may be looking for a camera and likely have the money to pay for it. You'd also get to keep the camera—if you also post a Facebook note to all your friends about how good the camera is and you tell the company about how tourists react to the camera.

If you take the job, you'd be in the business of "stealth" advertising, in which ad recipients do not know they heard an ad.

➤ **What do you do?**

Questions
- **What's your problem?**
- **Why not follow the rules?**
- **Who wins, who loses?**
- **What's it worth?**
- What else do you need to know?

Thinking it Through

1. Is this an ethical issue? Why or why not?

2. Do you take the advertising job?

   A. If you say "yes":

      a. How do you justify your decision?

      b. What do you say to tourists who ask you at the end of your spiel: "Wow, you must really love that camera. Are you working for the company or something?"

      c. Do you feel bad that your advertising relies on people doing you a favor because they think you are a fellow tourist who needs help?

      d. What about doing a Facebook posting in exchange for keeping the camera? Is your decision different when you are doing stealth marketing on your "friends"? Why or why not?

   B. If you say "no":

      a. How do you justify your decision?

      b. What changes would the ad agency have to make to its Learning Tower sales pitch for you to take the job?

3. Is there another choice you could make? If so, how do you defend that choice?

4. Would it be better if you offered to take pictures of the tourists using your camera but their memory card, so you wouldn't be wasting their time and they'd be getting something from you even as they heard the stealthy sales pitch?

5. Have you ever realized that you were on the receiving end of a stealth sales pitch without knowing at the time it was an ad? How did it make you feel?

6. Today's advertisers know that many people in the public are immediately defensive and cynical when they see an ad. How can advertisers solve this problem in what you perceive to be an ethical manner?

■ ■ ■

CASE 9.5 **Entertainment: To Screen, or Not to Screen**

You work in media relations for Freedonia Films, which releases 20 or so feature-length motion pictures a year for view in first-run theaters. You spend much of your time coordinating previews, making sure that movie critics from newspapers, television, and influential blogs see your company's movies before wide release. Typically, the writers publish their reviews in conjunction with the film's release. As you'd expect, some movies receive terrific reviews, and other movies are savaged; you can generally predict the tenor of the reviews long before you see them.

The newest movie that Freedonia Films will release is the sequel to a movie that was widely panned by critics but made enough money to warrant a sequel. At a meeting to make marketing plans for the movie, the department head says she wants to hear what everyone thinks about withholding the movie from critics and releasing the movie as a "cold opening." She says the critics likely will hammer the movie with reviews even worse than the original. This would be the first time the company has withheld a movie from critics.

To support her plan, she cites an academic study that says that while only a few movies are actually withheld from critics, those movies make about 15 percent more money at the box office than they otherwise would. The research (Bartlett, 2010) argues that while withholding a movie from critics should suggest to moviegoers that the movie isn't very good, the reality is that many potential moviegoers don't know or care that a movie was withheld from critics.

As you sit in the meeting, several competing ideas run through your head:

1. On one hand, you can expect a backlash and negative publicity if this occurs.

    On the other hand, it will be difficult to know whether the backlash will have short-term or long-term consequences.

2. On one hand, you think it's wrong because it acknowledges that you are merely "using" reviewers for your own purposes.

    On the other hand, the critics "use" you, too. They make money through advertising around stories about your films. Even if you withhold some movies from advanced screenings, those critics have no choice but to continue to give you publicity because the public craves news about movies.

3. On one hand, the public may not be well served if they don't have an opportunity to know much about a movie before they decide whether to go on the opening weekend.

    On the other hand, news travels fast, and people will quickly hear whether a movie is worth watching through word-of-mouth or critics' second-day reviews.

4. On one hand, if we're so worried about a movie that we don't want people to know about it in advance (except for our own marketing efforts, of course), then we ought to make better movies.

   On the other hand, this is a business. We make movies so we can make money. Whatever it takes to drive people to the box office is what matters; if withholding an occasional movie from a critical pounding is what it takes, then that's OK.

➤ **When your time comes to speak, what do you say?**

Questions
- **What's your problem?**
- **Why not follow the rules?**
- **Who wins, who loses?**
- **What's it worth?**
- What else do you need to know?

Thinking it Through
1. Is this an ethical issue? Why or why not?
2. Yes or no: Should all your movies be previewed for critics?
   A. If you say "yes":
      a. How do you justify your decision?
      b. Provide a rank order of the four "on-the-one-hand" arguments, from what was most important to you to what was least important to you.
      c. How do you argue against bottom-line focused people at the meeting?
      d. Do you tell any of the critics that your company was considering plans to stop previews of some movies? Why or why not?
      e. How can you compete with movie companies that do not preview some movies? Is there a way to use this decision to your advantage?
   B. If you say "no":
      a. How do you justify your decision?
      b. Provide a rank order of the four "on-the-one-hand" arguments, from what was most important to you to what was least important to you.
      c. How do you argue against people at the meeting who argue that it's wrong to "use" critics like that?
      d. How do you break the news to critics that the rules will change? How can you mitigate the short-term PR damage?
3. This case study gave you four reasons for or against the decision. What other reasons might exist, and how might those reasons influence your decision?

Who's Whispering in Your Ear?

The fifth section of this book turns to philosophers and their moral theories. This means we are now considering the wisdom of the ages, consulting authoritative voices who have created an impressive body of advice about examining and living a moral life. It should not be surprising to notice that these philosophers disagree about many things. There are subtle differences in basic terminology, and significant differences in ideas about what constitutes the moral imagination, the moral life, and appropriate ways to engage in moral reasoning.

> In general—and specifically in this case—which school of philosophy or set of moral principles provides you with a moral compass?

Thousands of years of talking about and doing ethics have resulted in theories framed by several distinct principles. We find it helpful to cluster them under the principles of:

- consequentialism and utility—a focus on ends
- duty and obligation—a focus on means
- virtue and character—a focus on motivations
- justice and fairness—a focus on values
- care and reciprocity—a focus on relationships.

While some texts and perhaps most discussions of media ethics emphasize only a couple of the principles—usually utility and duty—we will range briefly across the territory, acknowledging contributions made by each of the five general schools of thought and pointing out where principles overlap. These principles are touchstones in our efforts to do ethics and to think critically about the media ethics environment. Because serious philosophers have come to blows over subtleties of terminology, forgive us for what looks like a superficial and pragmatic rendering of all those centuries of good thinking and careful categorization.

Many texts on applied professional ethics place this material in their opening chapters. We place it toward the end of the book. Our reasoning is seen in the ordering of the six questions that frame our text: We believe that to "do ethics" well, we should start by using our own judgment about the moral dimensions of the problem at hand; we next make a pragmatic consideration about which rules, policies, and conventions may or may not apply; and then we clarify and prioritize our conflicting personal, professional, and community loyalties and our moral and non-moral values. Up to that point we should have been exercising our own judgment when weighing the variables, instead of relying upon an authoritative voice to do our judging for us. After that, it seems appropriate to check our own good insights against the judgments of our tribal elders.

If we initiate the process by invoking a particular school of philosophy, there is some risk that our chosen philosopher might predetermine our answers for us. For instance, John Stuart Mill might automatically lead us to focus exclusively on utility, Immanuel Kant on moral duties, Aristotle on virtue, John Rawls on justice, Carol Gilligan on caring, etc.—all the while tempting us to overlook the importance of other moral principles and the nuances that should have emerged from doing our own heavy lifting: asking and answering our other questions.

Through intuition or practical experience, you may have already become utilitarians, or deontologists, or adherents of some other school of philosophy. This is all well and good. If that is the case, you will bring these principles into the decision-making equation. However, we would ask that you use the principles rationally, not dogmatically. Keep your minds open to the nuances, and respect the choices made by other stakeholders and observers who may be influenced by a different school of philosophy. And please don't retrofit your thinking so that all cases are simplified by mere invocation and *post-hoc* application of a bumper-sticker philosophy!

As we have suggested before, we are more interested in encouraging you to engage in a defensible process than we are in having you take too much comfort in always having the "right" answer. Ownership of a good process means you can apply it thoughtfully to any number of situations, which bodes well for your future as professionals and thoughtful critics of media.

Chapter 10 examines theories of utility and consequentialism. It recognizes that media are commercially based enterprises with great potential for bringing about benefits or harm to individuals and societies. The chapter tries to show the pros and cons of relying upon thinkers such as John Stuart Mill.

Chapter 11 takes a similar approach to theories of duty and moral obligation. In contrast with the ends-based thinking of consequentialists, it focuses on the means-based thinking of philosophers such as Immanuel Kant, William David Ross, and Bernard Gert.

These philosophers tell us that good choices come from adhering to a number of duties, and not from being obsessed over the impacts of those choices.

Chapter 12 offers an overview of insights from philosophers who have advocated principles of virtue and character, justice and fairness, and care and moral reciprocity. The list is selective; we cannot even pretend to describe all the works of all the good thinkers for the past several millennia. But we believe there is value in summarizing the thoughts of some leading thinkers and seeing what advice they might offer media practitioners struggling for morally justifiable responses to dilemmas.

We introduce five new case studies to be used throughout the three chapters, so you can see how applying different theories to the same set of facts might lead to different results.

In sum, these three chapters bring provocative and pragmatic insights to the media ethics environment.

---

1. **What's your problem?**

2. **Why not follow the rules?**

3. **Who wins, who loses?**

4. **What's it worth?**

5. **Who's whispering in your ear?**

6. **How's your decision going to look?**

CHAPTER 10

Consequentialism and Utility

This chapter:

- uses two scenarios to distinguish between consequentialistic and deontological reasoning

- defines utilitarianism and shows how media make cost-benefit decisions

- considers contributions from philosophers Jeremy Bentham, John Stuart Mill, and William Frankena

- outlines different varieties of utilitarian thinking

- offers practical applications and five original case studies for further study.

INTRODUCTION

JUST AS ethics demands decision making, ethical consistency also demands adherence to principles. Most of us would gladly describe ourselves as persons of principle. We might even say we adhere to "high principle"—whatever that redundant adjective adds. But we're likely to stumble for words when asked to describe the principles that guide our lives and decisions. To the extent that we claim to follow our principles, we probably envision that as meaning we "try to do what is right"—another rather abstract set of terms.

It seems reasonable to assert that the media have widespread—and sometimes problematic—influence on society and institutions, and that people working in mass communications have specific role-related duties motivating them to perform at a high level. Thus, many media ethics discussions are limited to principles of consequence and duty. The two principles are more rightfully known as *teleology* and *deontology*. Teleology and deontology both employ the suffix "-ology," which refers to "the study of . . ." The prefix "teleo-" is related to "cause and effect." The prefix "deon-" is related to "duty." We introduce both theories at this juncture, then devote the rest of this chapter to teleology. In Chapter 11 we will further develop ideas about deontology and the nature of personal and professional duties.

Teleology refers to philosophies concerned with desired ends or consequences; its adherents are called teleologists or consequentialists. We will use the terms "consequentialism" and "teleology" when talking about "ends-based" utility or the effects of our choices.

Deontology is a summary term dealing with philosophies concerned with moral duties or rules-based ethics, and the "means-based" people who espouse it are called deontologists. (Our terminology will be more basic when we discuss insights from philosophers who advocate other principles; in our Chapter 12 discussion we will call these the ethics of virtue, justice, or care.)

This chapter explores the objective moral theories of consequentialism, with particular attention to utilitarianism. By looking at case studies, we will see that one way to justify our actions is to consider the nature of the consequences of those acts. For instance: Have we figured out which consequences are morally relevant, and to what extent? Have we considered the interests of all the stakeholders? Are more people helped than harmed? Is the benefit spread widely? Is there a greater amount of good than harm? And if there is more harm than good, is the balance of harm over benefit minimized? These are not simple questions to answer, but to "do ethics" while a consequentialist is whispering advice in our ear, we should do our best to take all these questions into consideration.

When modern media institutions and practitioners offer moral explanations for their behaviors, they often tend to use a consequentialist or utilitarian calculus. In their quest for sales and ratings, media try to avoid being overly offensive; advocates try to persuade gently rather than attacking audiences' deeply rooted beliefs; entertainers try to maximize pleasure and eye appeal without being overly distracting; broadcasters try to inform without being too boring; reporters reveal systems failures but try to avoid causing apathy or hopelessness. These are rational justifications, coming from commercially based, relatively unregulated media whose successes or failures are usually measured in terms of subscribers, dollars, and impact on public opinion. However, as we will see in this chapter, there are pros and cons to doing a rudimentary cost-benefit analysis when making moral decisions. The theories we're about to explore demand far more of us than merely counting up the "goods" and "bads" that occur when we enter the media ethics environment.

SETTING THE STAGE

Two case studies help us set the stage. The first is an edited version of a true case written by one of our former media ethics students, who worked at the university's student-run newspaper. The second is hypothetical. The basic moral questions in these cases relate to concerns over consequences and duties.

As you work through the two cases, try to avoid thinking that consequentialistic thinking is morally permissive and that deontological thinking is morally restrictive. Utilitarians don't "do whatever it takes," and duty-based philosophers don't always "just say no." It is much more complex than either conducting a simplistic cost-benefit analysis or following an arbitrary set of moral rules.

In the first case, the students' decisions are clearly explained, and you are asked to critique them. In the second case you are asked to make—and then defend—your own decisions.

CASE 10-A **The Temptation to Deceive**

Three of us were sitting around in the student paper newsroom shooting the breeze, yelling at copy editors and doing the whole college journalist shtick when we got word of an explosion in the physics lab. College papers live for that sort of thing. It's a steak dinner with all the trimmings in a regular bland diet of Student Government senate stories, campus political reports and student-makes-good biographies. We tossed our soda cans and made a mad scramble for Physics Hall.

Inside of 30 minutes we knew what happened, the names of the injured parties, and the other standard information from police. Then, when I interviewed a student who wasn't hurt, she said that the lab instructor may have given permission to the student to pour liquid nitrogen into a glass soda bottle. I pulled my fellow-journalist away from some guy describing for the umpteenth time that the explosion sounded like a shotgun and dragged him to his car, leaving the daily newspaper reporter and the rest of the pack wolves to do their features. WE HAD THE REAL STORY! We knew the name of the kid who bottled the nitrogen and that he was rushed in an ambulance to the Regional Medical Center.

We had dealt with the Regional Medical Center and their people a lot—the illegal abortion series, traffic accidents, etc.—so we discussed our chances of talking to the guy. We knew their policies. They are restrictive. You get more out of a monk under a vow of silence.

The issues involved that we discussed were these: Our readers will want to know why the kid pulled such a bone-headed stunt; students have a right to know if the labs—physics or otherwise—use unsafe procedures; whether the University is hiring incompetent lab instructors, thus endangering students further; that we were on a tight deadline and if we didn't get it now we'd be beaten; that it could place blame in the public's mind that the kid did it on his own; that if we went through the public relations department or identified ourselves as reporters we'd be given the runaround; and that if we just published the official report that other journalists were going to publish, then we wouldn't be doing our job.

Our decision was to lie and say we were friends and family members of the injured kid. We decided that was our only recourse. We told the duty nurse in the trauma center that I was the brother of the kid injured. She walked me to his trauma-room door. I walked into the room alone and identified myself as clearly as possible. "I'm John Doe with the campus newspaper. I'm a reporter. I'd like to get your story." (I think all reporters at one time or another love that kind of melodrama.)

The kid told me from his hospital bed everything that happened. My buddy got a confirmation from the kid's other two classmates. With that, confirmation from two uninvolved kids from the class and a "no comment" from the lab instructor and the University powers-that-be, we went with the story—triple by-line and 60 inches. Front page and two days ahead of any other news media.

In the days that followed, we kept up pressure on the University and the investigators. We showed that there were unsafe lab practices, the lab instructor was at fault, and that even the slowly moving

continued

wheels of University fact-finding committees could spin at high speed when properly greased. As a result, lab procedures have been made safer, the lab instructor, though not officially punished, was asked not to return the next semester, and the University paid the bills for all those injured. The editor, managing editor, and the entire staff of the paper, including our rigid ombudsman, stood by our decision to use deception.

Let's run it through the checklist to see if the same answer comes up.

1. **What's your problem?** We were faced with lying to get the whole truth about a story with great impact.

2. **Why not follow the rules?** We briefly thought about the student newspaper's policy manual and the SPJ code of ethics. Both stress truth telling and fair play, while leaving us a small loophole or two (references to seeking truth as an ultimate goal made us think about capital-T truth and small-t truth). Besides, our ombudsman is a pretty thoughtful person; he holds us accountable, and we're willing to face him.

3. **Who wins, who loses?** The stakeholders included the injured student, other students who might be at risk, the lab instructor, the nurse, the University PR folks, our readers, and ourselves (ambitious student journalists). The injured student deserved our highest loyalty. We had reasonable cause to believe that students' lives were endangered by unsafe lab practices and an incompetent lab instructor. We had an obligation to protect life by finding out if that was indeed true, which it was. Even if it wasn't true, I believe we would have still been justified in our actions because the protection of life is a paramount value that outweighs truth. Our decision set into motion a chain of events that made sure life would be safeguarded in lab classes.

   Our second loyalty is to the readers. They deserve all of the truth and the whole story, but they cannot be expected to believe us if we make a regular practice of lying to sources. In life and death situations, however, this must be subordinate to the protection of life, just as truth must take precedence over what the readers want. A newspaper is published in the readers' interest, but it is not necessarily tailored to their needs. I'm sure many readers would like it if all we published were happy, happy stories and if we never dredged up the banalities of reality. But we have a higher commitment to the truth. (Besides, we are ambitious; we're loyal to ourselves.)

4. **What's it worth?** Several values were on the line. Lives may have been at stake if the University was using unsafe lab procedures. Second, there is truth. The whole truth might not have been told if we published the official version—just that the kid filled the bottle and it exploded. The values conflict is that we had to lie to get the whole truth.

   We had to think about the value of responsibility—in two ways. First, we are responsible to readers—we have an obligation to get all of the facts. Second, the campus paper is the closest

continued

thing to a media watchdog for the University administration. If they are not telling everything, then we are responsible for getting whatever it is they are sweeping under the rug. Given our past dealings with hospital officials, we knew we couldn't interview the people actually involved with the explosion unless we told them we were friends and family.

Lastly, and this should not be understated, we want to be the best. Ambition. We have to do all we can to satisfy the rest of our values. We wanted to get the whole story because we wanted to beat the other media. We may not have the resources other media have, but by God, if something happens on campus, we should have the most complete coverage.

5. **Who's whispering in your ear?** I have always believed, in spite of its flaws, that utilitarianism best suits a newspaper. Our alternatives were: (a) tell the truth, (b) lie to the nurse, or (c) print what one source, uninvolved but at the scene, said without confirmation from the directly involved parties. Persons directly affected: sources at the hospital, sources in the explosion, our readers, the University administration, co-workers.

Likely consequences: By telling the truth to the nurse, we would have had the same incomplete story as everyone else and it might not ever have come out that the lab instructor and the University were at fault; the University would have kept the same unsafe practices; our readers would have been cheated; and the kids would have been blamed. We would have done no better than our competition.

By lying to the nurse, we would get the whole story, the University would have to admit to its errors, and we would beat our competition. It could also have left a bad impression on our other less-experienced personnel that we advocate lying to get the truth in all situations; the hospital would be more wary of us and might start making it harder to see real relatives in their care; and some might ask, "Why should we believe you when you lied to get the story?" Major benefits of lying to the source: the University paid the medical bills, it changed practices in the lab, it "asked" a poorly qualified instructor not to return, readers got the whole story, the kids were exonerated, we beat the competition, and we fulfilled our responsibility.

Major harm: The hospital will be more wary of media and may be more careful in scrutinizing visitors; an instructor was essentially fired; young campus newspaper staffers might get the wrong impression; some readers might question our reliability when we lied to the nurse.

6. **How is it going to look?** Given that the greatest amount of good for the greatest number of people was done by our lying to the nurse, and the least amount of harm was done to the least amount of people, I'm willing to go public; I feel that our decision was ethical and justified. (*Note: We'll talk more about this question in Chapter 13.*)

CASE 10-B **Marketing Your Movie**

You are writing the script for an action-packed fantasy movie that you expect a film distribution company to make. It's a "popcorn" movie, aimed at making a splash during the summer height of the movie season. The plot is solid, and you can make the movie as tame or racy as you want.

The movie's producers have two requests. They want you to:

1. Aim the script so it will receive a PG-13 rating, which cautions parents that "some material may be inappropriate for young children." Aiming for a PG-13 rating means the movie will be more likely to draw teenagers and older viewers, since a mere PG rating might make older moviegoers think the movie is boring or "for kids." To hit that PG-13 rating, you must add a few curse words, shed a little more blood, toss out some double-entendres, and include a sex scene that shows no nudity but leaves little to the imagination.

2. Make sure there's a cartoonish character in it, so the film company can make a marketing deal with a well-known fast-food chain that would include the characters as the toys in kids' meals.

At one level, you're fine with the decision because your movie isn't exactly high art, and it means more marketing power and money for the movie. Besides, it's been done before with kids' meals for PG-13 movies such as *Incredible Hulk* and *Transformers*.

However, when driving home from the meeting with the producers, you pass an elementary school and see a class of 10-year-olds on the playground. They'd be able to buy the kids' meal, but they may not be allowed to go see the movie. (They'd certainly pester their parents about going to see it.) And if the kids saw the movie, they would be exposed to language and scenes that the movie raters say may be inappropriate for children.

➤ **What do you do?**

STOP!

Before you continue, jot down your thoughts about what the student journalists (10-A) should have done and the script writer (10-B) should do, and how they could morally justify their decisions.

CONSEQUENTIALISTIC AND DEONTOLOGICAL JUSTIFICATIONS

Now, read the following sets of responses regarding the student journalist and film marketing cases.

Student Journalist Justification No. 1

The journalists who deceived the nurse did what morality required because, aside from embarrassing a few members of the University community, they held the University accountable for its hiring and supervision policies, helped make the university safer for students and staff, and let them tell a more complete story than competing media. They gave the injured student a voice, a chance to be heard, which was something that authorities sought to take from him without his direct consent. The positive payoff was certainly worth the price of one relatively insignificant lie!

However, even if their primary goal was to bring about good results, the students might have come to the opposite conclusion. They could ethically decide to "sit" on the story out of concern that they may have made a rash mistake about the university's culpability; they may sense that publishing a potentially erroneous and dubiously researched story might seriously harm their newspaper's reputation and independence and their own future job prospects; they may conclude that young journalists should not accept duplicity as a reportorial tool.

Student Journalist Justification No. 2

Although the journalists may have acted with good intentions, they were morally wrong because they deceived the nurse, using her as a means to their own end, and violated the hospital's privacy policies that had been established to protect vulnerable patients. All of these are inherently immoral actions. After all, how can news media claim they are fighting for honesty and integrity while acting less than honestly in gathering and reporting their story? Two wrongs do not make a right! The end does not justify the means! Besides, all of this utilitarian argument is *post hoc*; what would the journalists have said if their lie had backfired and caused additional harm? And how could they possibly know the long-term consequences of their action; what if none of their sources will trust them (or other journalists) again?

However, a similar duty-based rationale may have motivated the student journalists to conduct the deception and publish the story—especially if their immediate sense of obligation to the majority of their stakeholders clearly overshadowed their obligation to abide by some rather abstract ethics codes and privacy policies. The minor moral transgression against the nurse was not intended to de-humanize her, but to help the journalists meet a higher obligation to full and complete story-telling. Some duties are more compelling than others.

Movie Marketing Justification No. 1

In today's complex marketplace, it makes good sense to attract the largest audiences to our productions. It is much better to produce a film that appeals to children and teenagers (and probably lure a large number of their parents into the theater) than to produce one that will appeal to only one of those two demographics. We know that it's good marketing to admit that "some material may be inappropriate for young children." We're not hurting anyone by spicing up our script. Little kids have probably heard a few curse words and seen a bit of blood, so we're not breaking any taboos here. Besides, their parents will either accompany them or give them permission to see the film. The marketing tie-in is crucial, if we want our movie to stand out from the rest of the summer's films. The tie-in reduces the production company's costs. A good cartoon character will generate the buzz that is essential if we hope to do a sequel. The production company and I and the fast food industry will all do very well, thank you, and nobody's really going to get hurt in the process.

However, even if we remain focused on the bottom line, we might come to an opposite conclusion, attempting to improve viewership and marketing by appealing to the "family values" market. In the short run we may sell a few more tickets if we include some material inappropriate for young children, but we may run the risk of offending a significant demographic. In the long run our marketing tie-ins may have an enormous appeal to families with young children. The "Toy Story" phenomenon has proven that you don't have to be offensive to be successful.

Movie Marketing Justification No. 2

A number of rules, regulations, and codes should be invoked in this case. Some of them say that pandering to vulnerable populations is unethical. Most of them say we ought to display respect and decency. Common sense tells us that if we make this film needlessly crude and violent, we're using children for our own benefit. It doesn't matter whether children are actually hurt by the film's production and fast-food marketing; what matters is that we're violating some fundamental rules about how to treat people. It is wrong to market a movie to an audience younger than the suggested rating. There's no way we could make any sort of general principle about "do whatever you're inclined to do when you're producing stuff for the mass media."

However, if we're concerned primarily about meeting our obligations, we may conclude that we have a duty to help the film producers meet their commitments to their underwriters; we should do all we can to make the film financially successful within the established rules of the ratings system. Our role-related obligations are to write good scripts; parents' role-related duties are to help their children make informed decisions. It is not unethical to write a PG-13 script and promote the film with marketing tie-ins.

Examining the Justifications

Does your reasoning more closely align with justifications No. 1 or No. 2? (Note: We didn't ask if your *conclusions* aligned with any of the justifications, but only how you processed the problem. The distinction is significant.) Or, do you have yet another approach to justify your view on the cases?

In each case, justification No. 1 captures the teleological or consequentialist approach to moral theory. Consequentialists believe that the moral status of an action is a function of the consequences of performing the action. More precisely, consequentialists are ethical absolutists who believe that whether a particular action has or lacks the property of being obligatory is a function of that action's results—its "payoff." Crudely stated, then, consequentialism is the view that the end justifies the means.

According to the consequentialist, the kind of action performed is irrelevant to its moral evaluation; to evaluate an action morally, one need only evaluate the consequences of performing that action. Note that in No. 1 the justifications focus on the outcome of deceiving the nurse and embarrassing the university *vis-à-vis* the benefit to other stakeholders, or whether the filmmakers and fast-food marketers benefited without causing too much harm. The justifications did not emphasize the kinds of conduct in which the journalists and entertainers engaged to achieve their results.

Justification No. 2 captures a radically different approach to moral theory known as deontology. First, deontologists reject the consequentialist view that an action's moral status is a function of the results it produces. Second, deontologists believe that some actions just are the right kinds of actions to perform, and other kinds of actions are inherently wrong to perform. Duties—some role-related, others universal—and rules are important considerations. In other words, some actions are obligatory; they ought to be performed just because they are the kinds of actions they are—regardless of their consequences. And, as we'll explore in Chapter 11, not all obligations have equal moral weight.

Deontologists believe that whether a particular action is obligatory is a function of the kind of action it is. In justification No. 2, the reasons for critiquing the student journalists' enterprise do not involve the good or evil that resulted from the investigation, or which stakeholders gained specific benefits or suffered specific losses from converting a PG film into one rated PG-13. Rather, the justification involves the *kinds of actions* and *moral duties* or *obligations* that should have motivated the student journalists interested in exposing possible incompetence and filmmakers attempting to market their merchandise.

Repeating an important point raised earlier: As you can see from the eight paragraphs of justifications for our two cases—and as this chapter will try to clarify—consequentialists aren't fixated on "getting away with stuff," and deontologists don't always wag their fingers while saying "No."

Both theories are morally compelling.

UTILITARIANISM DEFINED

Utilitarianism has many definitions. The *Encyclopedia of Ethics* says utilitarianism holds that human conduct should promote the interests or welfare of those affected (Lyons, 2001). A shorthand definition is that utilitarianism insists the right action is that which benefits the greatest number of people or harms the least number of people. Another says that the sole ultimate standard of right, wrong, and obligation is the principle of utility, which says that the moral end to be sought in all we do is the greatest possible balance of good over evil (or the least possible balance of evil over good) in the world as a whole (Frankena, 1973).

This utilitarian approach has a fundamental justification: The theory seems democratic. It allows for equal treatment of people and provides a calculus to determine right action, which is fairer than merely letting the strongest person get his or her way. In this sense, the theory is more philosophically mature than ethical egoism (allowing everyone to do whatever pleases them) and ethical relativism (concluding that each person or culture defines what is right). On the other hand, utilitarianism is readily faulted if it judges each individual act's rightness or wrongness solely on the basis of imagined benefits or harm, or if it disregards any unnecessary harm as being an incidental by-product of a cost-benefit calculus. It is certainly problematic if the theory is trotted out to justify social injustices by saying that, so long as the majority benefits from the practice, tough noogies. Finally, the appeal to utilitarianism tends to overlook our fundamental duty to do right for its own sake.

Utility and Disutility

Consequentialists grapple with key concerns of utility and disutility:

Utility	Disutility
benefits	costs
goodness	badness
pleasure	pain
happiness	unhappiness

Utility and disutility exist in individual as well as social contexts, and all our decisions are made in a certain amount of uncertainty—that is, we are never completely sure of the outcome of our choices. Note also that individual utility is more easily applied decision making than is social utility. In the former, the concern is with greatest good for me. In the latter, the concern is with the greatest good for the rest of society.

Media constantly face utilitarian questions of functions and dysfunctions. Information, entertainment, persuasion, and general transfer of culture from generation to generation are all "functions" of media. But for every function there may be an approximately equal and opposite dysfunction, whether intended or not.

It is silly to believe that entertaining (function) movies dealing with the mafia or street gang violence were made expressly to create more real-world mayhem (dysfunction). A graphic news photo may alert readers and viewers to danger (function) but may paralyze them or make them believe the world is scarier than it really is (dysfunction). A public relations campaign may draw attention to an important issue (function) but provide only a one-sided view that crowds out opposing views (dysfunction). An ad campaign may help a company sell its product (function) but may make people feel inferior because their lives don't match the ad's ideal (dysfunction). A movie that blurs the lines between "docu" and "drama" has important functional and dysfunctional components (is its message powerful and truthful enough to outweigh its deception?). Some media fare that was intended to make a profit and to entertain (functions) may also bring about antisocial effects (dysfunctions). In consequentialist terms, these are matters of utility and disutility.

The major concern over utility and disutility may be "values," the subject we explored in Chapter 6. We have gone through values clarification exercises to identify a variety of values, but big questions remain: How do we measure the effects of good and evil, truth, love, friendship, security, a world at peace, etc.? How do we know when we are maximizing benefit to self and to society? What are the tradeoffs between and among conflicting values? How much of one value needs to be compromised in order to maximize another value?

These are the types of questions utilitarians try to answer. The next part of this chapter focuses on the thinking of philosophers Jeremy Bentham, John Stuart Mill, and William Frankena. Each brought subtle (and not-so-subtle) differences to the topic.

JEREMY BENTHAM:
Hedonic Calculus

The first philosopher to articulate a full-blown theory of utilitarianism was Jeremy Bentham (1748–1832). He was interested in everything from the structure of to the ways to reform numerous social and political institutions, including public policy, legislation, and political administration. He took up prison reform, ending capital punishment, relief for the poor, representative democracy, birth control, sexual liberation, and treating animals humanely (Postema, 2001). Because he was convinced that many institutions muddled along on moralistic (or amoralistic) and non-scientific "business-as-usual" standards, he advocated a structure of rigorous, practical, rational, and readily accessible decision making.

Bentham said moral judgments need to be justified, and the best way to proceed was to use language that anyone could understand. Hence, he put the everyday notion of "happiness" front and center in his decision-making schema. To calculate whether happiness would trump unhappiness in any given situation, Bentham worked out a hedonic calculus of pleasures and pains, impartially and publicly calculated. In doing the calculus, Bentham said that from the moral point of view, everyone's happiness is of equal significance: each person counts as one, and no one counts as more than one. The goal was not just to maximize that one individual's happiness, but the greatest happiness of the greatest number, while preventing unnecessary pain.

Happiness was measured along seven dimensions:

- **Intensity**: The more intense the pleasure/reward, the more it is sought.
- **Duration**: The longer the benefit lasts, the more it is sought.
- **Purity**: The more clear cut the pleasure utility, the more it is sought.
- **Certainty**: The more certain we are of the results, the more it is sought.
- **Fecundity**: The more a utility/pleasure leads to something else beneficial, the better it is and the more it should be sought (fecundity means fruitful, versus something that is dead).
- **Propinquity**: All else being equal, take the near at hand over the remote or aloof.
- **Extent**: How widely do you apply the effects/conclusions? (i.e., to the greatest number?)

The first six of Bentham's dimensions of utility apply neatly to individuals; the seventh factor considers society. Rather than thinking solely in terms of pleasure and pain, Bentham said the calculus can also be used to assess profit, convenience, advantage, benefit, emolument (payment for work), happiness, and so forth (on the plus side); and evil, mischief, inconvenience, disadvantage, loss, or unhappiness (on the negative side). To perform the calculus, Bentham said we should sum up all the values of all the pleasures on the one side, and all the pains on the other. To take an account of the number of people whose interests appear to be concerned, repeat the process with respect to each (Cahn & Markie, 2002).

To many, it seems bizarre to calculate happiness objectively, even though we do this when we draw a line down the middle of a paper and list the "reasons for" on one side and the "reasons against" on the other. Despite its quaintness, however, a hedonic calculus has merit. Consider how these seven categories can be applied to decision making in the media environment. How a journalist defines news, how a PR person or advertiser decides about a particular campaign, how an entertainer chooses among themes and story lines, how a videographer chooses what shots to take and how to display them, etc., are often done through a calculus somewhat similar to that of Bentham's.

For instance, again consider the nature of "news judgment" (hearkening back to Chapter 6). The traditional news elements sound a lot like Bentham: All else being equal, journalists seek out and report things that entail:

- **Proximity**: Select things that happen close to home, or to people we know.
- **Timeliness**: Tell people what just happened.
- **Prominence**: Talk about important people, or people who are already known.
- **Consequence/Impact**: The greater the potential impact, the more newsworthy.

- **Oddity/Novelty**: The more something is unusual, the more newsworthy it is.
- **Conflict**: The clearer the battle lines, the easier it is to tell the story.
- **Currency**: Keep things that are newsworthy percolating on the agenda.

Relatively blind application of this tried-and-true calculus may explain why the news media focus on the latest exploits or meltdowns of our favorite celebrities; why we receive breathless updates on political horseraces and the stock market; why we have so much more news about disasters and two-sided conflicts, with clearly identifiable good guys and bad guys, than on things that are going well (which helps explain our obsession with sports and massive oil spills in the Gulf of Mexico); why we report on the cats who get stuck in the trees rather than the ones who climb down on their own. Held captive by a hedonic calculus, focused on pleasing audiences with predictable news, little wonder journalists produce a pattern of predictable news stories.

Even Jeremy Bentham would conclude that it is not enough to simply bring momentary pleasure to people. He would expect more from news media. As he did with other institutional reforms, he would ask the media to consider the widespread and long-term benefits of their "product." He would likely ask journalists to redefine individual and social "happiness," thinking of it as a principled utility, based on fully and publicly justified moral judgments. He would conclude that it is morally insufficient to fill the news pages or minutes with titillating, sensationalistic, novel information that brings about no real "good." He would ask persuasive communicators to consider more than their own goals and points of view. And he would ask entertainment communicators to focus on the societal impact of their products.

JOHN STUART MILL:
Building Upon Bentham

British philosopher John Stuart Mill (1806–1873) built upon Bentham's utilitarianism to offer a much more nuanced set of insights for people facing moral dilemmas. He started with the familiar Bentham guiding principle: Ethical decisions should seek the greatest amount of happiness or benefit to the greatest number of people while at the same time they should seek to harm the least amount of people. But he extended Bentham's framework in claiming that when balancing the benefit of one (or many) against the harm of one (or many), people should recognize that some benefits are better than others and some harms more painful than others. Therefore, the measure is whether you are seeking the greatest possible balance of good over evil, and whether you are distributing this good as broadly as possible. It is a question of the aggregate good—benefits for all the stakeholders who might possibly be affected by the decision. And, while considering the aggregate benefits, Mill would have us provide "special protection for individuals who might otherwise be sacrificed for the good of the whole" (Elliott, 2007, p. 100). These decisions should be made objectively and impartially; decision makers cannot give themselves any special privileges, especially if they are stakeholders in the case at hand.

Mill argued adamantly that there is more to life than simple hedonistic pleasures, so happiness should be defined broadly. Whereas Bentham described pleasure or pain in terms of their intensity and duration, Mill advocated higher level pleasures, such as the pleasures of imagination, intellectual pursuits, and others that are qualitatively different from base-level pleasures. One of his famous explanations was that it is better to be a human being dissatisfied than a pig satisfied; better to be Socrates dissatisfied than a fool satisfied (Mill, 1863/1988; Peck, 2007).

If John Stuart Mill Were Sharing Your Office

Mill would tell you to test your decisions by:

1. Compiling a complete list of possible actions you might take. (You need a good sense of potential outcomes to do this thoroughly.)
2. Listing the stakeholders likely to be affected by the decision. (Public relations and advertising practitioners would be sure to include their clients, co-workers, superiors, stockholders, public, and themselves in the equation; journalists would include their sources, news subjects, editors, co-workers, readers, advertisers, stockholders, and themselves in the equation.)
3. Deciding the likely consequences from each option, being attentive to the number of people likely to benefit or be harmed and the extent to which anyone's legal or moral rights would be violated.
4. Asking whether someone who might get harmed actually *deserves* to be harmed. (After all, some folks who have done wrong or violated public trust ought to be publicly criticized.)
5. Choosing—impartially—the consequence that would seem to provide the most benefit to the largest aggregate of people or the least harm to the smallest number of people.
6. Concluding whether some harm could be justified because it promotes the overall good of the community or whether the community might be harmed if you were to take no action. (Sometimes, more harm is caused by "burying" an issue than by publicizing it; copping out or choosing not to decide has consequences!)

As we will see in the next section, this justification process cuts across categories. On one hand, it seems that Mill asks people to choose which act will maximize happiness, but on the other hand, he implies that people should follow rules or principles to bring about the best results. Many philosophers say Mill tends to fall into the category of "rule utilitarianism." That is because, despite his deserved reputation as a consequentialist, Mill's approach includes a good degree of deontological thinking.

Categories of Utilitarianism

Philosophers have proposed at least three variations of utilitarianism: act, general, and rule utilitarianism.

1. Act Utilitarianism

Act utilitarianism is a teleological perspective that says a person should use the principle of utility when considering what is right in specific cases. In other words, we should try to see which specific action will—or is likely to—produce the greatest balance of good over evil in the universe. There are no rules; everything is situational. Act utility is invoked on a case-by-case basis, not necessarily connected to prior situations. This seems to provide a lot of moral wiggle room, and it can be faulted for not taking into consideration the influence of ignorance, prejudice, and other contaminating variables in our decision making.

From some utilitarians we hear the hedonistic argument that an act is morally obligatory—not just permissible, but obligatory—if and only if (IFF) it produces happiness or pleasure, and IFF it results in the absence of pain. A better description of act utilitarianism is that an act is morally obligatory IFF it produces happiness; IFF it produces more pleasure than pain; IFF it produces the greatest utility; and, in case of a tie, IFF there is no other act that produces greater utility than that act.

This gives rise to interesting questions, such as: At what cost do we maximize pleasure? Over how long a time does the pleasure need to be maintained? How can we calculate variables to figure out what the balance of plus/minus will be? Can we quantify pleasure and pain on a "hedometer"—a modification of Bentham's approach?

$$-10\ -9\ -8\ -7\ -6\ -5\ -4\ -3\ -2\ -1\ /\ 0\ /\ +1\ +2\ +3\ +4\ +5\ +6\ +7\ +8\ +9\ +10$$

Advocates of the hedometer say we can quantify our options, adding and subtracting units of pleasure and pain. For instance, if we wanted to look at this in terms of the news media environment, we could calculate the likely functions or dysfunctions of each gatekeeping decision about proximity, timeliness, prominence, impact, novelty, conflict, or currency. Of course, we could (and probably should) go beyond these non-moral, craft-based variables and calculate how each of them could be relied upon to maximize the short- or long-term, narrow- or widespread benefits for all stakeholders.

2. General Utilitarianism

General utilitarianism is a more deontological approach to consequentialism. It holds that we should not ask in each situation which action has the best consequences, but neither should we merely invoke some rules. According to general utilitarianism, we should not ask: "What will happen if I do so and so in this case?" or "What rule should I follow?" Rather, we should ask: "What would happen if everyone were to do so and so in this case?" If something is right for one person in a certain situation, then it is also right for anyone else who is similarly situated. Hence, a person cannot ask simply what effects one's proposed action will have in a particular case. (The principle of universalizability is combined with the principle of utility, making this a sort of an act deontological theory, and not strictly a teleological one.)

3. Rule Utilitarianism

Rule utilitarianism, as we have seen from our discussion of John Stuart Mill, is pretty much a deontological theory, because it emphasizes the centrality of rules in morality. It insists that we are generally, if not always, to decide what to do in particular situations by applying a "useful rule" (such as the rule of truth telling, promise keeping, etc.—rules that would be useful if they were applied universally) instead of by asking what particular action will have the best consequences in the situation in question.

Unlike strict deontology, however, it adds that we are always to determine our rules by asking which rules will promote the greatest good or general welfare for everyone. The question no longer deals with which *action* will have the greatest utility, but which *rule*. For many philosophers, this approach squares with practical decision making in everyday life for people working through dilemmas. As we see elsewhere in this book, rule utilitarianism seems to fit fairly well in the media ethics environment, as media practitioners and institutions try to figure out ways to inform, educate, entertain, and influence society while keeping in mind the best interests of society as a whole.

An action, practice, or rule may maximize the sum of good in the world yet be unjust in how it distributes this sum. (Affirmative action may seem unjust to groups not in the minority; excess amounts of free speech may offend the sensitive; etc.) So a less beneficent action, practice, or rule that is more just may be preferable to it. Therefore we must talk about justice and a principle of utility—a double principle that tells us to try to (1) produce the greatest possible balance of good over evil, and (2) distribute this as widely as possible. (We'll say more about "justice" in Chapter 12.)

WILLIAM FRANKENA:
Theory of Obligation

In the media ethics environment, we might do well to discard "pure utilitarianism." We can replace it with William Frankena's (1973) "theory of obligation," recognizing a principle of justice to guide our distribution of good and evil that is independent of any principle about maximizing the balance of good over evil.

This is essentially a mixed rule, or mixed deontological-teleological theory. Frankena says we have no moral obligations, prima facie or otherwise, to do anything that does not, directly or indirectly, connect with what makes somebody's life good or bad, better or worse. The guiding question behind Frankena's theory of obligation can be read into a provocative question raised by William James: "Take any demand, however slight, which any creature, however weak, may make. Ought it not, for its own sole sake, to be satisfied? If not, why not?"

All this leads to principles of beneficence and justice. Frankena's principle of beneficence is a modification of basic utilitarianism. It holds that we ought to do the act, or follow the practice or rule, that will or probably will bring about the greatest possible balance of good over evil in the universe. Frankena adds that this principle, of course, is based on another one that is more basic: that we ought to do good or avoid doing harm. The bottom line of this consequentialistic principle of beneficence is that we are expected to *do* good and not evil, and not just to *want* or will to do so.

According to Frankena, the foundation of the principle of beneficence contains four obligations:

1. One ought not to inflict evil or harm (what is bad).
2. One ought to prevent evil or harm.
3. One ought to remove evil.
4. One ought to do or promote good.

SUMMARY AND CONCLUSIONS

It should not be surprising that theories of consequentialism and utility are controversial. In theory if not in practice, a single-minded focus on consequences could result in an obsession with bringing about the greatest benefit to me, and the heck with everybody else. As one wag put it, "I always try to serve the greatest number. The greatest number is Number One!" Yes, this self-interest would count as a teleological or consequentialistic perspective, but it's morally questionable.

Utilitarianism is particularly problematic when over-simplified as merely "doing the greatest good for the greatest number." It is much more than that, as Bentham, Mill, Frankena, and others have explained, and as the chapter's opening case studies demonstrate. It demands careful consideration of values, stakeholders, principles of justice and beneficence, and higher level notions of happiness.

In practice, consequentialism may expect too much of us. It seems to ask decision makers to be clairvoyant, able to make judgments based on intended consequences. Can we call an action "right" because something good followed? What if it were simply a case of "moral luck?" Who can ever know all the short-term and long-term impacts of any of our actions or choices? We can try to do a sophisticated cost-benefit analysis; experience teaches us what seems to work and what doesn't. But we lack 20/20 foresight, which means that a strictly consequentialistic theory may not suffice.

In theory, the fundamental notion of consequentialism also has come under fire. Media ethicist Clifford Christians (2007), for example, says even a mature version of utilitarianism does not require any broader philosophical or theological justification; "it presumes no foundational or universal propositions" (p. 115). In other words, consequentialism and utilitarianism fall short of the mark by not considering the motives or character traits or moral obligations of decision makers, and by focusing on the individual rather than the wider community.

On the other hand, a lifetime of decision making should count for something. Media professionals recognize when they get satisfactory results from producing a particular kind of entertainment product, or an advertising or public relations campaign, or a print design, or a website, or a series of news stories. They take the lessons learned and apply them to the next set of decisions, the next media products. Sometimes they are surprised when something that worked once doesn't work again under different circumstances. But each episode provides a learning experience. An open-minded, diligent professional who attempts to improve the general welfare of readers, viewers, listeners, and consumers by doing the right thing, with the right motivations, cannot be considered morally bankrupt.

For reasons we have already mentioned (including the commercial and institutional nature of the media and the pragmatism of its practitioners), a sophisticated application of utilitarianism still makes a good deal of sense in the media ethics environment.

As you read the four practical applications and five case studies that follow, ask yourself whether each one displays defensible consequentialistic and utilitarian reasoning. If you decide that it doesn't, be ready to explain why, and open yourself to a search for an alternative decision-making process.

■ ■ ■

CHAPTER VOCABULARY

Note: Definitions are available at this book's companion website.

- act utilitarianism
- Bentham, Jeremy
- deontology
- ethical egoism
- ethical relativism
- Frankena, William
- general utilitarianism

- hedonic calculus
- Mill, John Stuart
- IFF (if-and-only-if)
- reciprocity
- rule utilitarianism
- teleology
- theory of obligation

PRACTICAL APPLICATIONS

1. Have you ever used some version of Bentham's "hedometer" to make a decision in your personal life? How justifiable was it?

2. Return to Freedonia and the two cases from Chapter 1. Focus on the intended and likely consequences of each action the major players in the case are considering. Use Mill's checklist to see which of those actions are justifiable.

3. Do a content analysis of a day's newspaper, or newscast, or your favorite magazine, website, television show, or film. Can you discern which of the gatekeeping decisions were utilitarian and which were not? How can you tell? In your own mind, are any of the decisions unjustifiable?

4. William Frankena's theory of obligation expands utilitarianism to include notions of beneficence and justice, independent of any principle about maximizing the balance of good over evil. How would Frankena's four points apply to the first two case studies in this chapter; that is, how would the student journalists and the script writer meet the theory of obligation?

■ ■ ■

CASE STUDIES

Note: We'll use these case studies for Chapters 10, 11, and 12, to show you that listening to different philosophers whispering in your ear might lead to very different (but ethically justifiable) decisions. Be sure to write your answers to these questions and keep them available when you move to the chapters that follow.

CASE 10.1 **Journalism: How (and Whether) to Cover a Prank**

You are campus editor of the student newspaper at Freedonia University. You're a junior who hopes that the student body will elect you as editor next year, since the job comes with paid tuition and other perks.

Your roommate is a member of Gabba Gabba Hey, a greek social organization. Many of your friends—including the person you are dating—also are members.

Late one night, your roommate arrives in your residence hall a little drunk and shaken up. Your roomie tells you that Gabba Gabba Hey members just stole a horse from the university's stable and took it into the dean's office. The prank backfired when the horse had a heart attack and died there, and Gabba Gabba Hey members left the carcass in the dean's office as they fled. They swore themselves to secrecy.

Your roommate wakes up the next morning and, after you start asking questions in your reporter mode, realizes that you know what happened. Your roomie tells you that you will lose your many Gabba Gabba Hey friends if the story ends up in the paper. A few hours later, the person you are dating makes you the same promise—and promises that you'll have Gabba Gabba Hey's support when you run for editor in the spring if the story isn't printed. Having that organization's active support would be enough for you to be elected to the job.

As you walk around campus the next day, you notice that no one is talking about the incident. You find an excuse to walk past the dean's office and find nothing out of the ordinary. You are not surprised, given that the school works hard to keep its image polished by sweeping bad news under the rug. It's as if it never happened. No police report has been filed.

It just so happens that the dean once was a professor in Freedonia University's communication department. It's a small department, and the dean taught both journalism and public relations classes. You've had two classes with the dean, who recruited you to Freedonia University. In a brief conversation in the dean's office (which suspiciously smells like disinfectant, by the way), the poker-faced dean tells you on the record that the university will have no comment. Off the record, the dean tells you that even asking questions about something like this (which of course didn't happen) could really hurt the university's fundraising efforts, which could lead to job cuts for staff and higher tuitions for students.

Deadline for the homecoming edition of the paper is three days away. It's the most important edition of the semester, because it's seen by alumni who include editors who might one day hire you.

➤ **What do you do?**

Questions

- **What's your problem?**
- **Why not follow the rules?**
- **Who wins, who loses?**
- **What's it worth?**
- **Who's whispering in your ear?**
- What else do you need to know?

Thinking it Through

1. Is this an ethical issue? Why or why not?

2. Make a list of the people (including yourself) and groups who are stakeholders in your decision.

3. Organize that list in order of who you consider most important to least important.

4. Which sets of stakeholders are most in conflict with one another? How, if at all, can these conflicts be reconciled?

5. What moral and pragmatic arguments can you make for either pursuing or not pursuing the story?

6. Take a sheet of paper and create a "utilitarian calculus"—a chart to help you balance offsetting factors that might help you decide which choice would do the most aggregate good or the least harm.

7. Can you make a decision that would fulfill Frankena's theory of obligation?

8. The bottom-line question: Would you pursue the story?

    A. If you choose not to pursue the story:

    a. Why? Who wins and who loses? What in the utilitarian argument helped sway your decision?

    b. What happens a few months from now, if the story ends up being talked about on campus? (As a quote ascribed to Benjamin Franklin goes: "Three can keep a secret if two of them are dead.") What if it came out that you knew about the prank but didn't write anything? How might the utilitarian argument change?

    B. If you choose to print the story:

    a. Why? Who wins and who loses? What in the utilitarian argument helped sway your decision?

    b. What happens if Gabba Gabba Hey and the person you are dating keep their promise to shun you?

    c. How do you answer the issues raised by the dean and Gabba Gabba Hey folks? Which utilitarian argument works best?

CASE 10.2 **New Media: Do You Take the Ads?**

As the head of www.freedonialive.com, you make most of your money by selling ads on your site to local companies. About a fifth of the key ad positions—at the top of the page and on the far right side of the page, adjacent to the site's content—go unsold to local advertisers each month. You fill the unsold space with promos for your website and free ads for worthwhile nonprofit organizations.

Now, a national company has offered to buy whatever unsold space you have each month and fill it with its advertising.

The good news: Your site makes money it would not have made otherwise, even when selling the leftover space to the national company at a discount. The deal is flexible, meaning you can still sell those unsold spots to local advertisers and the national company takes what is left.

The bad news: Some of the banner ads promise "free" products for customers, but the ads do not disclose information about what the customer must do to qualify for the "free" offer. Other ads look like Windows warning messages, and people who think they're closing the box by clicking "OK" actually go to the advertiser's website.

Also, some of the ads down the side of the page, next to your content, are designed to resemble news content. Those ads' links read like headlines but go to "display" ads or ads that look like news stories but actually are selling a product. An example is an ad with the heading "For Your Health" with links such as "Four secrets to a tighter tummy" and "Doctor announces new way to lose weight" that go to a site promoting a diet drug.

➤ Do you take the offer to sell your site's leftover ad space?

Questions
- What's your problem?
- Why not follow the rules?
- Who wins, who loses?
- What's it worth?
- Who's whispering in your ear?
- What else do you need to know?

Thinking it Through
1. Is this an ethical issue? Why or why not?
2. Make a list of the people (including yourself) and groups who are stakeholders in your decision.
3. Organize that list in order of who you consider most important to least important.

4. Which sets of stakeholders are most in conflict with one another? How, if at all, can these conflicts be reconciled?

5. What's the relationship between the "means" and the "ends" in your decision?

6. Get a sheet of paper and create a "utilitarian calculus"—a chart to help you balance offsetting factors that might help you decide which choice would do the most aggregate good or the least harm.

7. Do this "utilitarian calculus" for both types of ads. To what extent, if any, do you come up with different answers for the different types of ads?

8. What responsibility, if any, does a company have for the content of the advertising it accepts?

9. Can you make a decision that would fulfill Frankena's theory of obligation?

10. Yes or no: Do you take the ads? Justify your decision.

■ ■ ■

CASE 10.3 **Public Relations: The Big Weekend**

You are on the in-house public relations staff of the Freedonia Hospital Foundation, an organization whose aim is to raise money and awareness for the nonprofit Freedonia Hospital, which has a national reputation for its breast cancer treatment. Among the staff's responsibilities is to raise awareness about the hospital and develop programs that help raise money for the hospital. This occurs through programs that focus on research, cancer risk and education, early detection, rallying survivors and their families, and building support communities for friends, families, and others affected by cancer.

The foundation's big focus is what it calls "The Big Weekend," which includes a Friday night banquet with about 500 participants and a Saturday morning "The First Lady's 'Give Cancer a Beatdown'" walk that draws thousands of people. The advertising and literature for both events note that proceeds will go toward patient care and research.

The banquet highlight is an appearance from a high-profile celebrity who has survived cancer or lost a loved one. Tickets range from $150 per person to $3,000 per sponsored table, and it draws key community leaders, politicians, major donors, and potential major donors. Nearly 100 seats are given at no cost to cancer survivors and families whose lives were affected by cancer.

The "Give Cancer a Beatdown" walk costs $20 per participant, and groups (such as churches, families, and businesses) are encouraged to team up. The governor's wife, who lost her mother and a sister to breast cancer, is the walk's honorary leader. Nearly 11,000 people participate in the Saturday morning walk.

Your office works to make sure local news media cover the events, and you have partnered with one of the local television stations for special access to the celebrity in exchange for free promotional commercials on the station and the station's logo on the back of the "Beatdown" T-shirt given to every walker. Other news media also cover the event, with photos of the walk and interviews with walkers who carry pictures of loved ones as they talk about helping raise money and awareness for breast cancer.

What is not well known is that The Big Weekend has little net proceeds after expenses. After paying for the banquet (including the famous speaker's $50,000 fee), the meals, buying shirts, hiring police, paying for portable toilets, and other expenses, the events have a net profit of about $20,000 from revenue of $300,000.

All told, that's about 7 percent of the revenue going toward research and patient services—actually less considering overhead spending such as the PR department's salaries, etc., which is not factored into the weekend's finances. The event falls short of Better Business Bureau guidelines that a nonprofit's fundraising costs should be less than 35 percent of related contributions.

It is legal, because Freedonia Hospital Foundation files accurate annual financial accounts with the government each year. It does not break out revenue/profits from The Big Weekend, because it is not required to. As a result, very few people outside the Foundation know the bottom financial line on the event.

At a first-of-the-year staff meeting of top Foundation officials (including your boss but many others not in the PR department), conversation runs hot and heavy about the need for The Big Weekend. Some say the value of the weekend—for awareness, building community, and laying the groundwork for future donations—is worth the small financial payback. Others say the weekend is a financial drain that could become a PR headache if the true finance picture became public.

➤ **The PR department is told to write a report with recommendations about The Big Weekend. Since you were at the meeting with your boss, the task of the first draft falls to you. What do you decide?**

Questions
*   **What's your problem?**
*   **Why not follow the rules?**
*   **Who wins, who loses?**
*   **What's it worth?**
*   **Who's whispering in your ear?**
*   What else do you need to know?

Thinking it Through
1. Is this an ethical issue? Why or why not?
2. List the people (including yourself) and groups who are stakeholders.
3. Organize that list in order of who you consider most important to least important.
4. Which sets of values are most in conflict with one another? How, if at all, can these conflicts be reconciled?
5. What moral and pragmatic arguments can you make for:
    A. continuing with the status quo?
    B. ending "The Big Weekend?"
    C. doing something else?
6. Take a sheet of paper and create a "utilitarian calculus"—a chart to help you balance offsetting factors to help you decide which choice would do the most aggregate good or the least harm.
7. Can you make a decision that would fulfill Frankena's theory of obligation?
8. The bottom-line question: What do you recommend about The Big Weekend? Should it stay? Be eliminated? Or changed? How and why?

CASE 10.4 **Advertising: The Nathan Freedonia Ad**

Your advertising agency's biggest client is Nathan Freedonia, whose chain of "Unpainted Freedonia" furniture stores blanket your area with stores—and television commercials. Nathan Freedonia stars in his ads and has become a celebrity. You wrote the tagline to his ads—"And if you can find lower prices anywhere, my name ain't Nathan Freedonia"—that made him famous, and he has been loyal to you and your ad firm.

Tragedy struck his family a few weeks ago, when a car crash slightly injured him but killed his son, Nathan Jr.

The other driver, a teenager, was sending a text message instead of paying attention to the road, which led to the crash.

A week after the funeral, Nathan, still showing the scars from the crash, comes to see you. He wants your agency to produce an anti-texting TV commercial aimed at teenagers.

He wants the ad to show a head-on collision caused by a texting driver, including the blood spilled by the dead driver and a dead toddler impaled in the crash. He wants to appear at the end of the spot—with his surviving children, and his new wife, and say: "If texting while driving isn't stupid and deadly, then my name ain't Nathan Freedonia."

He tells you not to worry whether the TV station in your market will air such a graphic ad, because his best friend is general manager and he'll pull all his advertising from the station if it doesn't run the ad.

"All you've got to do is make it bloody," he said. "Make it real. I don't care if anybody doesn't like it. We've got to scare them."

A few days later, Florence Freedonia, the ex-wife of Nathan Freedonia and mother of the late Nathan Jr., comes to your office. Her eyes are still red from crying as she begs you not to make the ad. "My ex-husband's just too impulsive and angry," she says, saying his anger problem was why she felt compelled to leave him. "I think I'll die inside every time I see that ad on TV. You and he can't do this to me."

➤ You have a meeting scheduled in a few days with Nathan Freedonia to discuss the ad. What do you do?

Questions
- What's your problem?
- Why not follow the rules?
- Who wins, who loses?
- What's it worth?
- Who's whispering in your ear?
- What else do you need to know?

Thinking it Through

1.   Is this an ethical issue? Why or why not?

2.   What's the relationship between the "means" and the "ends" in your decision?

3.   Get a sheet of paper and create a "utilitarian calculus"—a chart to help you balance offsetting factors that might help you decide which choice would do the most aggregate good or the least harm.

4.   What responsibility, if any, does your company have for the assignments it accepts? Can you balance accepting an assignment even if you don't agree with its approach?

5.   Can you make a decision that would fulfill Frankena's theory of obligation?

6.   Yes or no: Do you make the ad?

■ ■ ■

CASE 10.5 **Entertainment: The VIM Kids**

You are a movie executive who has just received the option to make a movie based on an underground comic book called *The VIM Kids*. VIM stands for "Vengeance Is Mine," and the kids are an 11-year-old set of twins, a boy and girl, who seek vengeance after they see a gang leader randomly kill their parents. The kids become heavily armed martial arts experts who, with the help of an older uncle who serves as a mentor, find themselves in all manner of fights with bad guys in search of their parents' killer.

The movie's story treatment includes scenes where the girl stabs a man who won't provide information about their parents' killer, the boy decapitates a thug who threatens him, the girl fights off a would-be rapist, and the boy gets an eyeful of topless dancers while sneaking into a club to find a bad guy. After the final bloody scene in which the kids shoot (at point-blank range) their parents' killer, they both smoke victory cigars they find in his humidor. And throughout the movie, both kids use foul language that we won't repeat here. The movie would be rated R, so children under 17 would not be admitted without a parent or guardian.

The comic book has received little national attention but sells well, and its publisher thinks it's precisely because the VIM Kids are so young. While the book isn't sold to minors, many of the readers are young teens and pre-teens who live vicariously through the kids.

The story is compelling; young actors work cheap; and the possibilities of sequels are endless.

➤ **Is this a movie you decide to make?**

Questions
- **What's your problem?**
- **Why not follow the rules?**
- **Who wins, who loses?**
- **What's it worth?**
- **Who's whispering in your ear?**
- What else do you need to know?

Thinking it Through
1. Is this an ethical issue? Why or why not?
2. What's the relationship between the "means" and the "ends" in your decision?
3. Get a sheet of paper and create a "utilitarian calculus"—a chart to help you balance offsetting factors that might help you decide which choice would do the most aggregate good or the least harm.

4. What would utilitarian theorists say about a movie whose main actors would not be allowed to see it without parental permission? How can a movie maker balance the needs of the story with the needs of youngsters who work as actors? What might what we know about the later lives of child stars mean in our calculations?

5. Can you make a decision that would fulfill Frankena's theory of obligation?

6. Compare and contrast this case with Case 10-B, "Marketing Your Movie." How might the utilitarian calculus be the same and different?

7. Yes or no: Do you make the movie?

CHAPTER 11

Deontology and Moral Rules

INTRODUCTION

THIS **CHAPTER** picks up where Chapter 10 leaves off. Recognizing limitations of making decisions based upon the potential conse- quences, we now turn to a major alternative approach. Three major deontologists help us explore the territory: W.D. Ross, Bernard Gert, and Immanuel Kant.

Ross and Kant provide different spins on the same sort of decision making. Ross, sometimes known as a "soft" or "mixed-rule deontol- ogist," would have us carefully sort through several conflicting duties, with an eye on their consequences, and choose the most defensible answer. Kant, the "strict deontologist," would have us make absolutist and universalized decisions that have little to do with consequences. Gert's version of moral rules bridges the two perspectives.

We will revisit the two case studies presented at the start of Chapter 10, this time assessing the decision making in deontological rather than teleological or consequential terms. In doing so, we will find ourselves raising questions about media practitioners' notions of duty and obligation. We will find them asking "to whom do we *owe* something," or "what *ought* we do, all things considered?" Terms such as right and wrong, good and bad, become part of the discourse. Means and ends are downplayed.

The previous chapter noted that modern media institutions and practitioners tend toward consequentialistic moral reasoning. This chapter considers why a duty-based thought process has merit, but why it is challenging to the 24/7, competitive, bottom- line oriented media. When we consider media codes of ethics and instances when practitioners face public accountability, we find plenty of examples of deontological

> **This chapter:**
>
> - **further distinguishes deontology from consequentialism**
> - **considers contributions from three deontologists**
> - **shows how media make duty-based decisions**
> - **offers practical applications for further study**
> - **challenges you to apply deontology to five case studies.**

reasoning . . . although it is often tempered by concern over the consequences of their choices.

FROM TELEOLOGY TO DEONTOLOGY

You'll recall that teleological theories deal with the consequences of acts. Mill, Bentham, and others say that the act itself is less important than the consequences of the act. There is a great deal of concern over means and ends. From the Greek, we get the terms "teleo," meaning goals or aims, and "logos," meaning logic; hence, teleology is the logical analysis of our goals or aims. With this in mind, it is no surprise to find teleological arguments based on such concepts as good, bad, desirable, undesirable, better than, best, the greatest good, etc. Looked at in another way, Mill and Bentham are teleologists because, to them, an act of morality is a function of its consequences.

Deontological theories, on the other hand, concentrate on the motives or intentions behind the acts. Again, from the Greek, the word "deontos" refers to duty or obligation, meaning that deontology is the logical analysis of our duties or obligations. Kant, Ross, Gert, and others have devoted their intellectual lives to working out these notions of general or role-related duties and obligations. Deontological discussions employ these terms, along with fundamental notions of right or wrong.

W.D. ROSS:
Mixed-Rule Deontology

Let's consider the nature of duties. What are some of the duties you have as a student, duties that college students share? Off the top of your head, you might list:

- Do my assignments.
- Go to class.
- Pay tuition.
- Get my money's worth from class.
- Absorb knowledge for knowledge's sake.
- Do my work honestly.
- Prepare for a career.
- Etc.

Meanwhile, what are some of your professors' duties? Their list might include:

- Be prepared.
- Show up for every class.
- Engage students in learning.
- Treat students with respect.
- Conduct research to create new knowledge.

- Be lifelong learners.
- Do professional and community service.
- Etc.

These are examples of "role-related" or "particularist" duties. They are not universal obligations everyone is expected to meet. Deontologists are interested in both role-related and universal duties. However, to introduce the basic notion of duty, it is sometimes easier to narrow our search, to think in terms of "particular" and personal duties.

Your intuition may have told you these lists—stated in positive rather than negative terms—consist of things students and professors *ought* to do. There is no master list, passed down by a moral arbiter from on high, demanding that these duties be fulfilled. If you agree that these duties are pertinent, can you rank order each list? Which duty filters to the top of the list? Which duty ranks last? And what's the connection between obeying these duties and whatever happens to the various stakeholders?

This is generally what British philosopher William David Ross (1877–1971) did in answering "What does it mean to be a good person?" and "What makes right acts right?" He presented his answers in terms of physiological and social/psychological needs. These needs are not unique to each individual, he said, but are shared. (Again, while our lists for students and professors are role-related, it's possible to follow Ross and generate a list that would apply to everyone.) Using our intuition and life experiences, we can extrapolate from human nature a list of duties to conclude that all else being equal, we need to do certain things.

It may seem that we're putting the cart ahead of the horse by introducing the twentieth-century Ross before discussing the more famous eighteenth-century Immanuel Kant (1724–1804). There are two reasons why: First, Ross neatly bridges consequentialism and deontology—a bridge we hinted at when introducing William Frankena's theory of obligation at the end of Chapter 10. Second, frankly, is that for most students Ross seems to have a higher GOR ("grip on reality") than Kant. His intuitive arguments about how we sift through competing obligations sounds more like real-world decision making than Kant's rather rigid philosophy. Ross offered a simple list of "common sense" prima facie duties/rules or "conditional" duties that we should generally follow, which fit well in the pragmatic media ethics environment.

The title of his major book, *The Right and the Good*, shows that Ross (1930) is concerned about the connection between duty and consequence. "Right" actions are duty driven, undertaken after careful reflection and application of good intuition; "good" is a consequentialist question "rooted in (often unforeseeable) outcomes" (Meyers, 2003, p. 84). Ross was a pluralist, maintaining there can be more than one way to define and to choose what is right and what is good (Regan, 2001). And, because people are not omniscient, we cannot know all possible outcomes so, unfortunately, not all right actions result in good acts. Intuition, experience, and maturity should help us recognize what's right and what's good in the long run.

"What Makes Right Acts Right?"

Ross begins his discussion by noting the type of moral conflict we face when we have promised to do something such as encountering an accident on our way to a job interview. We may be in a position to do some good if we stop to aid the victim, but doing so will mean we'll miss our appointment.

Let's compare and contrast how Ross and utilitarians would have us act in such a situation.

If you are an act utilitarian, you'd find it perfectly OK to break a promise if better consequences would develop from an alternative act. A deontologist or rule utilitarian, however, would say that "all else being equal, I should keep a promise." Unfortunately, all else is seldom equal, so people like Ross make us ponder the conflicting duties and obligations.

The teleologist might say you should help an accident victim and miss the interview because doing so brings a better result/end. Ross, the deontologist, would have us consider two moral duties: the duty to help the accident victim and the duty to keep our promise. But if these duties conflict when life is at stake, the duty to help ranks higher than our promise to be on time. Deontologists would say it is more *morally incumbent* upon us to stop and help.

Prima Facie and Actual Duties

Immanuel Kant advocated pure rules, based on "duties of perfect obligation" to fulfill our promises, pay our debts, tell the truth, etc. We are expected to follow these rules no matter what. Ross, on the other hand, asks us to consider both prima facie and actual duties, which are different from Kant's pure rules.

Ross said that circumstances in a given case help us decide which prima facie duties are morally incumbent or obligatory (Cahn & Markie, 2002). In other words, they make intuitive sense "at first glance" or "on their face." Ross says these rules are general, deeply rooted, and readily apparent. Several prima facie duties may be relevant in any situation.

Actual duties, or "duties proper," on the other hand, emerge from specific situations. Once we have calculated which prima facie duties pertain to the situation, we determine which duty trumps the others and should be performed; that is, which duty has become morally incumbent.

To apply these ideas, Ross would say that everything else being equal and there being no other moral considerations, we have a moral duty to keep our promises (or other prima facie duties) and, if possible, we have a moral duty to help. It is inherently right to keep promises, and it's inherently right to be beneficent. We must decide which is the duty proper—which duty will outweigh other prima facie duties. (It's always interesting to do brain games with this theory: For example, what if our lunch appointment is very important, and there are several people with cell phones and first aid kits attending the accident victim?)

Returning to the first case study in the text of Chapter 10, the student journalists had a moral duty to tell the truth to all stakeholders as well as a moral duty to expose a dangerous problem at their university. Deceiving the nurse violated the truth duty. Was the exposure of danger to students more morally incumbent than not deceiving? What is the duty proper? Ross would say this is where we must do our own hard thinking.

In short, there is a prima facie (conditional) duty to do a certain act if no conflicting act carries a greater duty. An actual duty (duty proper) to do a certain act emerges once we have rationally assessed the relevant prima facie duties. Ross's way out of the problem of how to prioritize these duties is to suggest that an act is morally obligatory if and only if there is a prima facie duty to perform that act and there is no other prima facie duty more *incumbent* than the prima facie duty to do the act.

(One other type of duty discussed by Ross and others is known as **supererogatory** behavior: acts that are good but not necessary. Such acts are over and above our minimal duties. Examples would include helping a handicapped person across the street, or going out of our way to be nice to someone with no expectation of a payoff. For journalists, it would be supererogatory for reporters to call their sources after a story appeared on the air or in print, and ask sources if they thought they were treated fairly.)

Ross then explained how we identify and act upon our obligations. He outlined seven prima facie duties. In no particular order of importance, and with comments about how they might be applied to the media ethics environment, they are:

1. **Non-maleficence**. Don't purposefully do harm—even to ourselves, let alone to the rest of society—or we'll destroy community. It's not "do no harm," but "do not cause harm on purpose." In the media environment, we "minimize harm" as we gather and report information that citizens need, although it may offend some. As we persuade or entertain, we strike a balance between the needs and interests of receptive and non-receptive/vulnerable audiences.
2. **Fidelity**. Keep all our explicit and implicit promises, and don't let down people who count on us. Some promises are imposed upon us, some are taken on as formal contracts, and others are assumed. What promises have we made to ourselves, to our employers, to our publics, etc., when we take a job or task? In the media environment, what have we tacitly promised our audiences, our colleagues, our clients, our sources, or other stakeholders? What efforts are we making to keep those promises?
3. **Reparation**. Pay back debts to make up for previous wrongs. News media, advertisers, and public relations practitioners sometimes publish retractions, corrective advertising, or clarifications of previously published releases. Ideally, Ross says, one would not have made the error or caused the harm in the first place; that is, non-maleficence precedes reparation. But if we err, we should be transparent and accountable, and find a way to make up for it as best we can.

4. **Justice**. Ensure an equitable distribution of reward, pleasure, and other good insofar as it is within our power. Distribute it on the basis of merit and need, not tit for tat. People should be treated as ends, not as means to ends. When doing investigative journalism, take care to "comfort the afflicted and afflict the comfortable." When making deals with sources, subjects, or clients, be fair-minded for all stakeholders. All media—including advertising, PR, and entertainment media—should be sensitive to the needs of vulnerable populations and not pander to the elites.

5. **Self-improvement**. Improve our own virtue, intelligence, and skills. We should try to be as professional as possible: follow the literature and issues in our fields; be active in professional organizations; learn new skills and to seek better ways to do our jobs.

6. **Gratitude**. Be good to people who have been good to us. Treat our sources, subjects, clients, colleagues, and mentors with the respect they deserve, and try not to use any of them solely as means to an end.

7. **Beneficence**. Strive to make the world a better place. All of us, every day, should be motivated to help others improve their lot in life. We are not just doing a job; we are entrusted with the power to help society self-govern, to increase everyone's welfare insofar as we can.

Scholar Jonathan Dancy explained why Ross's list may trouble people who want a careful ranking or prioritization of the prima facie duties. People may want to know in advance which duty always trumps another duty, he wrote,

> But no such ranking fits the facts. The plain fact is that sometimes one ought to keep one's promises even at an overall cost to others, and sometimes the cost of keeping one's promise means that it would be better to break it, for once. Ross would say that this sort of thing is just a feature of our moral predicament.
>
> (Dancy, 1991, p. 221)

Dancy said a neat and orderly world would help us rank our different prima facie duties once and for all. But they shouldn't be rank ordered; "there is just a shapeless list of them, which is no more than a list of the things that make a moral difference," Dancy concluded (p. 221). We're left with no choice other than having to think our way through them, relying on intuition and logic. And in the process we do not abandon any of those principles or duties; we merely put them in perspective. (A careful reading of Ross suggests that he would put non-maleficence and promise-keeping at the top of the heap—all else being equal, they are the most important to fulfill.)

If W.D. Ross Were Sharing Your Office

Ross would insist that you make ethical decisions by thinking about a set of intuitively obvious prima facie moral duties. If you are considering violating a law or custom, ask yourself if you would be willing to universalize the violation: Violate only the bad laws or customs that you think everyone else in similar circumstances would be justified in violating.

When faced with an ethical dilemma, if you were to follow the model of Ross you would:

1. compile relevant facts and reasons for following alternative actions
2. ask which considerations have the most weight in a prima facie sense
3. realize that if you are violating a prima facie duty when you follow through on a proposed action, you should justify that violation by appealing to other prima facie duties.

When doing the calculation, Ross would remind ethically conscientious people that the more significant the duty they are violating, the more duties they must have on the other side of the equation.

Mixed Duties in the Media Ethics Environment

Figuring out how to rank order or apply duties is a daily occurrence in the media ethics environment. Consider what the PRSA and the SPJ ask their members to do when making moral choices.

The PRSA's Code of Ethics describes six affirmative moral obligations for "responsible advocacy":

1. Advocacy
2. Honesty
3. Expertise
4. Independence
5. Loyalty
6. Fairness

The code describes each in some detail. But even at first glance, each is a prima facie duty and must be put in context with the others. For instance: If PR practitioners are expected to advocate for a client or cause and also are expected to be honest, must they fully disclose everything they know about their client's or cause's strengths and weaknesses? Does advocacy trump honesty? And what about fairness? Can they be honest and fair and faithful advocates? Meanwhile, how do the PR counselors prioritize their duties to be both independent and loyal? (Looking back at the case studies in Chapter 1, you may recall the public relations person's conflicting loyalties, and the duty to be an autonomous decision maker while recognizing the moral rights of the employer and other stakeholders.)

The PRSA code provides no answers. It merely asks practitioners to be aware of the compelling duties and obligations; it does not do their thinking for them.

The same may be said of the SPJ code. You'll recall that it is framed by four "principles and standards of practice" (a.k.a. prima facie duties):

1. Seek truth and report it.
2. Minimize harm.
3. Act independently.
4. Be accountable.

How do we turn these prima facie duties into actual duties? The student journalists in Case 10-A ("The Temptation to Deceive") wanted to seek out and report significant truths about their communities. They recognized that reporting administrative recklessness would create discomfort for some stakeholders—pitting SPJ duty No. 1 against duty No. 2. We've already seen that there's a dilemma built into the decision concerning whether it is OK to deceive in order to tell the truth; that, too, is a truth vs. harm issue. And we know that journalists try to avoid conflicts of interest or unnecessary "deals" with sources (duty No. 3); but how do they hold themselves accountable (duty No. 4) if they use unnamed sources, or if their "tipsters" might be harmed if their identities were revealed?

Media ethicist Kevin Stoker (2003) challenged journalists to draw from Ross in clarifying their duties "to society individually and collectively, the truth, themselves, and their news organizations." Stoker's Rossian model emphasizes the importance of retrospection and experience. Comparing the model to a compass, Stoker said journalists could use their own experience and intuition as cognitive landmarks to orient their moral compass to the terrain. In Rossian terms, the student journalists in Case 10-A had to rank the duties of non-maleficence, fidelity, justice, self-improvement, and beneficence. That's pretty rough moral terrain; it requires a good compass.

A different clash of duties occurs in Case 10-B ("Marketing Your Movie"). As a scriptwriter you would seem to have the prima facie duty of offering a film that is worth the price of admission: fidelity to the consumer. The same should hold true for the producer. Neither of you should set out to rip off your audiences: non-maleficence. In fact, both of you have an obligation to entertain without causing harm: non-maleficence, fidelity, and perhaps justice. But you find yourself facing other duties: fidelity and gratitude to your producer, without whom your script will never become a movie. As you debate whether to convert your tame PG film into a spicier PG-13, yet still market it to children, the duty of self-improvement enters the equation. How do you prioritize these? Which prima facie duties become the morally incumbent actual duties?

These are not no-brainers. They demand clear-headed and mature application of moral thinking. In Rossian terms, they demand heavy reliance upon the special human faculty known as ethical intuition, a form of "mental maturity" that is refined and honed throughout personal and professional lives.

Ross says ethical intuition is a sixth sense. Just as with our eyes we see color, with our tongues we taste peppermint, with our ears we hear a symphony, with our nose we smell a rose—similarly with our intuition, we sense that some things are wrong and other things are right. Our ethical intuition that "X" is prima facie right does not make "X" right; rather, it is via ethical intuition that we come to know that "X" is prima facie right, Ross has written. He adds that, so far as we know, humans are the only species with the singular faculties of experience and reason, and these alone are sources of knowledge . . . a sense of right and wrong.

A relativist might challenge this by saying that intuition differs from person to person, so who determines which intuition is on target and which isn't? Ross would reply that personal differences in intuition may be a matter of "refinement"—different people smell, taste, appreciate music differently after experiencing them. With an intuitionist theory it is impossible to have 20/20 foresight. Because of the confounding and unknown variables and unknowns, we cannot precisely predict the outcome of our behaviors. But we make the best guesses, based on our clearest thinking and our refined intuition.

While moral uncertainty bothers people who seek clear and absolute decision-making processes, others find real strengths in the Rossian approach. Christopher Meyers (2003) praises Ross for providing a "universalist contextualism": the abstract prima facie duties are universal, and the actual duties contextual. This, Meyers says, accurately reflects how humans engage in moral reasoning: We "grasp universal moral truth at the abstract level, but our moral decision making in actual cases is fraught with uncertainty and ambiguity" (p. 93). In addition, if we are sincerely trying to make good decisions, if our motives are correct and we try to get as much relevant information as possible before acting, we are hardly blameworthy if our "right action" fails to produce a good result.

BERNARD GERT:
A Modern Approach to Moral Rules

Dartmouth philosophy professor Bernard Gert (born 1934) cut across several philosophic boundaries to develop an alternative approach to deontological ethics. He has been characterized as "Kant with consequences, as Mill with publicity, and as Ross with a theory" (Gert, 1998, p. xi). He draws on Aristotle, Hobbes, and others in developing a complex theory that has a good deal of practical application.

In *The Moral Rules* and other books, Gert focuses on the importance of avoiding evil, and on rationality and impartiality. He believes the effects of evil deserve more attention because they are more significant than the effects of good deeds. He defines morality as an "informal public system" that applies to all rational people. Everyone ought to rationally understand and obey moral rules, ideals, and virtues while seeking to lessen evil or harm (1998, p. 13). He also believes that it is not always irrational to behave immorally, or to violate a moral rule.

Moral rules are embedded within the broader moral system and should be obeyed impartially, Gert says. By "impartially," he means the rules make no reference to person, group, place, or time, with regard to whom, when, and where the rules should be obeyed. That means the rules place no restriction on those who are to obey them. The process demands intuition, which harkens back to Ross.

Gert maintains that moral rules are discovered, not invented; they do not depend upon anyone's will or decision. Such moral rules require us not to cause evil for anyone; they do not require us to promote the general good.

He notes that while morality cannot provide unique answers to every moral question, it limits the range of morally acceptable opinions. Gert believes that some moral disagreements will never be resolved to everyone's satisfaction, but following his list of moral rules will benefit all stakeholders.

Gert's Ten Moral Rules are:

1. Do not cause death (permanent loss of consciousness).
2. Do not cause pain (or other mental suffering).
3. Do not cause loss of ability (mental, physical, or volitional).
4. Do not cause loss of freedom (to act or to be acted upon).
5. Do not cause loss of pleasure (or opportunities for pleasure).
6. Do not deceive.
7. Keep your promises.
8. Do not cheat.
9. Obey the law.
10. Do your duty (universal or particular/role-specific duties).

Gert says each rule should be obeyed by fully informed, impartial, rational people—unless those same people can publicly advocate violating them. He calls this process "the moral attitude" (Gert, 1998, p. 216). An action would be irrational IFF it increases a person's risk of being harmed by an "evil" on his list, the person knows of the risk, and the person committing the action does not have a good explanation for his or her action (Sinnott-Armstrong, 2001). It might be OK to violate a rule IFF after careful analysis you are convinced that other people, in similar situations, also would be permitted to violate the rule. But both you and they would have to be rational and insightful, able to anticipate the long-term consequences of any rulebreaking.

Note that the first five of Gert's moral rules deal with evils that rational people try to avoid. He argues that acts are evil IFF they significantly increase people's chances of encountering one of those variables (death, pain, disablement, loss of freedom, or loss of pleasure). These are not occupation-specific prohibitions, although the first half of his list is particularly relevant to the medical profession (Gert spent many years teaching at Dartmouth's medical school).

The second five rules apply more directly to the media ethics environment: truth telling, promise keeping, honesty, obedience to the law, and, in general, meeting the expectations of your trade. These ideas are nothing new. While not stated as rules *per se*, they have certainly been advocated in most media ethics codes and media criticism literature. And, as we have been doing ethics in several of the previous chapters, we recognize the problems arising when we violate a commonsense rule.

For instance: You're working in the communications field, and you want to live up to your obligations (Gert's rule No. 10). You've promised to meet a deadline (Gert's rule No. 7), and you don't want to do any harm (Gert's rule No. 2, and perhaps Nos. 3, 4, or 5). But the deadline is pressing in on you, and you consider whether to cut corners or cheat (violating Gert's rule No. 8). You may be tempted to plagiarize or violate copyright (violating Gert's rule No. 9). To apply Gert, you may tell yourself that you won't cause any real harm by yielding to temptation. However, would you want your colleagues (or anyone else) to think that they also could break these rules? Might the violations lead to more and more disruption in the media/societal environment—in ways you can only begin to imagine? Could all stakeholders—and any fully informed, rational, impartial witnesses—tolerate violation of any of these rules? It is unlikely. You probably would conclude that you are morally obligated to meet your deadline without cutting corners. You might ask your boss or client for an extension. And you may be more careful the next time you accept an unrealistic deadline.

On the other hand (why are there so many hands in philosophy?) if you review the situation very carefully you might conclude that if you don't violate one of the rules (perhaps Gert's rules Nos. 8 or 9), your ornery boss might cause you severe pain and mental suffering (violating Gert Nos. 2 and 3), or fire you (violating Gert Nos. 4 and 5). At that point you must decide whether violating a moral rule is rational, and whether other stakeholders and impartial witnesses would justify doing so.

Gert's books and lectures carefully spell out the rational process people should use when considering how to apply the rules. He has published widely in bioethics, the human genome project, business ethics, engineering ethics, and the ethics of scientific research. It takes only a small leap to see how his ideas can be applied across the media environment, whether to inform, entertain, or persuade.

If Bernard Gert Were Sharing Your Office

He would tell you to bear in mind his list of ten moral rules as you carefully:

1. gather all the morally relevant information you can before making a moral evaluation about whether to violate any of the rules; among other questions, you might ask:
   A. what evils or harms are you likely to cause, avoid, or prevent?
   B. what are the desires and beliefs of the person toward whom the rule is being violated?
   C. what is the power relationship between you and the other person?
   D. what goods or benefits are being promoted by the violation?
   E. why are you considering violating the rule?
   F. are there any good alternatives to violating the rule?
2. consider what would happen if other rational people in similar circumstances knew they could violate the same moral rule or rules (Gert, 2004).

IMMANUEL KANT:
The "Strict" Deontologist

German philosopher Immanuel Kant (1724–1804) lived a century before John Stuart Mill (1806–1873) and two centuries before W.D. Ross (1877–1971). Many consider him the most influential philosopher since Aristotle; he is certainly among the most provocative. Kant's work on ethics, including *Fundamental Principles of the Metaphysics of Morals* (1785), emphasized the irrelevance of the consequences of our actions and focused instead on the duties/rules inherent in acting morally. To Kant, an action is right when it is in accordance with a rule that satisfies a principle he calls the "categorical imperative," or the "moral law." But first . . .

The Autonomous Use of Rules

There are rules, and then there are rules. And there are different ways to understand and abide by those rules. At one level, we obey a general rule or principle when we have a basic understanding of it and can apply it in a specific case. For instance, once we understand how multiplication tables work, we can then apply them to new problems. Kant wants us to go further, particularly in regard to moral rules. He would say we're not moral unless we make *autonomous* use of ethical rules . . . unless we understand, take ownership of, and operate upon those rules from a sense of self-duty. Memorizing and merely following the Ten Commandments doesn't make us moral or ethical. Understanding the Ten Commandments and applying them autonomously, however, is altogether different. One is a matter of accepting rules imposed upon us by an authority, the other a matter of exercising what Kant called "pure reason" to generate and abide by self-imposed rules.

To sum up this point, Kant tells us that the morality of an action is based on:

1. autonomous reasoning—one has thought through the rule
2. acting from a sense of self-duty.

Maxims and Rules

Consider what happens when we ask ourselves: "What are the fundamental rules I should follow at this time and place in my life?" Recalling the list of duties of students and professor from our discussion of Ross, we may want to rephrase them: "If I am a student, I ought to do such-and-such." But would you say that all people, at all times, are morally obligated to pay their tuition, go to class, and do their assignments? No. These are situational, role-related, "particularist" duties that do not apply to all people at all times.

In the media ethics environment, "rules" say a journalist should not deceive others when gathering news, and advertisers should not deceive vulnerable consumers. We can turn around that rule and say: "When I am in circumstances like this, when I am gathering news, I will not deceive my sources." "When I am developing an advertising campaign, I will not deceive my audiences." Such rules, when stated thusly, are maxims. Kant says all reasoned and considered actions involve maxims.

We cannot force others to obey our own rules, so we shouldn't attempt to convert an idiosyncratic belief into a universal law. Ethics doesn't come from forcing obedience, but by creating rules that are *ipso facto* correct—that others will follow merely because each person, if he or she thought about it, would have reached the same right conclusion. Morality, for Kant, has its ultimate source in rationality. Moral rules are not mere arbitrary conventions or subjective standards, but objective truths that have their source in the rational nature of human beings.

Kant argues two main points dealing with "imperatives" (or "commands"); one has to do with *hypothetical imperatives*, the other with *categorical imperatives*.

Hypothetical Imperatives. Most of what people do in life is based upon hypothetical imperatives, which tell us what to do if we want to bring about certain consequences— such as happiness. *If* (we want something,) *then* (we do something).

Kant says we often act out of selfish desires, which arise out of calculations about how we can get what we want. For instance, some utilitarians say we do what's necessary to be happy. Advertisers may say they have a duty to do what persuades folks to buy the product; journalists may say they have a duty to get the story, etc.

Kant would suggest that such things entail good and bad actions but have nothing to do with morality. The maxims we employ to get the job done, reach happiness, etc., may be personal and subjective. They could be considered candidates for moral rules, but they are not in and of themselves moral rules. They cannot become moral rules unless they pass some severe tests. They must transcend merely personal and subjective rules to reach the status of objective rules of morality that hold for everyone and apply to all cases of the same kind. In other words, moral rules must have universalizability. We must be willing to see our rules adopted as maxims by everyone in a situation similar to ours. If this happens, these rules become categorical imperatives.

Categorical Imperatives. Categorical imperatives are universalized maxims or ethical principles of behavior, outside our wishes and desires. Such principles are unconditional, allowing for no exceptions, no fudging, no arguments about "close enough will do." They are known and obeyed by all rational creatures with an inborn conscience and the capacity to exercise "pure reason." And they exist with no consideration of the consequences.

Reconsider your list of fundamental rules that apply to fulfilling your roles as students. We have described how these can be expressed as maxims or hypothetical imperatives pertaining to your specific role: "If I am a student, I ought to do such-and-such." On the other hand, what about the duty of doing your work honestly? Could we not make a case for universalizing that duty, claiming that everyone else would follow our rule if they had thought about it and understood the universal validity of it? In making that case, we are appealing to a categorical imperative.

The categorical imperative has several components, including:

1. We should "act only on that maxim (principle) that we can at the same time will to become a universal law." We described this in the preceding paragraphs.
2. We should "always act so as to treat humanity, either yourself or others, always as an end and never as only a means." In other words, we should never exploit. We must treat people—including ourselves—as rational creatures and valuable entities in and of themselves. People should not have a "price" nor be used as mere commodities; they should have dignity. (Note that we can "use" our news sources as "means" of getting a story, or "use" an audience as a "means" of making money, just as we "use" the mail carrier as a "means" of receiving our mail. But they deserve more than that; we must value their dignity.) This component of the categorical imperative is sometimes called "the kingdom of ends."

To test the formulations, take a general act and universalize it. For instance, take the maxim: "I ought to deceive these people to get a good news story." Universalize that maxim, by saying something like, "Everybody who is a journalist ought to deceive their sources now and whenever the occasion presents itself." The statement is now universalized to all journalists and all sources.

But now consider how this might apply. What if the journalist finds herself the subject of a news story? Will she expect to be deceived? Not likely. She would have to consider deception from her own view, from her source's view, and from the view of a disinterested third party. The "disinterested third party" test demands total transparency—fully and openly disclosing all variables in the decision-making process. As Plaisance says, fully exposing our motivations, aspirations, and intents "allows us as rational, autonomous beings to assess each other's behavior" (2007, p. 187).

The test is through these three levels: How does this apply by:

1. me to others?
2. others to me?
3. disinterested others to others?

If it's rationally impossible, and if it's not universally applicable, we must change our generalization. We must be willing to universalize our maxim, even though on some other occasion it might work to our disadvantage. We have no good principles unless we've tested them on all three of the above levels.

Let's take similar examples of hypothetical imperatives: "When I'm on deadline, I'll publish whatever information I have to finish my story, even if it means I have not had time to verify information that might hurt someone." Or, "When I need to persuade someone, I'll use whatever legal means are at my disposal." Let's turn these hypothetical imperatives into categorical imperatives. Under the hypothetical imperative we can do either good or bad acts. We may be friendly to others either because it's our natural habit, or because we want to sell them something. But such is not the case under categorical imperatives. Categorical imperatives involve higher truths.

Kant makes a case for universalized higher truths: Right is right; it must be pursued regardless of the pressures to do wrong and even if it results in bad consequences. Tell the truth. Keep promises. Do not cheat or steal. Pursue benevolence. These higher truths—our moral obligations—are found not by a reasoning process but through their existence in our inborn conscience. As Clifford Christians describes it, "To violate one's conscience—no matter how feeble or uninformed—brings about feelings of guilt. Through the conscience, moral law is embedded in the texture of human nature" (Christians, 2005, p. 16).

Kant says there's nothing as important in the world as good will. If our *motivation* is to do the right thing (even if we're inclined to do otherwise), then it's morally good. Do we act out of respect for the moral order or an obligation to do the right thing? If we do the right thing, even if we don't want to do it, we're acting out of the categorical imperative.

As Christians concludes, categorical imperatives must be obeyed even to the sacrifice of all natural inclinations and socially accepted standards. These are ethics "with an austere quality, but they are generally regarded as having greater motivating power than subjective approaches to ethics that are easily rationalized on the basis of temporary moods" (p. 16).

Kant admits that his categorical imperatives demand obedience and faithful practice. They are rigid and hard to follow. To the extent that we're not pure and rational, Kant's strictness seems offputting.

Despite Kant's rigidity and other shortcomings to be mentioned later, many philosophers say Kant's ethical theories are the most substantive ones ever laid out. They capture many of our intuitive beliefs about what is right (not to lie, to treat people with dignity, to act benevolently). They supply us with a test to determine our duties (the categorical imperative) that is superior to the generalizations posed by utilitarians and others.

Imperfect and Perfect Duties

Kant distinguishes between two types of duties: perfect and imperfect. A perfect duty is one we must always observe; an imperfect duty is one that we must observe only on some occasions. This is somewhat (but not precisely) similar to Ross's prima facie and actual duties, with actual = perfect and prima facie = imperfect.

For instance, I have a perfect duty not to injure another person, but only an imperfect duty to show love and compassion. I must sometimes show love, but when and to whom are entirely up to me. The latter—imperfect duties—then, appear to be more like the supererogatory duties we discussed with Ross.

What perfect and imperfect duties do we have in mass communications? What's your list?

To sum up Kant:

1. No matter the consequences, it is always wrong to lie.
2. We must always treat people (including ourselves) as ends, not as means only.
3. An action is right when it satisfies the categorical imperative.
4. Perfect and imperfect duties give a basis for claims that certain rights should be recognized.

How does Kant resolve a flaw of utilitarianism—the problem with justice? (Remember that utilitarianism does not focus on the principle of justice, because what serves the interests of the majority may mean gross injustices to others.) The tentative answer is that Kant, by telling us that every individual is to be treated as an end and never merely as a means to an end, considers it impossible to legitimately exploit some for the benefit of others.

If Immanuel Kant Were Sharing Your Office

Kant would say that if you wanted to be an ethical communicator, you would abide by universal rationality. You would be a person of "good will." You would obey your duty and conform to certain rules that rest on two governing principles known as the "categorical imperative":

1. Never make any rule that you are not willing to universalize. Your rule should apply to you and to others, in all circumstances.
2. Respect the humanity in every person. Treat all persons as ends in themselves, not a mere means to some end.

Kant would tell you to:

1. Decide what you want to do.
2. Figure out what professional "rule" you would be obeying if you follow through on that decision ("Journalists should always seek out and report truth" and "Public relations practitioners owe a special allegiance to their clients" are conventional journalism and PR rules.)
3. Try to universalize that rule, making it apply to all people.
4. Question whether your rule, and thus your proposed action, respects the dignity and wellbeing of all people involved.
5. If you can answer "yes" to Nos. 3 and 4 above, go for it. If not, rethink your rule or action (Kant, 1785/1964).

Applying Kant to the Media Ethics Environment

If we accepted Kant's categorical imperative, how would it change how we do our business in mass communications? How can these ideas be applied to the two scenarios at the beginning of Chapter 10—the student journalists and the scriptwriter?

As suggested in the second set of justifications for each of the two scenarios in Chapter 10, a strictly Kantian decision would not have approved the student journalists' lying to get into the hospital. The story was significant, and the truth behind the explosion was important to reveal (to bring justice and accountability in that specific case and for the future health and safety of students). But the competitive motivations of the student reporters—to scoop other media—did not spring from "pure reason." They did not treat all persons as rational ends in and of themselves. They were not transparent. Alternative means of getting the full story received little consideration; the journalists quite readily used a utilitarian calculus to decide it was appropriate to deceive.

(Note that a "softer deontologist," such as Ross, could have approved the deception, because the obligation to serve the informational needs of a majority of the stakeholders may have trumped the obligation to be fully transparent with the nurse, or to dogmatically abide by the university's and hospital's privacy policies.)

Kant also would have problems if a film writer, motivated by commercialism, diddled with a script to convert it from a PG to a PG-13 rating that would be marketed to children under 13. One argument might be that institutional policies are already in place to address issues of decency and responsibility in cinema. However, it does not appear they were applied autonomously in this case. The intended audiences were being manipulated and not respected as rational creatures and valuable entities in and of themselves. Could filmmakers apply moral duties and notions of moral autonomy to their task of selling tickets and making commercial tie-ins? Only if they truly believed that people's self-worth and self-improvement could be addressed through entertainment. The "moral evil" might be diminished if consumers are expected to refine their reasoning processes. (This fits with Kant's advocacy of "casuistry"—the process by which children and immature philosophers are led to the right decisions by didactic examples, case studies, or experiences, after which they can act as autonomous moral agents.) All in all, however, the case study seems to encourage the filmmakers to cut some moral corners.

(Again, we might find Ross reaching an opposite conclusion. As described in the previous chapter, the script writer may be driven by an obligation to help the film makers succeed in the marketplace so long as they abide by the ratings system's rules. The "particularist" duties may include helping children and their parents make informed decisions about purchasing movie tickets and supporting marketing tie-ins.)

Criticisms of Kant

Kant has his critics. Ronald Munson suggests three things in *Intervention and Reflection: Basic Issues in Medical Ethics* (2007) that apply to the media ethics environment.

First, Kant's principles supply no clear way to resolve cases that have a conflict of duties. I have a duty to keep my promises, but I also have a duty to help those in need. Kant provides no rank ordering of our duties.

Second, a difficulty with the categorical imperative arises because we are free to choose how we formulate a maxim for testing. In all likelihood, none of us would approve a maxim such as "Lie when it is convenient." But what about "Lie when telling the truth is likely to cause harm to another"? We would be more inclined to make this a universal law. Or, "Whenever a physician has good reason to believe that a patient's life will be seriously threatened if he is told the truth about his condition, then the physician should lie."

A third problem with Kant's philosophy is his notion that we have duties to rational beings or people. Physicians, among others, have problems defining "rational beings or persons." Consider abortion: is a fetus a rational being or person? Is a 95-year-old senile man hopelessly tied to life-sustaining equipment? A newborn with an open spine, ill-formed brain, and other serious birth defects? These are serious questions for doctors and nurses.

Are there equivalent problems in defining "rational beings or people" for journalists and persuasive communicators? For instance, what does a photographer or cinematographer do when shooting film in an insane asylum? Or journalists who happen across totally hysterical survivors of a tragedy? Or, for the advertiser, the small children who are targets of commercials? Or the subjects of orchestrated public relations campaigns, who may not have full access to opposing information? Do these people possess "an autonomous, self-regulating will," as Kant perceived those to whom the categorical imperative applied? Without such a will, such people are not legitimately affected by the categorical imperative, are they? They cannot "give consent" to be treated the way the photographer, film maker, reporter, PR practitioner, or advertiser is using them.

Note that these three maxims could be applied to the same situation. Since Kant does not tell us how to formulate our maxims, we can act virtually any way we choose if we merely describe the situation in detail. We might be willing to have everyone act just as we are inclined to act whenever they find themselves in exactly this kind of situation. The categorical imperative, then, doesn't seem to solve our moral problems quite as neatly as it first appears.

SUMMARY AND CONCLUSIONS

This chapter describes three philosophers' arguments in favor of duty-based rather than strictly consequentialistic ethics. British philosopher William David Ross asks us to use our intuition to sort among competing prima facie duties, then to act upon our actual duties (which may or may not entail consequentialism). American professor Bernard Gert provides us with a list of moral rules to be applied with rationality and impartiality.

German philosopher Immanuel Kant invokes notions of universal rules and persons-as-ends. All three promote rational thinking. Each has strengths and weaknesses.

These deontologists believe that the basic nature of our behavior—our moral actions—is more significant than the nature of the consequences. Each advocates freedom, respect, and happiness for all, including ourselves (slight variations on the Golden Rule). To varying degrees, each asks us to be morally mature, to use clear-headed reasoning, and to rely upon our consciences when making moral choices. All would advocate "front-loading" our decision making, carrying well-formulated notions of right and wrong, good and bad with us before we enter the daily moral wars.

Readers may discern the authors' slight tilt toward W.D. Ross. The perpetual moral tugs-of-war that occur constantly in the media ethics environment suggest that Ross provides us with a "grip on reality" worth attending to. The daily choices are often the right-versus-right choices that a mixed-rule deontologist can help us with. Using our best judgments, drawing upon our intuition and experience, we can keep one eye on the goal line ("teleos") while obeying our moral duties ("deontos"). This is not to disrespect Kant or Gert—or Mill and other utilitarians, for that matter. All of them, as well as the philosophers discussed in the next chapter, have much to offer.

Many claim deontology is a reasonable and workable principle, and that it assures us of maintaining the moral order. Others wonder how we can do right or wrong without considering the consequences of our actions, or whether we've ever considered whether we're being dogmatic absolutists. Still others concede that our intuition tells us that right acts should be categorized in terms of highest priority. Keeping a promise is right, but circumstances of higher ethical priority might cause us to break that promise. It is right not to hurt others, but many would not hesitate to cause harm to defend themselves or loved ones. It is right not to deceive, but if deceiving serves a more morally justifiable goal (such as protecting the innocent from unnecessary and/or significant harm), it may be appropriate to fudge the truth.

This book includes many "moral duties" for media. Media ethics codes tell practitioners to tell the truth, minimize harm, be independent, be accountable, be loyal, advertise honestly, honor promises, safeguard privacy, be impartial, be accurate, maintain confidences, be loyal, avoid conflicts of interest, avoid being offensive, show good taste, be sensitive, seek diversity, be courageous, expose wrongdoing, be responsible advocates, substantiate claims, etc.

This list of moral duties articulates standards of performance in traditional and emerging fields of journalism, public relations, advertising, and entertainment media. Some state minimal standards, while others express ideal expectations. Even though the codes' lists of duties were often embedded in a broader context of consequentialism or virtue or care or justice, each could stand alone as an expression of moral obligation. Each is a commandment, although some are more absolute than others.

Notice that the codes offer little guidance for practitioners trying to think their way through the conflicting rules. How does a journalist always tell truth but minimize harm?

How does a public relations practitioner remain simultaneously loyal and impartial? How does an advertiser communicate honestly but never offensively? How do you know when your intuition is correct or flawed? In life, we must choose. Unavoidably, some of those choices may lead us to violate even the best-intentioned rules concerning right and wrong.

■ ■ ■

CHAPTER VOCABULARY

Note: Definitions are available at this book's companion website.

- actual duty
- beneficence
- categorical imperatives
- deontology
- dogmatic
- fidelity
- Gert, Bernard
- good actions
- gratitude
- hypothetical imperatives
- imperfect duty
- justice
- Kant, Immanuel
- mixed-rule deontology
- morally incumbent
- non-maleficence
- perfect duty
- prima facie duties
- reparation
- right actions
- Ross, William David
- self-improvement
- strict deontologist
- supererogatory duties
- universalist contextualism

PRACTICAL APPLICATIONS

1. Based on insights from the philosophers you met in this chapter, make two lists of moral duties or obligations: (a) those that apply to you in your personal life; (b) those that you think will apply to you in your professional life. Are they the same lists? Why or why not?

2. Which (if any) of the philosophers in this chapter resonate best with you? Which (if any) do not? Why is that?

3. The chapter described supererogatory duties as ones that are good to perform but not necessary. Consider your media specialization and describe a supererogatory duty. Could some of those duties actually put you at a disadvantage in competing with others? Can you think of such duties that would not put you at a competitive disadvantage?

CASE STUDIES

Return to the five case studies at the end of Chapter 10, and listen to the three philosophers you've met in this chapter. Remember how you answered each of the first four questions: What's your problem? Why not follow the rules? Who wins, who loses? and What's it worth? Now, resolve the same five cases by listening to the deontologists whispering in your ear.

CASE 11.1 **Journalism: How (and Whether) to Cover a Prank**

Thinking it Through

1. Ask, and answer:

    A. Which of W.D. Ross's prima facie duties help you make a decision?

    B. How does Bernard Gert's thinking help you make a decision?

    C. What "hypothetical imperative" or "categorical imperative" helps you make a decision?

    D. Kant argued that people should be ends unto themselves, not a means to an end. How does that statement tie into your decision?

    E. Do any of the deontologists imply that there is a way to run the story without violating any moral rules?

2. Do you publish the story? Yes or no?

3. So far, which type of ethical approach seems to work best for you: the utility-based approaches of Chapter 10 or the duty-based approaches of Chapter 11. Why?

4. Did your decision change—or at least become more difficult to justify—when moving from a utility-based approach to a duty-based approach?

■ ■ ■

CASE 11.2 **New Media: Do You Take the Ads?**

Thinking it Through

1. Ask, and answer:
    A. Which of W.D. Ross's prima facie duties help you make a decision?
    B. How does Bernard Gert's thinking help you make a decision?
    C. What "hypothetical imperative" or "categorical imperative" helps you make a decision?
    D. Kant argued that people should be ends unto themselves, not a means to an end. How does that statement tie into your decision?
    E. Do any of the deontologists imply that there is a way to accept the ad without violating any moral rules?

2. Given what you know about the state of web advertising, is there a type of web ad that you would not accept? (Chapter 9 lists web advertising types that include advertorials, in-text ads, kick-through ads, contextual link ads, pop-ups, pop-unders, fake dialogue boxes, interstitial or prestitial ads, and overlays.)

3. Is there a way to craft a rule-based decision that could lead you to take the ads?

4. What would a deontological philosopher say about your duty, if any, to the nonprofit groups that receive free advertising, which might disappear if you accept the company's offer?

5. Do you take the ads? Yes or no?

6. So far, which type of ethical approach seems to work best for you: the utility-based approaches of Chapter 10 or the duty-based approaches of Chapter 11. Why?

7. Did your decision change—or at least become more difficult to justify—when moving from a utility-based approach to a duty-based approach?

■ ■ ■

CASE 11.3 **Public Relations: The Big Weekend**

Thinking it Through

1. Ask, and answer:
    A. Which of W.D. Ross's prima facie duties are helpful as you write recommendations about changes, if any, to The Big Weekend?
    B. How does Bernard Gert's thinking support your thinking?
    C. What "hypothetical imperative" or "categorical imperative" helps you justify your proposal?
    D. Kant argued that people should be ends unto themselves, not a means to an end. How does that statement tie into your decision?
    E. Do any of the deontologists imply that there is a way to continue the current Big Weekend practices without violating any moral rules?

2. Given what you know about The Big Weekend, what recommendations would you make? What deontological arguments can you make? Which of the three approaches work best for you?

3. So far, which type of ethical approach seems to work best for you: the utility-based approaches of Chapter 10 or the duty-based approaches of Chapter 11. Why?

4. Did writing your recommendations change—or at least become more difficult to justify—when moving from a utility-based approach to a duty-based approach?

■ ■ ■

CASE 11.4 **Advertising: The Nathan Freedonia Ad**

Thinking it Through

1. Ask, and answer:
    A. Which of W.D. Ross's prima facie duties are helpful in justifying your decision?
    B. How does Bernard Gert's thinking support your decision?
    C. What "hypothetical imperative" or "categorical imperative" helps you justify your decision?
    D. Kant argued that people should be ends unto themselves, not merely a means to an end. How does that statement tie into your decision, especially considering concerns by Nathan Freedonia's ex-wife?
    E. Do any of the deontologists imply that there is a way to make the graphic ad without violating any moral rules?
2. To what extent, if any, did your "squeamishness" about making a bloody ad play a role in your decision?
3. Assuming that Nathan Freedonia is not willing to make changes to the ad's content, do you make the ad? Yes or no?
4. So far, which type of ethical approach seems to work best for you: the utility-based approaches of Chapter 10 or the duty-based approaches of this chapter? Why?
5. Did your decision change—or at least become more difficult to justify—when moving from a utility-based approach to a duty-based approach?

■ ■ ■

CASE 11.5 **Entertainment: The VIM Kids**

Thinking it Through

1. Ask, and answer:

    A. Which of W.D. Ross's prima facie duties are helpful in justifying your decision?

    B. How does Bernard Gert's thinking support your decision?

    C. What "hypothetical imperative" or "categorical imperative" helps you justify your decision?

    D. Kant argued that people should be ends unto themselves, not merely a means to an end. How does that statement tie into your decision?

    E. Do any of the deontologists imply that there is a way to produce the episode without violating any moral rules?

2. Kant might argue that using the 11-year-old twins is immoral because they are not fully "rational beings" able to show "pure reason," because they do not have fully developed senses of morality. What is your response?

3. So far, which type of ethical approach seems to work best for you: the utility-based approaches of Chapter 10 or this chapter's duty-based approaches. Why?

4. Did your decision change—or at least become more difficult to justify—when moving from a utility-based approach to a duty-based approach?

■ ■ ■

CHAPTER 12

Virtue, Justice, and Care

INTRODUCTION

So FAR, several philosophers have been whispering in our ear. They've suggested that we either make choices to maximize benefits or to follow a sense of duty and obligation. While these approaches may be the most popular, they are decidedly not the only basis on which to make morally sound decisions.

This chapter considers some reasonable alternatives. As we have said, philosophers disagree sharply about each set of moral principles. Our approach is only moderately idiosyncratic, but we find it reasonable to cluster significant principles under the categories of ethics of virtue or character; ethics of justice or fairness; and ethics of care or reciprocity.

AN OVERVIEW OF THE PRINCIPLES

If asked to identify your ethical principles, you might assert that your lives and your decisions are guided by a variation of one of the following principles, here stated in rather general, even colloquial, terms:

1. "I believe in doing whatever brings about the best results for the most people."
2. "I believe that right is right and wrong is wrong; and I should always do my moral duty."

This chapter offers:

- an overview of five principles, showing how consequentialism and deontology fit into the scheme
- a closer look at philosophers who have advocated virtue or character, justice or fairness, care or moral reciprocity
- a sense of how each philosopher informs our discussions about the media ethics environment
- a challenge to assess the strengths and weaknesses of each theory, and to avoid the temptation to assume automatically that "one size fits all"
- an opportunity to apply each principle to the five case studies used in Chapters 10 and 11.

3. "I believe in doing what my moral heroes and my own virtuous character motivate me to do."
4. "I believe the playing field should be level, and that everyone should be treated fairly."
5. "I believe in caring about everyone, and I hope they care about me."

Which of the preceding sounds like the position you are most likely to stake out? Let's explore each of these in a bit more detail and see how they emerge from and reflect the principles of utility, duty, virtue, justice, and care. In doing so, we'll note pros and cons of each. Then, we'll look at philosophers who have helped articulate these principles.

1. Consequentialism and Utility

"I believe in doing whatever brings about the best results for the most people."

This is a somewhat clichéd summary statement of the principle of utilitarianism, which we covered in Chapter 10. You'll recall that it is concerned with doing "the greatest aggregate good for the greatest number, and the least harm to the fewest." Put another way, the principle demands that our choices should lead to the greatest possible balance of good over evil, and to distribute this result as broadly as possible. It emphasizes utility, practicality, and end results (Mill, 1863/1988).

2. Deontology and Moral Rules

"I believe that right is right and wrong is wrong; and I should always do my moral duty."

This is an assertion of absolutism or unconditional moral obligation, as we said in Chapter 11. Many claim to believe in the assertion's supreme allegiance to duty, consistency, universalism—if it's right or obligatory for me to do, it should be right or obligatory for everybody; if it's right today, it should be right tomorrow. Some outstanding philosophers, and many conscientious individuals, adhere to this rule-based or deontological approach. They have their own checklist of "right" and "wrong" actions—moral rules, if you would (Gert, 1998; Kant, 1785/1964; Ross, 1930).

3. Virtue and Character

"I believe in doing what my moral heroes and my own virtuous character motivate me to do."

This statement endorses the mature application of good character, virtues, empathy, and practical wisdom to make "just" decisions. It also entails moderation, temperance, and compromise, as well as the recognition of alternatives. The measure of success is not whether a specific duty was being obeyed, or whether good consequences occurred. Rather, it is a question of whether the moral decision maker was properly motivated (Aristotle, 1962; MacIntyre, 1984, 2001).

One who claims this position might assert that a truly ethical person should lead a life of equilibrium and harmony. The call for "fair and balanced" news reporting may unconsciously reflect this philosophic principle, but it is important to note that a "fair and balanced" report does not occur at some mathematical middle point between the two loudest or most quotable news sources—"the idiots at either end of the spectrum." Like other professional practices, "fair and balanced" work should emerge spontaneously and clearly from conscientious virtues and good technical skills that have been learned from experience. It is passed down from good role models, and then so thoroughly internalized that it appears to be second nature.

Critics of this perspective would say that compromise has merit sometimes, but not if it means abandoning other valid philosophies that deserve supremacy. They might ask: How can you ignore—or even downplay—the consequences of your decisions or fundamental moral duties? And how do you decide which virtues or character traits are the most important? Such critics, who tend to view ethics through the lenses of either deontology or teleology, may be uncomfortable with this "virtue" approach.

4. Justice and Fairness

"I believe the playing field should be level, and that everyone should be treated fairly."

This admirable perspective focuses on the notions of rights and justice. A world filled with injustice demands sensitivity toward others—particularly to the downtrodden or disenfranchised. Anyone with the power to cause harm or to adjust the allocation of resources needs heightened empathy. In a society where information and knowledge bring power, an advocate of justice is particularly concerned about disparities between the information-rich and the information-poor. It's not just a matter of duty or utility, and it is not based strictly on intuition or virtues—it is a philosophical perspective all its own (Rawls, 1971, 1993; MacIntyre, 1984, 2001).

Media practitioners who have experienced life "up close and personal" know that professional pleaders and people who create pseudo-events don't always deserve the attention they receive. Advertisers, PR practitioners, entertainers, and journalists are well served by having a sense of the "other," of people unlike themselves, people whose stories ought to be told. Such a sense may release the creative juices or engender moral outrage. The general public interest will be served if such empathy is used wisely. However, media consumers can take only so many depressing news stories or appeals to their better selves, because at some point they suffer compassion fatigue and tune out and turn off (Moeller, 1999). Apathy is a media dysfunction, no matter how well intentioned the media practitioners.

Philosophers who focus on justice recognize that it's only human nature to be self-interested, and that sometimes we all need to be challenged to put the interests of others against our own. They talk to us about a social contract and distributive justice, about the need to recognize the inherent worth and dignity of everyone—including ourselves.

They seek ways, such as affirmative action, to compensate for past injustices and to build a just and equitable society.

Some critics of the justice approach to ethics call it loosey-goosey liberal claptrap. They say it is only natural to be self-interested to survive in a competitive world. They note that media practitioners generally do not emerge from the ranks of the underprivileged, and that empathy for the "huddled masses" sounds artificial when coming from the mouths of the media elite—especially if the media elite are white, upper-middle-class males. And, as suggested above, while media fare about justice issues may draw an audience, critics say that particular agenda doesn't have staying power.

Finally, we might wonder where this principle fits in the larger scheme of ethics. It sounds like an appeal to duty, and to utility, and to virtues, and to lovingkindness. To some extent it is all of these. Its advocates, however, claim it deserves its own category. They have a point.

5. Care and Moral Reciprocity

"I believe in caring about everyone, and I hope they care about me."

This is a basic and practical combination of feminist ethics and the Golden Rule, emphasizing respect for others and maintenance of reciprocal relationships. In terms of feminist ethics, it refers to everyone and everything we "care for" and "care about." We may have little trouble identifying who or what we care *for*, because those things and people are probably close by; we can reach out and touch them; we can feel their pain; we can be intimate. We may have, in addition, a number of things and people we care *about*, in a more abstract sense. I care for my family; I care about the homeless, the victims of disasters, the oil-soaked birds in the Gulf of Mexico. Some scholars say the key is to bridge that gap and care for and about people, things, and institutions both near and far. Feminist ethics tells us the goal is to sustain relationships and community through dialogue and with sensitivity. The Golden Rule—in all its permutations—tells us that sustaining those interdependent relationships will require a high degree of empathy (Becker, 2001; Gilligan, 1982; Noddings, 1984; Singer, 2001; Steiner, 2009).

Care and reciprocity are laudable concepts and worthy of general application, but they may be more idealistic than practical. This doesn't mean they should be abandoned, but we should recognize their limitations.

Real situations often involve complexities that make it impossible to apply these philosophies completely. A decision that "does right" by one person may unavoidably "do harm" to another. Only one advertising agency wins a contract; not all news stories land on page one; your excellent talents cannot be offered to multiple clients. And, as we have seen throughout our exploration of the media ethics environment, despite our best intentions it is practically impossible to gather and redistribute information/ persuasion/entertainment/etc. without harming or offending someone. Unavoidably, choices must be made in life. Some of those choices will favor one person, one institution, or one interest over another. As suggested in the preface to this text, the nature of media work may mean that we "care about" more things and people than we can "care for," and that universal empathy is elusive. Something's got to give.

WHO IS SHARING YOUR OFFICE?

As an exercise in ethical application, assume that you work in the media position of your choice, seeking to carry out your daily tasks in a consistently ethical way. Imagine that, as you seek to make the right choice when facing a dilemma, each of the following philosophers takes a turn sharing your office, whispering in your ear and influencing your decision making. Consequentialists and deontologists whispered in your ear in the previous two chapters; now it is time to hear from philosophers who advocate virtue and character, justice and fairness, and care and reciprocity.

IF ARISTOTLE, A VIRTUE ETHICIST, WERE SHARING YOUR OFFICE

Virtue Ethics

Aristotle (384–322 BC) and modern adherents of virtue ethics argue that it is not enough just to "do" ethics. They say we ought to "be" ethical. As Karen Lebacqz explained:

> It is normal to think about ethical issues not only in terms of right behavior, but also in terms of appropriate feelings, attitudinal responses, and ways of being. We urge the person to *be* a certain way, not just to *do* something.
>
> (1985, p. 77)

The starting point for virtue ethics is: What kind of persons are we, and what kind of persons do we wish to become? Louis Pojman said the virtuous person is constantly asking: "What sort of person should I become?" (2006, p. 156). Lebacqz put it this way: "When confronted with a difficult ethical dilemma, we can ask not merely, Is this the right thing to do? But, which act has the most integrity in terms of the kind of person I want to become?" (1985, pp. 85–86).

The difference between "being" and "doing" is philosophically and semantically significant. Our actions tell the world what we believe, who we are, what we value, what we think is virtuous, and what we think is wicked. Those actions emerge from deeply held character traits: virtues.

Virtues, according to journalism ethicist Edmund Lambeth, are "those traits of character or personhood that help one live up to or live out the principles of an ethical system" (1986, p. 54). William Frankena defined a virtue as "a disposition, habit, quality, or trait of the person or soul, which an individual either has or seeks to have" (1973, p. 64). These definitions are more precise than those of many other philosophers, who for eons have struggled over the degree to which virtues are character traits, dispositions, habits, skills, or innate faculties (Pincoffs, 2001).

Regardless of how virtues are defined, the following character traits or "habits of the heart" seem to belong on the list of factors that should produce and sustain a good community: benevolence, charity, civility, compassion, conscientiousness, cooperativeness, courage, dependability, empathy, fairness, generosity, gratitude, honesty, humaneness, humility, justice, kindness, loyalty, magnanimity, moderation, non-maleficence (non-malevolence), patience, peacemaking, persistence, self-control, sensitivity, temperance, thoughtfulness, tolerance, trustworthiness, and wisdom. The list is not comprehensive, but it demonstrates the qualities of virtuous people.

When discussing virtue ethics as a field of study, philosophers employ the following terms: practical virtue, practical wisdom or moral knowledge ("phronesis"), discernment, reason-based behavior, wisdom-enhanced judgment, internalized ethics, good character, moral development, moral agency, moral motivation, moral psychology, moral heroes, role models, good habits, mean, balance, equilibrium, harmony, living well, achieving excellence ("arête"), flourishing ("eudiamonia"), and happiness.

Virtue ethicists are uncomfortable with moral systems governed by rules that prescribe our duties (deontology) or what we must do to maximize payoffs (consequentialism). Virtues motivate us to be our best selves, to have admirable character traits that will lead us to make good decisions under all sorts of conditions, to flourish, to be good citizens, to have true happiness—not because we're following any particular moral rules or because we're doing a moral cost-benefit analysis. Critiques of virtue ethics by a number of scholars led one observer to conclude that "some forms of virtue ethics challenge consequentialism and deontology as the most plausible forms of ethical theory" (Quinn, 2007, p. 170).

Unlike deontological and teleological ethics that are action-governed/rule-governed and focus on "doing," virtue ethics emphasizes "being." Virtue-based systems are sometimes called "aretaic ethics" (from the Greek "arête," meaning "excellence" or "virtue"). Virtue ethicists consider how excellent people can live in excellent communities; how people who act out of spontaneous and deeply established convictions can inspire one another. Ideally, virtue ethics springs from true goodness. We are good without being prompted to be good; goodness has become a habit. We truly enjoy doing the right thing. Goodness is an end in and of itself.

In his *Nicomachean Ethics*, Aristotle considered moral virtue to be the appropriate starting point—the touchstone for acting well and engaging in reason-based behavior chosen for its own sake (Cunningham, 1999, p. 9). Moral virtue lies somewhere between the extremes of deficiency and excess. For instance, courage is the mean somewhere (not the precise midpoint) between cowardice and foolhardiness; generosity is the mean somewhere between stinginess and unrestrained giving. Aristotle described a number of things that we experience: fear, confidence, desire, anger, pity, and generally any pleasure. He said we may experience these deficiently or excessively, but not necessarily properly.

But to experience all this at the right time, toward the right objects, toward the right people, for the right reason, and in the right manner—that is the median and the best course, the course that is a mark of virtue.

(1962, Book 2, 1106b)

> To act from a moral virtue is to act in accordance with a mean between some excess and some defect, so that to fail in virtue is always to exhibit a vice of either excess or defect.
>
> —Alisdair MacIntyre (2001, p. 1757)

Aristotle said that the middle course of goodness "is no longer something easy that anyone can do. It is for this reason that good conduct is rare, praiseworthy, and noble" (1962, Book 2, 1109-a). In other words, being excellent is difficult. "It is not enough to do the right thing—even to do the right thing for the right reason; it is also important to do it with the right attitude and to have the right attitude and dispositions even when no action is possible" (Pojman, 2006, p. 172). Moral virtue is not merely a matter of *observing* the mean, but having an *aptitude* for choosing the mean. Ideal motives lead us toward the mean, while poor motives lead toward extremes.

Aristotle believed that the ethical life was impossible without good character traits and moral habits that emerged from a good upbringing and exposure to moral heroes. He was an aristocrat and admitted elitist: He didn't think women or barbarians could become fully developed people of virtue, let alone moral heroes. He thought it was easier to be virtuous if you were free, had resources, and lived in an inherently good community. This view is not surprising, given the time and circumstances in which Aristotle lived.

But the great works of many religions, the insights of scholars such as Thomas Aquinas, the writings of more recent virtue theorists (especially those who espouse "character education"), and common sense tell us that Aristotle was wrong: Everyone has the potential to lead the virtuous life. Pojman said "the saints and moral heroes are the salt by which the world is preserved" (2006, p. 164), and that all of us can be exposed to and influenced by these role models. Moral heroes and sheroes and their virtuous followers have emerged from the ranks of the downtrodden and disenfranchised, the agnostics and atheists. We're all responsible for our character. We can all be good, and we can all love the good.

Conclusions About Virtue Ethics

Contemporary virtue theorists, including Alisdair MacIntyre, have built upon Aristotle to argue that a character-based individual and professional life should lead to a virtuous community. In other words, virtuous individuals can become virtuous professionals, who can help virtuous communities flourish. Lambeth (1990) has argued that MacIntyre's modern virtue theory should encourage journalists to establish and maintain their own standards of excellence. Lambeth said that once established, these professional standards should lead to improved civic life.

Some argue that virtue ethics is superior to other moral theories because:

1. It offers a natural and attractive account of moral motivation—we do certain things, and avoid other things, because we are motivated to do so, not because we are governed by rules imposed upon us or because we are trying to maximize certain outcomes.
2. Unlike other theories that espouse the ideal of impartiality, virtue theory seriously doubts whether all stakeholders have an equal claim on us. Some virtues are partial, particular, and private (focused on people we know well, have a special relationship with, and care for) while others are impartial, general, and public (focused on people as a whole, those we may not actually know but still care about in the abstract).
3. Modern virtue theory has overcome Aristotle's sexism and the dominant male-oriented theories focused on advocacy, contracts, and cost-benefit analyses. The new applications embrace feminist considerations of intimacy and connectedness (Rachels, 1993).

On the other hand, limitations to virtue ethics include arguments that:

1. Virtue theory doesn't always tell us what to do, or what constitutes the "morally right action." The theory merely describes what virtues should be brought to the table. Thomas Bivins is concerned that:

    > . . . since the emphasis is on character and not on action, there is no easy way to determine a right action from a wrong one. Virtue ethicists simply insist that a virtuous character will result in virtuous actions.

    > (2004, p. 101)

2. Being virtuous does not necessarily mean doing the right thing. Lebacqz said the

    > . . . link between virtue and action, being and doing, is not a simple one-to-one correlation in which a right act always indicates a virtuous person and a wrong act always indicates a nonvirtuous person. A wrong act is not necessarily a vicious act, not does it point to a vicious agent. A right act is not necessarily done by a virtuous person.

    > (1985, p. 93)

3. Virtue theory doesn't prioritize the ideal character traits. It provides little help in knowing what to do when a conflict occurs, for example, whether honesty should trump loyalty, or compassion should trump justice.
4. Virtue theory is incomplete. It doesn't provide a character trait for every moral action.
5. Good character is often overwhelmed by institutional and situational pressures, especially in the absence of clear-cut ethical rules (Levy, 2004).

What Would Aristotle Advise?

He would tell you to act as a "virtuous communicator" or as a "good person communicating well." He would propose starting with a thoughtfully chosen "mean," and argue that moral virtue lies somewhere between the extreme options of "excess" and "deficiency."

He would ask you to rely upon fundamental virtues that you have internalized as you make good choices. You would make these choices for their own sakes, not because you expect some reward, and not because you "owe" somebody. Your choices should have the quality of moral excellence, in and of themselves. They should be character-grounded and wisdom-enhanced, and they should result in personal and professional competence.

He (and more contemporary virtue theorists, such as MacIntyre) would maintain that these virtues do not develop randomly, but emerge from exposure to good role models, and conscientious—habitual—testing. Ultimately, the virtues become innate; they define who or what we are. They may appear to be second nature but are much more than that. They indicate that we have learned wisely, that we have discernment and judgment. If we say, "I can't do that; it's just not the kind of person I am," we are describing a habit of the heart, a system of virtues. When we say it on deadline, without a great deal of time for contemplation, it is a thoroughly integrated ethic, and not just a dogmatic and tenaciously held prejudice.

IF JOHN RAWLS, A JUSTICE THEORIST, WERE SHARING YOUR OFFICE

Theories of Justice

Harvard political theorist John Rawls (1921–2002) offered an alternative to both strict deontology and consequentialism. His comprehensive social and political theory is a contractarian (that is, based on a "social contract") view of justice, integrating ideas from John Locke (1632–1704), Jean-Jacques Rousseau (1712–1788), and Immanuel Kant (1724–1804). Rawls placed the principles of justice and fairness at the heart of a social contract for anyone attempting to build a democratic society. Like Kant, he wanted all people to be treated as ends in and of themselves, not merely a means to someone else's ends.

In the spirit of many other philosophers, Rawls wanted to know how people could find happiness. Drawing from Aristotle, Rawls described a "plan of life" conception of happiness (1971, p. 432). As Pojman put it:

> There is a plurality of life plans open to each person, and what is important is that the plan be an integrated whole, freely chosen by the person, and that the person be successful in realizing his or her goals. This view is predominantly subjective in that it recognizes the person as the autonomous chooser of goals and a plan.
>
> (2006, p. 73)

But Rawls thought there ought to be an objective component to this life plan, so that in an ideal world "primary goods" or social values would be distributed equally unless an unequal distribution of any, or all, of these values is to everyone's advantage (Rawls, 1971, p. 62). These "primary goods" include rights and liberties, powers and opportunities, income and wealth, health and vigor, intelligence and imagination.

Rawls depicted democracy as a cooperative venture, a search for the good, in which all participants seek mutual—not selfish—advantage. Cooperation increases the flourishing of primary goods and social values. Citizens are expected to agree upon the importance of these primary goods, and then seek to distribute them fairly and consistently. However, the goals of justice and fairness are difficult to achieve because society consists of rich and poor, powerful and powerless, and numerous other involuntary conditions. In addition, while it might be nice if all these primary goods were distributed equally, an unequal distribution may actually benefit everyone (affirmative action and compensatory justice might be examples, if one took a longer view of justice). Therefore, Rawls proposed that society create its ideas about justice and fairness from an "original position" or starting point—a level playing field.

Parties in the original position would be under a "veil of ignorance." They would have no knowledge of their specific positions in society. They would not know their race, class, gender, or profession. Until the veil is removed at the end of the negotiations, they would not know whether they are among the winners or the losers. Without these biases or preconceptions, the only way they could make reasoned decisions is on the basis of some general knowledge that would be available to all.

They are all mutually disinterested "moral persons" with a strong sense of justice and the ability to develop and pursue a conception of what is good for everyone and not just for themselves.

The "veil of ignorance" means the decision maker does not know "his place in society, his class position or social status . . . his fortune in the distribution of natural assets and abilities, his intelligence and strength, and the like" (Rawls, 1971, pp. 12, 137). Rawls called this position of "ideal observation" an extension of Kant's categorical imperative. He noted that Kant, who believed actions should be promoted to universal laws of nature, would assume that none of us knows our place within this imagined system of nature when deciding whether an action would be ethically justifiable.

Once behind this veil, principles of justice are chosen so that:

> . . . no one is advantaged or disadvantaged by the outcome of natural chance or the contingency of social circumstances. Since all are similarly situated and one is able to design principles to favor his particular condition, the principles of justice are the result of a fair agreement or bargain.
>
> (Rawls, 1971, p. 12)

This veil, of course, is imaginary; Rawls acknowledges that the reverting to the original position is a "purely hypothetical situation so as to lead to a certain conception of justice" (1971, p. 12).

Rawls maintained that if everyone were in an "original position" when they began to develop their notions of fairness and justice, they would create a system that would demand autonomy and rationality for all stakeholders. They would be unlikely to opt for a strictly utilitarian model, in which a majority or a power bloc might increase its strength while a minority or the disadvantaged face even more suffering. This would be especially true if none of the stakeholders knew where they might land in the scheme of things once they emerged from beneath the veil of ignorance. If they were not sure if they would end up being enfranchised or disenfranchised, they would most likely envision a system of justice that would not discriminate against any stakeholders; they would treat persons as ends and not as means. Korsgaard and Freeman explained it this way: "Not knowing what their social positions are, eager to advance their particular conceptions of the good, and aware that this exercise is a one-time gamble on which everything depends, the parties try to ensure that even the worst position in society is as good as possible" (2001, p. 1456). (When you were a child, did your parents let you cut the cake but make it clear that your siblings would get the first slice?)

The process does not demand consensus. Indeed, it would be surprising if all stakeholders had identical moral imaginations and emerged with identical concepts of fairness. Instead of seeking unanimity, Rawls's system attempts to maximize individual liberty while protecting the weakest parties. The process, which he called "reflective equilibrium," would permit some inequities, but they would be fewer and less egregious than if the playing field were uneven. However, reflective equilibrium would expect the principles of justice selected by stakeholders in their original positions to match their "most deeply held convictions about what is just" (Korsgaard & Freeman, 2001, p. 1457).

Basically, Rawls was arguing for ethical actions focused on creating social contracts that lead to two principles of justice:

1. Each person has an equal right to the most extensive scheme of equal basic liberties compatible with a similar scheme of liberties for others.
2. Social and economic inequalities are to be arranged so that they are (a) reasonably expected to be to everyone's advantage, and (b) attached to positions and offices open to all (Rawls, 1971, p. 60).

Justice as Fairness in the Media

Many media ethicists have found the Rawlsian "justice as fairness" model to have enormous moral appeal. This book alludes to the model when discussing theories of moral development and values; news media experiments with public or civic journalism; and media codes of ethics calling for fairness, balance, diversity, compassion, and respect for privacy.

Most news media ethics codes seem at home with Rawls. "Justice" is the sixteenth word in the Society of Professional Journalists' ethics code and highlighted as an overarching purpose of journalism. SPJ asks journalists to "give voice to the voiceless," to "examine their own cultural values and avoid imposing those values on others," to "support the open exchange of views," and to "invite dialogue with the public." The Society for News Design code tells its members to:

> . . . accept the responsibility to understand our communities and to overcome bias with coverage that is representative of the constituent groups in the community. Over time, all groups, lifestyles, and backgrounds should see themselves and their values represented in the news.

Similar appeals appear in codes for broadcasters, photographers, and bloggers.

Appeals to justice and fairness also are found in some of the public relations, advertising, and marketing codes—but sometimes with a subtly different "spin." The PRSA asks its members to be "faithful to those we represent, while honoring . . . public interest," and to "respect all opinions and support the right of free expression." The IPRA code asks practitioners to "establish the moral, psychological and intellectual conditions for dialogue, and recognize the rights of all parties involved to state their case and express their views." And the AMA draws most directly from Rawls when it tells marketers to "foster trust in the marketing system," to "embrace ethical values" of "fairness, respect, transparency and citizenship," to "acknowledge the social obligations to stakeholders that come with increased marketing and economic power," and to "balance justly the needs of the buyer with the interests of the seller."

If we relied solely upon these codes for insights into media commitments to justice and fairness, we would probably conclude that all media are on the same page. However, the reality may not mesh with the theoretical.

One reason Rawls may not fit particularly well with non-news media is that he is suspicious of free-enterprise capitalism and the potential harm against individuals caused by what he called the exploitative economic aristocracy—essentially, the organizations likely to hire or otherwise use public relations and advertising practitioners and producers of entertainment fare. Martinson said calls for justice are particularly troublesome for persuasive communicators who define ethics "in individualistic terms" as relationships among people instead of focusing on society at large (1998, p. 144). He maintained that pluralism—but not universalism—is a key concept in relating Rawls's theory to public relations, because practitioners view their task as helping clients insert their positions into the marketplace, allowing the self-righting process to protect the greater common good and public interest. When public relations, advertising, and marketing groups focus on "corporate social responsibility," they don't necessarily refer to justice and fairness. They may call for two-way symmetrical communication, but they operate from a fiduciary model, which means they are not playing on a completely democratic playing field.

> The demands of distributive and social justice require that practitioners not function primarily as facilitators who will enable powerful and privileged interests to transform the marketplace of ideas into a conduit for control and manipulation of the political—economic—social agenda.
> —David Martinson (1998, p. 146)

By their very natures, public relations and advertising are about advocacy, which implies that the "original position" of the advocates is to choose a side and remain loyal to it, communicating messages for their clients' own gain for mutual benefit. You'll recall that in Rawls's original position, all of the mutually disinterested "moral persons" are driven by a strong sense of justice and the ability to develop and pursue a conception of what is good for everyone and not just for themselves. That position may make it theoretically challenging for advocates to achieve Kohlberg's highest stages of moral development and to engage in distributive justice and fairness toward a whole universe of stakeholders. (However, as we'll see momentarily, one of the most powerful criticisms of both Rawls and Kohlberg comes from feminists who say justice and fairness are masculine traits, and that the highest stages of moral development ought to reflect the feminist "ethic of care"—an ethic that can incorporate the moral ideals of justice.)

Conclusions about Justice

John Rawls is properly credited with shifting political philosophers away from a strictly utilitarian model of how democratic institutions ought to function. In doing so, he did not merely argue for a return to strictly Kantian deontology. Rather, he proposed a sophisticated and nuanced challenge for a just and fair society founded on a rational consensus of morally motivated and empathetic stakeholders. That consensus, achieved behind a hypothetical veil of ignorance, would do more than serve the needs of the majority; it would protect the weakest members of society.

Rawls has been a lightning rod for criticism. Some critics fault him for being too liberal, for presuming that ordinary persons have moral sensitivities that extend to the ends of the universe and that they have particular sensitivities to the most disadvantaged creatures in that universe. Others don't agree with how Rawls connects justice and morality, or his connection between "the focus on basic social institutions and the focus on persons' conduct and character" (Pogge, 1989, p. 3). Others think the veil of ignorance exercise has little pragmatic application.

A review of best media practices tells us that Rawls deserves our serious attention. When journalists make tough decisions about whether to invade privacy, use deception, comfort the afflicted or afflict the comfortable, they often employ a modified version of the veil of ignorance. At editorial board meetings or daily planning sessions they will bring a number of voices to the table, including the "imagined" voices of their story's stakeholders. They ask such questions as "Who will benefit, and who will suffer? How much benefit and how much suffering will this story or campaign produce? Is everyone's voice being heard? Is anyone getting favored treatment? How would I feel if I were the target of this news story? Would I deserve it?" This dialogue is more likely to occur in a larger news media organization than within the heads of individual bloggers, but it is reasonable to expect even isolated journalists to put on the veil of ignorance. Thinking about justice should convince them that pleasing their sources (or, sometimes, even their managers) is less important than a higher loyalty of delivering lower-case "t" truth to citizens (Kovach & Rosenstiel, 2007).

Rawls also has much to offer in other media environments. Advertising and public relations and media entertainment practitioners can use the veil when organizing a campaign or production and when meeting with clients. The job may be more challenging because of fiduciary loyalty commitments and because the weakest members of society cannot afford highly paid spokespersons. Loyalties struggles are never easy, but too often those struggles go no farther than loyalty to self (or firm) *vis-à-vis* loyalty to client.

Bringing Rawls to the table should pay dividends, helping persuasive and entertainment communicators consider how they can honor their vows of loyalty to those they represent, while honoring their obligations to the public interest. The decision-making model will shift from asymmetrical to two-way symmetrical to truly interactive, as the needs and interests of customers, consumers, and all members of the public are borne in mind. Discussions will not merely center on making a profit, moving product, or delivering eyeballs to advertisers. Those considerations remain on the table, where all the stakeholders will be seated at a level surface.

Using Rawls will help identify stakeholders not previously considered and whose omission could lead to unintended consequences. And once a more-complete identification of stakeholders has occurred, media practitioners then can more fully place justice among the considerations needed when finding a proper ethical balance between client loyalty and public interest. For advice on how this ideal relationship would look, media practitioners would do well to read carefully the AMA advice on fostering trust, embracing fairness and respect, and acknowledging their social obligations to all stakeholders.

What Would Rawls Advise?

He would insist that you and your cohorts wear a "veil of ignorance" as you grapple with your ethical dilemmas. He would say, for instance, that you can go about making your decisions as the normal, self-interested, egoistic persons you are. The only catch is that, in making the decision, you each must put aside your own identity and make the decision by momentarily adopting the viewpoints and interests of others who are involved—all the stakeholders.

Test your decision by:

1. Making a list of all people who will be affected by the decision—including the audience, sources, subjects, clients, co-workers, superiors, stockholders, yourselves, etc.

2. Putting yourself behind a "veil of ignorance." Give up your identity and assume the identities, in turn, of the other people affected by your decision.

3. Assuming a discussion taking place among the various players, with none of the participants knowing for sure what their ultimate identities will be until the veils of ignorance are removed. The optimal decision is the one on which all people involved could reach agreement. At the very least, all participants in the exercise should have had their senses of empathy tweaked.

IF CAROL GILLIGAN, AN ETHICIST OF CARE, WERE SHARING YOUR OFFICE

Women's issues emerged dramatically in the 1960s, with pragmatic concerns over reproductive rights, gender discrimination, pornography, and the plight of women in developing nations. The major theories of ethics at the time tended toward Kantian approaches, or justice-based/social contract rights-based assumptions that all moral agents were "free, equal, independent, and mutually disinterested" (Jaggar, 2001, p. 528). This, however, was not the lived experience of many women. Based on their own experiences, and the research of developmental psychologists and philosophers, feminists said it was time for revisions in ethical discourse.

We noted in the Chapter 4 discussion of moral development that feminists have been justifiably critical of traditional Western moral theories. They note that Aristotle said good women are characterized "by obedience, silence, and faithfulness." The domestic environment—unlike the economic or political spheres—was seen as a place where true excellence was unlikely to occur.

Aristotle, Kant, and others suggested that women are inferior at moral reasoning. The Western tradition emphasizes supposedly masculine values such as independence, autonomy, intellect, will, wariness, hierarchy, domination, and product. Western tradition also deprecates the supposedly feminine values of interdependence, community, connection, sharing, emotion, trust, absence of hierarchy, nature, process, and peace (Jaggar, 2001, p. 530). The Western tradition is preoccupied with impartial application of rules or contracts and following narrow lists of duties and morally acceptable actions.

These biases have not disappeared from ethics literature. Consider the concepts of justice in the relatively recent works of political theorist John Rawls and moral psychologist Lawrence Kohlberg: Men, who for centuries had controlled the public sphere, made the laws and policies that were to be applied impartially and somewhat unfeelingly.

Feminist scholars say the female experience differs. It embodies experiences and relationships in context, and resolves differences by means of caring and empathetic, deep listening. As stated in Chapter 4, Gilligan (1982) said that while men rely upon moral rules—particularly concerning justice, fairness, and equality—women abide by an ethics of care, relationships, and maintaining community. Gilligan said women develop morally from a self-centered care, to a sacrificial care of others, to a universal sense of care. Nel Noddings (1984) said that maternal caring was the moral ideal—an intimate "care- for" relationship between mother and child and, by extension, between people in specific and limited relationships. Other feminist theorists extend both these perspectives, examining how people care for (beneficence) and care about (benevolence) individuals, institutions, causes, and the universe.

Feminist ethics is eclectic in scope and practice. It may have started as a reaction to male-dominated moral philosophy, but it has developed a literature and authority of its own across many academic disciplines. Along the way, it has branched out. Linda Steiner (2009) mentions ten terms describing those branches: ethics of care, feminine ethics, feminist ethics, female ethics, womanist ethics, dialogic female ethics, ethics of agape, feminist communitarian ethics, ethics of solidarity, and expressive-collaborative morality.

While the field has expanded, some of its premises are being revised. Scholars have had mixed success in blending notions of care with notions of justice and other virtues (Steiner, 2009; Steiner & Okrusch, 2006; Porter, 1999; Tronto, 1995). Concerns once thought to be limited to women have expanded to include men, children, and institutions near and far. "Special interests" are seen increasingly as "human interests"—from the local workplace to developing nations. Feminist ethics are articulating concerns over race, class, and age. This may be due in part to ethicists' increased sensitivity to disadvantaged people and the institutions that discriminate against them. It is no coincidence that women are disproportionately overrepresented in the world's poor, illiterate, and oppressed peoples (Jaggar, 2001, p. 536).

This raises an empirical and pragmatic matter: As the world evolves and the workplace more accurately mirrors the world's gender mix, men and women are seen as equally capable of reflecting an ethic of justice and/or care. On various motivational scales, men who work in managerial or administrative jobs tend to score high in "justice," while women who work at home tend to score high in "care." But men and women score similarly when education and occupation are taken into consideration. Therefore, the moral gender gap may be diminishing as theories of feminist ethics mature. The issues, values, and experiences are not easily defined as being exclusively male or female (Held, 1999; Jaggar, 2001). Most values are not gender- or culture-specific; enough variance exists to motivate a great deal of conversation, research, and policy decision making.

Care in the Media

Media practices and policies tend to reflect Western liberal theories of rights that can be applied in a value-free manner. Objectivity is a perfect example of a standard that might emerge from deontological, utilitarian, virtues, or rights theories. We have always talked about "news judgment," but somehow presumed that media judgments about proximity, timeliness, conflict, impact, etc., could be made in a non-moral, value-free environment. Yet social responsibility theory demands something else of media practitioners. The literature and recent codes of ethics say that media work should entail transparent moral judgments, a consideration of the needs of stakeholders, and a commitment to improve the world. They articulate a strong case for an ethics of care.

> The question is not whether journalists may or should care, but about what or whom journalists should care.
> —Steiner and Okrusch (2006, p. 104)

Advocacy is another problematic construct, according to feminist ethics. Advocacy is a Western masculine "power ethic" that downplays the importance of interdependence, trust, and care. It presumes a polarization of views, instead of a conversation. It could be that the advocacy demands of public relations sometimes limit the universal care ethic espoused by feminist theorists, leading to "racialized and marginalized groups of men and women remaining invisible to campaign planners and researchers" (Aldoory, 2009, p. 120). As discussed in Chapter 9, media practitioners should redefine moral advocacy to encompass far more empathy than found in the fiduciary relationship between client and advocate. We envision a blend of traditional and feminist ethics when we ask advocacy to include non-maleficence, extended loyalty, and accountability.

Entertainment media (and advertisers who underwrite them) would also do well to take feminist ethics more seriously. Despite new broadcast and online networks aimed solely at women, and recent successes by sensitive producers and "talent," much of their work product still objectifies, commodifies, and trivializes women. It tells them who they are, how they are to be seen by others, and what they can achieve. The pictures are not always pretty. We're not just describing pornography, although that remains a significant problem area. We're also talking about sit-coms, commercial films, popular magazines, music videos, websites, and music. To the extent that any media stereotype or demean *any* group, they need to be called out.

What Would Gilligan Advise?

She would join other feminist scholars in advocating an ethics of care. She would challenge media notions of justice, balance, and neutrality, claiming that these perspectives are promulgated by men and/or privileged people who have the luxury of not taking a moral stance. These people advocate autonomy over community, separation over connectedness.

She and her colleagues might say journalists who advocate objectivity and rely on non-moral news values are not as compassionate or sensitive as they ought to be. Advertisers, public relations counselors, and special pleaders who "talk at" rather than "talk with" audiences and clients would be accused of misusing their power. When she and her colleagues speak in terms of connectedness, they focus on both caring for and caring about, on care giving and care receiving, on conversation, on building and maintaining relationships. They would dissuade you from sitting silently while injustice unfolds. They would rather you displayed professional competence and compassion by taking a stand—but not jam your position down anyone else's throat.

Caring is a virtue that may deserve to be on the same pedestal as the virtue of justice. (Feminist scholars disagree about this point.) As Aristotle might have put it, we learn to care by having it modeled for us, by practicing it, and by internalizing it. It is grounded in our sense of and commitment to human flourishing. Gilligan noted that the least morally mature individuals are selfish, thinking only of themselves; the conventionally moral think of and care for others, but in the process may sacrifice themselves to others' needs; the most morally sophisticated individuals care for themselves as well as for others, both known and unknown.

In short, "care" is a way of knowing, and it is particularly important for knowledge-seeking and knowledge-sharing professions (Belenky et al., 1986). People who advocate the ethics of care would ask you to develop, know, and use your own "voice"; to consider the welfare of intimates and strangers alike; to leave your campsite better than you found it.

IF AN ADVOCATE OF MORAL RECIPROCITY AND THE GOLDEN RULE WERE SHARING YOUR OFFICE

If any theory is a principle of universal ethics, moral reciprocity, as expressed in the Golden Rule, belongs on the short list. In one version or another, the Golden Rule has developed over thousands of years in almost all religious communities, under many different political cultures, and in several philosophic systems. Its various formulations make a compelling argument for principles of altruism, appreciation, autonomy, benevolence, caring, compassion, cooperation, dignity, empathy, gratitude, justice, love, moral reasoning, non-maleficence, rationality, respect of others, self-respect, and tolerance.

Strictly speaking, mutual respect for one's neighbor—and by extension everyone and everything within the interdependent web of existence—is neither a deontological nor consequentialist principle. It alludes to moral duties but does not focus specifically on them. It also alludes to utility but is not limited to a cost-benefit analysis. It is not a formulaic theory of justice, nor is it a virtue, *per se*.

Reciprocity is not necessarily a moral or ethical enterprise. It may simply be a tit-for-tat or non-moral exchange of like for like—such as an eye for an eye, a dinner invitation for a dinner invitation, money for goods. However, reciprocity and ethics are sometimes mentioned in the same breath, especially if the conversation is about justice, gratitude, and friendship (Becker, 2001). When we tie reciprocity to the Golden Rule, we are not making a connection that all ethicists would be comfortable making. For that reason, we use the term "moral reciprocity."

Moral reciprocity may appear to belong with the feminist ethic of care, but since it predates that theory by several millennia and covers more philosophic turf, it deserves its own category in the ethics lexicon.

As philosopher Harry J. Gensler (2010) argues:

> The golden rule is best seen as a consistency principle. It doesn't replace regular moral norms. It isn't an infallible guide on which actions are right or wrong; it doesn't give all the answers. It only prescribes consistency—that we not have our actions (toward another) be out of harmony with our desires (toward a reversed situation action). It tests our moral coherence. If we violate the golden rule, then we're violating the spirit of fairness and concern that lie at the heart of morality.

Knowledge and moral imagination are necessary for anyone hoping to apply the Golden Rule consistently and adequately, according to Gensler: "We need to know what effect our actions have on the lives of others. And we need to be able to *imagine* ourselves, vividly and accurately, in the other person's place on the receiving end of the action."

Critics of the Golden Rule have suggested that the rule is imprecise and not helpful as a guide to action; that it asks people to do irrational things (Singer, 2001, p. 616). They note that a narrow reading of the principle might result in harm, if the "other" happens to be a masochist. They wonder how we are supposed to know how others want to be treated. They ask how it can be applied to the competitive worlds of business and sports, where victory is a goal. They question whether the principle truly can be applied to people who are outside one's own cultural/ethnic/racial/nationalistic arenas of understanding. Meanwhile, to some cynics the pragmatic reading of the Golden Rule is either to "Do unto others before they do unto you," or to admit that "Whoever has the gold makes the rules."

Critics notwithstanding, principles of reciprocity as explored through the Golden Rule have prima facie value for human rights and cultural pluralism, "if every participant of the dialogue is willing to apply it in a way of full empathy as a sign of respect for the other" (Bordat, 2007).

Many changes might result if mass media practitioners—and media consumers—paid close attention when a Golden Rule theorist whispered in their ears. At several points we have tried to make the case that expanded empathy and other components of reciprocal relationships have the potential for enhancing the media ethics environment.

Historical Quotations about Reciprocity and the Golden Rule

The following quotes show how various philosophers and religions have referred to the ethic of reciprocity, or the Golden Rule. The list comes from many sources, not all of which used the same translations (Bordat, 2007; Gensler, 2010; Gerwith, 1978; NationMaster.com, 2010; Religious Tolerance.org, 2010; Shared belief, 2010; Scanlon, 1998; Singer, 2001; Teaching Values.com, 2010). Take this not as the final word on the subject, but as general insights into the historical, religious, and philosophic dialogue.

Aristotle:

"To the question how we should behave to friends, he (Aristotle) answered, 'As we should wish them to behave to us.'" (Singer, 2001, p. 614)

Bahá'í Faith:

"And if thine eyes be turned towards justice, choose thou for thy neighbour that which thou choosest for thyself." (Epistle to the Son of the Wolf)

Brahmanism:

"This is the sum of Dharma [duty]: Do naught unto others which would cause you pain if done to you." (Mahabharata, 5:1517)

Buddhism:

"Hurt not others in ways that you yourself would find hurtful." (Udana-Varga 5:18)

Christianity:

"So in everything, do to others what you would have them do to you, for this sums up the Law and the Prophets." (Matthew 7:12, New International Version)

"Do to others as you would have them do to you. If you love those who love you, what credit is that to you? Even 'sinners' love those who love them. And if you do good to those who are good to you, what credit is that to you? Even 'sinners' do that. And if you lend to those from whom you expect repayment, what credit is that to you? Even 'sinners' lend to 'sinners,' expecting to be repaid in full. But love your enemies, do good to them, and lend to them without expecting to get anything back. Then your reward will be great, and you will be sons of the Most High, because he is kind to the ungrateful and wicked." (Luke 6:31–35, New International Version)

Samuel Clarke:

"Rule of equity: Whatever I judge reasonable or unreasonable that another should do for me; that, by the same judgment, I declare reasonable or unreasonable, that I in the like case should do for him." (Singer, 2001, p. 615)

Confucianism:

"Do not do to others what you would not like yourself. Then there will be no resentment against you, either in the family, or in the state." (Analects 12.2)

"Tse-kung asked, 'Is there one word that can serve as a principle of conduct for life?' Confucius replied, 'It is the word 'shu'—reciprocity. Do not impose on others what you yourself do not desire.'" (Doctrine of the Mean 13.3)

The Dalai Lama:

"Every religion emphasizes human improvement, love, respect for others, sharing other people's suffering. On these lines every religion had more or less the same viewpoint and the same goal." (Religioustolerance.org)

"If you want others to be happy, practice compassion. If you want to be happy, practice compassion." (Nationmaster.com)

Epictetus:
"What you would avoid suffering yourself, seek not to impose on others."

Alan Gerwith:
"Do unto others as you have a right that they do unto you." (Gerwith, 1978)

Hinduism:
"This is the sum of duty: do not do to others what would cause pain if done to you." (Mahabharata 5:1517)

"That one I love who is incapable of ill will, And returns love for hatred." (Bhagavad-Gita, Chapter 12, Verse 18, 19)

Islam:
"Hurt no one so that no one may hurt you." (The Prophet Muhammad's Last Sermon)

"None of you [truly] believes until he wishes for his brother what he wishes for himself." (Inman Al-Nawawi Forty Hadiths, Number 13)

"The most righteous of men is the one who is glad that men should have what is pleasing to himself, and who dislikes for them what is for him disagreeable." (Conversations of Muhammad)

Isocrates:
"Do not do to others what would anger you if done to you by others."

Jainism:
"Just as sorrow or pain is not desirable to you, so it is to all which breathe, exist, live or have any essence of life. To you and all, it is undesirable, and painful, and repugnant." (Acaranga Sutra, Sutra 155–156)

"Just as pain is not agreeable to you, it is so with others. Knowing this principle of equality treat other with respect and compassion." (Suman Suttam, 150)

Judaism:
"What is hateful to you, do not do to your fellowman. This is the entire Law: all the rest is commentary." (Talmud, Shabbat 31a)

"Do not seek revenge or bear a grudge against one of your people, but love your neighbor as yourself." (Leviticus 19:18.)

John Stuart Mill:
"To do, as one would be done by, and to love one's neighbor as one's self, constitute the ideal perfection of utilitarian morality." (Mill, 1863)

Native American Spirituality:
"Do not wrong or hate your neighbor. For it is not he who you wrong, but yourself." (Pima proverb)

Plato:

"May I do to other as I would that they should do unto me."

Shinto:

"Be charitable to all beings, love is the representative of God." (Ko-ji-ki Hachiman Kasuga)

Sikhism:

"No one is my enemy, none a stranger and everyone is my friend." (Guru Arjan Dev, AG 1299)

Socrates:

"Do not do to others that which would anger you if others did it to you."

Sufism:

"The basis of Sufism is consideration of the hearts and feelings of others. If you haven't the will to gladden someone's heart, then at least beware lest you hurt someone's heart, for on our path, no sin exists but this." (Javad Nurbakhsh)

Taoism:

"Regard your neighbor's gain as your gain, and your neighbor's loss as your own loss." (Tai Shang Kan Yin P'ien)

Unitarian Universalism:

"We affirm and promote respect for the interdependent web of all existence of which we are a part." (UU Principles)

Zoroastrianism:

"That nature alone is good which refrains from doing unto another whatsoever is not good for itself." (Dadistan-i-dinik 94:5)

SUMMARY AND CONCLUSIONS

This brief excursion is a crib sheet of a handful of perspectives and a few of the people who have developed them. As we said, this clustering of theories is somewhat idiosyncratic. We make no claim that this excursion would be acceptable to all philosophers, but we hope it is helpful and that we have not done a disservice to the good thinkers who have dedicated their lives to each of the subtopics.

The goal of this chapter has been to outline a number of principles that should have value for people attempting to understand the media ethics environment. As Marcus Singer has eloquently argued, principles are guides that challenge us to work out things for ourselves.

> A principle can be a general guide to action without telling us exactly just what to do in each set of circumstances. This requires judgment, which in turn requires character, moral sense, and discernment, and to look to precise principles for exact direction is to surrender both autonomy and responsibility for one's own judgments and decisions.
>
> —Marcus G. Singer (2001, p. 617)

By examining the philosophical assertions in this chapter (and in the two previous chapters), it should be obvious that each has merit worthy of consideration. However, each has potential weaknesses if we are tempted to apply them to every ethical dilemma. One size does not fit all. That is why we present these three chapters as tentative answers to the question, "Who's whispering in your ear?"

We urge you to compare your own personal principles with those of the philosophers—not just so you know what kind of philosopher to call yourself, but so you can more carefully articulate and apply your own philosophy.

■ ■ ■

CHAPTER VOCABULARY

Note: Definitions are available at this book's companion website.

- arête
- Aristotle
- compassion fatigue
- contractarian
- empathy
- ethics of care
- eudaimonia
- feminist ethics
- Gilligan, Carol
- Golden Rule

- justice
- MacIntyre, Alisdair
- moral reciprocity
- original position
- phronesis
- pseudo-events
- Rawls, John
- social contract
- veil of ignorance
- virtue

PRACTICAL APPLICATIONS

1. Look again at the two cases in the text of Chapter 10—the student journalists tempted to lie in order to get access to an important story, and the script writer tempted to turn a PG film into a PG-13 film in order to draw a larger audience. As you review the three new pairs of principles introduced in this chapter, consider:

    A. What specific advice would each of the philosophers give you?

    B. Which advice do you find to be the most compelling?

    C. Which is the least compelling?

    D. How will you resolve each of the two cases?

2. Talk with a former journalist who has become a public relations practitioner. Ask how the applications of the approaches taken in this chapter—virtue, care, and the Golden Rule—may be applied differently based upon the communicator's goal.

3. When people think media have a greater effect on themselves than others, that's called the "third-person effect" of mass communication (Davison, 1983). As an example, you might hear someone say: "Violence doesn't bother me on TV, but we should limit it because it will cause other people to be more violent." How does that theory tie into the media messages you personally consume and create? How might this theory be applied when considering ethical considerations of virtue, justice, and care?

■ ■ ■

CASE STUDIES

Return to the five case studies at the end of Chapter 10, and listen to all of the philosophers you've met in the present chapter. Remember how you answered each of the first four questions: What's your problem? Why not follow the rules? Who wins, who loses? and What's it worth? Now, resolve the same cases by listening to what the Chapter 12 theorists whisper in your ear.

Case 10.1   Journalism: How (and Whether) to Cover a Prank

Case 10.2   New media: Do You Take the Ads?

Case 10.3   Public Relations: The Big Weekend

Case 10.4   Advertising: The Nathan Freedonia Ad

Case 10.5   Entertainment: The VIM Kids

Thinking through each of the five cases:

1. What else do you need to know?
2. Is this an ethical issue? Why or why not?
3. What would Aristotle say about this moral quandary? What would the virtuous communicator have to consider, and what decision would he or she make? What are the extremes of excess and deficiency, and what are the satisfactory means?
4. Put on Rawls's veil of ignorance. Define the stakeholders and make your decision based on principles of justice. What is your decision?
5. Now, consider the "ethics of care." What decision do you come to when you use feminist ethical theory? Is it different from what (and how) you originally decided?
6. How useful is the Golden Rule in making a decision for each case?
7. Of all the ethical approaches discussed in Chapters 10 through 12, which worked "best" for you? Which was the most difficult for you? Which led you to decisions that were at odds with other decisions? Which led you to decisions that were at odds with your original choices?
8. The bottom line for each case: What do you do? How do you justify it? Which philosophy do you choose?

■ ■ ■

How's Your Decision Going to Look?

This book's final chapter deals with accountability, transparency, and credibility. It describes numerous internal and external systems that help media practitioners be accountable to themselves and to others. These topics are significant variables when answering the sixth and final of the "5Ws and H" questions we believe should be asked when

> State your conclusion, and imagine what your friends and people you respect will think about your decision making.

doing ethics. The question—"How's your decision going to look?"—expects introspective decision makers to consider the stakeholders who can hold them to an accounting.

Ethical justification is much more than *post-hoc* rationalizing or moralizing once all the decisions have been made and actions have been taken. As we have stressed since the outset of the book, ethical justification should be front-loaded, thought about well in advance of the deadline. If the problem has been well articulated and the choices about loyalties and values and principles are made rationally and openly, the decision makers have gone a long way down the path of accountability.

Unlike the work of many other professional groups, the product of mass communicators tends to be public, and it can affect the lives, feelings, and fortunes of many stakeholders. Nearly anyone has the moral authority to call mass communicators to an accounting, because every member of the audience and the media industries is a stakeholder. Even the most articulate moral justification and transparent performance will fail to satisfy some of the stakeholders, but the media practitioners who hold themselves truly accountable should be able to sleep more comfortably at the end of the day.

1. What's your problem?

2. Why not follow the rules?

3. Who wins, who loses?

4. What's it worth?

5. Who's whispering in your ear?

6. <u>How's your decision going to look?</u>

CHAPTER 13

Accountability, Transparency, and Credibility

INTRODUCTION

BAD NEWS, advertising practitioners: Only 11 percent of Americans think you have high standards of ethics and honesty, which ranks you just above insurance salespeople and members of Congress (Gallup, 2009). The numbers are slightly better for journalists: a third of Americans call journalists immoral and a threat to democracy (Pew, 2007), and only 23 percent say journalists have high standards of honesty and ethics. Meanwhile, many people see public relations practitioners as "flaks" who would do almost anything to polish their clients' problems, bloggers as narrow-minded score settlers who cannot get real media jobs, and people in the entertainment industry as soulless ladder climbers who are amoral on their best days and immoral most of the time. If you are contemplating a career in media primarily because you want to be loved (or even understood) by the general public, you may need to reconsider your motivation. There's a reason for the phrase "kill the messenger."

However, this bad news should cause you little concern if you agree with this book's argument that what others think about your ethics is not necessarily a gauge of how ethical you actually are. Ethics is a matter of substance, not just image. On the other hand, making ethical decisions requires that decision makers be able to defend their decisions in truthful, logical, and ethically sound ways. They need to pass Sissela Bok's (1978) "test of publicity." This is especially true in mass media, a peculiar enterprise in which our products and

> **This chapter:**
> - defines accountability, with a special focus on media accountability
> - places accountability in the context of moral development, transparency, and credibility: moral development helps us understand to whom we feel accountable; transparency is one way to show our accountability; credibility is the perceived result of our efforts to be accountable
> - considers various accountability systems in place for media practitioners and the effectiveness of those systems
> - concludes with practical applications and asks you to revisit case studies and focus on justification and accountability.

actions are designed to be seen (and judged) by audiences. The old saying that "journal-ists print their mistakes; doctors bury theirs" is true for other mass communicators, too.

Accountability, transparency, and credibility are the focus of the sixth and final of the "5Ws and H" questions we propose asking when doing ethics. The question—"How's your decision going to look?"—requires decision makers to reflect not only on the ethical justifications of their decisions, but also to consider to whom (and to what extent) they may be accountable. In doing so, they are well advised to behave with transparency, and to pay some attention to their credibility.

Some of the issues in this chapter are aimed at individual people. Other issues are more focused on institutions as small as individual newsrooms or ad firms, or as large as entire media categories such as television news, or advertising, or "Hollywood." Finally, some of these issues are projected to the large yet largely undefined "media" that the public is so quick to blame. While you can ultimately be responsible only for your own actions, it may be useful to consider some of the issues in this chapter in personal terms, even if you play a small role in large organizations and industries.

Note that each of this book's first five questions contributes to how decision makers answer this final question. The question "How's your decision going to look?" is import-ant to consider when answering questions related to rules, loyalties, values, and principles. Without satisfactory answers to those questions, trying to justify your deci-sions to others (and yourself) can be a painful, humiliating experience. With satisfactory answers, however, decision makers can be more confident when making the call, ready to answer the internal and external critics who inevitably ask them for an accounting.

ACCOUNTABILITY

Defining Accountability

The word "accountability" derives from Latin words that combine to mean "to reckon together." That idea of reckoning can be powerful, as it conjures the image of standing alone in front of a judging audience to explain your irrevocable action. That judge may be your own conscience. More likely, that judge may be a jury that includes any number of stakeholders demanding an explanation. Defining those stakeholders—and the extent to which you owe them loyalty or accountability—is central to the "who wins, who loses" question posed in Chapter 5.

That term "accountable" might make you think of accountancy, the task of setting financial standards, measuring a business' value and adherence to those standards, and communicating the results. The comparison is useful for ethics, because financial and ethical accounting requires clear-eyed, bottom-line approaches.

The people who have been "whispering in your ear" from the previous three chapters have a great deal to say about ethical accountability. In Book 3 of *Nicomachean Ethics*, for example, Aristotle says people are morally responsible for an act if they had the choice of whether to act and whether they knew what they were doing. (He excuses ignorance to a degree, and like some teleologists wonders whether holding people accountable is worthwhile if it does not change their behavior.) Kant, on the other hand, assumes that people are basically rational and have freedom of choice. This makes them morally responsible—a belief shared by most duty-focused philosophers. Jonas (1984) makes the environmental argument that the human race cannot survive unless we are accountable to one another. Someone wearing Rawls's "veil of ignorance" would consider account-ability for justice and other considerations when making a decision.

While the philosophical debate over moral responsibility is long and confusing, this book assumes that people (especially mass communicators, who willingly choose the craft) should be held accountable for their actions. We further believe that morally developed people consider accountability as they make decisions; a lack of sound justification suggests that the decision may be morally suspect. But a justification may be reasonable even if most stakeholders do not fully agree with it.

The term "accountability" has close ties to concepts that include:

Account-giving, or the act of providing excuses and justifications for actions. While this may be a moral necessity to account for lapses of "unanticipated or untoward behavior" (Scott & Lyman, 1968, p. 46), it could be argued that mass communicators, like others in the media spotlight, often must give an account even (or especially) when their decisions are ethically neutral or praiseworthy. The term suggests that such an "account-giving" occurs after the decision is made and the action taken, although that is problem-atic when it is merely "*post-hoc*" moralizing.

While you may have to give your account after the action is taken, it is important to consider what account you will give long before the decision is made and the accounting is required. In Chapter 7, we discussed the three-prong test to determine whether a lie is justifiable, which concludes with: "[W]hat would a public of reasonable persons say about such lies?" (Bok, 1978, p. 112). Bok's list is a reminder that accountability should be a front-end process, not a cover-your-rear-end effort that begins only after others demand an explanation.

Blameworthiness, or deciding whether people deserve censure for their actions. While many people (in and out of media) want to blame the media for messages they don't like, it's important to remember that we should only be held accountable for what we do. Reminding people who blame "the media" that you are only responsible for your individual actions in your individual "medium"—not the plural "media"—can help you sleep nights. (Critics may not know their Latin, but they still should know better than to overgeneralize about all media.)

Responsibility, a term that is often blurred with accountability. The concepts of social responsibility and accountability are inexorably tied in mass communication. As Chapter 3 noted, the First Amendment grants freedom to the press but makes no mention of the responsibilities media practitioners have to themselves or to others. The Commission on

Freedom of the Press (1947), better known as the Hutchins Commission, argued that media enjoy freedoms that are predicated on accountability:

> Freedom of the press for the coming period can only continue as an accountable freedom. Its moral right will be conditioned on its acceptance of this accountability. Its legal right will stand unaltered as its moral duty is performed.
>
> (p. 19)

Many news organizations saw the commission's report as an attack upon their freedom (Blanchard, 1977). The argument continues. At least one scholar says that while ethics and law are important, the only real accountability in media should be in the marketplace. In an open marketplace, media organizations "that people accept and support will survive and thrive; media that people dislike or reject will suffer and die," according to John Merrill (1989, p. 12). That is a minority view. For reasons that include the continued professionalism and corporatization of media, many journalistic organizations accept social responsibility as fundamental to their ethical foundations, not for reasons of First Amendment freedom but because organizations perceived as unethical may be hurt financially. Indeed, a writer opposed to Merrill's argument said the profit-driven demands of most mass media make organized accountability systems even more important (Raskin, 1989).

The term "responsibility" also has legal implications, including the act of acknowledging responsibility for a mistake. While law and ethics are different enterprises, they often intersect at accountability. Plenty of corporations pay fines without admitting guilt and apologize without making themselves publicly accountable (Cohen, 1999). Lawyers representing media organizations may tell their clients not to apologize because it could be used against them in a media malpractice lawsuit. At other times and in some states, however, a quick apology to a libel victim will free the plaintiff from paying punitive damages in a lawsuit. As said in earlier chapters, ethics goes beyond the minimum standards of law, so accountability is a concept that should begin well before a jury's decision or a government agency's fine.

The Dynamics of Accountability

It may appear that accountability is as simple as saying "I'm sorry" when you mess up, or as gratifying as justifying an action that is difficult yet ethically correct. It may well be nearly that simple with decisions made by individuals. It is not that simple in much of mass media, because the organizational structure of most modern media organizations makes it difficult to find that single person to hold accountable. It is even more difficult given that mass media rely on outsiders ranging from news sources to the clients who hire us and also have varying levels of accountability. "The dilution of accountability now common to most large organizations (including media organizations) frustrates onlookers who can't determine who is to blame when something goes wrong" (Bivins, 2009, p. 7).

Accountability is not a binary, "yes/no" construct. Plaisance (2000) describes it as much more fluid and complicated. He says accountability is best understood as a "dynamic of interaction" between a media messenger and "the value sets" of the people or groups who receive those messages (p. 258).

The concept of accountability considers:

- Agreements about the ethical standards to which a media practitioner or an entire media industry should be held. For example, while a journalist may be held accountable and sanctioned for weaving fictional details into a news story, a situation comedy script writer is expected to write fiction. This often confuses both the media practitioner and the public. Asking a dozen movie producers what is "right" might lead to a dozen answers; asking a dozen journalists what is right might give you nearly as many answers. When we can't agree on our standards, how can we expect the public to understand our standards or to have consistent standards of their own?
- The power of the government structure in which media operate (Gordon & Merrill, 1988). For example, in Chapter 3 we noted that while media are accountable to the monarchy in a typical authoritarian society, media accountability is less clear in a libertarian society. The laws relating to media help define some level of account- ability but fall short in an ethical sense. We'll take up this issue when talking about the role that law plays in media accountability systems.
- The power of the people and organizations that seek to hold media practitioners accountable. "Those with the power can demand that those over whom the power is held give an account, explain, or justify themselves and their acts" (Newton, Hodges, & Keith, 2004, p. 166). Internally, that may be a boss requiring a worker to explain a sin of commission or omission. Externally, it could be a powerful advertiser, politician, or interest group whose complaints can hurt the media organization's prestige or pocketbook. How the media organization responds to an accountability request may depend upon how the organization views the power of the requestor.
- The power of the media organization itself, as communicators may feel varying needs to be accountable in order to gain or keep power. For example, a PR practi- tioner may not feel the need to be accountable to PR practitioners with competing messages, to groups the practitioner does not see as stakeholders or seeks to develop a two-way symmetrical relationship with. However, that practitioner likely feels primarily accountable to the client paying the bills. Another example would be an entertainer who falls short of ethical standards but acknowledges that failing out of genuine contriteness, or at least to keep his or her career alive.

Accountability in Context

It is almost certain that your instructors in this course will make you take tests, because people act differently when they know they are being watched and will be held accountable. Your syllabus probably explains your accountability for the material, how that accountability will be measured, and how your level of accountability is reflected in your grades. Accountability may work both ways—at semester's end, you likely will be asked to rate your teacher anonymously. Consistently high or low ratings should affect how the course is taught in the future, and may impact your teacher's continued employment. Despite the differences in who holds power in the student-teacher relationship, these accountability systems can lead to both of you to behave properly.

For mass media, as in much of real life, accountability isn't so simple. The vital question in any consideration of accountability is: "To whom am I accountable?" The answers: To yourself, and to others.

Accountability to Self

The first answer is easy: You must be accountable to yourself. Nature, nurture, education, and your lifetime of experiences have combined to create your schema of what you believe to be right and wrong. Part of any rational decision-making process includes knowing that you must live with that decision both inside and outside your body. Making a decision that falls within your ethical framework can be easily justified. But when that decision is at odds with your ethical framework, the result will be cognitive dissonance—the discomfort that occurs when your beliefs don't match your actions, or when your brain has two competing thoughts (Festinger, 1957). To regain that internal harmony of your thoughts, you must (1) reject one of those competing thoughts, or (2) justify (or rationalize) your thoughts or actions.

This internal accountability can help you clarify your beliefs, acknowledging that you acted ethically or unethically. Or it can be a dangerous time when you reject what you know to be right in order to live with yourself. Consider Jayson Blair, fired in 2003 for multiple counts of fabricating and plagiarizing in the *New York Times*. Reviewers noted that his 2004 memoir, *Burning Down My Master's House*, looks like an example of self-accountability but falls short as Blair "rappels down Mount Excuse, blaming everybody but himself for his offenses" (Shafer, 2004).

It also is worth pointing out that Jiminy Cricket was wrong—you cannot always let your conscience be your guide. The term "conscience" is what most people call what "seems to spring spontaneously from the depths of our human constitution" when we face a moral question (Rogers, 1931, p. 144). Over time, continuous rationalization of unethical decisions may sear your conscience to the point that you do not recognize the need to answer Question 1—"What's your problem?"—because you are unaware that a problem exists. (Remember that in the original story—not the Disney version—Pinocchio squishes the cricket with a mallet.)

A seared conscience—perhaps better known as callousness—is a chief complaint against media practitioners. Journalists who repeatedly report on crime and tragedy may lose their sense of tact and inflict more pain on the victims they photograph or interview. Or PR practitioners may feel bad the first time they use a white lie to "spin" the truth, but by the thousandth spin they don't even notice how far their moral compass has strayed from true north. Or after being careful at first, bloggers may think nothing of spewing invective that they wouldn't dare repeat to the face of the people they are criticizing.

Accountability to Others

Once we move past self-accountability, the answer to the question becomes more difficult. The short answer comes from Chapter 2, which stated that communicators have accountability to the government, to fellow practitioners, and to the public. But what we mean by "public" seems fuzzy. The Chapter 1 discussion of relationships (assigned, contracted, and assumed) can clear up that fuzziness, because accountability is a part of being in a relationship.

Another way to consider accountability is through the prism of moral development theories discussed in the Chapter 4 question of "Who wins, who loses?" Even as theorists disagreed about the definitions, they defined categories of pre-conventional, conventional, and post-conventional levels of moral development. Using Kohlberg's (1981) cognitive-social approach to answer the question "To whom am I accountable?" it can be said that accountability in:

- Pre-conventional levels of moral development is about self-interest. People at these levels may feel accountable only to people who can reward or punish them (Level 1) or to people who can help them in their self-interests (Level 2). Journalists at this low level may feel accountable to bosses who can fire or promote them, or to sources who can make or break a story. People in the entertainment industry may feel accountable to bosses or more powerful people, such as well-known actors, to whom they can hitch their wagon.
- Conventional levels of moral development are about conformity and following the rules. As stated previously, many of the rules involve accountability—especially when those rules are violated. For mass communicators, juries decide accountability when considering cases of libel, invasion of privacy, copyright violations, and similar issues. The legal rights of persuasive communicators have changed as legislatures, regulators, and courts have defined limits to commercial speech and created ways to hold violators legally accountable for their actions. Meanwhile, over-the-air broadcasting rules require that communicators should be socially responsible and operate in "the public interest, convenience and necessity" because the public gives broadcasters access to the scarce commodity that is the electromagnetic spectrum. Most of us live our lives at this conventional level, accountable to rules and rule-makers, in part because our "tribes" understand our justifications when we follow their rules. Mass communicators operating at this level of moral development may feel accountable to the codes of ethics that guide their craft, and to fellow practitioners. This might include advertising practitioners who follow Federal Trade Commission rules and the AAF and Better Business Bureau code of ethics, so they can point to those rules when required to make an account of their actions. The notion that mass communicators must serve "the public" is implicit in these rules and codes, but sometimes following the rules does not relieve media practitioners of accountability. The advertising practitioner may craft ads that meet federal guidelines and the letter of the code, yet still have ads that are misleading, ethically suspect, and difficult to justify on grounds other than saying that the ad

"meets federal guidelines." This is why ethicists want people to operate at higher levels of moral development.

- Post-conventional levels of moral development are about accountability to the greater society. They might require a journalist to deceive, or a filmmaker to show violence unflinchingly, in order to reveal a greater truth. Those sorts of acts generally draw a great deal of attention and require a high level of accountability, just as Martin Luther King, Jr.'s *Letter from a Birmingham Jail* justified his decision to break racist laws he considered immoral. This can be tricky, as people operating at lower levels of moral development do not always understand or accept why the rules needed to be broken.

Communitarian and feminist ethicists also consider accountability, as they generally assume that higher levels of moral development require higher levels of accountability in our relationships with others and to the larger world. Ethicist Clifford Christians (1988) describes an example of the difficulties in tying together the various levels of accountability to ourselves, to people and groups with whom we have affiliation, and to society at large by introducing a TV station manager who also is a church member, second-generation American, and parent, which means he (and the rest of us) operate "with a sense of collective responsibility issuing from our humanity":

> In fact, much of what we mean by enlarging the scope of our accountability entails that our duties as experts become so intertwined with our communal relationships that our thinking and action are inseparably shaped by both our expertise and our basic humanness.

(pp. 54–55)

To summarize, the higher the level of moral development, the wider the collection of people and groups to which we feel accountable. (Recall that the title of our Chapter 4 is "Moral Development and the Expansion of Empathy.) Balancing that accountability is a consideration as we sort our values and loyalties, as discussed in Chapters 5 and 6. When we determine to whom we are loyal and to what values we cling, we can decide to whom we owe accountability.

TRANSPARENCY AND ACCOUNTABILITY

When we "give an account" to someone to whom we feel accountable, to some degree we reveal to them something about ourselves, our motives, and our decision-making process—we are being transparent.

Dictionary definitions of transparency include "capable of being seen through" and "without guile or concealment; open; frank; candid" (Neufeldt, 1997, p. 1422). Oliver's definition of communication-related transparency—"letting the truth be available for others to see if they so choose" and as "active disclosure" of information in a public context—has long been a concept in fields that range from political science to international finance (Oliver, 2004, p. 3). In finance, for example, the system of buying would collapse without trust and accountability, so the rules are designed to make transactions as transparent as possible. It is true in mass communication, too.

We are likely to trust those who show openness and accountability—assuming we agree with their justifications. People operating at higher levels of moral development may appreciate reasonable justifications and high levels of transparency, even if they disagree with the decision.

As mass communicators, transparency means treating our audiences as ends unto themselves by revealing ourselves and our motives. Plaisance (2006) called transparency a "first-order media ethics value" because communicators must be concerned not only with the content of their messages but also with "the form and nature of our interaction with others" (p. 3).

The source-message-channel-receiver definition of communication (Berlow, 1960)—which describes how a source sends a message over a channel to a receiver and receives feedback—provides a useful way to show how transparency plays a role in mass communication accountability with audiences (Roberts, 2007). Again, some of these notions are focused at the institutional level, as we consider how a particular medium or media organization is transparent. Other notions are aimed at the individual decision maker, inside or outside of a media organization.

Transparency begins with the *source* of message. Mass communicators cannot be accountable to audiences without revealing themselves and their motives. This suggests that "astroturf" public relations campaigns, "sock puppet" persuasive campaigns, ads designed to look like official government forms, hidden-camera journalism, journalists who fail to reveal real or potential conflicts of interests, and some forms of anonymous online communication may be unethical. Message recipients, and people "used" by mass communicators in creating messages, usually deserve to know the source and motivations of the messengers.

Source transparency also includes considerations of audience feedback. For journalists, it means allowing audiences to comment on stories or even actively soliciting sources during the course of reporting in order to have a more complete news report. For public relations practitioners, it may begin with two-way symmetrical public relations practices with the publics identified by the PR practitioner, but it moves into considerations of stakeholders who may be powerless yet are affected by the campaign.

Message transparency considerations include the reason for the message, because the audience deserves to know whether a mass media message is designed to inform, persuade, or entertain. This suggests potential ethical problems tied to stealth advertising, persuasive communication disguised as "objective" news reports, or broadcasters who do "news" reports highlighting their own entertainment shows without mentioning the connection. For journalists, message transparency means that the audience understands the extent to which the journalist can vouch for the information used, the sources of the information, the justification for using anonymous sources, and whether the audience knows the extent to which raw video was edited or otherwise changed. For entertainment media, it suggests that movie makers tell audiences where reality ends and fiction begins so audiences won't confuse the two.

A separate sort of message transparency involves special descriptions of content. News stories with possibly objectionable content, for example, may be topped with an "editor's note" or a warning from broadcasters about the content. The Recording Industry Association of America, under pressure from outsiders, asks its members to put a "Parental Warning: Explicit Content" label on CDs. Apple's iTunes store also labels songs with explicit lyrics, and its iPhone applications warn buyers that the apps could contain content inappropriate for children. The Motion Picture Association of America (MPAA) is perhaps the most famous organization for its voluntary ratings system, but the broadcast television industry and the video gaming industry also include ratings. All of these companies and trade groups say they provide the service as a voluntary act of accountability. On the other hand, the MPAA is not totally transparent as a messenger because it neither reveals the identities of reviewers nor publicly explains specifics in how it rates individual movies (MPAA, n.d.).

Channel transparency suggests that some ways to deliver messages can be more transparent than others because they allow more feedback. The Internet's rise of the "chat room" and open comment sections on news and other websites gives mass communicators many options in transparency. Transparent communicators make it easy for the audience to talk back to the messenger—and to each other. The question for communicators is what lines, if any, to draw letting the audience criticize the messenger, to require audience members to identify themselves, and to send messages that are racist, sexist, crude, wildly off topic, based on rumor and not fact, etc.

Receiver transparency is focused on the audience members' understanding of themselves. Just as mass communicators should be accountable for their messages and methods, audience members also have a level of accountability when it comes to understanding themselves, their ability to handle dissonant media messages, how aware they are of their own belief sets, and their level of media literacy. When audience members understand themselves and how media work, then they can be more reasonable, active, and formidable in demanding accountability.

CREDIBILITY AND ACCOUNTABILITY

Beyond the moral imperative that requires people to be accountable to themselves and to others, mass communicators often have a more pragmatic reason to be accountable: credibility. Mass communicators—whether journalists, entertainers, or persuaders —are more likely to be successful when audiences believe messengers and their messages.

The term "credibility" comes from the Latin word that means "to believe," and message recipients make ultimate decisions about credibility regardless of the message's truth or the messenger's morality. It bears repeating: Credibility is what people think about you, not what you really are. Unfortunately, perception often becomes reality for mass communicators, so credibility deserves special attention.

Ethicists as far back as Aristotle have studied credibility. The earliest research on mass media effects involved measuring the believability of messages, because a message perceived as true is more likely to be acted upon. Media practitioners who provide information and commentary seek to be perceived as credible, to persuade audiences that they are ethical and that their messages are believable. Entertainment communicators seek a different sort of credibility: that they are capable of telling powerful or entertaining stories in ways perceived as ethical by the public. Persuaders often seek credibility as a means to the end of reaching their organization's larger goal of promoting their own positions as they persuade the public to buy their goods or to believe in their cause. For journalists, credibility is an end unto itself.

Aristotle's *Rhetoric* (350 BC/1954) introduced credibility through the concepts of ethos, pathos, and logos. Ethos "depends on the personal character of the speaker." Pathos depends on "putting the audience into a certain frame of mind." Logos considers "the proof, or apparent proof, provided by the words of the speech itself." Stated more directly, ethos provides an insight into the creator of a message; logos considers the message; and pathos considers the audiences and their emotional reaction to a message and messenger. When combined, those three concepts add up to the list of ingredients that people use to decide whether they believe the message and the messenger.

Where does accountability fit in? It ties into ethos, because research and common sense show that messengers who are accountable are more likely to be perceived as trustworthy and therefore more credible. It also ties into logos, because messages that include information about the source of the message and the source of the information inside the message also are more likely to be perceived as credible.

Having said that, added transparency does not necessarily mean a corresponding rise in perceived credibility—especially at the institutional level. People may trust government less as it becomes more transparent; *New York Times* columnist David Brooks (2010) says "government should sometimes be shrouded for the same reason that middle-aged people should be clothed." The same may be true of some mass communication, as the veneer of objectivity has been replaced by opinionated talking heads on TV, as more coverage of the financial side of entertainment shows how profits are more important than art or "truth telling," and public relations practitioners find that revealing the true source of a message can backfire. Sometimes media fare, like law and sausage, is best not watched while being manufactured.

We close this section where we started, with the reminder that having credibility does not mean the same thing as having ethics. Transparency is required in order to have the accountability needed to be an ethical communicator, but it is not sufficient to boost credibility.

And it is clear that media are not trusted. An overview of 1,000-plus research studies showed that the American public's concerns are rising about what they see:

> . . . as excessive violence, gratuitous sex, and invasive advertising, repetitive news reports, excessive emphasis on crime and celebrity, truth telling (bias and sensationalism), and invasion of privacy.
>
> (Cooper, 2008, p. 16)

The study also showed that Americans are opposed to totally free speech, see the media as too negative and contributing to the decline of democracy, don't trust news reports as much as they used to, think children deserve more protection from media, and believe there's too much advertising in media. Nearly all subsets of society think media portrayals of them are inaccurate. No major type of communication went unscathed: In the overview of media studies, "perhaps three fourths of Americans' primary reported irritations about a medium or a genre seemed to be based on ethical concerns" (p. 25).

MEDIA ACCOUNTABILITY SYSTEMS

Earlier in this chapter we dredged up the adage that "journalists print their mistakes; doctors bury theirs." Mass communicators say it as if they get the bad end of the deal, but doctors know better because they are accountable for their life-and-death decisions. Most medical centers hold M&Ms—morbidity and mortality conferences—in which doctors regularly meet to discuss mistakes in patient care and to learn from those mistakes. While some worry that the frank discussions can lead to more malpractice lawsuits (a liability concern also held by many mass communicators), it does not seem to be the case in medicine (Stewart et al., 2006). Others are concerned that apologizing also can lead to medical (or media) malpractice lawsuits because apologies assume responsibility for actions, but those worries may be overblown (Wagatsuma & Rosett, 1986). Indeed, saying you are sorry is not only ethical but may be the right legal tactic, too.

Gawande (2002) says medical accountability meetings are paradoxical because, on one hand, they reinforce "the very American notion that error is intolerable. On the other hand, the very existence of the M&M, its place on the weekly schedule, amounts to an acknowledgement that mistakes are an inevitable part of medicine" (p. 62).

Mistakes are inevitable in mass media, too, but accountability systems are rarely as formal or consistent as in medicine. Borden (2007) says the freedom granted to media is precisely why media should be accountable. Part of her argument is the hope that journalism (and, perhaps, other forms of mass media) will be viewed as a profession, which comes with societal contracts that assume professionals will regulate themselves if they "act in society's interests" (pp. 110–111). While mass media's professionalism remains debatable (see Chapter 3), it is clear that mass communicators do not have accountability systems as formal as systems in more-established professions.

This section describes a variety of accountability systems. The late media ethicist Claude-Jean Bertrand (2003a) identified 60 types of accountability systems for journalism, which he categorized as text-based, individuals/groups, and processes. He noted that some are internal, involving individual mass communicators, their employers, or immediate members of their tribe. Others are external, involving government, recipients of media messages, and outsiders who also happen to be media practitioners. Still others involve cooperation between media practitioners and outsiders (see Box 13.1). All are useful, but none is completely effective.

Box 13.1 | MEDIA ACCOUNTABILITY SYSTEMS

Claude-Jean Bertrand (2003a) identified 60 examples of media accountability systems in three broad areas: internal to the media, external, and co-operative. Examples of his journalism-focused list include:

- **Internal**: Letters from the editor, corrections, reporters who cover media, in-house critics, ethics audits, audience surveys, codes of ethics, whistle-blowers, internal memos.

- **External**: Alternative media, trade publications, media-related web sites, higher education, required ethics courses, research, consumer groups, government.

- **Co-operative**: Letters to the editor, ombudsman, press councils, panels of media users, training.

Building upon Bertrand's journalism-oriented list, we expand our thinking to include key accountability systems for all media. They include government, codes, external ratings and internal standards, corrections, ombudsmen, news councils, and external critics.

Government Systems

The only accountability systems that all parts of society share come through the government's courts and regulatory agencies. The development of laws related to libel, slander, invasion of privacy, copyright, and others are aimed at curbing the most excessive abuses of speech. Other media-focused laws balance free speech against other concerns, such as defense or trial-related rights. American law has a sliding scale of speech protection, with political and news-based speech receiving the most freedom, followed by artistic speech. Commercial speech ranks lower on the continuum, as evidenced by state and federal rules against untruths, overstatements, and misleading speech. At the bottom is obscene speech, which receives little protection.

Courts and governments hold mass communicators responsible for the most egregious violations of ethics, which are described (and their penalties proscribed) by law. As discussed in Chapter 1, law is concerned with what we can or cannot do; ethics is concerned about what we should or should not do. We can act unethically while acting legally, so other accountability systems are needed to deal with actions that are legal yet wrong.

Bertrand (2003a) points out several problems in relying on law to force media accountability. Authoritarian nations use law to chill, harass, and punish media whose messages run counter to authority's dictates. In nations such as England, where defendants bear the burden of proof in libel cases, lawsuits and threats of lawsuits can make media run scared. And in the United States and other nations, law may not be the best way to seek accountability from media because the "law is slow, expensive, and so complicated that it scares off the common human being" (p. 13). Bertrand was a proponent of the next three types of accountability systems, which he described as non-governmental "means to insure that media provide good public service" (p. 16).

Code-Based Accountability

The category of accountability we've discussed most frequently in this book involves codes of ethics. In addition to their uses of teaching neophytes the standards of their craft, codes often hold sway in the court of public opinion, where peers and outsiders who perceive ethical violations by practitioners can use codes as a way to demand accountability.

Codes of ethics are almost always internally imposed systems, or at least accepted when a communicator freely chooses to join a trade group such as the SPJ or AAF. Most codes mention accountability, even as the codes also carry a call for independence in action. While freedom and external accountability seem contradictory, the two concepts are indeed related. Mass media practitioners say they cannot be accountable without being independent—even as media practitioners who do not act independently may be accountable for allowing themselves to lose independence. For example, a journalist who curries favor to gain advertising may be accountable to readers for failing to be fair and independent. Advertising practitioners who don't stop clients from making unsubstantiated claims for fear of losing the account also may feel accountability beyond the law.

The key issue involving codes of ethics is the repercussions of accountability. Organizational code of ethics, such as an individual newspaper's code, often are perceived as legal documents, and someone who violates the code's minimum standards could be reprimanded or fired. That is similar to—yet far from—codes for professionals such as doctors and lawyers, who can be stripped of their medicine or law licenses when found to have broken ethical standards.

As a practical matter in the media ethics environment, however, codes offer little accountability because they are generally unenforceable. The SPJ in 1987 removed a clause from its code that said "Journalists should actively censure and try to prevent violations of codes of ethics," which a First Amendment lawyer said made the code more constitutionally acceptable but destroyed "most of the code's public relations benefits" (Zenner, 1995). Not everyone was pleased, of course. The former head of the group's ethics committee called SPJ "an ethics wimp" (Bukro, 2000, p. 46).

The PRSA's code seems stricter in its accountability, with members asked to sign a statement acknowledging that they could be kicked out of the PRSA for legal misconduct or for breaking a code rule. But even if that happens, a PR practitioner (like a journalist or someone in nearly every other media job) could continue working as a professional communicator, because the First Amendment allows no barrier to entry. While the shame of being admonished by peers may be real, the practical effect may be tiny. Box 13.2 includes accountability and transparency statements from a variety of codes.

External Ratings and Internal Standards

Earlier in this chapter, we included entertainment industry ratings systems as an example of message transparency. They also can be used for accountability, especially when these voluntary ratings systems are challenged for being incomplete or faulty. Pressure on the movie industry, for example, led the Motion Picture Association of American to consider tobacco use when issuing ratings (Polansky, Titus, & Glantz, 2009). While the MPAA ratings system is voluntary, filmmakers who do not use it often encounter difficulties in marketing and distributing their films through normal channels.

The television industry holds itself accountable through "standards and practices" departments at the major networks. These departments "review all non-news broadcast matter, including entertainment, sports and commercials, for compliance with legal, policy, factual, and community standards" (Dessart, n.d.). The departments hold their own communicators accountable, before material is broadcast, for both legal and ethical reasons. The job ranges from making sure scripted shows don't break FCC decency guidelines to reviewing advertising. CBS is among the most recent networks to face questions after it broadcast a pro-life ad bought by the Christian group Focus on the Family, starring former University of Florida quarterback Tim Tebow, but it rejected an ad from a gay dating service showing "two football-watching men sharing a passionate kiss after their hands touch while reaching into a bowl of potato chips" (Stransky, 2010). The network questioned the dating service company's finances but did not elaborate about the ad's content beyond saying it did not meet broadcast standards.

Corrections

Another vehicle for accountability is corrections columns, in which journalists publicly acknowledge errors of fact or, to a lesser extent, lapses in taste, tone, or generally accepted reporting standards. Corrections columns can be useful because they seek to mitigate mistakes, can limit punitive damages in lawsuits, and serve as a public-relations reminder to audiences that the news organization is serious about accuracy. But research

Box 13.2 | WHAT CODES OF ETHICS SAY ABOUT ACCOUNTABILITY AND TRANSPARENCY

From the Society of Professional Journalists Code of Ethics:

Be Accountable

Journalists are accountable to their readers, listeners, viewers and each other.

Journalists should:

- Clarify and explain news coverage and invite dialogue with the public over journalistic conduct.
- Encourage the public to voice grievances against the news media.
- Admit mistakes and correct them promptly.
- Expose unethical practices of journalists and the news media.
- Abide by the same high standards to which they hold others.

From the American Society of Newspaper Editors' Statement of Principles:

ARTICLE VI—Fair Play. Journalists should respect the rights of people involved in the news, observe the common standards of decency and stand accountable to the public for the fairness and accuracy of their news reports.

From the Radio Television Digital News Association:

ACCOUNTABILITY: Professional electronic journalists should recognize that they are accountable for their actions to the public, the profession, and themselves.

Professional electronic journalists should:

- Actively encourage adherence to these standards by all journalists and their employers.
- Respond to public concerns. Investigate complaints and correct errors promptly and with as much prominence as the original report.
- Explain journalistic processes to the public, especially when practices spark questions or controversy.
- Recognize that professional electronic journalists are duty-bound to conduct themselves ethically.
- Refrain from ordering or encouraging courses of action that would force employees to commit an unethical act.
- Carefully listen to employees who raise ethical objections and create environments in which such objections and discussions are encouraged.
- Seek support for and provide opportunities to train employees in ethical decision-making.

continued

Box 13.2 | *continued*

From A Bloggers' Code of Ethics:

Be Accountable

Bloggers should:

- Admit mistakes and correct them promptly.
- Explain each Weblog's mission and invite dialogue with the public over its content and the bloggers' conduct.
- Disclose conflicts of interest, affiliations, activities and personal agendas.
- Deny favored treatment to advertisers and special interests and resist their pressure to influence content. When exceptions are made, disclose them fully to readers.
- Be wary of sources offering information for favors. When accepting such information, disclose the favors.
- Expose unethical practices of other bloggers.
- Abide by the same high standards to which they hold others.

From the Public Relations Society of America's Member Code of Ethics Pledge:

PRSA Member Code of Ethics Pledge

I pledge:

> To conduct myself professionally, with truth, accuracy, fairness, and responsibility to the public; To improve my individual competence and advance the knowledge and proficiency of the profession through continuing research and education; And to adhere to the articles of the Member Code of Ethics 2000 for the practice of public relations as adopted by the governing Assembly of the Public Relations Society of America.

> I understand and accept that there is a consequence for misconduct, up to and including membership revocation.

> And, I understand that those who have been or are sanctioned by a government agency or convicted in a court of law of an action that is in violation of this Code may be barred from membership or expelled from the Society.

From the American Marketing Association's Ethical Norms and Values for Marketers:

Transparency—to create a spirit of openness in marketing operations. To this end, we will:

- Strive to communicate clearly with all constituencies.
- Accept constructive criticism from customers and other stakeholders.
- Explain and take appropriate action regarding significant product or service risks, component substitutions or other foreseeable eventualities that could affect customers or their perception of the purchase decision.

shows that journalists correct only a small portion of their actual mistakes, and people who are the subjects of news stories find many more errors than are ever corrected ("Forget the error," 2007).

Ombudsmen

While they are few in number, some media organizations large and small hire people to investigate public complaints and tell others about the good and bad of the operations. Ombudsmen—the term is Swedish—usually are trusted outsiders who look into the organization that is paying them. (Some newspapers use the term "readers' representatives.") They often are hired for a set length of time and essentially answer to no one, giving them independence in accounting for that organization. ESPN, *The Washington Post*, *The New York Times*, and fewer than 40 other news organizations employ such people.

Nemeth notes that they can "fulfill public accountability and public-relations roles at the same time" (Nemeth, 2003, p. 144), but Glasser (2003) notes that few organizations have them because they must be paid, they can undercut management's authority, and "it hurts morale to have someone always second-guessing" (p. 177). Still, media ombudsmen provide more accountability than in other industries; whoever heard of a Fortune 100 company hiring someone to tell the world about its failures on a regular basis?

News Councils

One truth about accountability—as with any other ethics activity—is that it requires the accused to take a rational, dispassionate look at the issue. Knowing that is difficult to do, many efforts have been made to create third-party organizations that meet to consider complaints against media organizations, take and review evidence, and draw conclusions. These examples of arbitration are best known as news councils. At least 60 nations have them, and they range from being very independent to being just another vehicle authoritarian governments can use to keep journalists in check.

News councils have had limited success in the United States, even though one of their redeeming qualities is that they keep the news organization out of court (Bertrand, 2003b). A national news council in the United States collapsed in the 1980s after about a decade, because few media organizations wanted to relinquish their freedom. Only a few local councils survive in the United States.

External Critics, etc.

Because mass media show their work to the world, it's not unexpected for the world to seek to respond with praise and criticism. News organizations may print letters to the editor or ultimately control the online comment below stories, but outsiders are invited to participate and hold the organization accountable. Also, media often cover each other; "alternative" media criticize and praise mainstream media. Newspapers may cover television news; infrequently, TV covers newspapers. Reporters cover and critics praise and pan the entertainment industry. Trade publications also weigh on the industry that is their focus, such as *Editor & Publisher* and journalism reviews, *PR Week*, *Advertising Age*, and *Variety*. Bloggers criticize everybody. When these outsiders do their jobs properly, media practitioners and organizations are called to account for their actions.

Other outsiders may include groups who demand accountability based on their narrow or largely drawn interests. They are all across the political spectrum, from the conservative Accuracy in Media to the liberal Fairness and Accuracy in Reporting. They include different races, creeds, and perspectives, such as the Jewish Anti-Defamation League, the American-Arab Anti-Discrimination League, and the Gay & Lesbian Alliance Against Defamation. They include religious groups, such as the Catholic League, the American Family Association, and the Alternative Religions Educational Network. We can go on and on . . .

Accountability can require that you respond to complaints about a single sentence in a news story or a single line from a script, the lack of certain types of characters, or the portrayal of people who may be perceived as representing an entire group of people.

What to do when a group comes calling? The reflex may be to recoil, circle the PCs, and take up our defenses. But an ethical mass communicator takes calls for accountability seriously, even from people and groups with obvious axes to grind. An occasional error is human, but multiple, systematic complaints should require us to think about our methods and motives.

The authors' advice in responding to calls for accountability is to begin with humility. Accountability is, in many ways, an act of humility. It shows that you do not think so highly of yourself that you do not feel the obligation to explain yourself to others, and it reveals to them that you were thinking of them (among other stakeholders, we hope) when making decisions. We don't recommend it, but we are struck by the accountability method of H.L. Mencken, the famous journalist of the early twentieth century, who often replied to letters of complaint or praise with a note that said: "Dear Sir or Madame, You may be right."

SUMMARY AND CONCLUSIONS

This chapter helps answer the final question: "How's your decision going to look?" It discusses the importance of thinking about that question as the decision is being made, because trying to justify a decision after the fact may be no more than an exercise in moralizing, an attempt to find reasons to cover yourself. Accountability is a moral necessity, because autonomous moral agents should take responsibility for their actions. Thinking about accountability requires a decision maker to have answered many of the previous questions listed in this book, especially ones related to our conflicting loyalties and values.

Accountability is particularly important to mass communicators because their messages can draw a great deal of attention and affect the lives, feelings, and fortunes of audiences. Many internal and external systems are in place to help (or make) media practitioners be accountable to themselves and to others. Government may require minimal accountability, but systems seeking higher ethical accountability are often voluntary for mass communicators.

■ ■ ■

CHAPTER VOCABULARY

Note: Definitions are available at this book's companion website.

- accountability
- blameworthiness
- cognitive dissonance
- communitarian
- credibility
- ethos

- logos
- media accountability systems
- ombudsmen
- pathos
- transparency

PRACTICAL APPLICATIONS

1. Go back to the cases at the conclusion of Chapter 4, in which you were originally not asked to make a decision. Now that we've investigated all six questions in the book, go back and "do ethics" using those questions.

    As you work, be sure to consider how you would justify your answer if asked to do so in: (a) court, (b) by a stakeholder in the scenario who might be helped by your decision, (c) by a stakeholder in the scenario who might be hurt by your decision, and (d) a reporter from a trade publication asking for an explanation.

    A. **News**: This chapter touches briefly on the controversy of the Society of Professional Journalists' decision to remove the "censure" clause from its code of ethics. Do you think it was a wise decision? Why or why not? In what ways can the news business raise its credibility without cutting into its own autonomy?

    B. **Digital media**: At the advent of blogging in the late 1990s, it was said that the key to its success and accountability would be its transparency, in which readers can click to learn about the blogger and to see the evidence used in the blog. Now, more than a decade later, how well do you think that has worked out? Do you feel as if the practices of blogging make it more or less accountable than "mainstream" media? What are the ethics of anonymous postings?

C. **Public relations**: What accountability, if any, do PR practitioners owe to people and groups who are not part of their readily identified "publics?" Can practitioners be more accountable to those secondary publics without losing the edge needed to meet the clients' needs? And in cases in which practitioners' clients have poor reputations and low credibility, to what level should practitioners worry about their own accountability and credibility in the eyes of the general public?

D. **Advertising**: The start of this chapter noted that just 11 percent of Americans think that advertising practitioners have high or very high ethical standards. What can the industry do to raise that percentage (including, perhaps, an ad campaign)? How can advertisers be more accountable in an age with so much more advertising and the ever-rising need to find ways to draw attention to your ad?

E. **Entertainment**. The Motion Picture Production Code of 1930, known as the Hays Code, was Hollywood's way to stop governments from imposing content rules on movies. Go to the code, at www.artsreformation.com/a001/hays-code.html, and choose a section. List the groups to whom Hollywood felt it should be accountable in 1930. Next, list groups to whom Hollywood filmmakers feel the need to be accountable today, and try to find ways to justify something in the 1930 code that you think should (or should not) be applicable today.

2. The chapter sought to differentiate between personal accountability and organizational/group accountability. Think of a time when you justified an action (you may not have believed in personally) by appealing to your affiliation with an organization. (Example: You did something you didn't "want" to do, but it was expected because you were part of a group, or a journalist/persuasive communicator, etc.) How much cognitive dissonance did you feel? How convincing was your justification? Would you make the same decision again? Why or why not?

■ ■ ■

References

AdAge.com (1995). The Marlboro Man. Retrieved from http://adage.com/century/icon01.html.

Aiello, L., & Proffitt, J.M. (2008). VNR usage: A matter of regulation or ethics? *Journal of Mass Media Ethics, 23*(3), 219–234.

Albert, E. (1968). Value systems. In D.L. Sils (Ed.), *International encyclopedia of social sciences* (Vol. 16, pp. 287–291). New York: Macmillan Press.

Allison, M. (1986). A literature review of approaches to the professionalism of journalists. *Journal of Mass Media Ethics, 1*(2), 5–19.

Allport, G.W. (1955). Attitudes. In C. Murchison (Ed.), *A handbook of social psychology* (Vol. 2, pp. 798–844). New York: Russell & Russell.

Alsdoory, L. (2009). Feminist criticism in public relations: How gender can impact public relations texts and contexts. In R.L Heath, E.L Toth, & D. Waymer (Eds.), *Rhetorical and critical approaches to public relations* (pp. 110–124). New York: Routledge.

Alterman, E. (2003). *What liberal media? The truth about bias and the news.* New York: Basic Books.

American Marketing Association's ethical norms and values for marketers. (n.d.). Retrieved from www.marketingpower.com/AboutAMA/Pages/Statement of Ethics.aspx.

Aristotle. (1954). *Rhetoric.* New York: The Modern Library.

—— . (1962). *Nicomachean ethics* (M. Ostwald, Trans.). New York: Macmillan.

Baker, S. (1999). Five baselines for justification in persuasion. *Journal of Mass Media Ethics, 14*(2), 69–81.

—— . (2008). The model of the principled advocate and the pathological partisan: A virtue ethics construct of opposing archetypes of public relations and advertising practitioners. *Journal of Mass Media Ethics, 23*(3), 235–253.

—— . (2009). The ethics of advocacy: Moral reasoning in the practice of public relations. In L. Wilkins & C.G. Christians (Eds.), *The handbook of mass media ethics* (pp. 115–129). New York: Routledge.

Baker, S., & Martinson, D. (2001). The TARES Test: Five principles for ethical persuasion. *Journal of Mass Media Ethics, 16*(2 & 3), 148–175.

Barber, B. (1963). Some problems in the sociology of professions. *Daedalus, 92,* 665–668.

Barney, R. (2001). Foreword, *Journal of Mass Media Ethics, 16*(2 & 3), 73–77.

Barney, R., & Black, J. (1994). Ethics and professional persuasive communications. *Public Relations Review, 20*(3), 233–238.

Baron, M.W. (2001). Loyalty. In L.C. Becker & C.B. Becker (Eds.), *Encyclopedia of ethics* (2nd ed.) (pp. 1027–1029). New York: Routledge.

Barrett, D. (Ed.). (1961). *Values in America*. Notre Dame: University of Notre Dame Press.

Bartlett, T. (2010, January 12.) Hiding movies from critics. The *Chronicle of Higher Education* "Percolator" blog. Retrieved from http://chronicle.com/blogPost/Hiding-Movies-From-Critics/20457.

Bates, S. (1995). *Realigning journalism with democracy: The Hutchins Commission, its times, and ours.* Washington, DC: The Annenberg Washington Program in Communications Policy Studies of Northwestern University. Retrieved from www.annenberg.northwestern.edu/pubs/hutchins/default.htm.

Bebeau, M. (1998, July 21–25). New Directions for Research and Assessment. Seminar at the University of Minnesota.

Becker, L.C. (2001). Reciprocity. In L.C. Becker & C.B. Becker (Eds.), *Encyclopedia of ethics* (pp. 1464–1467). New York: Routledge.

Belenky, M.F., Clinchy, B.M., Goldberger, N.R., & Tarule, J.M. (1986). *Women's ways of knowing: The development of self, voice, and mind.* New York: Basic Books.

Bellah, R.N., Madsen, R., Sullivan, W.M., Swidler, A., & Tipton, S.M. (1985). *Habits of the heart: Individualism and commitment in American life.* New York: Harper & Row.

Bendick, M., & Egan, M. (2009, January). Research perspectives on race and employment in the advertising industry. Retrieved from www.naacp.org/news/press/2009-01-08/Bendick. Egan.Advert.Industry.Report.%28Jan%2009%29.pdf, pp. 34-35.

Bentham, J. (1970). *An introduction to the principles of morals and legislation.* J.H. Burns & H.L.A. Hart (Eds.). London: Athlone Press. (Original work published 1789).

Berkowitz, D. (1990). Information subsidy and agenda building in local television news. *Journalism Quarterly, 67*(4), 723–731.

Berlow, D. (1960). *The process of communication.* New York: Holt, Rinehart & Winston.

Bernays, E.L. (1923). *Crystallizing public opinion.* New York: Boni & Liveright.

—— . (1928). *Propaganda.* New York: Liveright.

—— . (1955). *The Engineering of consent.* Norman: University of Oklahoma Press.

Bertrand, C.-J. (2003a). A predicament and three solutions. In C.-J. Bertrand (Ed.), *An arsenal for democracy: Media accountability systems.* Cresskill, NJ: Hampton Press.

—— . (2003b). Press councils. In C.-J. Bertrand (Ed.), *An arsenal for democracy: Media accountability systems.* Cresskill, NJ: Hampton Press.

Bissell, K. (2006). Skinny like you: Visual literacy, digital manipulation and young women's drive to be thin. *SIMILE: Studies In Media & Information Literacy Education, 6*(1), 1–14.

Bivins, T. (2004). *Mixed media: Moral distinctions in advertising, public relations, and journalism.* Mawhaw, NJ: Lawrence Erlbaum.

—— . (2008). The future of public relations and advertising ethics. In T.W. Cooper, C.G. Christians, & A. Babbili (Eds.), *An ethics trajectory: Visions of media past, present and yet to come* (pp. 233–238). Urbana, IL: University of Illinois.

—— . (2009). *Mixed media: Moral distinctions in advertising, public relations, and journalism* (2nd ed.). New York: Routledge.

Black, J. (1992). Teaching media ethics. In M. Murry & A. Ferri (Eds.), *Teaching mass communication: A guide to better instruction* (pp. 235–255). New York: Praeger.

—— . (1995). Rethinking the naming of sex crime victims. *Newspaper Research Journal, 16* (3), 96–112; revised and republished (1996) in T. Thomason (Ed.), *Newspaper coverage of rape: Dilemmas on deadline.* Fort Worth, TX: Texas Christian University, pp. 14–24.

—— . (2001). Semantics and ethics of propaganda. *Journal of Mass Media Ethics, 16*(2 & 3), 121–137.

—— . (2004, August). Teaching and studying journalism ethics. *Quill*, pp. 6–7.

—— . (2009). The ethics of propaganda and the propaganda of ethics. In L. Wilkins & C.G. Christians (Eds.), *The handbook of mass media ethics* (pp. 130–148). New York: Routledge.

—— . (2010). Who's a journalist? In Christopher Meyers (Ed.), *A philosophical approach to journalism ethics* (pp. 103–116). New York: Oxford University Press.

Black, J., & Barney, R. (1990). Toward professional, ethical journalism? *Mass Comm Review, 17*, 2–13.

Black, J., & Ritch, S. (1995, February). Tracking students' values and moral development. Paper presented to the Institute on College Student Values, Wakulla Springs, FL.

Black, J., Rawlins, B., Viall, E., & Plumley, J. (1992, August). *Effects of a media ethics course on student values: A replication and expansion.* Paper presented to the Mass Communication and Society Division of the Association for Education in Journalism and Mass Communication, Montreal, Canada.

Black, J., Steele, B., & Barney, R. (1998). *Doing ethics in journalism: A handbook with case studies.* (3rd ed.). Boston: Allyn & Bacon.

Blackstone, W. (1899). *Commentaries on the law of England* (Vol. 2, Book IV). Chicago: Callaghan.

Blanchard, M. (1977). The Hutchins Commission, the press and the responsibility concept. *Journalism Monographs, 49.*

Bloom, P. (2010, May 3). The moral life of babies. *New York Times Magazine.* Retrieved from www.nytimes.com/2010/05/09/magazine/09babies-t.html.

Blum, L. (2001). Care. In L.C. Becker & C.B. Becker (Eds.), *Encyclopedia of ethics* (pp. 185–187). New York: Routledge.

Bois, J.S. (1966). *The art of awareness.* Dubuque, IA: Wm. C. Brown Company.

Bok, S. (1978). *Lying: Moral Choice in Public and Private Life.* New York: Pantheon.

—— . (1982). *Secrets: On the ethics of concealment and revelation.* New York: Pantheon.

Bond, E.J. (2001). Concept of value. In L.C. Becker & C.B. Becker (Eds.), *Encyclopedia of ethics* (pp. 1745–1750). New York: Routledge.

Borchert, D.M., & Stewart, D. (1979). *Being human in a technological age.* Athens, OH: Ohio University Press.

Bordat, J. (2007). The Golden Rule as a global ethos. *Marburger Forum.* Retrieved from www.marburger-forum.de/mafo/heft2007-1/Bor_gol.htm.

Borden, S.L. (2007). *Journalism as practice: MacIntyre, virtue, ethics and the press.* Burlington, VT: Ashgate.

Braxton, G. (2007, August 29). Buddy System. *The Los Angeles Times.* Retrieved from http://articles.latimes.com/2007/aug/29/entertainment/et-bff29.

Brecht, A. (1959). *Political theory: The foundations of twentieth century political thought.* Princeton, NJ: Princeton University Press.

Breckenridge, A. (1980). *The right to privacy.* Lincoln, NE: University of Nebraska Press.

British Broadcasting Corp. News. (2000, April 8). Bishop warns of "evil Internet." Retrieved from http://news.bbc.co.uk/2/hi/uk_news/706341.stm.

—— . (2008, December 18). Rwanda: How the genocide happened. Retrieved from http://news.bbc.co.uk/2/hi/africa/1288230.stm.

Brodkin, J. (2009, December 8). Facebook halts Beacon, gives $9.5 million to settle lawsuit. Retrieved from www.pcworld.com/article/184029.

Brooks, D. (2010, February 19). The power elite. *New York Times*, p. A27.

Bryant, G. (1987). Ten-Fifty P.I.: Emotion and the photographer's role. *Journal of Mass Media Ethics, 2*(2), 32–39.

Bukro, C. (2000, December). Society falls short on accountability. *The Quill, 88,* 46–47.

Burns, K. (2008). The misuse of social media: Reactions to and important lessons from a blog fiasco. *Journal of New Communications Research, 31,* 41–53.

Bush Hitchon, J., Reaves, S., Park, S., & Yun, G.W. (2008). *Consumer response to brands in fashion magazine ads and their public relations implications.* Paper presented at the annual meeting of the International Communication Association, Marriott Hotel, San Diego, CA. Retrieved from www.allacademic.com/meta/p111846_index.html.

Cahn, S.M., & Markie, P. (2002). In *Ethics: History, theory, and contemporary issues* (2nd ed.). New York: Oxford University Press.

Canadian Radio-television and Telecommunications Commission. (2009). Canadian content. Retrieved from www.crtc.gc.ca/eng/cancon.htm.

Carey, J. (1978). A plea for the university tradition. *Journalism Quarterly, 55,* 846–855.

Carville, J. (2000). *Stickin': The case for loyalty.* New York: Simon & Schuster.

Cases and commentaries. (1988). Larry Speakes: He did not check with the chief. *Journal of Mass Media Ethics, 3*(2), 73–77.

CBS. (1999). Unsafe haven. Retrieved from www.cbsnews.com/stories/1999/04/15/60minutes/main43232.shtml.

Chase, S. (1938). *The tyranny of words.* New York: Harcourt, Brace.

—— . (1954). *The power of words.* New York: Harcourt, Brace.

Child, J., & Falk, J. (1982). Maintenance of occupation control: The case of professions. *Work and Occupation, 9,* 155–192.

Christenson, J.A., & Yang, C. (1976). Dominant values in American society: An exploratory analysis. *Sociology and Social Research, 60*(4), pp. 461–473.

Christians, C.G. (1977, Autumn). Fifty years of scholarship in media ethics. *Journal of Communication, 27,* 19–29.

—— . (1985–1986). Enforcing media codes. *Journal of Mass Media Ethics, 1*(1), 14–21.

—— . (1988). Can the public be held accountable? *Journal of Mass Media Ethics, 3*(1), 50–58.

—— . (2007). Utilitarianism in media ethics and its discontents. *Journal of Mass Media Ethics, 22* (2 & 3), 113–131.

Christians, C.G., & Covert, C. (1980). *Teaching ethics in journalism education.* Hastings-on-Hudson, New York: Institute of Society, Ethics and The Life Sciences.

Christians, C.G., Fackler, M., McKee, K.B., Kreshel, P.J., & Woods, R.H. (2008). *Media ethics: Cases and moral reasoning* (8th ed.). Boston: Allyn & Bacon.

Christians, C.G., & Nordenstreng, K. (2004). Social responsibility worldwide. *Journal of Mass Media Ethics, 19*(1), 3–28.

Cirino, R. (1971). *Don't blame the people: How the news media use bias, distortion, and censorship to manipulate public opinion.* Los Angeles: Diversity Press.

Clarke, A. (2001, May 1). Sweden using EU to push for wider children's ad ban. Retrieved from www.brandrepublic.com/News/13740/Sweden-using-EU-push-wider-childrens-ad-ban.

CNN.com. (1999, April 23). Marlboro Man hangs up billboard hat: Outdoor tobacco ads being replaced. Retrieved from www.cnn.com/US/9904/23/tobacco.billboards/index.html.

—— . (2006, January 27). Oprah to author: "You conned us all." Retrieved from www.cnn.com/2006/SHOWBIZ/books/01/27/oprah.frey/index.html.

Cobb, W.D., & Elder, C.D. (1983). *Participation in American politics: The dynamics of agenda-building* (2nd ed.). Baltimore: Johns Hopkins University Press.

Cohen, J.R. (1999). Advising clients to apologize. *Southern California Law Review, 72,* 1009–1069.

Cole, R. (Ed.). (1998). *The encyclopedia of propaganda.* Armonk, NY: Sharpe.

Coleman, R., & Wilkins, L. (2009). Moral development: A psychological approach to understanding ethical judgment. In L. Wilkins & C.G. Christians (Eds.), *The handbook of mass media ethics* (pp. 40–54). New York: Routledge.

Combs, J.E., & Nimmo, D. (1993). *The new propaganda: The dictatorship of palaver in contemporary politics.* White Plains, NY: Longman.

Commission on Freedom of the Press. (1947). *A free and responsible press: A general report on mass communication.* Retrieved from www.archive.org/stream/freeandresponsib029216mbp.

Cooley, T. (1888). *A treatise on the law of torts* (2nd ed.). Chicago: Callaghan.

Cooper, T. (2008). Between the summits: What Americans think about media ethics. *Journal of Mass Media Ethics, 23*(1), 15–27.

Craig, D. (2007a). Wal-Mart public relations in the blogosphere. *Journal of Mass Media Ethics, 22* (2 & 3), 215–228.

——. (2007b). In-text ads: Pushing the lines between advertising and journalism. Cases and commentaries. *Journal of Mass Media Ethics, 22*(4), 348–361.

Cunningham, S. (2002). *The idea of propaganda: A reconstruction.* Westport, CT: Praeger.

Cunningham, S.B. (1999). Getting it right: Aristotle's "Golden Mean" as theory deterioration. *Journal of Mass Media Ethics, 14*(1), 5–15.

Cutlip, S.M. (1976). [Review of the book *Managing the socially responsible corporation.*] *Public Relations Review, 21,* 60–64.

Dancy, J. (1991). An ethics of prima facie duties. In Peter Singer (Ed.), *A companion to ethics* (pp. 228–229). Cambridge, MA: Basil Blackwell.

Davis, M. (2010). Why journalism is a profession. In C. Meyers (Ed.), *Journalism ethics: A philosophical approach* (pp. 91–102). New York: Oxford University Press.

Davison, W.P. (1983). The third-person effect in communication. *Public Opinion Quarterly, 41*(1), 1–15.

Day, L. (2006). *Ethics in media communication: Cases and controversies* (5th ed.). Belmont, CA: Thomson Wadsworth.

Deaver, F. (1990). On defining truth. *Journal of Mass Media Ethics, 5*(3), 168–177.

Deggans, E. (2008, September 14). Cable tops broadcast TV in reflecting diversity. *The St. Petersburg Times.* Retrieved from www.tampabay.com/features/media/article808305.ece.

Dessart, G. (n.d.). Standards and Practices. Retrieved from www.museum.tv/eotvsection.php?entrycode=standardsand.

Diversitynow.com (2009). Focal point: Ethnicity and the media. Retrieved from www.diversitynow.ca/article.jsp?content=20050401_093942_6320.

Doob, L.W. (1935). *Propaganda, its psychology and technique.* New York: Henry Holt.

——. (1948). *Public opinion and propaganda.* New York: Henry Holt.

Edelstein, A. (1997). *Total propaganda: From mass culture to popular culture.* Mahwah, NJ: Lawrence Erlbaum.

Electronic Privacy Information Center. (2010). Hot policy issues. Retrieved from www.epic.org.

Elliott, D. (1984). *Toward the development of a model for journalism ethics instruction.* Unpublished Ed.D. thesis, Harvard University.

——— . (1985–1986). A conceptual analysis of ethics codes. *Journal of Mass Media Ethics*, *1*(1), 22–26.

——— . (1988). All is not relative: Essential shared values and the press. *Journal of Mass Media Ethics*, *3*(1), 28–32.

——— . (1991, Autumn). Moral development theories and the teaching of ethics, *Journalism Educator*, *46*(3), 18–24.

——— . (2007). Getting Mill right. *Journal of Mass Media Ethics*, *22*(2 & 3), 100–112.

——— . (2009). Essential shared values and 21st century journalism. In L. Wilkins & C.G. Christians (Eds.), *The handbook of mass media ethics* (pp. 28–39). New York: Routledge.

Elliott, S. (2008, March 31). Is the ad a success? The brain waves tell all. *New York Times*. Retrieved from www.nytimes.com/2008/03/31/business/media/31adcol.html.

Ellul, J. (1965). *Propaganda: The formation of men's attitudes*. New York: Alfred A. Knopf.

——— . (1981). The ethics of propaganda: Propaganda, innocence, and amorality. *Communication, 6*(2), pp. 159–177.

Enron Corporation. (2000, July). *Code of ethics*, pp. 1–64. (No publication data included.)

Erwin, R.E. (1992). Loyalty and virtues. *Philosophical Quarterly, 42*(169), 403–419.

Farsetta, D., & Price, C. (2006). *Fake TV news: Widespread and undisclosed. A multimedia report on television newsrooms' use of material provided by PR firms on behalf of paying clients*. Madison, WI: The Center for Media and Democracy.

Festinger, L. (1957). *A theory of cognitive dissonance*. Stanford, CA: Stanford University Press.

Figdor, C. (2010). Objectivity in the news: Finding a way forward. *Journal of Mass Media Ethics*, *25*(1), 19–33.

Fitzpatrick, K., & Bronstein, C. (Eds.). (2006). *Ethics in public relations: Responsible advocacy*. Thousand Oaks, CA: Sage.

Fitzpatrick, K., & Gauthier, C. (2001). Toward a professional responsibility theory of public relations ethics. *Journal of Mass Media Ethics*, *16*(2 & 3), 193–212.

Flexner, A. (1915, June 26). Is social work a profession? *School and Society*, 902–911.

Forget the error. (2007, Autumn). *Wilson Quarterly, 31*(4).

Frankena, W.K. (1967). Value and valuation. In P. Edwards (Ed.), *The encyclopedia of philosophy* (pp. 229–232). New York: Macmillan.

——— . (1973). *Ethics* (2nd ed.). Englewood Cliffs, NJ: Prentice-Hall.

Freedom House. (2010, April 29). Freedom of the press. Retrieved from www.freedomhouse.org/template.cfm?page=16.

Freeman, C.P. (2009). A greater means to the greater good: Ethical guidelines to meet social movement organization advocacy challenges. *Journal of Mass Media Ethics*, *24*(4), 269–288.

Fuller, J. (1996). *News values: Ideas for an information age*. Chicago: University of Chicago Press.

Gallup. (2009). Honesty/Ethics in professions. Retrieved from www.gallup.com/poll/1654/honesty-ethics-professions.aspx.

Gans, H.J. (1979). *Deciding what's news: A study of CBS Evening News, NBC Nightly News, Newsweek and Time*. New York: Vintage Books.

Gartner, M. (1990, March 15). The scarlet letter of rape: A courageous victim fights back. *The Wall Street Journal*, p. A15.

——— . (1992, July–August). To The Staff. *Columbia Journalism Review*, pp. 54–55.

Gawande, A. (2002). *Complications: A surgeon's notes on an imperfect science*. New York: Picador.

Gensler, H.J. (2010). The Golden Rule. Retrieved from www.jcu.edu/philosophy/gensler/goldenrule.htm.

Gert, B. (1973). *The moral rules: A new rational foundation for morality*. New York: Harper Torchbooks.

———. (1988). *Morality: A new justification of the moral rules*. New York: Oxford University Press.

———. (1998). *Morality: Its nature and justification*. New York: Oxford University Press.

———. (2004). *Common morality: Deciding what to do*. New York: Oxford University Press.

Gerwith, A. (1978). The Golden Rule rationalized. *Midwest Studies in Philosophy, 3*, 133–147.

Gilligan, C. (1982). *In a different voice: Psychological theory and women's development*. Cambridge, MA: Harvard University Press.

Gillis, D.H. (1966–1967). Broadcasting as profession: A socio-economic approach. *Journal of Broadcasting, 11*, 73–82.

Glasser, T.L. (2003). The newspaper ombudsman and the aim of accountability in American journalism. In C.-J. Bertrand (Ed.), *An arsenal for democracy: Media accountability systems* (pp. 177–184). Cresskill, NJ: Hampton Press.

Goleman, D. (1995). *Emotional intelligence: Why it can matter more than IQ*. New York: Bantam.

Gordon, D., & Merrill, J.C. (1988). Power—The key to press freedom: A four-tiered social model. *Journal of Mass Media Ethics, 3*(1), 38–49.

Grcic, J. (1986). The right to privacy: Behavior as property. *Journal of Values Inquiry, 20*, 137–144.

Green, E. (2004, August 5). Quiznos pulls ads on "urban" radio stations. *Washington Times*. Retrieved from www.washingtontimes.com/news/2004/aug/05/20040805-104634-2167r/print.

Greenwood, E. (1957). Attributes of a profession. *Social Work, 2*, 45–55.

Grunig, J. (1993). Implications of public relations for other domains of communications. *Journal of Communication, 43*, 164–173.

Guanzhong, L., & Roberts, M. (2005). *Three Kingdoms: Chinese Classics*. Beijing: Foreign Language Press.

Harrison, K., & Cantor, J. (1997). The relationship between media consumption and eating disorders. *Journal of Communication, 47*, 40–63.

The Hastings Center. (1980). *The teaching of ethics in higher education*. Hastings-on-Hudson, NY: Institute of Society, Ethics and The Life Sciences.

Hatchen, W. (1981). *The world news prism: Changing media, clashing ideologies*. Ames, IA: Iowa State University Press.

Hayakawa, S.I. (1949). *Language in thought and action*. New York: Harcourt, Brace.

———. (1954). *Language, meaning and maturity*. New York: Harper & Brothers.

———. (Ed.). (1962). *The use and misuse of language*. Greenwich, CT: Fawcett Publications.

Held, V. (1999). Liberalism and the ethics of care. In C. Card (Ed.), *On feminist ethics & politics* (pp. 288–309). Lawrence, KS: University Press of Kansas.

Helft, M. (2010, April 27). Senators ask Facebook for privacy fixes. *New York Times*. Retrieved from http://bits.blogs.nytimes.com/2010/04/27/senators-ask-facebook-for-privacy-fixes.

Hendrickson, L., & Tankard, J. (1997, Winter). Expanding the news frame: The systems theory perspective. *Journalism & Mass Communications Educator*, 39–46.

Hiebert, R.E. (1966). *Courier to the crowd: The story of Ivy Lee and the development of public relations*. Ames, IA: Iowa State University Press.

Hill, T.E., & Zweig, A. (2002). *Kant: Groundwork for the metaphysics of morals*. Oxford: Oxford University Press.

Hirschman, A.O. (1970). *Exit, voice, and loyalty: Responses to decline in firms, organizations, and states*. Cambridge, MA: Harvard University Press.

Hobbes, T. (1968/1651). *Leviathan*. Edited by C.B. Macpherson. Harmondsworth, England: Penguin.

Hodges, L.W. (1983). The journalist and privacy. *Social Responsibility: Journalism, Law, Medicine, IX*, 5–19.

——— . (1988, Fall). Undercover, masquerading, surreptitious taping. *Journal of Mass Media Ethics*, *3*(1), 26–36.

——— . (1994). The journalist and privacy. *Journal of Mass Media Ethics*, *9*(4), 197–212.

——— . (2000). Unsafe haven; Cases and commentaries, *Journal of Mass Media Ethics*, *15*(4), pp. 269–270.

——— . (2009). Privacy and the press, in L. Wilkins & C.G. Christians (Eds.), *The handbook of mass media ethics* (pp. 276–287). New York: Routledge.

Hohenberg, J. (1969). *The professional journalist: A guide to the practices and principles of the news media* (2nd ed.). San Francisco: Rinehart Press.

Horiuchi, V. (2010, May 18). Want out? Here's how to delete your Facebook account. *The Salt Lake Tribune*, p. C2.

Hornsby, Jr., A. (1986). "Martin Luther King, Jr., Letter From a Birmingham Jail," *Journal of Negro History*, Autumn-Winter, pp. 40–41.

Institute for Propaganda Analysis. (1937, November). How to detect propaganda, *Propaganda Analysis, I*, 1–4.

Jaggar, A.M. (2001). Feminist ethics. In L.C. Becker & C.B. Becker (Eds.), *Encyclopedia of ethics* (pp. 528–539). New York: Routledge.

Jefferson, T. (1787, January 16). Letter to Colonel Edward Carrington. H.A. Washington (Ed.), *The Writings of Thomas Jefferson*, Vol. 2. New York: Riker, 1853.

——— . (1807, June 11). Letter to John Norvell. H.A. Washington (Ed.), *The Writings of Thomas Jefferson*, Vol. 4. New York: Riker, 1854.

Johnas, H. (1984). *The imperative of responsibility: In search of an ethics for the technological age*. Chicago: University of Chicago Press.

Johnson, W. (1946). *People in quandaries: The semantics of personal adjustment*. New York: Harper & Brothers.

Jordan, W. (2009). Wal Marting across America creates many ethical issues: How the new world of blogging has changed public relations. Retrieved from www.associatedcontent.com/article/2353610/wal_marting_across_america_creates.htm.

Jowett, G.S., & O'Donnell, V. (2006). *Propaganda and persuasion* (4th ed.). Thousand Oaks, CA: Sage.

Joyce, W. (1963). *The propaganda gap*. New York: Harper & Row.

Kakutani, M. (2008, February 26). However mean the streets, have an exit strategy. *New York Times*. Retrieved from www.nytimes.com/2008/02/26/books/26kaku.html.

Kant, I. (1953). *Groundwork of the metaphysics of morals*. (Translated by H.J. Paton as *The moral law*.) London: Hutchinson. (Original work published 1785).

——— . (1964). *Groundwork of the metaphysics of morals*. (H.J. Paton, Trans.). New York: Harper Torchbooks. (Original work published 1785).

Kaul, A.J. (1986). The proletariat journalist: A critique of professionalism. *Journal of Mass Media Ethics*, *1*(1), 47–55.

Kidder, R.M. (1994). *Shared values for a troubled world: Conversations with men and women of conscience*. San Francisco: Jossey-Bass.

——— . (1995). *How good people make tough choices*. New York: Fireside.

King, M.E.P. (1994, March 22). Should newspapers name the victim of a rape? *Philadelphia Inquirer*, p. A13.

Klaidman, S., & Beauchamp, T.L. (1987). *The virtuous journalist.* New York: Oxford University Press.

Kleinig, J. (2008, Fall). Loyalty. In *The Stanford Encyclopedia of Philosophy*, Edward N. Zalta (Ed.). Retrieved from http://plato.stanford.edu/archives/fall2008/entries/loyalty.

Knightley, P. (2002). *The first casualty: The war correspondent as hero and myth-maker from the Crimea to Kosovo.* Baltimore: Johns Hopkins University Press.

Kohlberg, L. (1969). Stage and sequence: The cognitive-developmental approach to socialization. In D.A. Goslin (Ed.), *Handbook of Socialization theory and research* (pp. 347–380). Chicago: Rand McNally.

——. (1981). *The psychology of moral development: The nature and validity of stages.* New York: Harper & Row.

Konvitz, M. (1973). Loyalty. In P.P. Weinder (Ed.), *Encyclopedia of the history of ideas* (Vol. 111, pp. 108–116). New York: Scribner.

Korsgaard, C.M., & Freeman, S. (2001). John Rawls. In L.C. Becker & C.B. Becker (Eds.), *Encyclopedia of ethics* (pp. 1454–1461). New York: Routledge.

Korzybski, A.H. (1948). *Science and sanity: An introduction to non-aristotelian systems and general semantics* (4th ed.). Lakeville, CT: Non-Aristotelian Library Publishing.

Kovach, B., & Rosensteil, T. (2007). *The elements of journalism: What newspeople should know and the public should expect* (2nd ed.). New York: Three Rivers Press.

Kuhn, M. (2007). Interactivity and Prioritizing the Human: A Code of Blogging Ethics. *Journal of Mass Media Ethics, 22*(1), 18–36.

Kultgen, J. (1988). *Ethics and professionalism.* Philadelphia: University of Pennsylvania Press.

Kurtz, H. (2006, October 12). *Post* photographer repays group for trip expenses. *Washington Post,* p. C2.

Kwitny, J. (1990, June). The high cost of high profits. *Washington Journalism Review,* 19–29.

Lambeth, E.B. (1986). *Committed journalism: An ethic for the profession.* Bloomington, IN: Indiana University Press.

——. (1990). Waiting for a new St. Benedict: Alasdair MacIntyre and the theory and practice of journalism. *Journal of Mass Media Ethics, 5*(2), 75–87.

Landsman, S. (1984). *The adversary system: A description and defense.* Washington, DC: American Enterprise Institute.

Lappé, F. (1989). *Rediscovering America's values.* New York: Ballantine, 1989.

Lebacqz, K. (1985). *Professional ethics: Power and paradox.* Nashville: Abingdon.

Lee, A.M. (1952). *How to understand propaganda.* New York: Rinehard.

Lee, I.J. (1941). *Language habits in human affairs* (2nd ed.). Concord, CA: International Society for General Semantics.

Levine, M. (1980). Privacy in the tradition of the Western world. In W. Bier (Ed.), *Privacy: A vanishing value?* (pp. 3–21). New York: Fordham University Press.

Levy, N. (2004). Good character: Too little, too late. *Journal of Mass Media Ethics, 19*(2), 108–118.

Lewan, T. (2009, March 1). More TV ads project images of racial harmony. Retrieved from http://multicultclassics.blogspot.com/2009/03/6495-multiculturalism-from-madison.html.

Lippmann, W. (1922). *Public opinion.* London: Collier-Macmillan.

Lyons, D. (2001). Utilitarianism. In L.C. Becker & C.B. Becker (Eds.), *Encyclopedia of ethics* (pp. 1737–1744). New York: Routledge.

MacDonald, J.F. (1989). Propaganda and order in modern society. In T.J. Smith III (Ed.), *Propaganda: A pluralistic perspective* (pp. 23–25). New York: Praeger.

Maciejewski, J.J. (2003). Can natural law defend advertising? *Journal of Mass Media Ethics, 18*(2), 111–122.

MacIntyre, A. (1984). *After virtue: A study in moral theory* (2nd ed.). South Bend, IN: University of Notre Dame Press.

———. (2001). Virtue ethics. In L.C. Becker & C.B. Becker (Eds.), *Encyclopedia of ethics* (pp. 1757–1763). New York: Routledge.

Marcellus, J. (2009, August 24). BMW excludes "urban" ad markets, highlighting ad industry's history of discrimination issues. Retrieved from www.findingdulcinea.com/news/business/2009/aug/BMW-Excludes-Urban-Ad-Markets.html.

Margolik, D. (1990, March 25). A name, a face and a rape: Iowa victim tells her story. *New York Times*, pp. A1, 28.

Marks, A. (2008, April 18). Privacy becoming more elusive for Americans. *Christian Science Monitor.* Retrieved from www.csmonitor.com/2008/04/18/p03s08-usgn.html.

Martin, L.J. (1958). *International propaganda: Its legal and diplomatic control.* Minneapolis, MN: University of Minnesota Press.

Martin, M.W. (2000). *Meaningful work: Rethinking professional ethics.* New York: Oxford.

Martinson, D.L. (1998). A question of distributive and social justice: Public relations practitioners and the marketplace of ideas. *Journal of Mass Media Ethics, 13*(3), 141–151.

Mazzetti, M., & Daragahi, B. (2005, November 30). US military covertly pays to run stories in Iraqi press. *Los Angeles Times.* Retrieved from http://articles.latimes.com/2005/nov/30/world/fg-infowar30.

McBride, G. (1989). Ethical thought in public relations history: Seeking a relevant perspective. *Journal of Mass Media Ethics, 4*(1), 5–20.

McGowan, W. (2001). *Coloring the news: How crusading for diversity has corrupted American journalism.* San Francisco: Encounter Books.

Mehegan, D. (2008, February 29). Author admits making up memoir of surviving Holocaust. *Boston Globe.* Retrieved from www.boston.com/ae/books/articles/2008/02/29/author_admit.

Merrill, J.C. (1985). Sound principle and wise deviation: Deontelic ethics for the journalist. *Social responsibility: Business, journalism, law, medicine, 11*, 14–24.

———. (1989). The marketplace: A court of first resort. In E.E. Dennis, D.M. Gillmor, & T.L. Glasser (Eds.), *Media freedom and accountability.* Westport, CT: Greenwood Press.

Merrill, J.C., & Lowenstein, R.L. (1971). *Media, messages, and men: New perspectives in communication.* New York: David McKay Company.

Merritt, D. (1995). *Public journalism & public life: Why telling the news is not enough.* Hillsdale, NJ: Lawrence Erlbaum.

Meyers, C. (2003). Appreciating W.D. Ross: On duties and consequences. *Journal of Mass Media Ethics, 18*(2), pp. 81–97.

Mill, J.S. (1947). *On liberty.* George H. Sabine (Ed.). New York: Appleton-Century-Crofts. (Original work published 1859).

———. (1988). *Utilitarianism.* Roger Crisp (Ed.). Oxford: Oxford University Press. (Original work published 1863).

Milton, J.S. (1644). *Areopagitica: Appeal for the liberty of unlicensed printing.* Retrieved from www.stlawrenceinstitute.org/vol14mit.html.

Moeller, S.D. (1999). *Compassion fatigue: How the media sell disease, famine, war and death.* New York: Routledge.

Moore, W. (1970). *The professions: Roles and rules.* New York: Russell Sage.

Motion Picture Association of America. (n.d.). Film ratings: Frequently asked questions. Retrieved from www.mpaa.org/Ratings_FAQ.asp

Moulton, J.F. (1924, July). Law and manners. *Atlantic Monthly, 134*(4), pp. 1–5. Cited by R.M. Kidder (1995) in *How Good People Make Tough Choices.* New York: Fireside, pp. 66–67.

Moyers, B. (2008, March 28). The Kerner Commission—40 years later. *Bill Moyers Journal.* Retrieved from www.pbs.org/moyers/journal/03282008/profile.html.

Munson, R. (2007). *Intervention and reflection: Basic issues in medical ethics* (8th ed.). Belmont, CA: Wadsworth.

Musa, B,A., & Domatob, J.K. (2007). Who is a development journalist? Perspectives on media ethics and professionalism in post-colonial societies. *Journal of Mass Media Ethics, 22*(4), 315–331.

National Press Photographers Association. (2010). Ethics in the age of digital photography. Retrieved from www.nppa.org/professional_development.

NationMaster.com. (2010). Ethic of reciprocity. Retrieved from www.nationmaster.com/encyclopedia/Ethic-of-reciprocity.

Navasky, V. (2005). *A matter of opinion.* New York: Farrar, Straus & Giroux.

Nelson, M.R., Wood, M.L.M., & Paek, H-J. (2009). Increased persuasion knowledge of video news releases: Audience beliefs about news and support for source disclosure. *Journal of Mass Media Ethics, 24*(4), 220–237.

Nelson, R.P., & Hulteng, J. (1971). *The fourth estate: An informal appraisal of the news information media.* New York: Harper & Row.

Nemeth, N. (2003). *News ombudsmen in North America: Assessing an experiment in social responsibility.* Westport, CT: Praeger.

Nerone, J.C. (Ed.). (1995). *Last rights: Revisiting Four Theories of the Press.* Urbana: University of Illinois Press.

Neufeldt, V.E. (1997). *Transparent. Webster's New World College Dictionary* (3rd ed.). New York: Simon & Schuster.

New York Times. (2003, January). *Ethical journalism: Code of conduct for the news and editorial departments.* New York: New York Times.

Newman, A.A. (2008, December 1). The minority report. *Adweek.* Retrieved from www.adweek.com/aw/content_display/news/agency/e3if0caf66d857a98ef2ef2650f5b99d631.

Newton, L.H., Hodges, L.W., & Keith, S. (2004). Accountability in the professions: Accountability in journalism. *Journal of Mass Media Ethics, 19*(3–4), 166–190.

Nissenbaum, H. (2009). *Privacy in context: Technology, policy and the integrity of social life.* Palo Alto, CA: Stanford University Press.

Noddings, N. (1984). *Caring: A feminine approach to ethics and moral education.* Berkeley: University of California Press.

O'Neill, O. (1991). Kantian ethics. In Peter Singer (Ed.), *A companion to ethics* (pp. 175–186). Cambridge, MA: Basil Blackwell.

Oleary, J. (2008, January 31). How marketers use targeting to reach consumers. Lecture presented to Propaganda and Media Ethics class, University of South Florida. St. Petersburg, FL.

Oliver, R.W. (2004). *What is transparency?* New York: McGraw-Hill.

Orzack, L. (1959). Work as a "central life interest" of professionals. *Social Problems, 7,* 125–132.

Ostwald, M. (1962). *Artistotle: Nicomachean ethics.* New York: Macmillan.

Overholser, G. (1989, November). We should not have to keep hiding rape. *The Bulletin* of the American Society of Newspaper Editors, p. 32.

Park, J. (2009, April 30). Margaret Cho's televisual trajectory: From all-American girl to *The Cho Show*. FlowTV (University of Texas at Austin). Retrieved from http://flowtv.org/?p=3800.

Parsons, T. (1935). Ultimate values in sociological theory. *International Journal of Ethics, 45*(3), 272–317.

Patterson, P., & Wilkins, L. (2008). *Media ethics: Issues and cases* (6th ed.). New York: McGraw-Hill.

Peck, L.A. (2007). A "fool satisfied"? Journalists and Mill's principle of utility. *Journalism and Mass Communication Educator, 61*, 205–213.

Peirce, C.S. (1877). The fixation of belief. *Popular Science Monthly, 12*, 1–15.

Perlmutter, D.D., & Schoen, M. (2007). If I break a rule, what do I do, fire myself? *Journal of Mass Media Ethics, 22*(1), 37–48.

Perry, R. (1954). *Realms of value: A critique of human civilization*. Cambridge, MA: Harvard University Press.

Perry, W.G., Jr. (1970). *Forms of intellectual and ethical development in the college years: A scheme*. New York: Holt, Rinehart & Winston.

——. (1981). Cognitive and ethical growth: The making of meaning. In A.W. Chickering & Associates (Eds.), *The modern American college* (pp. 76–116). San Francisco: Jossey-Bass.

Pew Research Center for the People and the Press. (2007). *Views of press values and performance: 1985–2007*. Retrieved from http://people-press.org/report/348/internet-news-audience-highly-critical-of-news-organizations.

Picard, R.G. (1982–1983, Winter/Spring). Revisions of the *Four Theories of the Press* model. *Mass Comm Review, 25*–28.

Pincoffs, E.L. (2001). Virtues. In L.C. Becker, & C.B. Becker (Eds.), *Encyclopedia of ethics* (pp. 1763–1768). New York: Routledge.

Plaisance, P.L. (2000). The concept of media accountability reconsidered. *Journal of Mass Media Ethics, 15*(4), 257–268.

——. (2005). *An assessment of media ethics education: Course content and the values and ethical ideologies of media ethics students*. Unpublished manuscript.

——. (2006, August 4). Transparency: An assessment of the Kantian roots of a key element in media ethics practice. Paper presented at the Association for Education in Journalism and Mass Communication, San Francisco.

——. (2007). Transparency: An assessment of the Kantian roots of a key element in media ethics practice. *Journal of Mass Media Ethics, 22*(2 & 3), 187–207.

——. (2009). *Media ethics: Key principles for responsible practice*. Los Angeles: Sage.

Plato. (1901). *The Republic (Book VII)*. New York: M. Walter Dunne.

Pogge, T.W. (1989). *Realizing Rawls*. Ithica, NY: Cornell University Press.

Pojman, L.P. (1990). *Ethics: Discovering right and wrong*. Belmont, CA: Wadsworth.

——. (2006). *Ethics: Discovering right and wrong* (5th ed.). Belmont, CA: Thomson Wadsworth.

Polansky, J., Titus, K., & Glantz, S.A. (2009). Two years later: Are MPAA's tobacco labels protecting movie audiences? Retrieved from http://escholarship.org/uc/item/5sr9w2s1.

Porter, E. (1999). *Feminist perspectives on ethics*. New York: Longman.

Postema, G.J. (2001). Jeremy Bentham. In L.C. Becker & C.B. Becker (Eds.), *Encyclopedia of ethics* (pp. 137–141). New York: Routledge.

Postman, N. (1985). *Amusing ourselves to death: Public discourse in the age of show business*. New York: Viking.

PriceWaterhouseCoopers (2010, June 15). Consumer behavior drives change; Entertainment & media players seek new roles in digital value change. Retrieved from www.pwc.com/gx/en/press-room/2010/E-and-M-players-seek-new-roles-digital-value-chain.jhtml.

Purtill, R.L. (1976). *Thinking about ethics.* Englewood Cliffs, NJ: Prentice-Hall.

Qualter, T.H. (1962). *Propaganda and psychological warfare.* New York: Random House.

Quinn, A. (2007). Moral virtues for journalists. *Journal of Mass Media Ethics, 22*(2 & 3), 168–186.

Rachels, J. (1993). *The elements of moral philosophy* (2nd ed.). New York: McGraw-Hill.

Rand, A. (1943). *The fountainhead.* Indianapolis: Bobbs-Merrill.

—— . (1957). *Atlas shrugged.* New York: Random House.

—— . (1964). *The virtue of selfishness.* New York: New American Library.

Raskin, A.H. (1989). The marketplace: A stacked court. In E.E. Dennis, D.M. Gillmor, & T.L. Glasser (Eds.), *Media Freedom and Responsibility.* Westport, CT: Greenwood Press.

Rawls, J. (1971). *A theory of justice.* Cambridge: Harvard University Press.

—— . (1993). *Political liberalism.* New York: Columbia University Press.

Read, M. (2008, February 28). A refugee from gangland. *New York Times.* Retrieved from www.nytimes.com/2008/02/28/garden/28jones.html.

Reaves, S., Bush Hitchon, J., Park, S., & Yun G.W. (2004). If looks could kill: Digital manipulation of fashion models. *Journal of Mass Media Ethics, 19*(1), 56–71.

Regan, T. (2001). William David Ross. In L.C. Becker & C.B. Becker (Eds.), *Encyclopedia of ethics* (pp. 1520–1521). New York: Routledge.

Religious Tolerance.org. (2010). Ethics of reciprocity (a.k.a. "Golden Rule."). Retrieved from www.religioustolerance.org/reciexce.htm.

Rest, J., & Narvaez, D. (1994). *Moral development in the professions: Psychology and applied ethics.* Hillsdale, NJ: Lawrence Erlbaum.

Rich, M. (2008, March 4). Gang memoir, turning page, is pure fiction. *New York Times.* Retrieved from www.nytimes.com/2008/03/04/books/04fake.html.

—— . (2008, March 5). Tracking the fallout of (another) literary fraud. *New York Times.* Retrieved from www.nytimes.com/2008/03/05/books/05fake.html.

—— . (2008, March 8). A family tree of literary fakers. *New York Times.* Retrieved from www.nytimes.com/2008/03/08/books/08fakes.html.

Rich, M., & Berger, J. (2009, December 28). False memoir of holocaust is canceled. *New York Times,* p. A12. Retrieved from www.nytimes.com/2008/12/29/books/29hoax.html.

Roberts, C. (2007, August). Measuring the relationship between journalistic transparency and credibility. Paper presented to Newspaper Division, Association for Education in Journalism and Mass Communication, Washington, DC.

—— . (2007–2008, Winter). When being ethical bites you back. *Ethical news: The newsletter of the AEJMC Media Ethics Division.* Retrieved from http://jcomm.uoregon.edu/~tbivins/aejmc_ethics/PDFs/MEDW07-08.pdf.

—— . (2010, August). Identifying values in media codes of ethics. Paper presented to Media Ethics Division, Association for Education in Journalism and Mass Communications annual conference, Denver, CO.

Rogers, A.K. (1931). Conscience. *International Journal of Ethics, 41*(2), 143–165.

Rogers, W. (2007). *Persuasion: Messages, receivers and contexts.* Lanham, MD: Rowman & Littlefield.

Rohan, M.J. (2000). A rose by any name? The values construct. *Personality and Social Psychology Review, 4(3),* 255–277.

Rokeach, M. (1960). *The open and closed mind: Investigations into the nature of belief systems and personality systems.* New York: Basic Books.

——. (1968). *Beliefs, attitudes, and values.* San Francisco: Jossey-Bass.

——. (1973). *The nature of human values.* New York: The Free Press.

Ross, W.D. (1930). *The right and the good.* Oxford: Oxford University Press.

Rotzoll, K.B., & Haefner, J.E. (1996). *Advertising in contemporary society: Perspectives toward understanding.* Urbana, IL: University of Illinois Press.

Royce, J. (1971). *The philosophy of loyalty.* (Reprinted from 1908. New York: Hafner.). New York: Macmillan.

RTDNA Ethics Committee. (2010). Guidelines for use of non-editorial video and audio. Retrieved from www.rtdna.org/pages/media_items/rtnda-guidelines-for-use-of-non-editorial-video-and-audio250.php.

Sackville, R. (2009). Let truth and falsehood grapple: Milton as a dubious guide to some questions about free speech. *Australian Journalism Review, 31*(1), 107–120.

Scanlon, T.M. (1998). *What we owe to each other.* Cambridge, MA: Harvard University Press.

Schwartz, S. (1999). A theory of social values and some implications for work. *Applied Psychology: An International Review, 48*(1), 23–47.

Schwartz, S., & Bilsky, W. (1987). Toward a universal psychological structure of human values. *Journal of Personality and Social Psychology, 53*(3), 550–562.

——. (1990). Toward a universal psychological structure of human values: Extension and cross-cultural replications. *Journal of Personality and Social Psychology, 58,* 878–891.

Scott, M.B., & Lyman, S.M. (1968). Accounts. *American Sociological Review, 33*(1), 46–62.

Shafer, J. (2004, March 4). "Burning down my master's house": The fabulist. [Review of the book *Burning down my master's house.*]. *New York Times.* Retrieved from www.nytimes.com/2004/03/14/books/review/14SHAFERT.html.

Shaw, D. (1991, August 18). Stumbling over sex in the press; Fluctuating between skittishness and sensationalism, editors and reporters keep fumbling—whether the subject is AIDS, rape or the behavior of politicians. *Los Angeles Times,* p. A1.

——. (1991, August 19). Gender of editors affects coverage of stories on sex—Media: Women tend to favor more candor in reports on rape, AIDS and the private lives of politicians. *Los Angeles Times,* p. A1.

Shoeman, F. (2001). Privacy. In L.C. Becker & C.B. Becker (Eds.), *Encyclopedia of ethics* (pp. 1381–1384). New York: Routledge.

Sichel, B. (1982). *Value education for an age of crisis.* Washington, DC: University Press of America.

Siebert, F.S., Peterson, T., & Schramm, W. (1956). *Four theories of the press.* Urbana, IL: University of Illinois Press.

Singer, M.G. (2001). Golden rule. In L.C. Becker & C.B. Becker (Eds.), *Encyclopedia of ethics* (pp. 614–619). New York: Routledge.

Singletary, M. (1982). Commentary: Are journalists professionals? *Newspaper Research Journal, 3*(2), 75–87.

Sinnott-Armstrong, W. (2001). Bernard Gert. In L.C. Becker & C.B. Becker (Eds.), *Encyclopedia of ethics* (pp. 608–610). New York: Routledge.

Smikle, K. (2007, December 19). FCC adopts proposal to eliminate "no urban dictates" practices. *Target Market News.* Retrieved from www.targetmarketnews.com/storyid12190701.htm.

Smith, T.J., III (Ed.) (1989). *Propaganda: A pluralistic perspective.* New York: Praeger.

Snopes.com (2007, August 6). Marlboro manslaughter. Retrieved from www.snopes.com/radiotv/tv/marlboro.asp.

Snow, N. (2003). *Information war*. New York: Seven Stories Press.

Spizziri, M. (2009). Ethical issues in online advertising. Retrieved from http://advertising.about.com/od/onlineadvertising/a/guestethicalads.htm.

Sproule, J.M. (1997). *Propaganda and democracy: The American experience of media and mass persuasion*. Cambridge, UK: Cambridge University Press.

Stanford Encyclopedia of Philosophy. (2005). Correspondence Theory of Truth. Retrieved from http://plato.stanford.edu/entries/truth-correspondence.

Steiner, L. (2009). Feminist media ethics. In L. Wilkins & C.G. Christians, *The handbook of mass media ethics* (pp. 366–381). New York: Routledge.

Steiner, L., & Okrusch, C.M. (2006). Care as a virtue for journalists. *Journal of Mass Media Ethics*, *21*(2 & 3), 102–122.

Stewart, R.M., Corneille, M.G., Johnston, J., Geoghegan, K., Myers, J.G., Dent, D.L., et al. (2006). Transparent and open discussion of errors does not increase malpractice risk in trauma patients. *Annals of Surgery, 243*(5), 645–651.

Stoker, K. (2003, March). A moral defense for the morally indefensible behavior of journalists. Paper presented at the Ethics Across the Professions Conference, St. Petersburg, FL.

Story, L. (2008, February 26). Nielsen looks beyond TV, and hits roadblocks. *New York Times*. Retrieved from www.nytimes.com/2008/02/26/business/media/26nielsen.html.

——— . (2008, March 10). To aim ads, web is keeping closer eye on you. *New York Times*. Retrieved from www.nytimes.com/2008/03/10/technology/10privacy.html.

Stransky, T. (2010). CBS rejects gay dating website's Super Bowl commercial. Retrieved from http://news-briefs.ew.com/2010/01/29/mancrunch-super-bowl-commercial-cbs.

Surlin, S. (1987). Value system changes by students as a result of media ethics course. *Journalism Quarterly, 64*(2 & 3) 564–568, 676.

Taylor, P.M. (2003). *Munitions of the mind: A history of propaganda from the ancient world to the present day* (3rd ed.). Manchester, UK: Manchester University Press.

Teaching Values.com. (2010). The universality of the Golden Rule in the world religions. Retrieved from www.teachingvalues.com/goldenrule.html.

Ticker, B.S. (1994, August 13). Ban the naming of rape victims? *Editor & Publisher*, pp. 37, 48.

Tronto, J.C. (1995). Care as a basis for radical political judgments. *Hypatia, 10*, 141–149.

Turk, J.V. (1986). *Information subsidies and media content: A study of public relations influence on the news*. Columbia, SC: Association for Education in Journalism and Mass Communication.

US Census Bureau. (2008). Resident population, by race and age. Retrieved from www.census.gov/compendia/statab/cats/population/estimates_and_projections_by_age_sex_raceethnicity.html.

Viall, E. (1992). Measuring journalistic values: A cosmopolitan/community continuum. *Journal of Mass Media Ethics, 7*(1), 41–53.

Wagatsuma, H., & Rosett, A. (1986). The implications of apology: Law and culture in Japan and the United States. *Law & Society Review, 20*(4), 461–498.

Wakefield, R.I., & Barney, C.F. (2001). Communication in the unfettered marketplace: Ethical interrelationships of business, government, and stakeholders. *Journal of Mass Media Ethics, 16*(2 & 3), 213–233.

Warren, S.D., & Brandeis, L.D. (1890). The right to privacy. *Harvard Law Review, 4*, 193.

Westin, A. (1967). *Privacy and Freedom*. New York: Atheneum.

Wilensky, H. (1964). The professionalization of everyone? *The American Journal of Sociology, 70*(2), 137–158.

Wilkins, L., & Christians, C.G. (2001). Philosophy meets the social sciences: The nature of humanity in the public arena. *Journal of Mass Media Ethics, 16*(2 & 3), 99–120.

——. (2009). *The handbook of mass media ethics.* New York: Routledge.

Wilson, C., & Guiterrez, F. (1985). *Minorities and media: Diversity and the end of mass communications.* Belmont, CA: Wadsworth.

Wilson, J.Q. (1993). *The moral sense.* New York: The Free Press.

Winch, S.P. (1996). Moral justifications for privacy and intimacy. *Journal of Mass Media Ethics, 11*(4), 197–209.

Wise, J. (2007, November). This is your brain . . . . *Popular Mechanics,* pp. 64–70.

Wong, K. (2004). Asian-based development journalism and political elections: Press coverage of the 1999 General Election in Malaysia. *Gazette, 66*(1), 25–40.

World Health Organization. (2007). Global youth tobacco survey: Senegal, ages 13–15. Retrieved from www.afro.who.int/en/divisions-a-programmes/dnc/tobacco/tob-country-profiles/doc_download/1766-senegal-national-gyts-2007-factsheet-ages-13-15.html.

Wreford, R.J.R.G. (1923). Propaganda, evil and good. *The Nineteenth Century and After, XCII,* pp. 514–524.

Wulfemeyer, K.T., & Frazier, L. (1992). The ethics of video news releases: A qualitative analysis. *Journal of Mass Media Ethics, 7*(3), 151–168.

Yin, J. (2008). Beyond the Four Theories of the Press: A new model for the Asian & the world press. *Journalism & Communication Monographs, 10*(1), 3–62.

Zenner, L.A. (1995). Codes run afoul of First Amendment. Minnesota News Council. Retrieved from www.news-council.org/archives/95code.html.

Zuckerberg, M. (2010, May 26). Making control simple. Retrieved from http://blog.facebook.com/blog.php?post=391922327130.

Permissions

A Blogger's Code of Ethics reproduced with permission, www.CyberJournalist.net.

American Advertising Federation (AAF) advertising ethics principles reproduced with permission, www.aaf.org.

American Association of Advertising Agencies (AAAA) standards of practice reproduced with permission, www.aaaa.org.

American Marketing Association (AMA) ethical norms and values for members reproduced with permission, www.ama.org.

American Society of Newspaper Editors (ASNE) statement of principles reproduced with permission, www.asne.org.

Black, J. (1984/85). A public relations dilemma. *Journal of Mass Media Ethics* 1(1), 78–79. Reproduced with permission, Taylor & Francis.

Black, J. (2001). Semantics and ethics of propaganda. *Journal of Mass Media Ethics* 16, 121–137. Reproduced with permission, Taylor & Francis.

Black, J. (2009). The ethics of propaganda and the propaganda of ethics. In L. Wilkins & C.G. Christians (Eds.), *The handbook of mass media ethics* (pp. 130–148). Reproduced with permission, Taylor & Francis.

Council of Better Business Bureaus, Inc. (BBB) code of business practices. Reprinted with permission of the Council of Better Business Bureaus, Inc. Copyright 2009. Council of Better Business Bureaus, Inc., 4200 Wilson Blvd., Arlington, VA 22203, www.us.bbb.org.

Deaver, F. (1990). On defining truth: The truth continuum. *Journal of Mass Media Ethics* 5(3), 169. Reproduced with permission, Taylor & Francis.

Free Speech Coalition code of ethics reproduced with permission, www.freespeech coalition.com.

Hodges, L. (2000). Unsafe haven. *Journal of Mass Media Ethics* 15(4), 269–270. Reproduced with permission, Taylor & Francis.

International Public Relations Association (IPRA) code of Brussels for the conduct of public affairs worldwide reproduced with permission, info@ipra.org.

Index

Page entries in *italics* refer to illustrations or boxed material.